"This book is a mystic's gift to us—carrying a vision of interdependence and offering guidance on how to create the beloved community with all of life."

Jack Kornfield, PhD, is one of the most influential Buddhist teachers in the West and co-founder of both the Insight Meditation Society and Spirit Rock Meditation Center. He is the author of the international bestseller A Path with Heart, which helped shape the modern mindfulness movement.

"For more than 35 years, Richard Flyer has carried Sarvodaya's vision into the West through his development of Symbiotic Culture. His book offers a compassionate, practical pathway toward world awakening rooted in community action and shared humanity. I invite all friends and well-wishers to join this vital work. *Birthing the Symbiotic Age* lights the way forward."

Dr. A.T. Ariyaratne
Founder, Sarvodaya Shramadana Movement

"In *Birthing the Symbiotic Age*, Richard Flyer shares his vision and decades of experience showing that a more loving, connected way of living is not something we must invent, but something already alive within and among us—waiting to be woven together. His book offers both gentle reassurance and a clear call to align in community service around a higher shared purpose, guided by love, trust, compassion, inclusiveness, and mutual respect, all for the greater good. Very inspiring, practical, and highly recommended."

Carolyn Anderson, co-author of The Co-Creator's Handbook 2.0, is an internationally respected author and pioneer in co-creative personal and social development. She has helped individuals and teams around the world discover purpose and build collaborative, love-based communities.

"*Birthing the Symbiotic Age* opens a clear path into a future of collaborative life, shared creativity, and generative movement-building."

Alan Hirsch, author of numerous books on movement spirituality, key contributor to the Missional Church Movement, and founder of the Movement Leaders Collective

BIRTHING THE SYMBIOTIC AGE

"Birthing the Symbiotic Age is a profound and practical community operating manual for our time. Born of decades of real-world experience, it reflects the work of Richard Flyer—one of those rare individuals who has remained true to his quest and carried it through to fruition. Going beyond activism toward root causes, he has uncovered the principles and pathways of harmonious community self-organization, grounded in consciousness and sacred order, and translated into practical community design. This book offers an excellent blueprint for getting us out of our shared mess—and practical guidance for rebuilding community from the ground up."

Foster Gamble is a filmmaker and systems thinker, best known as the co-creator of the globally influential THRIVE documentaries, which have been seen over a hundred million worldwide. For decades, his work has explored the root causes of global crises and pathways toward regenerative culture, integrating consciousness, systems intelligence, and practical solutions for societal renewal.

"Birthing the Symbiotic Age is a vibrational match for the evolutionary leap we are taking. Richard Flyer offers spiritual technology for rebuilding society through the Intelligence of the Heart—a powerful guide for co-creating the Beloved Community and living Love in action.

Michael Bernard Beckwith, founder and spiritual director of Agape International Spiritual Center in Los Angeles, is a leading voice in the contemporary spirituality and conscious-living movement, known for integrating inner transformation with compassionate action in the world and for his appearances on Oprah's SuperSoul Sunday.

"Many people complain about the state of the world. Some offer quick fixes. Very few dare to probe the deeper social and spiritual patterns that brought us here — or offer a clear, humane, hopeful path forward. Richard Flyer is one of those rare few, and *Birthing the Symbiotic Age* captures his vision with striking clarity. I hope you'll be one who dares to see what he sees."

Brian D. McLaren, bestselling author, public theologian, and widely respected voice in the movement for contemporary Christian renewal, known globally for inspiring faith-based social transformation.

"*Birthing the Symbiotic Age* turns our focus away from the fear of global crisis and back to where it belongs: the grassroots, where real change begins. Richard Flyer lifts up the local wisdom that Gandhi and Dr. A.T. Ariyaratne cherished—showing how cooperation, compassion, and community action enable people to rebuild their own futures. This book carries a rare clarity of heart. It reminds us that when people choose understanding over conflict and service over division, a more humane and peaceful society becomes possible. It offers real hope, especially for the younger generation longing for justice and renewal."

> **Rajagopal P. V.**, an acclaimed Gandhian activist, has spent five decades advancing land and resource rights for India's most marginalized communities. He has mobilized millions through historic nonviolent marches, strengthening grassroots governance, community empowerment, and global movements for dignity, peace, and people-led transformation.

"*Birthing the Symbiotic Age* is a timely beacon, offering the proof points we need to shift how we live. In an era of fragmentation, this deeply humanistic book is threaded with wonder and reverence for the sacred—the connective tissue that holds all. Richard Flyer invites us on a luminous journey, translating a life of experience into a profound relational worldview. By grounding the "ancient blueprint" we need to remember in practical, lived examples, the book does more than instruct—it reassembles our priorities. Its activation guidance charts a path from personal transformation to a culture of connection—and ultimately to a more virtuous economy and politics. A tour de force of practical hope."

> **Lyn McDonell**, MA, C.Dir, FCMC is a governance advisor, facilitator, and regenerative systems-thinker and practitioner. Her chapters in the 2nd and most recent 3rd edition of The Handbook of Board Governance advance accountability and long-term stewardship.

"*Birthing the Symbiotic Age* illuminates how the timeless wisdom of the Buddha can guide us in healing our communities. Richard Flyer shows that compassion, ethical action, and mindful cooperation are not just personal virtues, but the foundation for a society where all beings can flourish. This book is a profound invitation to bring Buddhist insights into practical, life-giving work in the world."

Bhikkhu Bodhi is one of the world's leading Buddhist scholars President of the Buddhist Association of the United States and the Founder and Chair of Buddhist Global Relief, a nonprofit addressing hunger and poverty through engaged Buddhist ethics.

"*Birthing the Symbiotic Age* is a timely and soulful contribution to the global search for renewal. Richard Flyer shows, with clarity and compassion, how the principles Gandhi lived and died for—truth, nonviolence, and the unity of humanity—can be reimagined for our fractured age. His call to build communities anchored in dignity, mutual trust, and shared responsibility echoes the deepest Gandhian traditions. This book invites us to rediscover the moral and spiritual strength needed to heal ourselves and our societies."

Prof. Dr. N. Radhakrishnan
Chairman, Gandhi Smarak Nidhi, Kerala
Founder of the G. Ramachandran Institute of Nonviolence

"Richard Flyer's *Birthing the Symbiotic Age* speaks to the heart of our shared humanity, inviting us beyond transactional systems rooted in separation into a culture of care and kinship rooted in love. Especially in these particularly polarized times, this book feels like an answer to a collective soul's call."

Ellen Davis, evolutionary wisdom teacher, yoga instructor, writer and photographer

"It is rare that we are given the privilege of seeing the convergence of God's work over the long arc of a person's life expressed so powerfully as we do in *Birthing the Symbiotic Age*."

Doug Tjaden, founder of Regeneco, works at the intersection of faith, stewardship, and community renewal to build resilient, biblically grounded economies

BIRTHING THE SYMBIOTIC AGE

AN ANCIENT BLUEPRINT TO UNITE HUMANITY

RICHARD FLYER

Birthing the Symbiotic Age:
An Ancient Blueprint to Unite Humanity

Copyright © 2026 by Richard Flyer
http://www.richardflyer.com

All rights reserved. This book may not be reproduced in whole or in part, stored in a retrieval system, or transmitted in any form without written permission from the publisher. The only exception is for a reviewer, who may quote brief excerpts in a review.

Cover and interior design: Ian Koviak: BookDesigners.com.

This book is a work of nonfiction that blends the author's personal experiences, reflections, and interpretations with historical, theological, and cultural analysis. While every effort has been made to accurately present events, conversations, and sources, some dialogue and descriptions are drawn from the author's memory and may be re-created for narrative clarity.

The information and perspectives offered here are general in nature and represent the author's views at the time of writing. The author does not make any guarantees or assumes liability for outcomes that may result from the application of concepts described in this book.

Library of Congress Control Number: 2025923377

ISBN (paperback): 979-8-9928550-1-2

ISBN (ebook): 979-8-9928550-0-5

ISBN (audio book): 979-8-9928550-2-9

First Printing, 2026

Printed in the United States of America

Dedication Note

This book is rooted in a universal vision of Divine Love that transcends any single religion or tradition. My own spiritual journey has been shaped through Jesus Christ—whose life revealed the Sacred Order I describe here. I honor every path through which people encounter Love, courage, and the sacred. This dedication reflects my lineage, not a boundary.

DEDICATION

To Jesus Christ, in whom the Sacred Order was made visible—not only in words, but in a life that revealed a Divine Design: how Heaven and Earth are meant to meet. And to those who followed in that pattern—Mahatma Gandhi, Dr. A.T. Ariyaratne, Dr. Martin Luther King Jr., Catalina Mendoza, and Václav Benda—and to the billions around the world who, often unseen, tend the sacred fabric of community with love, courage, and care.

To my parents, Eli and Roslyn Flyer, who loved me and gave me the freedom to explore my lifelong path.

I offer heartfelt thanks to my beloved family: my wife, Marta, whose unwavering support, patience, and love sustained this work from beginning to end, and my children, Isaac and Arlae, whose encouragement carried me forward. Thank you for the sacrifices you made—especially during these last four years of daily writing.

This book carries your fingerprints, too.

I couldn't have done this without you.

CONTENTS

Preface vii
Note to the Reader xiv
Introduction xv

SECTION 1: FORMATION

CHAPTER 1
The Luminous Web
A Presence I Couldn't Yet Name 3

CHAPTER 2
The Ancient Blueprint
Love, Logos, and the Awakening of the Authentic Self 19

CHAPTER 3
Embodying the Blueprint
Jesus, Virtue, and the Foundations of a Symbiotic Society 29

CHAPTER 4
Nature's Web
Lessons from the Living World 46

CHAPTER 5
Awakened by Wonder
A Deepening Awareness of the Sacred Order 58

CHAPTER 6
From Separation to Symbiosis
The Next Evolutionary Leap 74

CHAPTER 7
Science, Indigenous Wisdom, and Jesus 88

CHAPTER 8
Jesus Sends Me a Buddhist................120

CHAPTER 9
Crisis to Community
Weaving Belonging from Breakdown..................140

CHAPTER 10
Beyond The Charity Industrial Complex................152

CHAPTER 11
From Social Enterprise to Parallel Society
The Kingdom of Heaven and a Culture of Connection........163

SECTION 2: APPLICATION

CHAPTER 12
Building the Foundation of a Virtuous Economy...........181

CHAPTER 13
Living Systems, Loving Structures
From Control to Co-Creation.....................199

CHAPTER 14
The Spiritual Wealth of Nations
Virtue, Kinship, and the Network Commons...............212

CHAPTER 15
Conscious Community Network
Foundations of a Culture of Connection................234

CHAPTER 16
Food as Foundation
Weaving the Threads of a New Community..............243

CHAPTER 17
Prelude to a New Pattern
Rediscovering What Unites Us 259

CHAPTER 18
Decoding Symbiotic Culture DNA
A Living Framework from Divine Design 269

CHAPTER 19
Re-Villaging Our Communities
Starting with Love Thy Neighbor 300

CHAPTER 20
The Ancient Blueprint and Its Living Legacy
A Pattern that Works 316

CHAPTER 21
Seeking the Holy Grail of Community
Recovering the Inner Ground 324

CHAPTER 22
The Art of Community
Festivals, Culture, and the Collective Field 341

SECTION 3: INTEGRATION

CHAPTER 23
The Replatforming of God
Restoring the Sacred in the Public Square 359

CHAPTER 24
Reclaiming the Ancient Blueprint and Establishing a Relational Worldview 370

CHAPTER 25
Recovering the Sacred Whole
From Siloed Systems to Symbiotic Circles 385

CHAPTER 26
Connecting the Good
Using the Internet to Serve the Outernet 402

CHAPTER 27
OneSphera
A Digital Framework for Fractal Empowerment 420

CHAPTER 28
The Heart-Centered Way of Symbiotic Culture 445

CHAPTER 29
Sarvodaya, Revisited
Coming Full Circle. 457

CHAPTER 30
Living the Truth
Building a Parallel Polis Within a Spiritually Hostile Regime. 470

CHAPTER 31
The Spirit of the Polis
How Love Outgrows Empire 484

CHAPTER 32
Society's "Come to Jesus" Moment. 502

SECTION 4: ACTIVATION

CHAPTER 33
Symbiotic Culture DNA as a Relational Worldview Lens 530

CHAPTER 34
Building a Parallel Society
Who Are the Players?. 544

CHAPTER 35
Activating Symbiotic Kinship
Uniting the Threads of a Living Network Commons. 553

CHAPTER 36
From Polarized Paralysis to Parallel Polis
How We Get There From Here **575**

CHAPTER 37
Tell-A-Vision
A Joyous Universe and Your Place in It **606**

EPILOGUE
The Still Point at the Threshold of a New World **626**

Acknowledgments **631**
About the Author **633**

PREFACE

LIVING BETWEEN WORLDS

At the age of twelve, something happened to me that changed my life forever. As I lay in the liminal space before sleep, I was immersed in a non-ordinary, ineffable encounter I was unprepared for—an overwhelming, loving presence that I would later interpret as a glimpse of a deeper, sacred Transcendent reality beyond what we normally see. It was at once awesomely beautiful yet frightening.

I didn't have words for it then, but I knew it was real. What began in a single instant continued to unfold over many years. I called it the Luminous Web—a radiant sense of interconnectedness, as if every leaf, bird, and heartbeat were part of a vast and loving whole.

I was no longer separate. I was part of something sacred, intelligent, and alive. Despite life's ups and downs, I felt an absolute trust and faith in that reality.

It wasn't an idea I read about in a book, or a belief grounded in tradition. It was a direct experience that stirred something within me that never faded. At the time, I didn't link it to any religious figure. As the years went by and my journey deepened, I realized that the Reality I encountered as a boy was the same Love I would later find in the life and presence of Jesus Christ.

And yet, when I returned to everyday life, the world I saw seemed the opposite of that Love.

The society I re-entered taught me something else entirely:

- You are alone
- Others are threats and rivals, not kin
- All that matters is matter
- Compete, consume, and control
- The Sacred is irrelevant

Our systems, even the most well-meaning ones, seemed to be built on fragmentation, fear, and material striving—a world designed around separation.

That contradiction broke my heart.

> *If life were truly one, why were we living as if we were separate, cut off, divided, estranged from one another and the sacred source that binds us?*

I didn't have the language to name it back then, but now I call it the Culture of Separation.

My father, sensing my heartbreak, asked me a simple question that became my life's compass:

"Well, son...what will you do about it?"

That question haunted me—not in a burdensome way, but in a way that awakened purpose. It set me on a path that would take decades to walk. I spent the next fifty years searching for answers.

Preface

I studied. I built. I made mistakes. I fell in love. Got married. Had children. Got divorced. Remarried. I tried to live according to what I had seen. I founded organizations, started companies, ran networks, and facilitated community movements that attempted to embody the coherence I once glimpsed as a boy. Along the way, I drew from every way of knowing I had access to—trained as a scientist, shaped by poetry, grounded in the concrete practice of community work. I welcomed wisdom from Indigenous elders, priests, Buddhist scholars, systems theorists, diverse spiritual traditions, forests, and pilot whales.

For years, I followed the thread of that early luminous experience, trusting the sense of belonging and sacred wholeness I had once touched. Everything changed in 1990, when that same Presence seemed to pursue me again—in a form I never expected.

It came while I was driving through Mexico, still grappling with how to translate that early glimpse into something practical and embodied. Out of nowhere, the veil lifted—not revealing what I was seeking, but what I had been longing to see. I saw a figure on the road—Jesus Christ.

He appeared not as a metaphor or a dream but as a vision imprinted on my soul. I felt lifted upward, and suddenly, I saw the planet from above. Instead of the lights of cities, I saw golden rays rising from the hearts of billions of people—streams of light converging into a great, radiant heart. It pulsed with a Love so total it dissolved all boundaries.

Only later did I recognize what I had seen: this was the heart of Jesus, not a distant ruler, but the very Love I had sensed as a child, now made visible, made personal. It was not a symbol or a belief but the living pattern of Divine Love pouring into the world.

What I had witnessed was not a new religion to be imposed but a sacred map—what I later called the Ancient Blueprint—a Sacred Design embedded in reality itself.

BIRTHING THE SYMBIOTIC AGE

It was a living web of connection—of people, hearts, and communities joined by Love and service— a new worldwide web of Love and Life.

This vision revealed more than Love as a feeling—it showed me Love as a structure.

The radiant heart above Earth formed a vertical thread: the connection between the Transcendent and the Immanent. It wasn't abstract theology—it was an actual reality. I began to see how the Divine pattern could be mirrored on Earth—not just through personal devotion, but in how we live, relate, and build together.

That vertical descent of Love demanded horizontal embodiment: shaping community, economy, and belonging from the inside out. What I had seen from above, I now felt called to bring to the ground below.

The luminous, loving presence I had once seen in all things stood before me in the person of Jesus. It wasn't a different reality; it was that same sacred coherence from childhood, now embodied—not as a doctrine, but as a living pattern of Divine Love.

That vision gave me direction. If my first experience had raised the question, "How can a world so whole produce lives so fractured?"—this second experience began to offer an answer:

We are here to bring Heaven down to Earth, unite what has been separated, and reweave the world with Love.

I didn't suddenly become a pastor, but realized I had been given a "ministry"—one I was already living.

My work in community—from apprenticing with an Indigenous/Christian medicine woman to developing local food systems, economies, and civic networks—became a form of spiritual

Preface

inquiry. Could the coherence I saw at twelve become a living pattern among us? Could Divine Love form structurally in neighborhoods, economies, and everyday relationships?

Over time, I began to see the pattern. I recognized it in Jesus' teachings, especially his radical call to Love God and Love Others—not as a poetic metaphor or a call to be a good person, but as the hidden framework of Reality.

I saw it in the early Christian ecclesia, and again in Mahatma Gandhi's village movements, Dr. A.T. Ariyaratne's Sarvodaya Shramadana network of village economies, and in the Parallel Polis movement created during the communist rule of Czechoslovakia. I saw it in Indigenous councils and recovery circles.

In each case, Love was not an ideal. It was the infrastructure.

This book is the fruit of that journey. It's not a memoir, though it tells my story. It's not a manual, though it offers models. It's not a theology, though it touches the sacred.

It's a field guide for remembering how we were meant to live.

As I wrote this book, I saw more clearly how deeply our civilization has "de-platformed" the Divine. Even those who believe in a higher power often leave it out of our civic life, governance, and design frameworks. That, too, is part of the Culture of Separation.

Here's the more profound truth I've seen: Most people I meet believe in something greater. Call it God, Spirit, Divine Love, the Sacred. Surveys say nearly 90% of us believe in a higher power. Yet our society is organized as if the sacred is private and irrelevant—as if love is too soft to structure a culture, and virtue is admirable but insufficient for survival.

Family, religion, and education teach us to be kind, generous, forgiving, and truthful. And yet, to function in today's systems, we're often forced to compete, hoard, dominate, and deny the truth we know in our hearts.

This split is not just a moral tension—it is the spiritual crisis of our time. Deep down, we know that we belong to a loving, relational universe, yet we live as if we are alone.

At the heart of this crisis is a misunderstanding of Virtue itself.

By Virtues, I don't simply mean admirable behaviors or moral ideals. To me, Virtues are enduring capacities of the soul—like Love, compassion, courage, humility, and truthfulness—that harmonize us with the deeper structure of Reality. These are not just ethical preferences; they are holy habits of the heart that draw us into deeper communion with Divine Love and reveal how life was always meant to flourish—in harmony with the sacred rhythm of the Creator and creation.

Virtues have endured because they echo something we already know—they align with the deeper design of Reality. And yet, despite knowing the truth of the Virtues, we've been conditioned to act otherwise: to take rather than give, to protect rather than trust, to perform rather than be.

That dissonance wears us down. Some compartmentalize, others give up and numb out. Many—especially our youth—experience ongoing anxiety or depression. Still others fight against "the system," addressing symptoms rather than the prime cause: separation.

And still, no one escapes the ache of living out of alignment with who we truly are.

That ache is not a flaw. It's the signal of something sacred breaking through. I have felt that ache myself since I was a young boy, standing between worlds: the "joyful cosmos" I had experienced as profoundly true, and the world I was expected to survive in.

This book is for those who feel that signal and want to respond—not with despair but with creativity, not by retreating but by participating in the birth of something new.

Preface

*I believe we are being invited into a great remembering,
to help bring Heaven to Earth,
starting with each of us.*

Not of a utopia that never was, but of an ancient truth that still lives beneath the noise: that we are made for communion. That love is the organizing design principle of reality. That the sacred is not just somewhere else. It is here, awaiting our attention, to align our lives with the grand design.

That's how we begin to build a Culture of Connection, what I call Symbiotic Culture.

I'm not just inviting you to read a book. I invite you to walk with me on a journey of a lifetime—decades of learning what works and what doesn't in building real communities of care.

You may hear echoes of your own story along the way, because this isn't about me. It's about us, and what becomes possible when we begin exactly where we are.

You're already part of this story. And it's time.

Let's begin.

BIRTHING THE SYMBIOTIC AGE

NOTE TO THE READER

While the heart of this book is inspired by Jesus's teachings, who he was, and the lineage of Love he revealed, it is written for anyone who longs for a more connected and compassionate world. The sacred pattern described here—the Ancient Blueprint—is woven into creation itself. It has surfaced repeatedly across cultures, movements, and moments when people remembered how to live in right relationship with one another, the Earth, and the Divine. Whether you come from a faith tradition or no tradition, or are simply seeking a better way forward, you are welcome here.

I share this journey because I hope this book will show how anyone—with an open heart—can bridge even the deepest divides: between religious and non-religious worldviews, between differing spiritual paths, and across every other separation that fragments our common life, from political allegiances to competing interests. The work of building a culture rooted in Love depends on finding this meeting place, where shared purpose outweighs our differences and trust grows through relationship.

This is a book about Love made visible—in neighborhoods, in networks, and in the very structures of society. My hope is that, as you turn the page, you will begin to see how this pattern can take shape in your own life and community—and perhaps feel called to help bring it to life.

This book unfolds in spirals, not straight lines. Each chapter revisits core themes with deeper clarity, mirroring how communities grow and how love forms structure. If it feels meditative or repetitive at times, that is intentional—each iteration opens a new layer of understanding.

INTRODUCTION

THE TURNING POINT WE'VE BEEN WAITING FOR

There's a question echoing within the human heart today—a quiet longing beneath the chaos of politics, polarization, and planetary crisis. It's not just "Why can't we all get along?" but something more profound:

> *Is there anything strong enough, true enough, to bring us together?*

We're flooded with information and good intentions, but trust erodes. We build movements for justice, systems for change, and technologies for connection, yet still drift apart. Even our most inspired efforts hit the same invisible wall: fragmentation, fatigue, and disillusionment.

But what if the problem isn't just institutional or political? What if it's existential, rooted in a cultural architecture that teaches us to relate to one another, the Earth, and the Divine as separate, competing parts instead of one interwoven whole?

That question has haunted me and guided my life's work.

This book is not a memoir, a manual, or a thesis. It offers a cultural turning point—an invitation to look beyond ideological debate and remember a deeper reality we've forgotten: a shared foundation beneath our systems, stories, and suffering.

I call it the Ancient Blueprint. By this, I mean the sacred pattern of reality—spiritual, social, and ecological—that has guided thriving communities and cultures throughout history. It holds the key to birthing what I now call the Symbiotic Age: a new era of human flourishing rooted in mutuality, sacred design, and connection.

LOVE AS THE STRUCTURE OF REALITY

If this book has a single conviction, it is this: *"Love God and Love Others."*

This isn't just a metaphor, moral teaching, or call to be nice—it's a revelation of how reality is structured. When Jesus gave this command, he wasn't offering personal advice or religious doctrine. He was unveiling the deep pattern within Creation.

> *The original protocol was Love—not as a feeling, but as the deep structure of reality, the architecture that holds everything together.*

He was revealing the nature of existence: that we live in a relational universe. Everything is connected—nothing exists in isolation. From the subatomic bonds that hold matter together to the ecosystems that sustain life and the communities that shape our humanity, reality is woven through relationships.

Introduction

This Love, revealed in Jesus and made available to all, is not a vague force but a living Presence and Power—calling us into relationship and service. This is the Kingdom of Heaven: not merely a future destination, but also a present reality—made visible wherever love, justice, and mutual belonging reign. It is the divine order manifesting when we align with the sacred pattern that holds everything together.

Love is more than an ethical ideal. It is the foundation for building a culture that unites rather than divides.

This Love is not sentimental, but the sustaining power of life itself—the generative force that binds the cosmos— the blueprint by which life flourishes.

Whether you call it Divine Love, the Spirit, or simply the presence of God, this Love is not distant. It is alive, personal, and draws us into communion.

Received by grace, Divine Love awakens in us a desire to love in return—not just upward, but outward. Love seeks the other— healing, bridging, belonging.

This movement of Love—outward, connective, generative— doesn't stop with individuals. It forms the scaffolding of communities, offering a tangible structure for how we live, relate, and build together.

THE LINEAGE OF LOVE

Not only is this structure of Love written into the cosmos, but it is also embodied in human lives and culture. It is a sacred pattern passed down not just in texts but in communities of practice, courage, and compassion.

> *This understanding—*
> *that Love is the very fabric of reality—*
> *runs through every page of this book.*

It's also the lineage that has informed and inspired me, from Jesus to Mahatma Gandhi to Dr. A.T. Ariyaratne, and is carried forward in the community movements I've helped co-create—living patterns of love and service that repeat and adapt at every scale, from small circles to whole bioregional economies.

This "lineage of love" is not only moral—it's structural. Jesus, Gandhi, and Dr. Ariyaratne were not merely good men; they left a legacy of cultural infrastructure. Each one translated Love into systems and communities that honored the dignity of every human being. They refused to confine spiritual truth to private experience or political ideology. Instead, they showed us how to build what I now call Symbiotic Networks—containers that can gather people across human-made divisions.

This is the shift from "love as sentiment" to "love as structure." But that sacred pattern has been overshadowed and obscured by a competing cultural logic that distorts love into control and relationship into rivalry.

THE CULTURE OF SEPARATION: THE HIDDEN WOUND

Much of the suffering we see today isn't merely the result of bad actors or flawed systems. It's the predictable outgrowth of something more profound and harder to see: the *Culture of Separation*.

This culture functions like an unseen operating system. It subtly whispers:

Introduction

- You are alone.
- The material world is all there is.
- Power means control.
- Success requires domination.
- The sacred is irrelevant.

And other people? *They are threats, not kin.*

These messages don't need to be taught in classrooms or preached from podiums. They're embedded in our media, institutions, economic assumptions, and unconscious habits of thought. Even our most well-meaning social change efforts often reflect this hidden worldview. It's what turns noble intentions to bring people together into isolated silos that keep them apart. That's why we create more programs, launch more campaigns, and publish more content—yet still feel more fragmented and powerless than ever.

Most tragically, this culture convinces us that our deep yearning for wholeness is naïve or weak.

But here's a deeper truth: our desire for connection is not a sign of weakness—it's evidence of a profound structure breaking through. That structure—the *Ancient Blueprint*—still resides within us. It doesn't need to be invented; it needs to be remembered and reclaimed.

CULTURAL RECOVERY: HEALING FROM THE ADDICTION TO SEPARATION

Reclaiming this loving legacy requires a radical shift to what the 12-Step recovery movement calls "a new way of life"—from our collective addiction to separation, to a conscious practice of connection. Put another way, to *recover from* the wounding of the

Culture of Separation, we must simultaneously *recover our connection to* this Ancient Blueprint.

Like healing from addiction, cultural recovery begins with the courage to see clearly and the humility to try something new. The first step is to acknowledge that we are addicted to old ways of thinking and doing: domination, division, control, and the illusion of separation. We keep reenacting the same patterns—from new systems and structures to reforming, protesting, attacking, and seizing power—hoping they'll deliver different results.

But how's that working for us? It isn't. It can't.

As you'll see throughout this book, the second and third steps in the recovery journey require turning our lives over to a higher power. I suggest that higher power is the Transcendent, and the Ancient Blueprint is the sacred design for how that power flows through our lives and communities.

Think about it. Our crisis isn't just political or institutional—it's spiritual.

We've built political, economic, cultural, and even religious systems with good intentions. But over time, many have become disconnected from the very Source they were meant to reflect: Divine Love. When competition replaces cooperation, dominance eclipses humility, and power outweighs compassion, we lose touch with the sacred pattern of communion that was always meant to guide us.

We've arranged our lives into silos—tribes, factions, political parties, gangs, cartels, ideologies—trapped in loops of fear and rivalry, unable to see beyond the identities we've inherited and the cultural habits we're addicted to. We talk about "thinking outside the box," but we're still operating *within* the logic of the box: domination, usury, control. We've mistaken conformity for wisdom and outsourced discernment to distant authorities.

Introduction

Cultural recovery is not about tearing everything down. It's about building something alongside what exists—a parallel society aligned with sacred design. It's about reweaving the Transcendent back into our civic and cultural lives.

The issue isn't a lack of goodness. This sacred recovery is already happening. It manifests in ordinary people performing extraordinary acts daily—quietly serving, helping, and healing. That's why so many local acts of goodness—billions of them—occur outside the spotlight of institutional power and media.

The Culture of Separation ensures that these acts remain scattered, isolated, and invisible to each other.

This book invites us to face that challenge—and offers the hope of gathering the scattered embers into a coherent flame. Throughout history, others have faced this same rupture and responded not by seizing power but by embodying Love in action.

A LIVING LINEAGE: EMBODYING THE ANCIENT BLUEPRINT

This is the path I've chosen to walk. It is both personal and cultural, born from deep spiritual conviction and expressed through practical action. It follows the lineage I mentioned—a living thread stretching through history, weaving through cultures, communities, and courageous lives. This lineage first revealed itself to me through Jesus, the essence of what I now call the Ancient Blueprint: a sacred architecture rooted in Divine Love.

In this realm, the last are first, the peacemakers are blessed, and the humble inherit the Earth. This was more than symbolic—it was a declaration that another way of being is not only possible, but already alive...in those who choose to live from Love.

Jesus built not so much a religion but a counter-cultural movement—embodied and practiced by the early Christian ecclesia.

These small, local kinship assemblies lived out the Kingdom of Heaven within the empire, forming networks of mutual benefit in the face of domination. They didn't aim to overthrow Rome with swords. Instead, they lived a different truth, and in doing so, they seeded a parallel society.

That pattern—the Ancient Blueprint—did not disappear. It has re-emerged wherever people remembered who they were and organized around what matters most. I observed it in Gandhi's vision of Sarvodaya, a commonwealth of self-reliant village republics.

I saw it again in the work of Dr. Ariyaratne, who established a network of over 5,000 villages across Sri Lanka based on shared virtues, mutual uplift, and spiritual awakening. These were not programs but living organisms—parallel societies grounded in the transcendent, embodied in the local.

PARALLEL SOCIETIES ACROSS HISTORY

And I saw it in the Czech Parallel Polis: a civic resistance movement born under communist rule that refused to fight the empire on its terms. Instead, it created a culture of truth, moral coherence, and community in the shadow of oppression. Like the early Christians and the Sarvodaya villages, the Parallel Polis didn't seek to conquer. It sought to cohere.

This lineage of the Ancient Blueprint spans from Jesus' vision of the Kingdom to Gandhi's Sarvodaya, Dr. Ari's village networks, and the Czech Parallel Polis.

> *Together, these movements show how Divine Love can be embodied in real societies across time, culture, and context.*

Introduction

Though arising from different cultural and spiritual roots, each movement gave form to the same sacred architecture—a living echo of the Ancient Blueprint in action.

I recognized the same recurring pattern in these diverse communities and movements: ordinary people rediscovering their divine dignity, that they were made in the image of God, organizing around shared Virtues, and building communities of mutual benefit. Not through hierarchy, but through humble coherence. Not through ideology, but through love made visible.

That is what Symbiotic Culture seeks to become—a Culture of Connection, emerging from the grassroots—from the lived reality of local communities, where relationships, trust, and mutual care are built face-to-face, neighbor to neighbor, and the existing regional networks are connected.

It is a parallel society rooted not in dominion but in community—a quiet revolution of belonging that undergrows and then outgrows the Culture of Separation.

This is how we apply the Ancient Blueprint to bring Heaven to Earth—not all at once, not through a sweeping act of policy or power, but step by step, soul by soul, neighborhood by neighborhood, community by community.

FROM PRINCIPLE TO PRACTICE: TRANSLATING LOVE INTO SYSTEMS OF BELONGING

If the Ancient Blueprint revealed a sacred pattern, the challenge was translating these Divine Design principles into grounded practice. For me, it began with a haunting question:

BIRTHING THE SYMBIOTIC AGE

How do we translate "Love God and Love Others" from spiritual conviction into civic design?

Models for community change usually start with external solutions—new systems, institutions, and technologies, all of which require formal organization and funding. In places like Logan Heights and Sherman Heights in San Diego and later Reno, Nevada, we learned that true transformation must be revealed, not imposed. It has to grow organically from the people, the place, and the presence of the Divine.

We weren't simply launching new projects—we were testing whether Divine Love could become the organizing force of civic life.

And it can.

What emerged wasn't another nonprofit, initiative, or ideology. It was a living network ecosystem: Symbiotic Culture. Within it, we recognized a consistent logic—there was a structure beneath the structure, a spiritual code that enabled communities to thrive across silos.

The repeatable pattern that appeared in neighborhood gatherings, local food systems, and living economy networks became what we later called Symbiotic Culture DNA—a set of living principles and protocols that could spread and scale virally in many communities simultaneously. It resembled the organic mycelium network beneath a forest—quiet, alive, and connective, linking people and efforts through trust, love, and shared purpose.

The community doesn't need to be formally or "professionally" designed when we align with that living system. It emerges naturally, like cells organizing into a body. This is why the heart of Symbiotic Culture is not an institution. It's a way of being that acknowledges we live in a relational universe, where everything is indeed interrelated.

Introduction

FROM LOVE TO STRUCTURE: SYMBIOTIC NETWORKS AS A CIVIC ECOSYSTEM

Over the years, one of the most powerful embodiments of relational design—the idea that different groups, systems, or entities are meaningfully interconnected—has taken shape in what I call Symbiotic Networks.

> *Symbiotic Networks serve as relational containers—spiritual and civic ecosystems—that connect personal transformation with collective life.*

They are not top-down institutions or loosely structured gatherings. When aligned, they foster trust, reveal common needs, and unite people across differences, enabling lives, vocations, and worldviews to come together in mutual service.

These networks decentralize agency rather than centralize control. They don't demand ideological conformity. They invite alignment around universal Virtues, shared values, and common community needs.

In this book, I will share examples from my community work in low-income, multicultural, gang-affected neighborhoods in San Diego, where we addressed public safety, and in Reno, Nevada, where we strengthened a local living economy, built a Local Food System Network, and established a neighbor-to-neighbor network, along with an arts, culture, and sustainability festival.

These Symbiotic Networks can take shape in any neighborhood or an entire region, and by the end of this book, you will see how it's been done, and how you can be a "node of change" in your community.

This isn't a lofty theory or ideal—it's a time-tested way of organizing civic life—one node at a time.

Each node is more than a point on a map; it's a living cell in a greater body, a local hub of trust, relationship, and purpose.

Whether it's a neighborhood, a faith community, a main street business, a grassroots nonprofit, or a circle of friends, every node becomes a vessel of mutual care and sacred interconnection—woven into a networked ecosystem of renewal.

These lived experiments represent more than a method—they embody the cultural shift this book aims to catalyze.

A CULTURAL CHANGE MOVEMENT, NOT A PROGRAM

This book is not about scaling a toolkit. It's about catalyzing a cultural movement—a shift from separation to connection, scarcity to generosity, and domination to service. It's about revealing a possibility that has always existed: that we are already one body, interdependent, and part of a greater whole that longs to manifest in the real world.

The practical outgrowth of that vision is what I call the birth of a Symbiotic Age—a global commonwealth of regional economies rooted in trust, virtue, and local belonging.

These are not pipe dreams. The Sarvodaya Movement established an ecosystem of 5,000 village societies in Sri Lanka. In the Czech Republic, the Parallel Polis demonstrated how spiritual communities can survive and thrive under oppression. In our work, we witnessed fractured communities and cities begin to heal, not through ideology but incarnated love.

We are not starting from scratch, we are not building a utopia. We are remembering something ancient and weaving it into the fabric of our lives today.

Introduction

You are already part of it, right where you are. I hope this book will help you see your role in this shift. That change begins with how we see reality, what we assume about people, power, and the nature of the world we inhabit.

The Symbiotic movement we are building requires more than new structures or systems. It calls for a deeper way of seeing—a lens that can sustain transformation beyond moments of urgency or crisis.

That lens is a worldview.

A RELATIONAL WORLDVIEW: MAKING SENSE IN A FRACTURED AGE

Our worldviews shape everything—what we notice, how we relate, and what we believe is possible. Many of today's political, ecological, and economic crises are interrelated. They are symptoms of a more profound spiritual crisis rooted in fragmented and competing worldviews. Yet most of us don't realize we have a worldview because we don't see it—we see the world through it. Like a pair of invisible lenses, it shapes how we interpret everything around us.

So, given the diversity of competing worldviews, how do we unite?

Here's the good news.

> *We don't need a single dominant worldview to replace the rest; we need a relational one capable of building bridges between them.*

Let me explain.

A relational worldview does not erase difference. Instead, it offers a deeper shared language, not merely of words but of understanding and orientation. This language is rooted not in control or separation but in communion, participation, and mutual recognition. It provides a common way to perceive, relate to, and act across cultures and traditions.

This worldview is implicit in the Sermon on the Mount, Indigenous cosmologies, and the Gospel of John's vision of the Logos—the divine pattern of wisdom and relational order woven into all creation. It is not a belief system, but a way of being—one that aligns with the reality that everything is connected and nothing exists in isolation.

That's what I mean when I say the ideas in this book are grounded in reality, not merely idealistic or technocratic. You will learn how local communities organically develop through trusted third-party connections, person-to-person, and network-to-network. You'll discover how this process of emergent community operates in the real world, enabling you to replicate it in your region or network.

WALKING THE PATH TOGETHER

The title of this book—*Birthing the Symbiotic Age*—is not metaphorical. It's literal. I've come to believe we are in the midst of a planetary passage from an age of extraction and domination to one of mutualism and service.

This isn't something that can be engineered from the top down. It must be birthed from within—from within families, communities, circles of care, and ordinary people aligned with something higher and more profound.

The tools I present are not meant to replace what's already working. They are designed to amplify and magnify it by "Connecting the Good." By 'the Good,' I mean the people, projects, and institutions already aligned with compassion, justice, healing, and mutual uplift—efforts like building local economies and food systems, faith-based service, neighborhood care networks, regenerative culture, mutual aid networks, civic engagement, and much more.

Connecting the Good means weaving these often-isolated efforts across organizations, faith communities, businesses, local governments, and mutual aid groups into living ecosystem networks of cooperation and shared purpose. It's a way of transforming scattered acts of service into a coherent Power for renewal—perhaps humanity's greatest untapped resource and superpower.

WHAT YOU'LL DISCOVER IN THIS BOOK

In the pages ahead, I'll walk you through more than forty years of community experiments, show how the Culture of Separation shaped my early life, and how encounters with mystics, communities, and crises led me back to a truth older than any ideology: that Divine Love, when received and lived, creates a new kind of society.

You'll read stories of re-villaging neighborhoods, closing drug houses, building buy-local campaigns, and forming multi-sector networks without a single formal institution. You'll meet people who chose to show up not because they agreed on everything, but because they were willing to love, serve, and build together.

In the final chapters, you'll find a five-stage roadmap for forming or joining a Symbiotic Circle. You'll also explore the Network Commons—a new collaborative, decentralized civic engagement model that empowers local groups to connect without losing their distinctiveness or autonomy.

You'll be invited to discern your place in the lineage—from Jesus to Gandhi to Dr. Ari to the people in your community who are waiting to connect, waiting to trust again, and waiting to belong.

THE BOOK'S FOUR ARCS OF TRANSFORMATION

This book unfolds in four arcs that mirror my development and the unfolding of transformation itself.

Formation begins with my personal story and the rediscovery of the Ancient Blueprint. It traces how I came to view Divine Love not only as a spiritual principle but as the sacred ordering system of life, and how that truth began reshaping how I perceived people, community, and culture. Readers will uncover the roots of our shared disconnection and be introduced to a sacred architecture that has quietly sustained life for millennia.

Application examines how these principles were applied in real-world experiments across neighborhoods, cities, and regional economies. From addressing gang violence to supporting local food systems and economies, as well as neighbors helping neighbors, this section presents concrete stories of how Love transforms into civic scaffolding. Readers will discover how to nurture trust-based collaboration and develop living networks of mutual support without the need to control or formalize everything.

Integration unites the spiritual and the structural. It shows how sacred design influences not just interpersonal relationships, but entire systems—economic, ecological, and institutional. You'll learn how the logic of communion can shape everything from governance to technology, and start to see how new patterns of belonging can emerge. You will gain a framework for coordinating community efforts.

Finally, in Activation, you are invited to walk the path yourself. This final arc provides a roadmap for carrying this work into your context and community, through approaches like Symbiotic Circles and Networks, the Network Commons, and practices of relational leadership that empower collective transformation from the ground up. You'll see yourself reflected in this movement because you are part of it.

You don't have to go through this alone.
The pattern is already established. The relationships
are already developing. The wisdom is already present.

THE SYMBIOTIC AGE:
A CULTURAL MOVEMENT ROOTED IN LOVE

We're witnessing the beginning of a new age—the Symbiotic Age—where mutual benefit, deep connection, and sacred design guide how we live and lead. *Birthing the Symbiotic Age* means nurturing a culture in which individuals, families, neighborhoods, and entire communities rediscover how to live in right relationship with one another with the Earth and with the Divine pattern of the Ancient Blueprint.

This blueprint is not abstract—it has been embodied throughout history by those who lived its truth: from Jesus and the early Christian communities, to Gandhi's Sarvodaya movement, to Dr. Ariyaratne's village-based awakening in Sri Lanka, to the Czech Parallel Polis.

It points toward a global commonwealth of regional
economies rooted in trust, virtue, and local belonging—
what I call the Virtuous Economy.

Rooted in timeless Virtues—compassion, integrity, generosity, and courage, this economy reflects the sacred logic of love in motion, circulating resources to strengthen relationships, meet real needs, and regenerate the commons.

INVITATION

Symbiotic Culture invites us to step into a life where love becomes the new organizing principle of society and its economy.

If you've sensed something essential is missing in how we live and relate...

If you've longed for a more beautiful, just, and sacred way to belong to this world...

These pages present a path of reconnection to your purpose, people, and the deeper pattern that holds us all. This renewed world—this Symbiotic Age—won't be imposed from above. It will be birthed and built by people like you.

And...you are not alone.

Across the globe, threads of reconnection are weaving into a living movement—once scattered, now coalescing into a whole-cloth emergence from the grassroots.

The Symbiotic Age is not a theory; it's already taking form.

This book invites you to find your place in it—and join what's already unfolding. Let's begin.

SECTION 1

FORMATION

REMEMBERING THE PATTERN OF LOVE

*Before we can rebuild the world,
we must first remember
what the world was meant to be.*

BIRTHING THE SYMBIOTIC AGE

With my dog Duke, early 1970s—just outside Alexandria, Virginia, before everything changed.

CHAPTER 1

THE LUMINOUS WEB: A PRESENCE I COULDN'T YET NAME

Until I was twelve years old, I enjoyed what could be called a typical American childhood.

I grew up in a middle-class Jewish family in Alexandria, Virginia, in the 1960s and early '70s. I did typical boy things—playing soldier in the forested Coast Guard land near my home, building tree forts, ice skating along the frozen narrow streams, and going with my dad to rock quarries to look for minerals and gemstones.

But then, at age twelve, something happened that would change my life forever. I contacted a deeper reality than we usually see on life's surface.

One night, I was in bed, getting ready to sleep. I rested in the liminal space between waking and sleeping, where images sometimes stream from a deeper part of ourselves and come into awareness as we drift off into slumber. This night was anything but normal.

Suddenly, I felt a deep vibration, like electricity inside the lower part of my back. The vibration spread upward toward my chest and finally into my head. My whole body was now vibrating—every part not just alive, but radiantly, unmistakably alive, fully awake, as if life itself were surging through me and I was being animated from the inside out by something beyond this world.

With my eyes closed, I felt illuminated and enveloped in bright white light and then pure golden light. Soon, purple and gold lights began flashing as if I were watching thousands of spectators at a stadium, simultaneously taking pictures with flashbulbs.

I heard a sound, then individual notes that became a crescendo, a celestial symphony. The intensity of the sound became overwhelming in my head, like the roar of a thunderous cascade of water, as if I were mere steps away from Niagara Falls. Then I entered and exited a tunnel filled with radiant light, seeing a thousand stars exploding simultaneously. I was awestruck!

My entire being was activated and energized during this fully immersive experience. As I write this, I can remember the radiant light, first cool and then filled with warmth.

The joy was overwhelming and brought me to tears.

I felt as if I were immersed in the sun's raw power, like I was being blessed by Love itself.

Suddenly, things shifted again into the most profound part of the experience. I was plunged into darkness, like falling into an unknown land, a void no words could possibly describe. I was no longer observing or even "experiencing"; somehow, there was a knowing.

It's hard to describe a pure knowing beyond all constructs—no sound, light, color, thoughts, sensations, perceptions, or concepts. Words escape me. Tears rolled down my face at the peace, the harmony, the great silence.

At some point, my sense of ego identity returned, but then I felt as if I was losing awareness, like I was dying. It became too much. It must have been an instinctual urge for self-preservation that helped me pull out of this state, and after a short while, I fell into a regular sleep.

It was a non-ordinary, ineffable encounter I was unprepared for—an overwhelming, loving presence I would later understand as a glimpse of Ultimate Reality.

In this book, I call it the Transcendent. Others might call it God, the Divine, or Love. At the time, I didn't know how to name it. Yet, I somehow knew that this Presence was authentic, personal, and calling me into something far beyond myself. It felt more Real than "reality," and it was as if I had broken through to the true foundation beneath what we think of as "normal" life. That experience left me feeling connected to something larger than myself—connected to everything.

Luminous visitation, age 12—Alexandria, VA, early 1970s. The night Divine Presence awakened deeper Reality.

This luminous experience happened several times a week for years. I told no one—not my parents, family, friends, or schoolteachers. No one around me was aware that this was going on. Some deep knowing told me to keep these experiences to myself, not out of embarrassment or shame, but because somehow it was necessary to let this "work through me" over time.

THE SACRED STRUCTURE BEHIND THE WORLD

Despite the combination of joy and incredible fear, unfamiliarity, and unknowing in my mind, I started to sense a peaceful trust that things were as they should be. Years later, it grew into an experience of great surrender, perhaps the first time I began to have a visceral understanding of trust.

By the time I reached my mid-teens, I knew I had been given a glimpse into the luminous infrastructure of existence—an absolute knowing that there was an unseen foundation both "under and above" the physical ground. I knew I could count on it, through thick and thin, through the vicissitudes of life—I felt a pure presence.

> *I sensed a benevolent power guiding and protecting me, with an underlying order to the world, and that I was here on Earth for some greater purpose.*

Later, as a young adult, I was told I probably had a "Road to Damascus" experience—like Saul of Tarsus (Paul) getting "struck by enlightening" by what Christians would call "Divine Grace" or Spirit. From an Eastern perspective, someone else said it sounded like a "Kundalini awakening." In either case, it was an experience often associated with deep religious practice or spiritual awakening.

I was neither religious nor a meditator. The experience seemed to come out of nowhere for no reason. However, having my experience acknowledged and named by various religious traditions gave me the impression that, though uncommon, it's happened to individuals across many religions, paths, and cultures over the last 3,000 years.

I would later discover a universal pattern, an operating system, recognized across cultures, that shapes spiritual experience and unites diverse traditions.

Christian apologist C.S. Lewis, venturing outside Christian theology eighty years ago, described an underlying, Absolute, objectively Transcendent, ordering principle—what some Eastern traditions call "The Tao." Lewis went so far as to call The Tao "the moral grain of the universe." He wrote:

> "The Chinese speak of...the greatest thing called The Tao. It is the reality beyond all predicates...the Way, the Road. It is the Way in which the universe goes on, the Way in which things everlastingly emerge, stilly and tranquilly, into space and time.
>
> It is also the Way which every man should tread in imitation of that cosmic and super cosmic progression, conforming all activities to that great exemplar.... This conception in all its forms, Platonic, Aristotelian, Stoic, Christian, and Oriental alike."

Lewis's recognition of this universal moral grain echoed what I had discerned intuitively: an Ancient Blueprint underlying historic wisdom traditions.

As a 12-year-old, I had no idea about any of this. There was no one—parents, siblings, clergyperson, sympathetic adult—I could talk to about it. In hindsight, I realize it was better I didn't tell anyone—I'm sure I would have been poked and probed and eventually put on medication with the thought that I had a mental illness I needed to be cured of.

It turned out not to be a mental disorder at all, but rather an opening to an expansive connection to a vast cosmos and its deeper foundation, referred to by many as the Transcendent, what was called Wisdom in the Old Testament, and what the Greeks and Christians called the Logos.

To me, it seemed like the very Sacred Structure of Reality, the Transcendent unity that underlies all life. This "Luminous Web" has lighted my path ever since. I came away from this experience knowing a sacred reality exists beyond the limits of the material world and human ego.

What I've come to call the Transcendent is the source of all meaning, coherence, and love, permeating everything while remaining greater than all things. Though unseen, it can be directly experienced through the heart, calling us into deeper relationships with life, others, and the Divine.

GROWING UP IN A CULTURE OF SEPARATION: A STRANGER IN A STRANGE LAND

While this new vision opened my heart to wonder, it also sharpened my awareness of the fractures and falsehoods in the world around me—an atmosphere marked by fragmentation, separation, and competition. As I re-entered daily life after these luminous visitations, I couldn't unsee what I had touched. The contrast was jarring.

Looking back, I can now see that, like most middle-class American kids, I was being shaped by an invisible field—what I

The Luminous Web

later came to call the Culture of Separation. This wasn't a phrase I had at the time, but it described the water I had been swimming in. It's a way of life and a worldview that disconnects us from the Divine, each other, the Earth, and our deepest selves. It tends to prize control, competition, and individualism, fragmenting communities and reducing life to transactions.

This cultural matrix was so immersive and all-encompassing that it felt like the only reality. But those early mystical experiences offered a broader horizon. They "broke the trance" of normality and revealed an entirely different vision.

I now had a tangible connection to a deeper, Transcendent ordering principle—something that guided me with a radically different logic than what I saw playing out around me.

Paradoxically, while I felt connected to all that is, I also felt profoundly different from those around me. Having touched something luminous and interconnected, I now felt the alienation of walking through a world that often felt one-dimensional by comparison. The phrase Culture of Separation would only come much later, but even then, it named something I had long felt. The world around me was rich in systems but poor in meaning. I knew—somehow—that something essential was missing.

This inner contrast between transcendent unity and cultural fragmentation eventually led me to seek answers through history, philosophy, and theology. I sensed that much of what society taught me about reality—that we are isolated individuals, and only the material world is real—was not just incomplete, but untrue.

No wonder we've ended up on a competitive battlefield instead of a cooperative playing field—and we believe that is normal!

You could say the Transcendent experience was indeed "trance-ending"—ending the trance of separation. But the price of that awakening was a persistent feeling of otherness. While my peers mainly seemed at home in the dominant "consensus reality," I often felt like an alien, a stranger in a strange land.

THE MISSING PIECE IN OUR CIVILIZATION

In time, I came to believe that what's missing in our modern civilization is not intelligence or technology but a commonly shared sense of Transcendent Power—a deeper coherence that unites us. In this unseen sacred reality, Love governs. This unifying Transcendent principle has been replaced by materialism and consumerism—the new "gods" of the globalist marketplace.

Today, this sense of separateness is reinforced by mainstream culture and intensified by social media algorithms, fragmenting us into customized or personalized realities. I used to think the division of society into tribes and silos was a symptom of the Culture of Separation. I now realize it is a "feature," not a bug. That is, it's not a glitch in the program; it IS the program.

Right now, exponential technologies like AI are entrenching this divide further. We are being conditioned into a "me vs. you" world—one that makes it hard to remember:

> *We are already profoundly interconnected,*
> *woven into a living web of life and Love.*

This dissonance between inner union and outer division left me suspended between two worlds. I felt like the man in the middle.

Yet this opening also brought a kind of sorrow, the sharp dissonance between the wondrous, beautiful, luminous Reality I had touched and the broken, conflicted world around me. The sorrow was no longer abstract—it was personal.

The contrast between what I had touched and what I saw around me broke my heart.

One night at a Passover Seder with my family, I suddenly felt overwhelmed by compassion for the suffering I sensed worldwide. I burst into tears, creating quite a scene. My very practical father, trying to make sense of it, said:

"Well, Richard, when you wake up each day, what will you do about it?"

With this question burning in my heart, I became endlessly curious about the world. It was as if I were an alien from another world, sent to Earth to observe and report back. Like in the movie *Starman*, I looked at everything with fresh eyes. Beneath the surface of ordinary life, I began to perceive hidden connections—patterns, energies, meanings that others seemed to overlook.

That's when I first recognized the Luminous Web— not as a metaphor, but as the hidden framework of ordered reality.

Having experienced both the ache of disconnection and the beauty of transcendence, I wondered: What kind of understanding could hold them both?

Could Love be the bridge?

THE VOICE OF THE HEART OF LOVE

Around that time, I became interested in astronomy. I mowed lawns to save up to buy a telescope. Every night, I would sit in the yard, gazing at the vastness of the visible universe, feeling that I was a part of something much bigger than myself.

Stargazing in Alexandria, VA, 1970s— longing not just to observe the cosmos, but to belong.

A sense of purpose welled within me that I was here on Earth for some deeper reason—that there was a grand, Divine plan, and I had a small role in it.

This growing sense of agency—that I was an active participant in something larger—became stronger with time. Several years later, as a young adult, I wrote a poem celebrating what the 7th century Orthodox Christian monk, St. Maximus the Confessor, called "Divine Love"—to me, the glue that underlies and connects reality, serving as the builder and sustainer of Creation.

Rather than being an impersonal force, Love began to gain a Voice—what I called the Voice of the Heart of Love started to speak directly to me like a kind and wise teacher. I could feel it in my heart and hear it in my head. It felt at once intimately close and infinitely vast—a tenderness that was both within me and beyond me. At the time, I knew it only as the Voice of the Heart of Love—gentle, steady, and deeply personal.

In hindsight, the tone and tenderness felt unmistakably like the voice I would later come to recognize as Jesus Christ. This Love didn't feel abstract or distant. It felt personal and alive. One poem from that time captured what this Voice revealed to me:

> Love isn't sentimental, but the glue connecting and binding the Universe. From the tiniest sub-atomic

particles to the creation of life, to the flowering of plants, animals, human beings, planets, stars, galaxies, built into it all, Love is there.

The Voice of the Heart of Love nurtures me, saying, "Can you feel my living presence inside and all around you? Like a slow-moving stream through a thick forest on a warm day, moving continuously, always there.

This loving, guiding voice comforted me and provided context, setting the stage for deeper unfoldment. What began as a quiet inner voice soon expanded into a new form of spiritual experience—this time through dreams.

DREAMS OF LIGHT AND LIVING WATER

In 1975, after my family moved to Monterey, California, I entered what now seems to have been the second phase of integrating my earlier experiences.

Over the next few years, I began having recurring dreams. In these dreams, I was lying on a white sandy beach near the water beneath a vivid blue sky. The air and water felt pleasantly warm, probably around eighty degrees. The ocean was very calm, lapping gently at my skin. As I lay there, looking into the deep blue sky, a warm golden light beamed from the sun, entering and enveloping me. The sun seemed to be a carry-over from my earlier experiences.

I felt my heart open as a golden light burst forth from within, surrounding me. It expanded from below my heart, rising upward, enveloping my chest and head until the upper part of my body was bathed in a soft, radiant, spherical halo of light.

Unlike my earlier waking dream, where I ultimately felt as if I were dying, this experience carried a sense of warmth and protection. I felt a deep, steady peace throughout my being. The illuminating light's gentle radiance filled me with joy, Love, and a bliss unlike anything I had known—"joy within joy," as if drawn from an inner well of ever-flowing waters.

I felt the sensation not just on the surface, but within the core of my body, as if energy and awareness were flowing together beneath my skin. As I became aware of the "water" moving through me, I felt more alive than ever before, as if I had discovered the source of life. I realized that what we perceive as life on Earth is merely the surface. Beneath this exterior, life is nurtured by "living water" from a deeper Source that flows through and sustains us.

Reflecting on my Jewish tradition, I am reminded of the wisdom literature of the Old Testament that echoed my experience: "When you find me, you find life, real life." (Proverbs 8:35)

I began to experience Divine Love not as an impersonal force, but as a Presence reaching out to meet me in relationship.

These expansive experiences further heightened my empathy and compassion for others, as I became more attuned to the people in my immediate environment and worldwide.

In my early twenties, these experiences deepened further, no longer limited to dreams or inner sensations. I began perceiving the light of the Divine in the external world. This time, it happened while I was fully awake, and that inner golden light became "externalized." I began to see the light within and around objects in the world—the world as a whole was alive.

On one occasion, while gazing at a palm tree, I saw its "energies" in the glowing light emanating from and surrounding it. I felt an inexplicable connection with that tree and recognized the light around it as an expression within creation, within nature, a "reflection" of the Luminous Web itself.

In Chapter 4, you will learn how Nature's Web and its ecosystems reveal a sacred, Transcendent pattern—one I would later recognize as the Living Logos at the heart of all creation. If this idea feels abstract, think of the Logos as a divine pattern that unites reason, love, and creation.

I share these experiences not because they are significant in themselves—ultimately, they are not. There is something far more important.

Spiritual experiences, no matter how profound, can become distractions if they do not guide us toward what truly matters: becoming transformed human beings capable of truly loving one another.

These experiences set me on that path, shaping and guiding my understanding of reality. Over time, they naturally led to what I've described as a relational worldview, grounded in the practical work of building flourishing, real-world communities rooted in Divine Love.

In the years that followed, I came to see that this same Transcendent power is not reserved for mystics or monks—it is accessible to everyone. Ordinary people and everyday communities can draw upon it in ways that elevate and empower, allowing us, as many spiritual and religious traditions have long affirmed, to bring Heaven to Earth.

Looking back, I can now see that these unfolding, extraordinary experiences were not random. They formed part of a natural progression—a deepening awareness that pointed toward something larger, more connected, and profoundly real.

Helping everyday people and real-world communities apply this 'super-power' has become my life's work. This sacred pattern of Divine Love—a power that often feels elusive in society—is, in fact, the organizing structure of reality itself. In walking with others through this process, I've understood how this Love moves beneath the surface of our lives, shaping what we build, relate to, and become.

DIVINE LOVE AND LOGOS: THE LIVING LOGIC OF THE UNIVERSE

Earlier, I described how Divine Love and the Logos manifested in the stillness of my earliest luminous experiences—as intimacy, presence, and peace. Here, those same realities began to reveal their structural nature: the relational architecture of belonging and the connective tissue of all creation.

You may notice that I use several terms interchangeably throughout this book to describe this organizing pattern—Transcendent, Logos, and Divine Love. The Divine Love I experienced felt like an underlying, unifying power that flowed through all of creation and is embodied within each of us.

I wondered if this was the same power Jesus described when he commanded us to Love God and Others. Love here is not a feeling; it goes beyond romantic, friendship, and parental love, and seems more expansive than even unconditional or agape love.

> *St. Maximus saw Divine Love as a real, creative power binding all things, and called us to "gather the cosmos in Love," participating in the very work of creation.*

Elsewhere, St. Maximus writes that love is the goal, source, and Highest of all Goods, and *"all the forms of Virtue are introduced, fulfilling the power of love, which gathers together what has been separated, once again fashioning the human being by a single meaning and mode."* Even after thirteen centuries, Maximus's vision still resonates—as if he were describing the very architecture of reality.

In this book, I hope to demonstrate that being rational about Transcendent experience isn't an oxymoron. Instead, it represents two parallel and complementary ways of knowing—two ways of encountering reality. I share this ancient wisdom not as theory, but as practical guidance to help us build stronger, more connected local communities.

Recognizing Love as the living logic of the universe reframes Jesus' commandment in the Sermon on the Mount—"Love God and Love Others"—as more than metaphor, poetry, or moral guidance. Love is built into the structure of reality. Just as Einstein revealed the relationship between energy and matter through $E=MC^2$, Jesus revealed the relational "equation" at the heart of existence—one that unites Heaven and Earth. Love isn't just a Virtue; its creative power holds everything together and harmonizes them.

Love God + Love Others = Heaven on Earth.
A spiritual equation embedded in the fabric of reality.

In this simple and powerful commandment, I began to glimpse what I've come to call the Ancient Blueprint—a sacred pattern woven into the cosmos, encoded not in doctrine but in relationship. Though often forgotten or obscured, this blueprint reveals how Heaven and Earth are meant to meet through lives of love, service, and community interconnectedness.

If that's true, it leads to a practical, guiding question that would shape the rest of my life:

How do we bring this luminous reality of Divine Love into our communities?

What began as an encounter with light became a call to action—an invitation to bring that same relational harmony into the world around me. I saw that this wasn't just a personal transformation—it pointed to a social and cultural invitation already stirring in communities worldwide.

As I described in the book's Introduction, a relational worldview does not seek to erase difference, but to build bridges across the silos of competing—and often polarized—worldviews. Where the Culture of Separation erects walls, this way of being cultivates relationships.

Over the decades, I began to discover pieces of the answer. As I worked to build bridges across the silos that separated people and organizations, I witnessed something unexpected: a new kind of culture beginning to emerge—not through power or conflict, but through connection. I would eventually call it Symbiotic Culture—a way of being, a way of life, born from the sacred act of bringing together what has been separated.

In the next chapter, I'll explore the roots of this discovery: the previously mentioned Ancient Blueprint that guides us toward wholeness, interconnection, and the possibility of a new way of life.

But before building anything outwardly, I had to wrestle inwardly—learning to translate the mystery into a lived pattern. This inner integration became the foundation for everything that followed—a bridge between spiritual illumination and embodied service. In the next chapter, I'll explore how this led me to the Ancient Blueprint: a sacred pattern pointing toward wholeness, relationship, and a new way of life.

CHAPTER 2

THE ANCIENT BLUEPRINT: LOVE, LOGOS, AND THE AWAKENING OF THE AUTHENTIC SELF

After encountering the Luminous Web, I sought a way to understand my experience—a language or framework that could express what I had seen. Eventually, I discovered something that felt both ancient and urgently relevant, which I refer to in this book as the Ancient Blueprint. It was a pattern interwoven through religious traditions, natural law, and the very structure of reality itself.

This foundational, unifying pattern has guided every project I have participated in—whether a food network, a nonprofit alliance, a local economy, or our neighbor-to-neighbor campaign.

Why is that important?

The fragmentation of our global political and economic systems—marked by silos, tribes, and a loss of shared meaning—impacts everything and everyone from international relations to our local communities. I began to notice how leaders across the spectrum exploit these divisions, using the ancient tactic of divide et impera—divide and rule.

BIRTHING THE SYMBIOTIC AGE

I longed to find a way for human beings to build bridges across these "man-made" tribes and silos and work together for their own and the common good.

This calling—to reconnect what has been divided—has faithfully led my life's work for five decades. In this chapter, I'll share how this calling led me to rediscover three ancient realities—Love, Logos, and Metanoia—each forming the foundation of a symbiotic society.

To rediscover these foundations, I first needed to find a framework that could encompass both my mystical experience and the longing I observed all around me—a deeper structure of order and meaning. That's when I encountered the ancient concept of the Logos.

THE LOGOS: A UNIVERSAL ARCHITECTURE OF MEANING

This universal pattern of Divine Love closely aligns with what ancient philosophers and religions have understood as the Logos—an ordering presence recognized for millennia as a philosophical, spiritual, and foundational principle.

For the Greeks, the Logos represented the Divine pattern of wisdom and reason—a cosmic architecture interwoven into everything. Early Christians embraced and transformed this concept, recognizing the Logos not merely as a principle but as a person: Christ, the Word made flesh.

In this view, the Logos is eternal and unchanging, binding everything together, predating religion, philosophy, and even the human mind, and serving as the source and sustaining pattern behind all true knowledge, order, and meaning.

The Ancient Blueprint

Early Christian communities sought to live in harmony with this Divine pattern. They understood the Logos to be embodied in Jesus Christ and practiced a new way of being in the world through Him. Even in the heart of the brutal Roman Empire, they lived a radically alternative, countercultural life: interconnected, interdependent, non-materialistic, and rooted in shared virtues and mutual love.

Their vision was nothing less than the Kingdom of Heaven—with a community built not on dominance but on self-giving love. Jesus' Sermon on the Mount became their blueprint, redefining the true essence of power and community.

During my teens and twenties, as I grappled with luminous experiences I couldn't share with anyone, I knew nothing of the Logos, the Tao that C.S. Lewis described, or even the idea of Divine Love—not as concepts, anyway. They weren't in my vocabulary.

I had no religious background, theological framework, or inherited belief system. I experienced raw and unfiltered emotions—an overwhelming connection that dissolved boundaries and transcended concepts. I didn't just feel part of something larger than myself; I felt part of everything.

This was my first true awareness of participation and agency. I could see—and feel—my role in Creation.

I also sensed that these experiences were preparing me for a deeper calling. Despite not knowing where it would lead, I felt a quiet certainty: I needed to keep listening. There was trust, guidance, and even joy in the uncertainty. A voice was awakening within me—what I've already referred to as the Voice of the Heart of Love.

Looking back, I now understand this inner guidance as the quiet prompting of the Holy Spirit—a name Christians give to the Divine Presence that dwells within and among us, awakening us to deeper truth and calling us toward love.

Understanding and living from this inner center is essential for embodying the Ancient Blueprint. However, knowledge alone is not enough—we must live it. That journey begins within, by tuning into the part of us that is most aligned with the Transcendent: the sacred self that knows it is already connected to Love.

DISCOVERING THE AUTHENTIC SELF: A SACRED PORTAL, NOT A SELF-IMPROVEMENT PROJECT

At this point, you may wonder how someone without a dramatic, spontaneous, or luminous experience like mine can connect to this same transcendent reality. Can anyone hear the "Voice of the Heart of Love"? The short answer is yes, but the path will look different for each of us.

The Transcendent is not reserved for mystics or spiritual outliers. It speaks quietly and persistently at the center of our being, inviting us into alignment through conscience, intuition, love, and longing.

I've come to call this center the Authentic Self—our deepest, most relational identity, beyond personality or cultural conditioning.

I chose the term "Authentic Self" to distinguish the Voice of the Heart of Love from the other competing voices outside us and within our minds. This authentic voice has guided me onto an entirely different trajectory, a path I recognize as more aligned with the Transcendent. Accessing this "truer" voice radically changes our relationship with God, others, and everything.

When this living power flows through us, we become a healing, unifying, and transforming presence in a broken, fragmented world.

When the term "Authentic Self" came to me, it didn't feel like a "thing" but more like a "portal," describing a two-way gateway to and from that luminous Transcendent Power. I was curious how others defined the Authentic Self, so I Googled the term. I was astounded to find that there were 500 million entries!

The popular "self-help" view of the Authentic Self is the exact opposite of what I mean by it. Society now sees the Authentic Self as "a way to fulfill one's dreams," wishes, and even purpose, often related to an individual's self-actualization. The bottom line is that it's like the ego on steroids.

This individual focus should not be surprising, given how immersed we are in the Culture of Separation—where it's all about our "individual" desires, even in religious and spiritual circles. The modern world, unsurprisingly, views the Authentic Self as an independent, separate "thing" not connected to a community.

> But for me, the Authentic Self is a "shared self,"
> a two-way portal, one side facing the Transcendent
> and the other facing our neighbor,
> the "other" in a community.

While many in the self-help and human potential movements view self-actualization as the goal, I see it as merely the beginning—a doorway into a deeper spiritual and community life. Could such a radical transformation not only liberate us from the grip of the ego but also invert the entrenched pyramid of economic and political power in the world?

I believe it can.

To understand this deeper life, I had to rediscover something many traditions already teach—that there is an inner compass guiding us home. I saw it as a living connection between the heart and the Eternal.

For some, it begins with silence. For others, through suffering, wonder, or a longing they can't explain. This voice often arises when we listen deeply, tell the truth, or choose love over fear. However it comes, it's never far away—it dwells within the heart, always seeking reunion with the Source.

A BRIDGE BETWEEN HEAVEN AND THE HUMAN HEART

This inward voice—subtle yet persistent—has been named differently across spiritual traditions. In the Christian lineage, it is often called conscience: not merely a moral judge, but a sacred faculty that connects the soul to the voice of God. My understanding of the Authentic Self resonates with this view. I see conscience as the "still, small voice"—God's whisper in the depths of our being—gently guiding us toward truth, compassion, and right action. In this sense, it becomes a living bridge between Heaven and the human heart.

As we will see later, this inner guidance system is accessible to everyone, regardless of their religious beliefs or lack thereof. Dr. A.T. Ariyaratne, a Buddhist visionary, called it "personality awakening." It became the foundation of the Sarvodaya Movement in Sri Lanka and played a key role in shaping what would become Symbiotic Culture.

The Authentic Self illuminates our understanding of universal principles and Virtues, enabling us to express profound, universal Love and act in alignment with the Transcendent.

What C.S. Lewis described as a sacred architecture, I see as a universal operating system known by different names across cultures and religions in the East, West, and Indigenous communities. At its core, the Authentic Self serves as the living interface with the Ancient Blueprint, representing the unique way Divine Love speaks within each of us, guiding us to live in harmony with the sacred pattern woven into all of creation.

This connection between our interior life and the larger world is no accident. This inner alignment is not merely personal—it's the seed of a larger transformation that calls us to participate in healing our world.

Recognizing the Ancient Blueprint—with the Law of Love written on our hearts—is not just about individual awakening. It sets the foundation for healing our shared cultural fabric. As more of us connect with this sacred design, we begin to break down the false patterns of separation and rediscover a more profound unity, rebuilding the bonds of trust, belonging, and mutual care that enable collective life. This reconnection paves the way for a new kind of society to emerge, one rooted not in domination but in Divine Love.

Even so, when this pattern first emerged through luminous experience, I lacked the language to understand it.

The resistance to these experiences isn't just personal—it's woven into the assumptions of our age. Perhaps the reason I struggled to articulate what I encountered lies in the culture itself. One reason may be that although these experiences are universal and more common than we are led to believe, the Culture of Separation has no "use" for the Transcendent.

It prioritizes control, material success, and measurable outcomes, leaving little room for mystery, inner transformation, or unseen sources of wisdom. In such a framework, the transcendent is often dismissed as irrelevant, irrational, or unproductive.

Consequently, terms like *Logos* and the one I'm introducing in this next section, *Metanoia*, may seem archaic, relegated to quaint irrelevance in a Culture of Separation. They are as real and present as my experience was. I choose to refer to these terms rather than create new ones to emphasize the universality of this Transcendent experience.

METANOIA—A TRANSFORMED WAY OF BEING

As I've already hinted, this deeper transformation—what Christian tradition names *Metanoia*—is far more than a shift in thought or feeling. In Greek, *Metanoia* signifies a profound change of mind and heart: a complete turning from the self-centered patterns of the Culture of Separation toward a new life shaped by self-giving Love.

This Divine Love, revealed fully in Christ, forms the foundation of a new Culture of Connection. It calls for authentic inner regeneration—a reorientation of how we live and love. Yet too often, Christian tradition has reduced metanoia to penance and punishment, rather than recognizing it as the transformative leap it truly is—from caterpillar to butterfly, from old self to new creation.

> *Metanoia is not just a change of attitude,*
> *a point of view, or a new philosophy—*
> *it is a change of being.*

The paradox is that you can't get "there" through concepts, thinking, feeling your way there, or even trying to get there. It's a real-world, embodied experience that reflects transformation. It's not something you can make happen; it's something that happens to you.

So, what exactly is Metanoia, and how does it relate to my life-changing experience? Perhaps the most clear description of Metanoia comes from a 5th-century monk, St. Diadochos of Photiki in Greece. For those of you who follow other religious traditions or none at all, I share this to convey a deeply felt experience, even though these words come from a religious perspective. St. Diadochos writes:

> "Those who truly love God never lose their longing for spiritual illumination—until it burns in their bones and transforms them completely. They live in the body, yet their souls journey ceaselessly toward God. Their hearts blaze with Divine Love, having once and for all transcended self-love in their love for God."

His words confirmed what I already knew: Metanoia isn't just a religious obligation, it's the spirit-led unfolding of a heart awakened by Divine Love.

I've never had a clearer understanding of what happened to me, the changes it sparked in my life, and the path it set me on. The Metanoia experience—being catapulted from ordinary reality to see the extraordinary and recognize the ordering structure beneath and beyond everything—activated my conscience and connected me to my Authentic Self.

Just as Western civilization has long conflated repentance with penance, many of us have been taught to view conscience as merely a constraint, like a brake on our worst impulses. Yet, by its truest definition, repentance means "to rethink." Paradoxically, rethinking arises not from the head but from the heart.

For instance, when we are about to do something wrong, our conscience might stir—a sense of "pre-guilt" that prevents us from acting in a non-virtuous way. This serves an essential function. Conscience, in this sense, supports order and integrity in a healthy society. However, that represents only a small part of what conscience means.

As a child, my experience of conscience resembled a transmission—a direct infusion of wisdom from what I would later understand as the luminous architecture of reality. It wasn't restrictive; it was joyful, vast, and liberating. Rather than being filled with "shalt nots," it felt like one big, life-affirming shalt.

Over time, I recognized this alignment—metanoia—most fully in the person and path of Jesus, but the turning had already begun long before I found the words for it.

Metanoia is a Spiritual Revolution of the Heart—an embrace of a life aligned with the Transcendent, guided by love, and rooted in community, shifting away from conformity to the systems that fragment us.

This inner movement wasn't about rejecting the world but about shifting my relationship with it. It was a reawakening to a deeper, transcendent reality—the heart of my "conversion" experience. This turning inward wasn't about doing without; it was about returning to the world with transformed eyes and a re-centered heart.

Turning away from the world in the spirit of Metanoia doesn't mean escaping to a cave, monastery, or ashram. It means reinhabiting the self with a different source at the center—becoming a new creation, animated by a new direction. As Saint Paul wrote, "Do not conform to the pattern of this world, but be transformed by the renewing of your mind." (Romans 12:2)

Metanoia reorders the soul, but it also reshapes the world. As my heart aligned more fully with Divine Love, I could no longer separate my spirituality from the suffering around me.

The transformation that began within demanded expression through virtue, action, and community.

The next stage of my journey would reveal that this sacred pattern was not meant to stay internal. It was meant to be embodied.

CHAPTER 3

EMBODYING THE BLUEPRINT: JESUS, VIRTUE, AND THE FOUNDATIONS OF A SYMBIOTIC SOCIETY

After awakening to the transcendent reality within, I could no longer view the world the same way. The luminous experiences I had encountered were not private treasures to be concealed; they were invitations to serve, act, and co-create a world more aligned with what I had seen and felt.

But this raised a deeper paradox:

> *How could something so beautiful, unified, and radiant with Love coexist with a world so fragmented, unjust, and wounded?*

Instead of retreating into a spiritual bubble, I was drawn more deeply into the world, seeking to understand the paradox I encountered at such a young age—the harmonious, unified order of luminosity on one hand and the fragmentation and disharmony on the other. That paradox continues to guide my life. It helps explain why my development diverged so sharply from that of my peers—and why I still find myself questioning our modern world:

"What's wrong with this picture?"

My inner grief didn't fade—it became fuel. I wasn't merely posing a philosophical question. It was a cry of the heart, as I was drawn into the world's suffering and invited to respond with Love.

LOVE AMID SUFFERING: A POETIC AWAKENING

I asked myself a question I've spent most of my life trying to answer: while I experience a deep sense of connectedness and illumination that seems to underlie and permeate all of life, why doesn't society operate this way? While hurricanes, floods, and fires are part of the natural world, what about the suffering caused by "unnatural disasters"—like war and poverty?

I made an absolute commitment, a vow to accept the suffering within myself and the entire world as my responsibility—and to do what I could to align the world with the Luminous Web I had experienced, bringing Heaven to Earth.

The following poem emerged from a season of profound inner turmoil and traces the journey from isolation to connection, ego to surrender, and the realization that we are never truly alone. Even in our suffering, Divine Love is always present.

Suffering is Never Alone but Shared
I feel the flow of life and death.
within and around me.

Embodying the Blueprint

Sometimes I resist in despair:
Why this senseless misery?
Tears are unleashed—
 a puddle, then a pool, then an ocean of sorrow
 from all the suffering.

The flesh cries out in confusion.
My small ego reels, torn by the sight.
Surely life is more than birth, sickness, pain,
old age, and fear of death.

Some drown the ache in distraction: drugs, possessions,
fame, power, sex, religion, politics, or social movements—
but none of it satisfies now.

Naked and raw,
I stand with nowhere to hide,
facing the elemental forces of creation.

Then—glorious surrender.
A veil of darkness breaks.
The Spirit of the Great Mystery moves through me.
 I feel connected to all beings.

Suffering is never alone but shared.
It is not aimless—there is an underlying direction.
It pushes us to let go—
of our silly games, our pretenses, petty lies and deceits—
until we contact the Truth within.

And in that naked Truth, we remember we were made
in the image of God—meant to reflect the Divine in Love.

We glimpse the eternal
beauty behind the cycle of creation and destruction,
life and death—
all of it yearning,
striving for awareness
of the Great Mystery.

Suffering and supreme peace—
they fit together
like hand and glove.

I began to realize that it's not about rejecting the world itself, but rather the patterns of the world that divert us from "what's written in our hearts," the beautiful life of the Spirit, and what Charles Eisenstein has called "the more beautiful world our hearts know is possible."

This deeper perspective reshaped how I viewed the world, which is why I felt like an alien, and still do. Maybe this is what Jesus meant when he said we are meant to live "…in the world but not of it." That tension between illumination and worldliness opened me to a deeper transformation previously mentioned—Metanoia, echoed across spiritual traditions, especially Christianity.

METANOIA AS A UNIVERSAL EXPERIENCE

Metanoia, while rooted in the Christian tradition, is echoed across cultures and movements. This is what Sarvodaya's Dr. Ariyaratne meant by "personality awakening"—that is, awakening beyond the limits of our egotism and recognizing that this awakening occurs within individuals, families, and an awakened physical, local community.

Dr. Ari wrote:

> "All our cravings for power, position, status, and wealth originate from egotism. Living among others with similar tendencies leads to competition, ill will, hatred, and ultimately, violent conflict. When a person undergoes spiritual awakening, these tendencies diminish, and relationships become healthier."

Reading this quote deepened my understanding of Metanoia and the awakened personality:

Metanoia isn't about acquiring more of what we think we desire. It's about being so radically transformed that our desires change entirely.

That's what happened to me. It has helped me understand how a Culture of Connection can arise from within a Culture of Separation.

In the fifty years since my first luminous experience, my path in life has been to reweave connections within myself, among individuals and organizations, and across nature and society. At the core of this work lies what I believe to be the most critical missing ingredient in today's movements for societal change: a Transcendent foundation of reality.

In retrospect, I realize I wasn't just brushing up against this Ancient Blueprint—I was being shaped by it. The Logos, this Divine ordering principle, imprinted on my life. For me, Metanoia represented a rite of passage: not an escape from the world, but a transformation that rooted me more deeply in it—no longer conforming to the dominant culture but learning to live from a different source.

But this turning wasn't just mine. I started to notice a pattern—others were awakening too, guided by the same inner impulse toward wholeness. What unfolded in my heart now seems to be awakening on a global scale—a quiet Metanoia stirring across humanity.

MASS METANOIA AND HUMANITY GROWING UP

Whether we know it or not, the "quickening" process of Metanoia is taking place, in one way or another, within many individuals and the communities to which they belong. Those in seemingly separate movement threads are being guided to come together, weaving a beautiful tapestry of a new Culture of Connection.

Guided by the Spirit into Metanoia, we can observe beyond today's polarized political, religious, and societal narratives—a new awareness essential for tackling our challenges.

By moving beyond the ideological and political constructs that subtly shape our identities, we uncover what it means to be a *Uniter* rather than a *Divider,* conscious agents of connection instead of unconscious tools of separation.

That leads us to a more hopeful question:

Could our entire species now be experiencing a sort of mass Metanoia, maturing from adolescence to adulthood, thus enabling us to turn our upside-down global Culture of Separation right-side up?

What if we're not merely children of God, but are evolving into adults of Good, called to embody the Divine Love we've received with maturity, courage, and compassion?

To awaken practically, we must first recognize—and then align with—the hidden ordering principle woven into the fabric of life. That sacred pattern became my sharpest focus through Jesus, who embodied this ordering principle with unmatched clarity.

JESUS AND THE ANCIENT BLUEPRINT OF LOVE

Fortunately, there is an antidote to the Culture of Separation—an ancient principle rooted in love that provides a pathway to a new Culture of Connection.

> *This Ancient Blueprint is not a distant ideal;*
> *it inspires a universal impulse for a*
> *Culture of Connection already alive deep within us.*

I sensed this during my Transcendent experiences, but it wasn't until I was introduced to Jesus and the Sermon on the Mount years later that I recognized the power and universality of the Ancient Blueprint as the sacred pattern of Divine Love.

While this message reached Western culture through Jesus, it is not based on or reliant upon any religion, spiritual following, philosophy, science, or institution. It stands alone as a proven template for functionality.

Although I was raised in a secular Jewish home, I would eventually see Jesus not only as a profound wisdom teacher but also as the living embodiment of the Voice of the Heart of Love that I had first encountered in a mystical experience. His life and teachings would later provide a personal form to a universal pattern I sensed long before I could name it.

As I've shared earlier, my own lineage on this path has been shaped most deeply by Jesus, whom I recognize as the clearest expression of the Ancient Blueprint—a sacred design I would also come to see reflected in other faith-rooted movements of love and justice, from the Gospel to Gandhi to Dr. A.T. Ariyaratne. That lineage of sacred action and relational wholeness continues to shape my life's work.

Jesus' primary teaching brings together two commandments from the Hebrew Scriptures:

> "You shall love the Lord your God with all your heart, with all your soul, with all your mind, and with all your strength."

And, *"You shall love your neighbor as yourself."*
There is no commandment greater than these.

Practiced together, they integrate and interweave the vertical and the horizontal dimensions of life. "Love God" is vertical and Transcendent. "Love your neighbor" is horizontal and immanent.

Love God and Love Others.

This prescription lies at the heart of the Ancient Blueprint to Unite Humanity—and holds the key to transforming our global Culture of Separation, beginning with ourselves and our communities.

But how does this blueprint truly manifest in the world? We start by embodying it through love in both its vertical and horizontal expressions.

VERTICAL AND HORIZONTAL LOVE: THE BLUEPRINT OF JESUS APPLIED IN THE WORLD

The Ancient Blueprint is not just a metaphor, story, superstition, or wishful thinking. It embodies a fundamental description of Reality—a Power that transcends and underpins the known physical forces of modern science, such as gravity and electromagnetism.

The Ancient Blueprint offers humanity a path forward and upward—through a radically transformed way of life and a fundamentally different view of the nature of power—by embodying and living in what Dr. Martin Luther King, Jr. called the Beloved Community. It is a timeless pattern through which the Transcendent becomes visible, shaping how we live, relate, and build the world.

The Culture of Connection, Sarvodaya, and the Symbiotic Networks I describe in this book illustrate how the patterning of the Ancient Blueprint of Divine Love can be directly translated into the formation of local community networks.

We serve as the translators of the Ancient Blueprint through our intentional, virtuous actions in the world.

As you will learn later, the Transcendent is expressed and embodied within us through universally recognized Virtues such as Love, generosity, sharing, faith, respect, kindness, compassion, self-control, trust, and charity, among many others.

These Virtues shape and unify our character, enabling us to serve others naturally and seamlessly. They unleash significant power that positively impacts those around us. Practicing the Virtues together doesn't just enrich individual lives—it nurtures the social fabric itself. The bottom line is that these virtues represent the living, real-world practice of the Ancient Blueprint.

Practicing the Virtues, we begin to quiet the inner fragmentation of conflicting thoughts and desires. Over time, this practice provides greater clarity and tunes us to a coherent, unified voice that rises from the center of our Being and resonates with Divine Love. This isn't merely a private spiritual achievement.

As I will explore throughout this book, that inner clarity—the alignment of heart, mind, and spirit—became the foundation for real-world transformation.

That's what happened for me.

The transformation I experienced affected not only my inner life but also my work in communities, economies, and civic systems. The path wasn't about retreating from the world but engaging with it through a different logic—one grounded in sacred relationality and expressed through concrete acts of love, justice, and co-creation.

As this inner coherence deepens within all of us, it naturally seeks expression in the external world. We begin by serving those closest to us—our families, neighbors, and local institutions such as churches, nonprofits, businesses, and civic groups. From there, this sacred impulse extends outward, connecting organizations and leaders and gradually creating networks of mutual benefit.

This is what I term *Connecting the Good*—linking the goodness and good works already present in our communities into something greater, reflecting the Ancient Blueprint and infused with the Transcendent.

> *When we embody the Transcendent,*
> *its power radiates throughout the relational web*
> *and animates the living nodes of grassroots,*
> *locally rooted communities.*

Embodying the Ancient Blueprint means allowing Divine Love to radiate through virtue, community, and the interconnected, living web of relationships. This sacred pattern, which I've come to recognize through my own luminous experiences, has been so obscured by the dominant culture that most people in postmodern society remain largely unaware of it.

If it appears that I am introducing many new terms right away, I am! Each of these terms—*Logos*, *Metanoia*, the *Transcendent*, and *Divine Love*—offers a way to make this unfamiliar world-view more accessible.

Perhaps this Ancient Blueprint feels so foreign to us because of our immersion in the Culture of Separation and the common, unquestioned beliefs we often mistake for reality.

To make the Ancient Blueprint more recognizable, we must first unearth and challenge the mental models that keep us bound to separation.

Turning an upside-down world right-side up requires a willingness to reexamine many of our inherited "truths"—including the Western myth of linear progress. One of these deeply embedded cultural assumptions appears in psychology's best-known model of human needs—Maslow's pyramid.

TURNING MASLOW'S PYRAMID ON ITS HEAD

Anyone who has come of age in the past century is familiar with psychologist Abraham Maslow's Hierarchy of Needs. At the base of his famous pyramid are survival essentials: food, clothing, shelter, and safety.

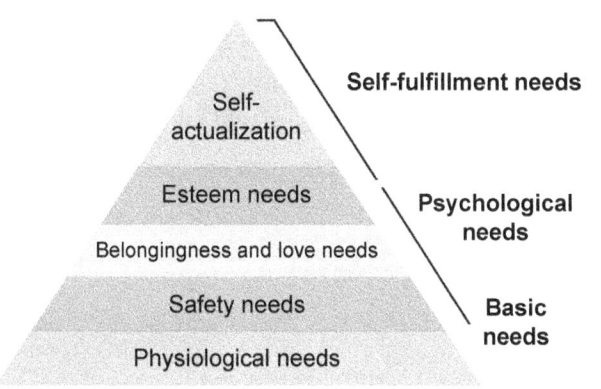

Maslow's Hierarchy of Needs—a classic model of human motivation.

Next comes self-esteem and family, meaningful work, and—at the pinnacle—self-actualization: the crowning achievement of the so-called Human Potential Movement. This may sound perfectly reasonable to the modern secular mind. From a worldview shaped by material progress divorced from spiritual grounding, it seems logical that higher needs can only be pursued once basic needs are satisfied.

But what if this framework has it backward or upside down?

What if the "actualized self"—that two-way portal to the Transcendent—is not the destination but the starting point of true growth?

Many ancient traditions—especially Indigenous ones—have long embraced this understanding. I was deeply encouraged when an Indigenous elder affirmed this view, stating bluntly that Maslow got it backwards.

In these traditional cultures, connection to "all that is"—to the Transcendent—is fundamental. Every action arises from that relationship, including how we care for our families, tend to the land, and engage with our communities.

We have a lot to learn from First Nations people. Their model of human flourishing emphasizes collective and relational aspects rather than individualism. It's not just about personal ascent but about community harmony. Among the Blackfeet Nation, whom Maslow studied, self-actualization was not a solitary climb but a shared journey, grounded in kinship, ecology, and the sacred.

Indigenous wisdom inverts Maslow's pyramid: self-giving love, not self-seeking growth, heals the world.

Embodying the Blueprint

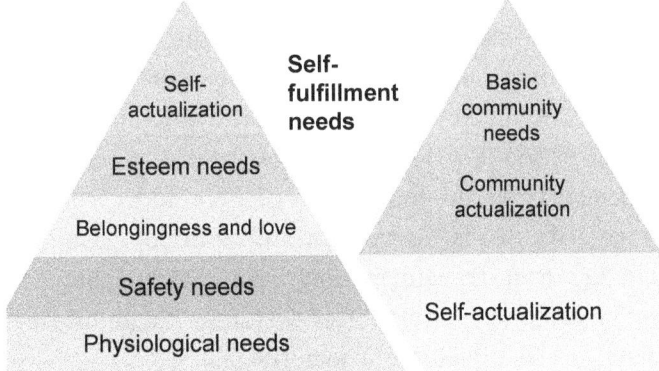

In this context, Maslow's pyramid illustrates not only a theory of needs but also the principles of a Culture of Separation. Spirit is separated from matter in this worldview, and the sacred is regarded as a final luxury rather than a foundational reality.

Western psychology and social movements, even when well-intentioned, often reinforce this separation by ignoring the foundational role of the Transcendent. They focus on feeding the hungry or building a new economy, yet they rarely confront the deeper hunger for meaning and connection that fuels so much of our brokenness.

This is where movements like Sarvodaya Shramadana in Sri Lanka provide prophetic insight. This sixty-five-year-old, Buddhist-inspired movement integrates the Ancient Blueprint into every aspect of daily life, affirming the same truths long recognized by Indigenous wisdom.

In Western terms, Sri Lanka may be seen as materially poor—many citizens are at the bottom of Maslow's hierarchy. Yet, spiritually, they often begin where Maslow ends. In Sarvodaya, the experience of sacred connection cannot be earned. It's the starting point.

Material service is not separate from spiritual truth. Feeding the hungry, building villages, and healing the land are all rooted in what Buddhist tradition refers to as the Four Sublime Abodes: compassion, loving kindness, empathetic joy, and equanimity. These Transcendent Virtues flow outward into practical action.

Virtues serve as the foundation of a community that collectively meets its needs. Sarvodaya and Symbiotic Culture both acknowledge that transformation isn't merely about feeding the hungry or constructing better systems—it's about nurturing self-giving love as the Heart of society.

Sarvodaya illustrates what's possible: a seamless connection between our inner and outer lives, the individual and the community. We don't need to reinvent the wheel; the principles are already present, waiting to be reawakened within us. If humanity is to pass safely through its rite of passage, we may need to invert more than Maslow's pyramid—we may need to invert the global pyramid of power that keeps us bound to scarcity, division, and ego.

Including the Western belief that spiritual connection comes last, not first.

Spirituality in the West is long overdue for a significant reboot—not just to survive, but to thrive.

True actualization—true service—begins not at the top, but at the root. This entails a personal inversion as well. Or perhaps, a conversion—turning the heart away from the conformity of the Culture of Separation and toward communion with the Transcendent.

This turning is not a retreat from the world, but a return to the Source that can heal and transform it. For me, that return began not with clarity, but with quiet trust in something I didn't yet understand.

Though I had no clear concept of God at the time—no theology, no religious framework—something unmistakable was guiding me. I didn't have the words for it then, but I listened.

Looking back, I understand that this inner guidance was what the Christian tradition recognized as the quiet prompting of the Holy Spirit—an ever-present companion who awakens us to more profound truth and calls us toward Love.

This return is also a step into what Jesus called the Kingdom of Heaven—an unseen but ever-present realm where Love reigns, and the last are first.

It is not far away, but near, already within and among us. That return also marks the rediscovery of something ancient and essential within us—our Authentic Self, the living bridge between the Transcendent and the world.

Inverting Maslow's pyramid is also an invitation to return to ourselves, not to the ego-driven self, but to the one rooted in sacred connection.

THE AUTHENTIC SELF: FOUNDATION FOR A NEW SOCIETY

By returning to the world with Transcendent Virtues that re-inhabit us with renewed minds and hearts, we gain the strength and capacity to help unite our communities and co-create a new society rooted in these universal principles.

That's why I am writing this book: To support those seeking a fundamental societal and cultural breakthrough, and who recognize that age-old wisdom and practical methods of whole-system change are necessary.

Once again, I am offering these insights in retrospect. It took me years—five decades—to integrate the awareness that emerged through me so unexpectedly. In those early years, I lacked clear language for what I was experiencing. Poetry became my refuge—a means to express what could not yet be fully explained, to give voice to the inexpressible.

In my early twenties, I wrote a poem that expressed humanity's universal unity, a pattern from the Ancient Blueprint that would serve as a beacon for me over the next fifty years. I am sharing only a part of it here.

WHO AM I?
>bound to the group, clan, or tribe to which I belong?

>I am American, Chinese, Russian—underneath,
>there is no country
>I am black, brown, white—underneath,
>there is no color
>I am Liberal and Conservative—underneath,
>there are no party politics.

>I am Jewish, Christian, Buddhist—underneath,
>we share a longing for the Transcendent.

>We each have our own universe of things important to us, and yet, I need you, and you need me, we strive for similar goals. We are brothers and sisters of Earth.

>We are all different and yet the same—part of one living system: Earth, our common home, entrusted to our care by the Creator.

It is a wonderful paradox, autonomy and dependence the necessary unity, with all the participants free from impunity.

The human world appears to be made up of many differentiated forms and tribes, and we identify with them, forgetting that underneath, we come from a deeper Transcendent reality; we are really One Humanity and One Family.

Are you ready to build a world that celebrates this diversity, yet unites us in the shared fellowship of Love and Service?"

Yes, you may feel this universal dream and soul longing, calling us into a deeper relationship with the Creator of all—and this sweet harmony, ringing throughout creation, the mirror calling us into a relationship with each other.

WHO AM I? I AM YOU.

The next step in applying this universal understanding to the human condition involves recognizing and engaging with another network that reflects the Luminous Web—the Web of Nature.

CHAPTER 4

NATURE'S WEB: LESSONS FROM THE LIVING WORLD

If the Logos offers the invisible architecture of meaning, then Nature provides the visible reflection—what I have come to call Nature's Web. While my previous out-of-this-world experiences propelled me into an interconnected, nonphysical Luminous Web, my growing love of nature brought me down to Earth.

*I began to sense that Nature's Web
was not fundamentally separate from the Transcendent,
but a living mirror of it—
woven into both the seen and the unseen.*

Throughout my teenage years and into my twenties, I continued to have extraordinary experiences that revealed the architecture underlying life itself. I lived in two worlds, and my heart and mind sought to understand and integrate these experiences while appearing normal on the outside.

Before graduating from Monterey High School in 1976, I experienced a series of adventures in nature that deepened my understanding. During high school, I was fortunate to find a fellow outdoor adventurer in a friend who had also moved to Monterey from Virginia. We were both drawn to outdoor activities that provided a sense of adventure and even danger, pushing us beyond suburban culture and our comfort zones.

While still in high school, we were invited to join a group of older students from the University of California, Santa Cruz, on a backpacking trip to the Sierra Nevada Mountains. We hiked with 60-pound packs along rugged, high-altitude trails in the Palisade Glacier region.

The summer after graduation, my friend and I had the opportunity to explore more of the natural world by working on a farm in eastern Oregon. Talk about being down-to-Earth!

We woke up each morning at 4 AM to move hand-line irrigation pipes, surrounded by curious cattle and bothered by swarms of mosquitoes. This experience provided me with a taste of rural small-town life and a direct understanding of the symbiosis between nature and the cycle of growth on a farm.

My friend and I continued climbing and scaling the walls of Yosemite and mountaineering in the Northwest, including Mount Rainier. The following summer, I worked as a station guard and Helitack firefighter in Idaho's Challis National Forest, sometimes rappelling from helicopters and hiking up to forty miles to combat wildfires. These experiences deepened my admiration for nature's vastness and made the routines of civilization feel small by comparison.

Yet even amid the outward adventures, a quieter inner pilgrimage was beginning—one that would reveal Nature not merely as scenery, but as a sacred teacher.

These wild places weren't escapes. They were initiations into a deeper communion with life itself.

HOW THE EARTH BECAME MY TEACHER

Throughout all these experiences, I was too occupied with the physical demands of climbing and firefighting to find much time for reflection. It wasn't until I reached my early twenties that I began to recognize Nature as a teacher, a guide, and a way to view human society in a larger context.

Growing up in a Jewish household, I had been exposed to the Hebrew Scriptures, even if I didn't understand their meaning then. Later, I would recognize that what I beheld in nature echoed the ancient wisdom of the psalmist, David: "The Heavens declare the glory of God; the skies proclaim the work of His hands" (Psalm 19:1).

*Even without theological language,
I began to sense the living testament of
the Creator's beauty, written into the world.*

These insights emerged from solitude in nature and manifested as poems, some of which I've already shared. They felt like divine promptings, arising almost effortlessly from a deep place within me—what some might recognize as the voice of the Holy Spirit, or the sacred speaking from within. At the time, I didn't know how to interpret these experiences. Looking back, I understand them as deep, intuitive reflections—stirrings of the heart awakened by the Spirit moving in and through creation.

Meanwhile, I began college at the University of California, Santa Cruz, with dreams of becoming an astrophysicist. However, mastering advanced quadratic equations and the required math was not as thrilling as the immersive natural experiences I had enjoyed in previous years. Looking back, it's no surprise that I returned to my newfound love for biology. As a child, I dreamed of combining my passion for the cosmos and the natural world by becoming an exobiologist and exploring other worlds.

I also became an admirer of Jane Goodall, the world-renowned primatologist. I was fascinated by animal intelligence and the possibilities for communication between humans and animals, which naturally sparked my interest in dolphins, pilot whales, and other marine mammals.

LISTENING TO THE DEEP: LESSONS FROM OCEAN LIFE

I spent several years researching pilot whales and, as part of that journey, lived on Catalina Island, thirty miles off the coast of California, for three months, immersing myself in their culture and society. I was also fascinated by how pilot whales and dolphins lived in symbiotic cooperation.

The dolphins learned from the pilot whales and even adopted their hunting strategy, following them closely. Rather than competing for territory and food, they worked together as a larger community.

In the ocean's silence, I heard the deeper call: to live in symbiotic harmony.

Of course, the natural world includes sharks as well as dolphins, and predation is as natural as symbiotic cooperation. Still, I couldn't help but wonder why human beings, with all their "superior intelligence," default to competition against one another.

In 1981, I moved to San Diego to pursue my master's degree in biology, aiming to unravel the mystery of whale and dolphin communication. That's when things became genuinely interesting, and I began to have experiences that extended far beyond my academic studies. The natural cooperation between marine animals stirred something deeper in me: A longing to understand why society, with all its brilliance, seemed to drift further from such harmony.

As mentioned previously, I kept my luminous experiences to myself. I didn't confide in anyone—not my parents, not my friends, not a rabbi, priest, or other spiritual teacher, nor a wise elder. Thus, integrating and reconciling the dissonance between the two seemingly contradictory worlds of the Luminous Web and the tangled web of society became an "inside" job.

In 1982, at 23, these internal churnings broke through, inspiring me to write poetry that felt as if it came from nowhere. I call it poetry, for lack of a better label. This continued throughout the decade. My time spent outdoors in natural settings inspired most of these early writings. The first occurred during a visit to my family home in Monterey, California, at Jacks Peak Park.

NATURE'S GREAT CHAIN OF BEING: THE FOREST AS BLUEPRINT

I walked alone in the pine forest on a bright, sunny, warm day. The rustling leaves, fragrant air, and subtle play of light and shadow created an ambiance of profound serenity and awe-inspired wonder. I lay on the ground to observe a slug eating a mushroom.

The forest didn't speak in words—but it revealed the Logos in every breath and being.

BIRTHING THE SYMBIOTIC AGE

Suddenly, a flood of images filled my mind, and I was overcome with emotion. Then, as if the voice of Love—the indwelling Presence—were speaking through the fibers of my being, a still, small voice rose from within, describing a direct and living experience of Nature's Web. The words came so clearly I had to write them down, as if taking dictation.

I didn't think about the words; they came almost automatically as a complete communication—a "download" of information that instantly made sense.

Little did I know that these spontaneous downloads would continue for years—and that it would take decades to fully absorb, live, and embody their more profound lessons in the world. They became a bridge, linking my childhood encounters with the Luminous Web to the living symbiosis of Nature and eventually to my mission of reconnecting a separated, suffering humanity.

As I lay on the ground watching the slug eat, I had an insight that informed my worldview. I realized that, despite the significant diversity in the forest, all creatures are directly or indirectly connected within the fabric of an extensive ecosystem. I could relate to the slug, the mushroom, and the interconnectedness of the entire forest. Individually, each is both a part and a whole—simultaneously integral to the ecosystem, intertwining mutual goals of survival, growth, and thriving.

In the forest, I saw the next reflection of the Transcendent... all this diversity happening in rhythmic accord. The slug and the mushroom are distinct organisms that have formed a symbiotic relationship within the larger whole of the forest. I sensed that behind this intricate symphony of life was the signature of a loving Creator—an unseen Artist weaving together every living thing into a greater whole.

So, why is this important?

Nature's Web

Nature reveals that cooperation is not only possible in our society but also our most natural path to thriving. To understand how Nature's Web reflects the deeper Luminous Web, I've found the concept of a "Holon" incredibly helpful. A holon is both a whole and a part, just as you are a complete individual and a member of a family, a community, a species, and a planet.

This concept is derived from the Greek word Holos, meaning "whole," and implies that reality is made up of nested systems—wholes within wholes, parts within parts.

> *Nature arises from a deeper reality,*
> *forming self-organizing, nested structures*
> *shaped by a Transcendent pattern,*
> *from subatomic particles to galaxies.*

You and I function as holons. We're more than just collections of atoms, cells, and organs—we're also smaller parts of larger holons: families, neighborhoods, ecosystems, humanity, and the universe. We live in a dynamic relationship with every level of this great chain of Being. This realization helped reconcile my longing for spiritual depth with my calling to practical community transformation.

One powerful example of this natural holonic pattern is the connection between trees, mushrooms, and fungi in a forest. A Smithsonian article, "Do Trees Talk to Each Other?" describes how mycorrhizal networks—a kind of underground symbiosis—link the root systems of trees to microscopic fungal threads.

> "The trees provide sugar to the fungi, which gather nutrients like nitrogen and phosphorus from the soil. In return, the trees absorb these nutrients. Trees even 'talk'

through this system—sending chemical, hormonal, and slow electrical signals to warn each other of danger or share resources.

Scientists have even recorded root-level crackling sounds at 220 hertz—inaudible to human ears—suggesting that a kind of sonic communication may also be taking place."

*Not a single command given, yet perfect order—
mycelial networks reveal creation's deeper, symbiotic design.*

SELF-ORGANIZING WEB OF NATURE

This network evolved over millions of years. It's a living template—a self-organizing, interdependent whole. It's a beautiful metaphor for how nature works and a living template for how human communities might evolve.

In these vast networks of mutual nourishment, I perceived more than how forests function—I saw a mirror of what we had forgotten: a sacred blueprint for connectedness, care, and collective well-being. It revealed a model for how human communities might reclaim their lost coherence and learn, once again, to thrive in interdependence.

The intelligence of these systems doesn't come from a central command, but from the relationships themselves—life emerges through connection.

This is an example of self-organization: the spontaneous emergence of order from the interactions of individual components without any external direction. This principle is found in biology and applies to human society.

*Nature has no boss directing its order;
its systems emerge from an intensely patterned reality
that shapes their nested structure.*

This led me to a deeper question. What's the underlying reality driving the system of creation, and how do humans fit into and connect with it? Before I share my observation, I must admit that I often feel like a rhizome—part of a living mycelial network—driven to connect silos within human communities. I know many of you feel the same, and I hope my story inspires more of this connective impulse.

Humanity self-organizes like forests, emerging from parts into wholes. First, tribes and then specialized silos grow as populations expand, requiring complex coordination and institutions. Unlike Nature's Web or the Transcendent Logos, however, as human culture has gained complexity, it has lost coherence. Though we follow nature's part-whole structure, society now divides and categorizes itself into isolated silos. To restore wholeness, we urgently need new forms of network coordination.

BIRTHING THE SYMBIOTIC AGE

RESTORING THE SACRED DESIGN: HEALING THE ROOTS OF DIVISION

Historians Arnold Toynbee and Oswald Spengler outline the rise and fall of civilizations, illustrating how domination hierarchies, while effective in the short term, eventually break down under their own weight. What begins with promise—such as individual freedom, market growth, and rapid technological progress—can devolve into a global system marked by division, disconnection, and control.

The control systems of empire follow the same old pattern Julius Caesar called Divide et Impera—divide and Rule. Today, this logic remains active, shaping a worldwide economic system—corporatism aligned with political elites—that has turned us into isolated consumers, conditioned to chase pleasure instead of purpose, superficial transaction instead of deep trust.

But this isn't just a social or economic problem; it reveals a deeper spiritual rupture. It reflects a profound disconnection from the Transcendent—from the original harmony and coherence of the Sacred Design, where the One and the Many exist in unity, and all things serve mutual benefit.

Beneath the surface of this breakdown, however, lies a forgotten order. Just as nature flourishes by following an invisible but trustworthy blueprint, human communities were meant to grow through patterns of mutuality, not domination. This ancient ordering principle—the Logos—offers more than a metaphor. It's a real, living structure rooted in Divine Love, waiting to be remembered and lived into once again.

That vision has become the heart of my life's work.

In the same way that the mycelial network nourishes an entire forest, the Logos pattern has guided me to weave communities into networks of mutual nourishment and connection, bridging silos and healing the divides that fragment society.

> *To "unite the cosmos in Love" is not just poetry—it's the only Power strong enough to counteract the atomization of modern life.*

When we reconnect the Logos of the Transcendent with the principle of connection in Nature's Web, we participate in its restoration, unleashing Divine Love as the driving force of social regeneration.

In the next chapter, we'll explore how this sacred pattern—stretching from forest floor to star-studded sky—is more than symbolic. It is a living blueprint for how our communities can evolve, reweave belonging, and remember what it means to be truly human.

CHAPTER 5

AWAKENED BY WONDER: A DEEPENING AWARENESS OF THE SACRED ORDER

The forest didn't just stir awe—it uncovered order.

Beneath the beauty of the trees and the stillness of the wilderness, I discovered a living network: the mycelial web. It revealed a more cohesive and cooperative social structure than anything I had witnessed in humanity. Immersing myself in these patterns, I perceived something profound: nature doesn't merely survive by competing—it flourishes by connecting. This insight transformed my perspective on humanity.

> *What if the forest's design—the invisible threads of trust, exchange, and mutual nourishment— offered humanity a blueprint for coexistence?*

What if the connection between trees and fungi wasn't just a metaphor, but a reflection of a deeper pattern woven into the fabric of reality? This insight unites nature, Spirit, and society—a principle echoed across wisdom traditions for millennia.

These threads—the ecological, the mystical, and the moral—converged in my own experience through what I recognized as the Luminous Web. It was not merely symbolic; it was visceral and real. And it pointed me toward the deeper architecture of love that binds all things.

THE LUMINOUS WEB, NATURE'S WEB, AND THE PATTERN OF LOVE

As I reflected on my luminous experiences, the Logos revealed itself as the highest and most Transcendent ordering principle, known as Wisdom in the Old Testament and by the Greeks and early Christians as the source of order and meaning. The Logos is both the builder and sustainer of reality, embodied most clearly in Jesus' Great Commandment: "Love God, Love Others."

This command reflects the Ancient Blueprint inscribed in reality—a timeless invitation to a New Creation and a new Beloved Community.

> *To truly transform society, we must begin by healing our separation from the Transcendent, nature, one another, and ourselves.*

This realization became the touchstone of my life—not just an insight, but a daily call to action. The Culture of Separation tempts us to look away from suffering—or to ease it without confronting its roots. A Culture of Connection calls us to face the world's pain—its suffering and fragmentation—because, to reiterate St. Maximus' prescient words, we are meant "to unite the cosmos in Love."

Each of us can embody this sacred pattern—"Love God, Love Others"—in our families, neighborhoods, and communities, becoming bridges that reconnect Heaven and Earth. By uniting the cosmos in love—linking the silos of people, institutions, and causes—we begin building a world grounded in Love and Wisdom. In doing so, we help restore Creation's original harmony.

This isn't just a spiritual insight—it's the foundation for a new way of organizing society.

What I discovered in solitude in nature was profoundly different from my earlier adventures. Free from the distractions of city life and human noise, I began to experience myself as part of something infinitely larger. Immersed in that stillness, I sensed something inescapable—an underlying universal order in every leaf, wind current, and birdsong.

I was no longer just an observer of nature's web—I was a participant. I felt myself both part of and whole within the Great Chain of Being, a living reflection of the Luminous Web. Fractal patterns of unity and diversity emerged, revealing the Transcendent intricately woven into creation. Nature's web didn't just mirror ecological systems—it revealed a spiritual architecture, echoing the Divine harmony I had first glimpsed at twelve.

Here's one of the poems I wrote that captures this experience:

> I am alone in a snow-covered meadow—just me, a coyote, birds, trees, and rocks.
>
> But I'm not afraid. Here, I see my Authentic Self, reflected like an undistorted mirror.
>
> I love the Earth, her life forms, her moods,
> both wild and calm.
>
> Creation itself is a mirror of a deeper Reality—
> Transcendent, and known by many as God.

Often, when alone in nature, I found myself surrounded by fierce weather. It was as if I were part of a universe in motion, sensing nature's energy around me and surging through my own being. During one storm, as the wind howled and hail struck the ground, a poem emerged from deep within me:

> The storm's center draws me in—its swirling
> heart pulsing with the rhythm of the universe.
>
> Can you see creation and destruction, life and death,
> light and darkness, and past, present, and future at the
> center, where peace lives and breathes?
>
> I press forward—lightning, wind, hail, and ice engulf me.
> But to go further is to be lost, overwhelmed by the storm's
> power.
>
> So many of us are caught here, lost in the world, mistaking
> the storm of our minds for reality, forgetting our deeper
> purpose, forgetting the truth.

These experiences, first felt in the depths of my being, soon reshaped how I saw the world, illuminating society's disconnection and the urgent need for reconnection. I sensed a deep thread linking the Luminous Web and Nature's Web in these spontaneous downloads. It intensified my curiosity: *Why was humanity so out of alignment with the harmony I now knew was possible?*

These encounters grounded me in a more conscious reality, revealing my place on the broader web and offering insight into what was unfolding in humanity at large.

This deep pattern of Love revealed itself everywhere—not only in scripture and philosophy, but also in the silence of snowfields and the rage of storms.

These moments didn't merely inspire me; they initiated me. They marked a turning point, showing my life as part of something larger. Wonder was no longer just a doorway; it became my compass, guiding me toward a deeper sense of purpose.

AWAKENED BY WONDER

As I shared in Chapter 1, my luminous experience set me apart from my peers and put me on an unexpected path—one that shaped the rest of my life.

Joseph Campbell famously described this archetypal passage as the "hero's journey," a call that echoes across cultures and time. In my case, the journey began not with a sword or a quest, but with wonder—with a direct encounter that shattered my assumptions and awakened a deep sense of purpose. Like many before me, I felt exiled from the familiar world, drawn into a liminal space where everything I thought I knew dissolved.

> *The call was not to become a hero,*
> *but to leave the ordinary behind,*
> *descend into mystery,*
> *and return bearing something sacred to share.*

What awaited me in that mystery was more than insight—it was initiation. For me, the Luminous Web and the Logos were not abstract ideas—they were revelations calling me to help restore harmony to a fractured humanity.

Then came another wave—an even deeper encounter with the Transcendent, one that clarified the Voice within and carried me further into the current of divine communion:

My whole body vibrates as I become immersed in your sweet harmony. The current moves through me—every cell, every molecule, every atom alive, conscious of life.

Like a stream winding through a lush forest, this force is gentle, warm, and soothing.

Oh, the light illuminates my inner vision. Glowing clouds of purple—forming, dissolving—now dance as waves, like still water stirred by a stone.

Waves rise from within. Inner voices converge into one voice; many notes become one liquid melody, attuned to the universe's song.

But there is only one voice, one chord in the depth of my soul.

I didn't break through to the Source of all things. The Voice of the Heart of Love rose from within me, and all was known.

What I encountered wasn't just a purification—it was a revelation. I felt myself aligning with a deeper, unifying principle of existence. It was as if I had pierced the veil of surface identities and egoic patterns to glimpse the Transcendent unity behind the world's multiplicity. This shift changed everything.

More than a religious conversion, my real experiences expanded my vision beyond the binary of belief and non-belief, faith and skepticism.

I'm neither a theologian nor a philosopher, but I've studied deeply how humans across cultures have tried to understand reality. Ironically, many of these systems—designed to reveal truth and foster unity—have instead become sources of division.

And so, awakened by wonder, I wondered:

> *How can we translate these inner realizations into outward transformation? How can we apply these inner revelations to address the world's brokenness? How can inner unity bring forth societal unity, despite our diverse and divergent worldviews?*

This marked a turning point. The next phase of my journey required me to confront division, not only within myself but also in societal structures. The crisis was not just internal but cultural, spiritual, and civilizational. What would it take to bridge these divides, not through uniformity, but through a deeper communion?

That's where we turn now.

THE CRISIS OF DIVISION AND THE CALL TO COMMUNION

It's natural for humanity to seek meaning through various worldviews—religious, spiritual, scientific, and cultural. However, when these perspectives become rigid silos, we lose sight of the deeper mystery that connects us all—and of what truly matters: living authentic Transcendence in community life.

Once institutionalized—whether by religion or politics—sacred truths can devolve into tribalism, self-interest, and territorial defense within a Culture of Separation.

Consider these differing—and often competing—religious worldviews:

- the "new age" view that God is in everything (Pantheism)
- the notion that God is the Universe (Monism)
- the segment of religious belief in a distant "Sky Daddy" God—an off-planet deity dwelling in an unreachable heaven (Hard Transcendence), and
- the scientific materialist worldview (Physicalism), which holds that only the material world is real, reducing any sense of the Transcendent to brain chemistry.

Although these perspectives differ, each can limit mystery, deflect responsibility, or keep us comfortably isolated in our own silos.

My own journey moved through several of them. My first awakening to Absolute Reality was a wordless knowing—beyond form and belief—that, over time, unfolded into a living relationship with a personal-yet-transcendent God. That placed me in a seeming contradiction: I was a "seeker," drawn to an abstract, impersonal Ground of Being, yet now deeply connected to a personal God who knows, loves, and calls us.

Reconciling these within myself became my first act of bridge-building—proof that what is reconciled within can also be reconciled between people.

In time, I came to see that the way of self-giving love—lived most clearly in the life and teachings of Jesus—offered a path that could hold both the personal and the universal. This realization didn't diminish my respect for other wisdom traditions; it deepened my conviction that any path rooted in such love can find common ground.

From that place of inner reconciliation, the larger calling became clear. We argue over ideologies while the world around us fractures. It's time to unite beyond all distinctions. Building a new parallel Symbiotic Society and Culture has become an all-hands-on-deck moment for all of us.

> *We must rise above narrow worldviews and concentrate on what unites us: nurturing local communities by honoring the Transcendent and practicing universal virtues, such as generosity, compassion, courage, and humility.*

These virtues are vital for uniting people around our shared human needs: food, water, energy, local economy, arts, culture, and care for the Earth.

And here's the hopeful part: studies show that 90 percent of people—whether religious, spiritual but not religious, agnostic, or even atheist—believe in a Transcendent higher power of some kind. Most of us sense there is more to existence than material reality alone.

Yet, the Culture of Separation—and those who profit from keeping us divided, distracted, and siloed—pushes us toward a different kind of "unity": a top-down, godless "religion" of global consumerism, techno-utopianism, and transhumanism, where algorithms replace relationships and convenience substitutes for community.

It's time for a new alliance. Whether their starting point is theism, non-theism, or something in between, leaders and seekers from religious, spiritual, non-religious, and civic traditions must come together in humility and courage—not in uniformity, but in shared commitment to restore the Transcendent to community life.

The measure is not uniformity of belief, but the shared practice of love and the honoring of what is truly sacred.

This book explores how that restoration is already beginning—and in Section 4, I'll share a practical framework for building it together. But before structure comes spirit. Before blueprints, we need being.

For me, that rediscovery began—again—in the quiet presence of nature, where wonder invites us back into communion.

FREEDOM AND THE SACRED CURRENT

Nature was the window that continuously revealed the cosmic and natural order to me, reflecting the organizing patterns of harmony, coherence, our divine impulses, and the profound pattern of love. It showed me that true freedom is not about following the whims of the ego, but rather becoming liberated from inner conflict, enabling me to hear and obey the voice of conscience and my Authentic Self.

Rather than being enslaved by the rulers and demands of this world, I found myself engaging more fully in life's deeper current. Just as the Luminous Web had come unbidden in childhood, these natural revelations arose from within me, not from external teachings but from a direct communion with creation.

We often call the spiritual path a "journey of seeking." But doesn't that imply what we seek lies somewhere "out there"? In contrast, my luminous experience sought me. I didn't chase it—it welcomed me unexpectedly and undeservedly. It was inescapable, yet it made me feel freer than I had ever felt before.

> *Paradoxically, freedom came not from striving but from surrender.*

It is the state I most associate with being immersed in the Luminous Web and encased in nature's embrace. But not the kind of freedom our culture glorifies: doing whatever we want, whenever we want, without consideration of others. Not the freedom to consume without consequence or pursue every passing desire.

Instead, I discovered a deeper kind of freedom—freedom from the push and pull of those desires, both my own and those broadcast 24/7 by what I now call the modern Tower of Babble.

The ancient story of Babel isn't just a myth—it's become an algorithm. Social media platforms, powered by AI, monetize and amplify our divisions while keeping us tethered to our devices. This has led to increasing fragmentation into isolated subcultures—political, religious, social, ideological—each speaking its own language.

Sound familiar? It's no accident.

Just as Babel once fractured human unity through language, today's technologies mimic that ancient confusion—only now, they're digitized and designed for maximum disconnection. Modern Babel isn't myth—it's code.

Modern Babel isn't myth—it's algorithmic.

The Tower of Babel has morphed into a Cell Tower of Babble. The memes and messages may feel connected, but they often create more separation than understanding.

We are "connected" but not united, informed but not formed by a shared reality or common purpose.

And yet, even amid this noise, I saw another way, not through ideology but through reorientation. Freedom was no longer about personal preference—it became about loyalty—a higher loyalty that transcended tribe, ego, and division.

HIGHER LOYALTY: THE PATH OF METANOIA

During this time, my understanding of freedom began to deepen—not as the license to do whatever I pleased, but as alignment with something greater: the sacred current of the Transcendent. I was no longer limited by the fluctuations of thought, feeling, or desire.

I began to understand what it meant to follow the natural order—not out of compulsion, but as an act of love and inner resonance. It felt like a liberation more real than any external permission. I captured this experience in a poem:

> A gem of the finest quality was waiting, one day, waiting to be seen.
>
> The wind's ebb and flow imprint on my mind—I'm not just watching, but participating with the trees in a universe set in motion.
>
> Could the gem reside in the wind? I can't see it, but it brushes my ears, whispering, *"I'm free—I follow the natural order."*

This was true freedom: not rebellion, but alignment.
These "gems" were Transcendent energies, alive in all creation.

Dirt and rock became precious, like jewels. The ordinary became miraculous.

Creation became scripture—a sacred text bearing God's fingerprints, inviting awe, humility, and reverence. As wind danced through trees and rivers sang over stone, I understood something essential: real freedom flows with—not against—the sacred pattern of life.

And yet, that was only the beginning.

A more profound liberation awaited—the discovery of the self beneath the surface self. I began questioning my inherited social identities and the labels I had accepted as "me."

Was I my profession, my nationality, my religion? Or was there something deeper waiting to be revealed?

I realized that true freedom is not found in isolated self-fulfillment, but in the mutual recognition of our shared humanity. It arises when we move beyond roles and masks and meet one another authentically—as whole persons.

> *There's no escaping identity,*
> *but we can choose where*
> *our loyalty lies.*

Reflecting on this shift in perception, I recognize it was crucial to the development of what I now refer to as misdirected loyalty. I first articulated this concept in a poem from Chapter 3, "Who Am I?", where I examined how we fragment ourselves by race, religion, profession, gender, politics, nationality, and tribe. While these divisions aren't inherently wrong, when they become the primary lens through which we relate, they confine us to silos and obscure our deeper sense of belonging.

Here is an excerpt from that poem:
> We are all of the same species, divided only by misdirected loyalties.
>
> If I say I am a child of Father God, holding this higher loyalty first—and also a part of beautiful Creation, Mother Earth...
> a brother to all her diverse peoples and life forms,
> many would scoff and call me a naive dreamer.
>
> But tell me honestly—does the old way still work?

Short answer: No.

This key insight—about where our loyalties lie—didn't come from philosophy. It emerged after experiencing union with the Divine order. From the Luminous Web I touched at twelve, to the web of nature that unfolded in my twenties, I was undergoing a more profound transformation—what I've already referred to as Metanoia: a turning of the mind and heart, a reorientation from illusion to reality.

I began to see how easily superficial divisions capture our loyalties, how we inhabit social bubbles that feel like community but often function as walls, and how true freedom—freedom in harmony with the sacred order—requires realignment. Realignment not just of identity, but of loyalty. Not to a political party. Not to a tribe. But to Divine Love.

Only from that ground can we begin to build a society not on domination, but on belonging. And...belonging requires more than emotional openness—it calls for a shift in how we think and what we believe is real. I soon realized that the deepest prison wasn't around me but within me. And it would take a long reckoning with the mind to find liberation.

BIRTHING THE SYMBIOTIC AGE

THE TYRANNY AND LIBERATION OF THE MIND

During this period of inner formation, I encountered what I later termed the "tyranny of the mind"—a deeply ingrained tendency to over-identify with thought, reinforced by the secular religion of materialism. This modern worldview disconnects us from the Transcendent source experienced in the Luminous Web and in Nature's quiet order.

This universal Transcendent—known by various names across cultures and eras—underlies reality's self-organizing patterns. Whether described by mystics, sages, or quantum physicists, each tradition points to the same truth: reality is more than what can be measured or reasoned.

Yet the rational intellect, when unanchored from the Transcendent, struggles to comprehend this depth. It attempts to reduce the sacred to data, mystery to mechanism, love to instinct, and meaning to chance.

In doing so, it forfeits access to the very dimension that defines our humanity.

Our modern mindset, shaped by centuries of materialist thinking, has come to treat anything intuitive, emotional, or spiritual as suspect—mere byproducts of brain chemistry, evolutionary detours, or childhood conditioning.

Meanwhile, advertising and media overwhelm us with countless options, conditioning us to consume rather than reflect. The sacred is buried under continuous stimulation. Our smartphones serve as both mirrors and masks, providing us with identity while depriving us of introspection.

We scroll, but we no longer see. We click, but we rarely connect. This disconnection represents the spiritual crisis of our time.

The Culture of Separation has denied that Virtue has a Source. In doing so, it has rejected the notion that principles like love, compassion, justice, and kindness are woven into the very fabric of reality itself. For 500 years, mind-made belief systems and mechanistic institutions have overwritten the Ancient Blueprint—the sacred architecture that once served as humanity's universal operating system.

The result? A world increasingly out of sync with the Web of Life and Love.

The "still, small voice" of conscience and connection is now harder to hear, buried beneath the noise of a distracted age. We've confused noise with knowledge, and data with discernment. But beneath it all, that Voice still calls. Not loudly. But like the whisper of wind through trees, it remains.

As I approached the end of this time of reflection and integration, I came to recognize two distinct ways of knowing that ran parallel within me and needed to be resolved: the methodical mind of the scientist and the mystic's unshakable inner knowing—the one that measures and the one that marvels.

Both ways of knowing were vital. Yet without their integration, each remained partial and prone to distortion. In their convergence, I began to perceive personal wholeness and a vision for cultural healing—a return to the Sacred Order that once guided human life before we split mind from spirit, matter from meaning.

CHAPTER 6

FROM SEPARATION TO SYMBIOSIS: THE NEXT EVOLUTIONARY LEAP

What would it take to reconcile two ways of knowing that had been torn apart for centuries?

As a developing scientist, I needed to resolve the apparent contradiction between science and religion. This divide dates back nearly 400 years, when science was granted dominion over the physical world, while the non-physical, non-measurable aspects remained within the religious realm.

This schizophrenic split—this cultural divorce—
is akin to having two key elements of our intelligence, each
necessary to achieve our individual and
collective human potential, not on speaking terms.

Now that's insanity.

This wasn't just a theoretical issue—it was a fault line running through my soul. To become whole, I needed to reconcile these two domains, both intellectually and in how I lived and perceived the world.

THE WOUND AND THE BRIDGE: RATIONALITY MEETS TRANSCENDENCE

Reflecting on the slug and mushroom experience, I saw a clear path to healing the split: combining rational science with Transcendent experience as complementary modes of knowing.

This integration revealed something more ancient and enduring—a sacred pattern so deeply woven into existence that civilizations throughout history have sensed it, named it, and sought to align with it. This sacred pattern—what some traditions call Logos, others Natural Law, and still others see in ecosystems and equations—has been recognized over time as the living code of reality.

It links the relational structure of biology, the moral arc of human conscience, and the deep intuition that love, not power, holds the cosmos together. I began seeing this same pattern everywhere—from the Sermon on the Mount to Einstein's awe, from the mycelium to the stars.

Of course, I could learn about the interconnection of forest ecosystems in my evolutionary biology and ecology classes—and I did. Like many other aspiring biologists, I found it exciting to discover how nature was organized: its interconnectedness, cycles, processes, and evolutionary adaptations.

Science reveals the structure—the How of things: patterns, systems, and complexity. But it is through Transcendent experience that we encounter the Why—the sacred meaning, purpose, and unity beneath it all.

Through this non-linear lens, I saw that nature's connections are not just concepts to understand, but realities to be lived and experienced from within.

Transcendence reveals that what seems separate is already unified at a deeper level.

Only this broader perspective can help us explore the "Why" of existence. Albert Einstein, though not traditionally religious, described a "cosmic religious feeling" that permeated his scientific inquiries. For him, the pursuit of truth was also a mystical journey.

Einstein famously said:

"The most beautiful thing we can experience is the mysterious. It is the source of all true art and science... revealing a Spirit vastly superior to man, before whom we must feel humble."

As I reflected on Einstein's cosmic reverence, I noticed a surprising harmony with the spiritual teachings I had long cherished. It wasn't just physics pointing to the sacred—ethics, too, flowed from this deeper order.

Einstein's perspective on wonder and humility resonates deeply with Jesus' Sermon on the Mount and Gandhi's "Law of Love." This universal truth spans disciplines and interweaves both scientific and spiritual ways of knowing.

As my understanding evolved, I began recognizing this cosmic pattern in ecosystems, equations, and sacred teachings across cultures.

I began to wonder: Was Jesus revealing more than moral guidance? Could he have been articulating the profound code of the universe—the same relational logic I sensed in the mycelium, the stars, and my own soul?

I reflected on the words in the US Declaration of Independence: that some truths are "self-evident." That phrase, too, points toward a deeper, universal order—what many have called Natural Law.

NATURAL LAW AND THE ANCIENT BLUEPRINT

Even pre-modern societies spoke of an underlying pattern called Natural Law, a built-in compass that guides us in distinguishing right from wrong. Natural Law exists across cultures as an innate sense of fairness and justice. It is not based on external commandments or rules but emanates from deep within us.

Consider this: Most people believe that stealing is wrong and helping others is right.

Natural Law inspired earlier Roman laws, English Common Law, the American Revolution and Constitution, the United Nations Universal Declaration of Human Rights, and many modern constitutions. So...the Ancient Blueprint and the Logos...Einstein's insight that spirit is fundamental to the "scientific" laws of the Universe...a sense of Natural Law that pervades and informs every human culture. Are we beginning to see a pattern here?

Transcendence, Ancient Blueprint, Natural Law, and Symbiotic Culture are not separate ideas, but three expressions of the same sacred pattern—a relational order woven into the fabric of creation, inviting us to align our lives, communities, and civilizations.

For me, this sense of universal order—natural, moral, and transcendent—began to point toward a social application. If the pattern was real, it must have real-world implications for how we live and relate. It could no longer remain an abstraction. It needed to take shape.

Drawing from my immersion in Nature's Web, I recognized a clear organizational pattern directing humanity toward a genuinely Symbiotic Culture and way of being. Eventually, I would refer to it as the Symbiotic Network.

By weaving a web of intentional mutual benefit, humanity can reconnect with and be guided by the Luminous Web and the Logos ordering principle.

I could see my path unfolding—though it would take years to fully understand how to navigate it. The greatest inspiration came several years later when I encountered Sarvodaya, a real-world Symbiotic Culture experiment that had been quietly thriving since the 1950s. More than just a model, I've come to see it as a mirror reflecting the vision I had glimpsed within.

I instinctively knew this was not just a source of inspiration—it was part of my life's calling. I now carried the seed of a larger vision: a world sustained by mutual benefit and spiritual coherence.

But how would I live it? How could I bring these luminous insights down to Earth?

And...insight alone wasn't enough. If this Sacred Order was real, it had to be lived—and tested—in the complexity of everyday life. I had to test the truth of what I had seen in relationships, communities, and practices. The next step would require courage—to move from inner revelation to outer expression and test these convictions in the living laboratory of community life.

THE EMPIRICAL MYSTIC: TESTING THE TRANSCENDENT IN REAL LIFE

As I sought to integrate my inner life with the outer world, I found myself in a unique position. No matter how non-ordinary my experiences were, I never stopped being a scientist. Applying what could be called an "empirical sensibility," I report my experience as "data."

When we truly follow science, we learn that productive inquiry requires a dance between the rational and the intuitive. Neither the rational nor the intuitive mind alone holds the answers, but when they work together, they guide us in the right direction. To be clear, I'm not codifying beliefs, starting a new religion, or prescribing what you should believe.

> *What I've encountered doesn't require adherence to a specific theology, but it invites us to live by the fruits of Divine Love, which many traditions affirm.*

That's why, as we will explore later, some versions of universal Virtues and principles, like the Golden Rule, can be found in every civilization and tradition. These universal Virtues reflect the underlying Ancient Blueprint—as Socrates famously said, Virtues "come from the Divine."

Yet, embodying these Virtues in ordinary life—especially in a fractured world—remains one of our most significant challenges. But if these virtues are universal and accessible, why do they often feel out of reach? The answer lies in how we relate to the Transcendent—in rare mountaintop moments and the sacredness of everyday life.

TRANSCENDENCE FOR ALL: ORDINARY PORTALS TO SACRED REALITY

As you read these early chapters, you may feel disconnected from the Transcendent experiences I shared. These extraordinary experiences have given me a unique perspective and a way to transform the conflicting voices of the surface ego into a coherent, purposeful one.

What about those who lack firsthand experience—who haven't undergone significant emotional events, near-death experiences, religious conversions, transformational psychedelic journeys, or the experiences I've described? While my experiences may be unusual, Transcendent experiences are normal and natural for human beings throughout time and across cultures.

*The longing to transcend the isolated self
is as primal as hunger, thirst, or desire—
yet it seeks not survival but communion, which holds
the key to healing our fractured communities.*

Even though I had an initiatory experience, I still needed a burning desire in my heart to continue experiencing the Transcendent and to make that journey my number one priority. We all possess the inherent potential and capability to embark on this personal journey and experience it for ourselves. To do that, we must learn to listen to our Authentic Selves amidst the chaos and confusion of human society and within our inner world.

Each of us touches the Transcendent in everyday moments—perhaps without recognizing it: the awe of a sunrise, the unconditional love for a child, the silent majesty of a star-filled night, the selfless service in a homeless shelter, the intimacy of caring for an aging parent, the harmony of Vivaldi's "Four Seasons," the sacredness of love between spouses, the exhilaration of carving fresh powder on a snowy slope, the Divine connection of liturgy, the beauty of poetry, or art. In all these glimpses, the sacred breathes through the ordinary.

Such glimpses offer more than inspiration—they invite a turning, a transformation of heart and mind that reorders our lives around love, virtue, and the sacred.

METANOIA: TURNING TOWARD LOVE AND VIRTUE

The depth we can experience through all of this is part of the ongoing "turning of our mind" towards a true conversion: a shift from external rewards to intrinsic Virtues and inherent worth, an increase in moral and ethical concern, the formation of resilient, virtue-shaped character, and doing the right thing. It means moving beyond limited, self-focused "love" toward a naturally expanded sense of Divine Love embodied within us.

This Love radiates outwardly in widening circles of self-giving—from our families to communities, cities, nations, and ultimately the whole world.

Over my lifetime, I have recognized the turning—Metanoia—as both a process and a practice. Simply being aware that such experiences are possible shows that any human can see through the veil of the world, discover a connection to a Transcendent order, and live from that foundation.

I hope that reading about my journey clarifies and deepens your own. Recognizing this potential for transformation within you will help you identify the cues and clues that might guide you in enriching your Transcendent, luminous experiences. You'll move toward your Authentic Self, hearing the inner voice more clearly until it rises above the noise and aligns you with Divine Order.

As you will read in subsequent chapters, these realizations did not completely liberate me from my egoic issues. In working with others in a symbiotic practice, I have had to face, acknowledge, and transform my limited ways of seeing and being—my shadow. I'm still in this process. Each day invites me to stay present, face my shadow, and grow into deeper wholeness.

I've come to see that this inner work is inseparable from the work of building community. In fact, the road between the two goes both ways.

What I've discovered turns the standard view of being a "conscious person"—thinking of yourself as "better" than others—upside down. Being a "conscious person" means knowing when I am *not* conscious and making self-corrections to realign with my Conscience and Authentic Self.

As you will read later, in addition to Jesus and the Sermon on the Mount, the most profound influence on my life's work has been Dr. Ariyaratne's movement in Sri Lanka, Sarvodaya. In retrospect, I realize I've repeatedly experienced Sarvodaya's wise theme and motto: We build the road, and the road builds us.

In Sarvodaya, that phrase captures the movement's belief that outer development and inner transformation are interconnected. As villagers work together to build roads and infrastructure, they foster a shared purpose, dignity, and spiritual growth, laying the physical and moral groundwork for a just society.

That same principle—a road that builds us as we build it—became a central metaphor for my own journey. It pointed not just to personal transformation but also to a societal one.

A VOW TO BEGIN THE WORLD ANEW

As I emerged from cultural restrictions and the tyranny of the mind to see life and nature from "the window of the Spirit," I envisioned how a symbiotic human society could arise from Nature's Web. In 1983, I wrote a poem, "The Well-Worn Path," summarizing the purposeful vow that set me on the "path less traveled," which has led to my life calling, this book, and the audacious mission and vision of a Spiritual Revolution of the Heart and a Symbiotic Revolution of society.

The Well-Worn Path
    I cannot take the well-worn path—
    the tried and true.
    I must take a chance,
    let down artificial barriers and opaque covers.
    I can be the role others expect,
    or I can connect to my Authentic Self.

    How do I find God—
    Transcendent reality—
    while living as a human being?
    What thread links me
    to the smallest atom,
    a crashing wave,
    another person,
    or the furthest galaxies?

    All I want is to be truly alive—
    to become a Human Being.
    Not an obedient, "organization man,"
    but my better self.

    How can I participate in society's Big Lie—
    that we are all separate—
    when the lie is magnified by my complicity?

BIRTHING THE SYMBIOTIC AGE

The answers aren't outside me—
not in movements, parties, cults, religions, or nations.
They do not hold the answers.

How do I live by the natural order
that emanates from the Luminous Web?
How do I make a bridge
so others can travel this path more easily?

It begins with a decision—
a declaration,
then an invitation and a challenge.

We must begin the world anew.
Circles and webs of light emerge from darkness—
small at first,
joining, growing—
shining with Spirit's radiance.

Can you see it?
The light? The beauty? The perfect harmony?
Desire this unity—
where everything is connected.

The Spirit spreads like firelight—
a chain reaction of moral force
countering the chain reaction of physical violence.
Spirit, once bound, is now unleashed.

Like healing waters,
this salve of reconciliation can mend pain and mistrust.

> People, awakened in inner peace,
> began to tear down their prison walls
> and share with one another.
> They rebuilt communities
> by working together,
> making real a more loving and united world.
>
> Begin with a decision.
> Act on what is true.
> Say no to blind obedience, cynicism, and fear.
> Say yes to healing division,
> to building a world of compassion and love.
> Take the first step
> on the not-so-well-worn path.
> Let it begin with each of us.

The poem was a vow and a vision—a call to live differently, build differently, and see the world as connected rather than compartmentalized. Over the decades, I've understood that this inner vow mirrored a deeper natural principle already at work in our world.

Over time, I came to name this principle Cultural Symbiogenesis—a pattern drawn from nature now offers humanity a path forward.

CULTURAL SYMBIOGENESIS: THE NEXT EVOLUTIONARY LEAP

From ancient forests to the architecture of living cells, nature reveals a stunning truth: life does not evolve through domination, but through relationships. It thrives in symbiosis. In biological terms, this is called symbiogenesis—a process through which distinct organisms merge to create new life forms. It's not just a metaphor; it's a scientific fact. Over time, what began for me as mystical encounters with the Luminous Web gradually crystallized into a practical framework—not just a new way of seeing, but a new way of becoming.

I came to recognize symbiogenesis as an evolutionary threshold—not only for organisms but also for civilizations. Just as symbiogenesis occurred 3.5 billion years ago, when single-celled organisms fused to form multicellular life, I saw that human culture now faces a similar chance. We can evolve beyond fragmented silos—beyond the isolated "cells" of competition and control—into relational networks built for mutual benefit, coherence, and life.

This is not an abstract vision. It is a path—spiritual, biological, and cultural. What I am calling cultural symbiogenesis is a shift from fragmentation to relationship, from domination to communion. In a sense, this realization is the culmination of my inquiry into the web of nature. What began in silence and mystery had now become a social imperative.

> *I began to see that the very pattern of life*
> *that connects cells, species, and civilizations*
> *was now inviting humanity into its next expression.*
> *The time had come to live it into being.*

And so, the first phase of my formation was complete: the direct encounter with the Luminous Web, the embodied insights from Nature's Web, and the integration of the Transcendent within myself—all culminating in the emerging formulation of the Symbiotic Network as both a vision and a path.

From Separation to Symbiosis

And...insight alone could not fulfill the journey. The pattern I discovered in solitude now needed to be tested and refined through human interaction—in the voices, wisdom, and presence of others. More experiences were yet to come that would reveal a traditional pathway to reconcile the mental, physical, and spiritual aspects.

My journey would soon lead me to Mexico, where an Indigenous—but deeply Christian—medicine woman named Doña Catalina would help me integrate the seemingly irreconcilable breach between science and spirit through ancient indigenous wisdom, embodied Christian faith, and relational healing.

CHAPTER 7

SCIENCE, INDIGENOUS WISDOM, AND JESUS

Science, Indigenous wisdom, and Jesus.

I know the title is provocative—and that's intentional. It may be difficult at first to imagine how these can coexist, let alone form a coherent whole. How can I—raised as a secular Jew, trained as a biologist, shaped by Tibetan Buddhist meditation, and apprenticed to an Indigenous Aztec medicine woman—now call myself a follower of Jesus? A Christian?

Welcome to the complexity of what philosopher Charles Taylor calls the *Secular Age*. In a world where religion is often commodified, politics polarized, and suspicion runs high, people instinctively ask: What's your angle? What are you selling?

So let me be clear.

I'm not here to sell or convert. I'm here to testify.

My life has been shaped by deep encounters with science, Indigenous wisdom, and Jesus Christ. Each offered a glimpse of reality—partial, profound, and, over time, convergent. What

Science, Indigenous Wisdom, and Jesus

I share in this chapter is not theory but lived experience. And I hope it invites you, wherever you stand—devout or doubting, religious or spiritual but not religious, agnostic or secular—to consider your own path toward the Transcendent.

> *Spirituality, for me, is humanity's innate longing to belong to something greater—to discover meaning, coherence, and sacred purpose.*

My search led me to align with the Transcendent through Jesus Christ, the Logos—the eternal Word through whom all things were made.

I introduced this concept earlier in the book, where I described the Logos as the living pattern that holds creation together. For those from non-Christian backgrounds, you might think of the Logos as the divine ordering principle of reality—what mystics, sages, and even quantum physicists have glimpsed through different lenses. In Christian understanding, this Logos is not abstract but personal—fully revealed in the life, death, and resurrection of Jesus.

This allegiance transcends all worldly identities—tribes, nations, ideologies, and even the reigning deity of modernity: materialism.

To me, spirituality is the embodiment of Divine Love, made visible through universal Virtues—kindness, gratitude, forgiveness, trust, service, and compassion. These are not doctrines to be memorized, but Love made manifest in how we live, walk, and act.

These words come easily now, but they have been carved by years of experience. So let me return to the path itself—where moments of the Transcendent met the ground of real people, movements, and communities.

BIRTHING THE SYMBIOTIC AGE

LIVING AT THE INTERSECTION
OF SCIENCE, SPIRIT, AND JESUS

As poetry emerged from my time in nature, I also found myself in serendipitous community experiences with remarkable individuals. These encounters helped me ground them into real-world action.

It began when I moved into a low-income, African American and Hispanic neighborhood in San Diego with an ex-Vietnam veteran—an intense man who had gone to war as a super-patriotic volunteer and returned a soul-wounded, disillusioned warrior.

He looked and spoke like an Old Testament prophet, with blazing blue eyes. A Christian on a mission to heal his trauma by ending ALL war, he called himself a "witness" for Jesus Christ and a conscious "advocate," living his faith as an anti-war activist. This was my first encounter with a Christian radically embodying nonviolence.

Together, we joined the global anti-nuclear 'freeze' movement of the early 1980s. That's when I first encountered Gandhi's use of Jesus' teachings in nonviolent resistance and Dr. King's Beloved Community. I was also introduced to Gandhi's vision of the Commonwealth of Village Republics, a structure that reflected that Beloved Community, and made it real in the world. These ideas planted early seeds of what I came to call the Ancient Blueprint.

FROM RESISTANCE TO RENEWAL:
TRANSFORMING EVIL BY CONNECTING THE GOOD

However, it didn't take long for me to grow disillusioned with the peace movement's strategy. Many participants seemed more like angry activists, speaking of peace while using tactics contradicting the ideals of nonviolence taught by Gandhi and Dr. King. This experience raised deeper questions in me that exposed the

Science, Indigenous Wisdom, and Jesus

disconnect between well-meaning political and social movements and the inner spiritual life.

The peace movement, within the Culture of Separation, lacked the deep metanoia I'd experienced. It never addressed the root cause: separation itself.

How can we overcome the madness if we constantly fight against what we don't like, yet fail to demonstrate what we stand for in our families, neighborhoods, and communities?

Dr. King's core message often gets ignored: without what he called a "Revolution of Values," we'll be marching for peace for the next thousand years. We haven't built the foundation that begins in the heart. Mother Teresa echoed this truth. She declared she wouldn't attend an anti-war protest, but would gladly show up for a demonstration of peace.

The peace movement overlooked the deeper issue of resisting evil, often viewing it as something external rather than acknowledging its presence in our hearts. As the cartoon character Pogo said, "We have met the enemy, and he is us." Former Czech President Václav Havel said it plainly:

> "The salvation of this human world lies nowhere else than in the human heart, in the human power to reflect, in human meekness and responsibility."

Much political activism has traditionally focused 'out there'—on systems and opponents—leading to blame and anger, and often trapping us in the dominate-or-be-dominated, villain-victim cycle. When disconnected from the Transcendent—the Logos—even our best intentions for compassion and justice can become distorted. History shows—and we still see it today—that if we're fighting on the battlefield of the Culture of Separation, those once oppressed soon demand "their turn"...to dominate.

Ironically, experiencing this disconnection deepened my understanding of the Ancient Blueprint, though I didn't yet have those words. Some factions of the peace movement, like Liberation Theology in the Catholic Church, had a spiritual foundation but still focused more on external political conditions than inner transformation. That is how, despite good intentions, many activists remained trapped in the Culture of Separation without realizing it.

Mahatma Gandhi understood the Ancient Blueprint, which linked the Transcendent with the immanent. He drew his vision of what he called an Eternal Law of Love from Jesus' Sermon on the Mount. He said:

> "Whether humanity will consciously follow the Law of Love, I do not know. But that need not disturb me. The law will work just as the law of gravitation works, whether we accept it or not. The person who discovered the Law of Love was a far greater scientist than any of our modern scientists. Only our explorations have not gone far enough."

Gandhi's approach to confronting the empire derived directly from Jesus, as echoed by St. Paul:

> "Do not be overcome by evil but overcome evil with good."
> — Romans 12:21

This is by no means passive. It's a radical call to create the Good, and that's just the beginning. To change structures, we must also Connect the Good—building networks of Love that can transform the world. We achieve this by creating a critical mass of positive spiritual consciousness that "flows" into new nodes of intersection, building our social network infrastructure to propagate Love tangibly.

In these times when darkness seems on the rise, we each have a role: to shine a light. By enhancing our fluency in embodying and extending Divine Love, we help create networks of love that counter despair and disconnection.

For me, that meant moving beyond the realm of ideas to literally embody the Eternal Law of Love. In the early 1980s, I collaborated with my veteran friend to establish a Christ-based intentional community in a diverse, low-income neighborhood of San Diego. We renovated a building and initiated street-level actions such as beautification projects, and meetings where we reflected on the Beloved Community. The project lasted only a few years, but planted something deeper within me.

Through encounters with nature and human nature, I maintained my childlike curiosity, which is essential for a scientist. However, I also began to wonder: Why do people committed to peace struggle to embody it? After grappling with the contradictions of activism, I realized that the transformation I sought would not come through outward struggle alone—it had to begin within, then ripple outward through love-infused action.

TRAINING THE MIND AND MEETING THE INNER MULTITUDE

After earning my master's in biology, I moved into a home transformed into a retreat center for a Tibetan monk sent by the Dalai Lama. I practiced various forms of meditation focused on breath, concentration, and mindfulness. This experience felt akin to a spiritual boot camp. I learned to engage with conflicting inner voices, cultivating both strength and clarity. I also began journaling my dreams and joined a group that used Jungian Active Imagination to interpret them.

Each night, I wrote down my dream experiences. I was fortunate to be part of a dream group led by a well-known Jungian psychologist who shared a method developed by Marie-Louise von Franz, one of Carl Jung's students. Processing and understanding my dreams became a powerful tool for grasping my "outside" world through "inside" insights.

I often woke up in the middle of the night to record these; sometimes, I would end up with two or three pages of dream content. I'm glad I recorded those experiences and the poems that came to me to more accurately share how this process eventually led me to a radically new way of building community.

In 1987, at 28, I had a waking vision in which I could combine the different parts of my personality into a coherent form.

Here is how I recorded it at the time:
> "I soared like a bird and landed on a flat plain. I walked along the path lined with diamonds on either side. Along the way, I encountered a variety of characters.
>
> At an oasis with trees and a natural pool, I saw my reflection turn into the face of an older man with long hair and a beard, smiling up at me. He wore a golden crown adorned with rubies and emeralds, and his eyes twinkled like stars. He walked with me along the path.
>
> Then came a cast of others: a queen who invited me on a journey—I declined; a 15-foot monster representing Fear; a man embodying Anger. Both joined me, and later, the queen returned.
>
> I spoke with each of them, discovering what they wanted from me. They agreed to unite, walk with me, and serve a higher purpose. As we continued, more characters

arrived—now a crowd—each one a part of me, traveling the same path.

We reached a mountain and began to climb. Ahead appeared a light—first a dot, then a radiant cross illuminating our way. There was a brilliant flash, and all my companions vanished in a wave of heat, like a crucible of light that united us all.

Suddenly, a voice echoed from everywhere and nowhere:

"Your friends are not gone. They are within you—emotions, thoughts, images, desires—pulling you this way and that, keeping you from awakening to the truth inside and around you. You have only just begun."

"To become what I ask, open yourself. Become clear and transparent. You will experience me in all things—from atoms to galaxies, from every life form to the people beside you. My pattern is written inside your heart."

"If you cultivate this relationship daily, you will grow in compassion, loving-kindness, and kinship with all that lives. You'll no longer feel divided—you'll see the spark of me in everything and yourself. You will find me everywhere."

I now walk down the mountain, free from fear, anger, greed, and envy—filled instead with strength, calm, compassion, joy within joy, and clarity to help heal and repair the world."

Looking back on this experience, I better understand what transpired.

When you connect to the light of the Transcendent, what was once a disorganized, chaotic "committee" of voices pulling in all directions without a sense of purpose or focus can be unified under the light of a higher-order Reality. Meanwhile, my experiences meditating with the Tibetan monk provided structure to my "out-of-this-world" experiences that began when I was twelve. I recognized that systematic practices evoked those experiences and used them for inner growth.

I sensed that my experiences prepared me for something, but for what? In the short run, they prepared me for a deeper understanding of applying the Transcendent in action, which came in a totally unexpected way.

MEETING DOÑA CATALINA: THE HEALER WHO LIVED THE ANCIENT BLUEPRINT

One of the teachers I met during this time was a student of Zen and Indigenous wisdom. Well-versed in multiple spiritual traditions, he was the perfect mentor to help me make the connections that would lead to my next steps. Through him, I met one of the most important teachers in my life: Doña Catalina Mendoza, a traditional *curandera*—a medicine woman who blended Indigenous Aztec wisdom with devout Christianity.

Her presence taught me more about spiritual unfoldment than any book or workshop ever could, revealing:

True spiritual authority flows not from titles, scriptures, or deeds, but from humility, alignment with the Transcendent, service, and living the truth.

The more your life revolves around self-giving love, the more you demonstrate your true spiritual credentials. As Jesus said in the Sermon on the Mount, reflecting the Ancient Blueprint:

"*You will recognize them by their fruits.*"

My journey—best described as an "initiation"—began one Sunday when I was invited to a small gathering at Doña Catalina's ranch in Tecate, Baja California, just an hour south of San Diego. Her home sat on several acres of arid land, featuring a water well, dirt floors, no electricity, wood fires for cooking, and gas lanterns for light.

Nearby stood Mount Cuchuma, a sacred site where Native peoples had held ceremonies for 5,000 years. That Sunday was her day of rest, and we spent the afternoon under the pepper tree with her children and grandchildren. She told us she received her calling at thirteen when God spoke to her in a church in Guadalajara and told her she would become a healer.

Doña Catalina in her healing room—embodying the Ancient Blueprint with prayer, presence, and self-giving love.

When I met her, she was 57. She was an herbalist and intuitive healer who worked through a "discarnate" physician named Don Arturo. Through prayer, she asked God and Don Arturo for guidance, used branches of the pepper tree for healing, and fully surrendered to her mission of service.

After my first visit, I returned home feeling exhausted and fell asleep early. That night, I experienced a series of dreams.

In the first, I led Doña Catalina through a forest toward a spring. When we arrived, we found Indigenous women joyfully bobbing in a natural pool. A white light glowed from beneath the water, illuminating the entire scene. Happy to reach the pool, Doña Catalina was now radiant with peace and joy. It felt like a direct transmission of her essence.

In the second dream, I was in a high mountain cabin. Four young men and women had just returned from a life-changing journey. They didn't speak, but somehow, I shared their direct experience of finding God.

The Waters of Joy, the Cabin of Encounter, and the Cosmic Map of Purpose— each unveiling a path from the heart of Indigenous wisdom to the Transcendent Source within.

In the third, I sat in front of a large poster board, explaining a set of charts to my brothers. These diagrams revealed the universe's origin, why we are here, my purpose on Earth, and a vision of a beautiful potential future—the first time I ever dreamed in color. The charts hinted at immense suffering but also redemption.

Those dreams got my full attention. They were a direct call from a deeper reality, pointing to my next step. I awoke with a sense of peace and purpose, knowing it might take decades to realize what I had seen.

Reflecting how I could begin to honor these dreams, I had an unusual thought: I needed to spend time in a cave on the hill across from Doña Catalina's property. Looking back, it made no sense from a rational standpoint—but something within me knew it was right. Something deep inside urged me to ask Doña Catalina for her blessing. What followed could only be described as my "initiatory vision quest."

Science, Indigenous Wisdom, and Jesus

A LIMINAL SPACE: A WORLD BETWEEN WORLDS

After she said yes, I packed a few belongings and drove to her land. I began the ascent with only the clothes on my back and a few water bottles, entering three days of silence, fasting, meditation, and prayer. The area was completely isolated—just sagebrush, lizards, chipmunks, ravens, and a single hawk.

When I emerged from the cave, I returned to find Doña Catalina seated as always. She told me a cloud had settled over the mountain while I was there, something she had never seen in over thirty years. When I asked what it meant, she said:

"You must have had a big healing."

As someone who'd just finished a Master of Science in Biology, this was a bit of a stretch! But in hindsight, I had chosen an experience that launched me beyond the ordinary.

> *I needed to bridge the two worlds I was straddling: The luminous Transcendent and a modern culture that revered science while dismissing spirituality as superstition.*

Even then, though less than now, we lived in a Culture of Separation, where opposites such as science and religion, spirit and matter, masculine and feminine, Western and Indigenous remained largely unintegrated. Today, that fragmentation has only deepened, intensified by digital life and hyper-specialization. At the time, despite my early mystical experiences, I still identified as a scientist. That gave me some detachment—an observer's mindset—even as I entered Doña Catalina's unfamiliar world.

There's a term for the space I entered—liminality—a threshold of ambiguity, openness, and uncertainty. In Indigenous cultures, it's often the space where boys transition into manhood, leaving behind the safety of childhood to face the unknown. That's why I view my time with Catalina as an initiation: it disoriented me just enough to realign my life toward a path of service and community.

Clearly, I was ready. After returning home, I asked her permission to move onto her land. I sold nearly everything I owned except for my car, pitched a tent, and became her apprentice. I lived there for about a year, sleeping in a small tent, even though winter nights were cold enough for snow. The fierce wind could cut like a razor. There was no running water, just a well with sweet, clear water. There was no electricity and no phones.

Taking a shower was a ritual in itself. First, you hauled water from the well in a bucket. Then, you chopped wood and built a fire to heat the water. After that, you stepped into a barn-like structure, undressed, poured the water over yourself, soaped up, and rinsed. All of this—sometimes in 26-degree weather!

While this doesn't exactly compare to an indigenous youth being released into the wilderness without food or a blanket, in many ways, I found myself in a "world between worlds." For one thing, I didn't speak Spanish and had to learn how to communicate quickly: How do I take a shower? Where's the wood that you want me to cut? How can I help you in the healing room? No classroom could have prepared me for the depth of this immersive experience, stepping into a worldview and culture completely unlike my own.

And this experience changed my life and perspective in several ways. What did I learn in my year with Doña Catalina? On the practical level, I learned some of what she knew, including methods of healing using hundreds of herbs, intuitive and spiritual healing, and what some may call "laying on of hands."

Science, Indigenous Wisdom, and Jesus

By the way, you may be asking if I "believed in" any of this. As a scientist, I observed what was beyond "belief" or "non-belief." It certainly expanded me beyond what I thought I knew! And...what Doña Catalina "did" was less relevant to me than who she was.

> *What moved me most wasn't her knowledge, but witnessing a holy life completely given over to God and selfless service.*

I experienced the essence of true religion and spirituality—love and Service.

It was all about connecting the Vertical/Transcendent and the Horizontal/Immanent nature of Reality—of the Logos. The essence of my "initiation" was to be with someone who loved God and embodied the Transcendent through her daily work. The fact that Catalina was both indigenous and Christian helped me see how completely different religious/spiritual systems, both reflecting the Ancient Blueprint, could harmonize in serving others.

She never charged for healing. People, primarily the very poor, including indigenous individuals from the surrounding mountains, came to heal their minds, bodies, and spirits. It was heartwarming to see them bring gifts in exchange for healing. They brought eggs, produce, milk, a pig, and many other offerings.

These gifts weren't payment or barter—they were love offerings mirroring Catalina's giving.

HEALING AS LOVE MADE VISIBLE

While I never attempted to conduct a scientific study of her work, I observed with all my heart and mind. She began her healing sessions as a Christian by praying to the Father, Son, and the Holy

Spirit. She asked God to make her an empty vessel so the Spirit could "fill" her, enabling her to help the person directly.

I witnessed numerous spontaneous healings, day in and day out—experiences my scientific mind could barely grasp. My heart, however, understood. Living with someone who allows themselves to embody God can directly influence us, much like osmosis—a direct transmission.

Around Doña Catalina, the strange became normal. Sometimes, in the healing room, I experienced sensations like the sound of a gunshot going off inside my head. I was flooded with love, joy, and sadness at other times. I learned directly what it means to have a heart for serving others and to accept the suffering occurring in others and the world, something others might call "sacrifice."

Yes, living this way requires giving up certain habits and preoccupations of our materialistic, everyday lives. However, I have found that the joy derived from simple service and authentic connections with others becomes a gratifying spiritual pleasure in its own right. So, while the world tends to view someone like her or Mother Teresa as selfless, we need to shift our frame of reference.

> *A person who gladly experiences*
> *the joy of serving God by serving others daily*
> *is truly the most "self-centered" person in the world!*

Let me explain.

As we go through our daily activities, we often forget that there is a place within us where acting out of love and compassion is normal and may be the source of life's most enduring pleasure. Gandhi, who did much of his work in direct service to poor villagers, spoke of this. A journalist once asked him if his purpose in serving the poor was altruistic. Gandhi replied:

Science, Indigenous Wisdom, and Jesus

"Not at all. I am here to serve no one else but myself, to find myself and God realization through the service of these village folk."

This certainly resonated with me as I observed Doña Catalina's work and how I felt in her presence—by helping others, we truly help ourselves. Every kindness, every act of compassion, and every word spoken with love nourishes us.

This is why I'm reminded again of St. Maximus the Confessor, the 7th-century Orthodox spiritual theologian whose mission bears repeating: to "gather the cosmos in love." His writings on union with God reflect the heart of Orthodox spiritual life. Maximus taught that to heal the world's fragmentation, we must reconnect with the Transcendent Reality of the Logos—Divine Love itself. Through this connection, we are empowered to embody the Virtues of kindness, compassion, forgiveness, charity, and more.

Yet Maximus also offered a profound insight: each time we practice a single Virtue, we access the fullness of Divine Love. The whole is found in the part. Every act of love draws us into communion with the Logos and contributes to healing the entire cosmos.

Virtues are the living interface between the Divine and our daily lives— where the Transcendent becomes immanent.

By practicing them, we are led back to the Transcendent in a Virtuous Circle.

The individual Virtues, or what St. Maximus called Logoi, are "Transcendent energies" that reflect the cosmic organizing principle and pattern of the Ancient Blueprint. They describe how the cosmos manifests an ordered, non-random pattern, even when considering nonphysical Virtues. The Virtues resemble fractals of the Logos—patterns of Divine Love that shape our inner world and the communities we create.

I use the term fractal because it best encapsulates my observation of this phenomenon within myself. A fractal is a pattern that repeats itself at various sizes or scales. When you zoom in, you see the same pattern recurring; when you zoom out, you also see the same pattern.

Back to the story!

LIVING TRANSMISSION AND THE DEATH OF A "SAINT"

I had many vivid dreams during my time with Doña Catalina. One was life-changing. In this dream, I observed a group of people at the base of a tall, sheer cliff that rose straight up. One moment, I saw a woman in the group float directly up alongside the cliff.

*She rose in light—her spirit ascending,
a living transmission of love beyond the veil.*

Science, Indigenous Wisdom, and Jesus

When I told Doña Catalina about the dream, she said rather matter-of-factly that it meant she, Catalina, would die in six months. I had never encountered anyone who knew in advance the time of their death, and I thought it was an odd comment. It turned out to be accurate, though. She died six months later at her home.

During the last two weeks of her life, she ate very little and stayed in bed. She shared her bedroom with some grandchildren in two other beds, and this became the scene of our final vigil as family and extended family arrived. On the last day of her life, I returned to my tent and found many scorpions and a few black widow spiders on the tent's surface. This certainly heightened my sense of impending death.

As I lay down to sleep, I saw Doña Catalina as a large rainbow-colored butterfly landing gently on my tent. The vision conveyed a sense of peace; I knew her time was at hand.

On her last day, the room was crowded with the people whose lives she had touched, all praying for her as she drifted in and out of consciousness. Towards the end, I was next to her and noticed that her body was becoming very cool to the touch. Only her upper body retained any warmth. At the moment she took her last breath, I stood beside her and gently touched her forehead.

I had a profound experience that is as vivid now as it was that day. In my vision, I saw a glowing cross of light. Then, another line was added, which now looked like a glowing asterisk of white light. This light began expanding dramatically, and I saw the whole room fill with light. I burst into tears of deep emotion, as did everyone in the room, wailing for this beautiful person.

For three days after her passing, I walked around in a state of bliss, peace, and joy. While I can't claim to have witnessed what happens after death, I felt that I was vicariously experiencing her crossing from this world to the next. It was blissful and pure light.

BIRTHING THE SYMBIOTIC AGE

In that moment, I lost the sting of my mortality and eventual death.

It was a strange yet peaceful feeling. My one-year experience of her life and death revealed more pieces of the mystery to me. What began in Chapter One, being struck by "enlightening," led to one level of embodiment of the Transcendent. That naturally led to the next level described in Chapter 4, where I could see the embodiment within Creation and nature directly.

The next step in my journey was to experience firsthand how a woman like Doña Catalina—deeply Indigenous and profoundly Christian—could embody the Transcendent. Her life was not just virtuous or devoted to others but a shining witness to a living relationship with Jesus. She did not preach doctrine or perform miracles; she lived the Gospel. Her humility, generosity, and unwavering attention to others' needs revealed the Divine Love she knew intimately through Christ.

In her, I glimpsed what it meant for Jesus's life to take root in a human being so completely that every word and gesture radiated sacred presence. That encounter reshaped my life. It awakened a calling to become a space-holder and convener of what would be called Symbiotic Culture, where Divine Love could once again find form in community.

The question remained: Could this same love shape systems, communities, and economies as it had shaped my soul?

I carried that question with me as I returned home from her funeral, still glowing with the imprint of her presence, yet increasingly aware that love of this depth would be tested in the world beyond her home. If Divine Love could radiate so clearly through one life, could it also transform the structures and relationships that governed how we lived together?

Science, Indigenous Wisdom, and Jesus

That's when I was confronted abruptly with the forces opposing such love.

CONFRONTING DARKNESS: THE DEVIL OUTSIDE THE TENT... AND INSIDE MYSELF.

Not long after I returned to San Diego, I found myself wrestling with how to embody the way of life I had witnessed in Doña Catalina. Her influence remained alive in me, yet one vivid memory from our time together kept resurfacing—an encounter that made it clear: walking in Divine Love also meant confronting the shadows within and without.

It had taken place about three months before her death, during a quiet evening at her house. Amidst the flickering kerosene lights (remember, there was no electricity), she turned to me and said in Spanish, "The devil is in town."

When I asked what she meant, she explained that the "devil" had taken the form of a new couple in our region doing "evil deeds."

She didn't seem very concerned, and when I asked her why, she told me that when you live a spiritual life and are connected to God, it becomes your shield of protection. "There is no need to fear evil," she told me, as the connection to the Transcendent power of light is within each of us, radiating from within and moving outward at every moment.

I knew Doña Catalina was a woman with a deep faith in a Transcendent God who, incidentally, had access to centuries of indigenous wisdom.

I felt I was being set up for a lesson—and I was right.

I retired to my tent and prepared for bed. It was very dark at the foot of the mountain, with no lights around. Suddenly, I sensed something outside the tent—an unmistakable presence of spiritual darkness. The air grew heavy, and something unseen pressed in around me. Was I imagining it? Had her warning planted a seed in my mind? That's how it felt at first. But the sense that the devil himself was outside the tent—palpable and undeniable—seemed to move through the very air around me.

Was I projecting? Succumbing to the power of suggestion? I didn't know.

But the feeling grew stronger, and fear welled up from deep within. I began to meditate and pray. That's when something even stranger happened. I found myself in a dialogue—not with a creature in the dark—but with a force I recognized from within myself. What I had first perceived as the "devil" outside the tent now mirrored my own inner fears and insecurities.

I realized this darkness wasn't only out there but also in here.

I wasn't possessed by evil. But I was being invited to see something essential: that the seeds of both good and evil live within every human heart. The "devil" took the shape of my hidden fears, unexamined wounds, and egoic shadows—the parts of me that resisted love, trust, and surrender.

I stayed in this inner confrontation for nearly an hour, wrestling and praying, until I became aware of a quiet light rising from within me. Just then, a gust of wind picked up outside, and the heavy feeling lifted. The presence vanished. The fear dissolved.

My "dance with the devil" was over. I was left in silence, utterly still, enveloped in peace.

In the shadow's presence,
her teaching became real:
the light of God is a living shield.

Science, Indigenous Wisdom, and Jesus

I still vividly remember this experience and how I was able to use prayer to dispel my fear and darkness by reaching "in" and "out" to the Transcendent, both "outside" and, at the same time, "inside." There was no theology attached to this, neither scripture nor scroll, just the contrast of dark and light and turning over my "will" in prayer to ask for God's help and the power of Love into my life.

AMAZING GRACE

Over the years, when people have heard the story of my time with Doña Catalina, they have commonly asked, "Did you become an apprentice? Did you become an herbalist? Do you do spiritual healing?" The answer is no. However, I received something infinitely more precious—immeasurable, beyond any physical gift or skill.

What I gained from the experience was the grace of being allowed to be in the presence of an enlightened being, a God-loving, indigenous version of Mother Teresa. This enlightenment reflected a remarkable ability to transcend the bounds of ego in everyday existence, turning the typical inclination for self-centered love into a self-giving Divine Love.

It's not about giving up the ego but about having the enhanced capacity to serve others, which is no different than being of service to oneself.

I came away with a direct experience of Doña Catalina's humility, which was transmitted into my being.

INTEGRATING SCIENCE AND SPIRIT, HEART AND HEAD

Having faced both light and shadow in the desert, I emerged with a clearer inner compass—but my integration work had only begun. Over the next thirty years, I would meet many celebrated pastors, rabbis, teachers, and healers, some highly competent, while others were merely competent at hype. I would also enter into fellowship with various religious faiths, primarily Christian churches and Buddhist Sanghas. I have yet to meet another individual with Doña Catalina's profound simplicity, other than Dr. Ari, whom I will discuss further in future chapters.

Doña Catalina was instrumental in my formation as a human being. In addition to demonstrating the Ancient Blueprint in action, she offered a key to resolving Western Civilization's deepest paradox and source of hidden pain, the separation of science and spirit, the linear and measurable from the intangible and intuitive, thinking from feeling.

These parts of me had been developing in tandem, though they previously didn't communicate as an integrated whole. Through this experience, I gained clarity about what lies deeper than the thinking and feeling functions—profound intuition.

*Intuition is a more profound knowing,
like a hotline to the Transcendent, that we can all access
and have it guide us beneath and beyond
the fears and worries of daily life.*

In the secular, scientific world I grew up in, there was no language for what I experienced at twelve and for years afterward. As a teenager, I immersed myself in nature, but I encountered only the masculine side: adventure and danger, with Nature as a challenge. Later, I developed the other masculine trait of measurement and observation as I sought to learn more about whales and dolphins.

Finally, I achieved true communion with nature as preparation for being with Doña Catalina.

Science, Indigenous Wisdom, and Jesus

And that's what made my time with her so significant. Through Aztec wisdom and Christian devotion, she demonstrated a way to make sense of both the physical and the non-physical. I never had to give up my perspective as a curious, scientific observer. I could hold all these encounters as experiences beyond belief. I don't mean they were unbelievable; what I mean is belief was not required to understand them.

> *The missing piece in Western science and theology is the feminine and indigenous sense that all nature is alive, even rocks.*

It then became clear that I had the best of both worlds—but now the roles were reversed. Where once the rational mind had been in charge, with intuition playing a secondary role, now the intuitive, Transcendent knowing led the way, and the rational mind served it. My rational mind still mattered, but it had found its rightful place: a vital instrument in service to the wisdom connected to the Transcendent order.

This deeper wisdom flowed from the heart—the seat of intuition and communion—rather than from intellect alone. The heart remembered what the mind had forgotten: that all of nature is alive, and that knowing comes through relationship, not just analysis.

LISTENING TO THE VOICE OF THE HEART OF LOVE: DISCOVERING JESUS CHRIST

Another gift Doña Catalina gave me was the gift of having a relationship with Jesus Christ.

Keep in mind that I was raised in a secular Jewish household, meaning we followed Jewish culture and traditions and tacitly celebrated certain holidays. Yet, there was never a concept of God in our family. I never had a childhood container of religious belief. There was no sense of Transcendent power, and, like many families I knew, the tangible and measurable was our guidepost.

My family identified as Jews, and Jesus was something that "religious Christians" believed in. However, as I got to know Doña Catalina and recognized her authenticity, I came to see Jesus anew. Perhaps it helped that she was also grounded in a deep Indigenous tradition, but her connection to Jesus sparked my connection.

> *Looking back, this was when my experience of the Transcendent shifted—from an abstract, impersonal force to a profoundly personal relationship with Jesus Christ.*

The personification of the Transcendent came naturally to me without having to arrive at it through a specific religious framework. To some extent, it seems as if I was already "converted" through decades of direct experience that led me to a place of "trust" and "faith" in God. Don't get me wrong—I'm not judging religion or non-religion, nor offering a new spiritual viewpoint.

I'm simply sharing my experience and how it led me to the Ancient Blueprint and its role in unifying the community.

After returning to San Diego from Mexico, I began working as a teacher in a school for children whose parents fled political persecution in Central America. During that year, I became friends with a Catholic woman who was later diagnosed with cancer. When she was in the final stages of dying, she began to deepen her relationship with God and spoke about Jesus Christ often. In her presence, I could see the peace that had come over her—it was as if a golden light enveloped her.

She died around my birthday in the late 1980s. I remember standing in a parking lot near San Diego State University, feeling a sense of peace and being overcome by love, and that's when I realized my friend had just died. In the last few weeks, there was so much light surrounding her, and at that moment in the parking lot, I could feel her love for everyone.

What an amazing human being! Instead of fearing death and lamenting her life, as many of us do, she expressed nothing but gratitude. Beyond her gratitude for life, she opened her heart to everyone. Through her, I received another glimpse of the love Jesus must have shown people.

With these encounters fresh in my heart, a new dimension of the Transcendent was about to break through—not as a concept, but as a Presence. What followed would forever deepen the meaning of the Luminous Web and the Ancient Blueprint I had glimpsed.

Later that night, I was at home. I lit some candles and prayed for a while. It was a very calm and quiet space. Suddenly, I felt a tapping on my left shoulder. I thought it might be a draft. But the tapping came again in the same spot.

Then, I felt a light on the top of my head, a beautiful golden light shining like a brilliant star. The light descended into my head and flowed further into my body. My inner awareness

Bathed in golden light, her soul passed on—but her love became my guardian presence, loving, guiding, and reflecting Jesus Christ.

was bathed in the radiant light surrounding me in my bedroom. I was filled with love, peace, calm, and joy.

Next, I heard a voice within my head saying, "I will watch over you and others as a guardian angel, guide and protect you, and help lead you to the peace and joy of God."

For days, I walked in a blissful state, reminiscent of when my dear friend Doña Catalina passed away. I knew that my friend spoke to me and was there for me. Whenever I thought of her, I felt the same joy and unconditional love, as if she were Jesus sacrificing for us while being present and available to us all the time as Spirit. She experienced such peace before her death, a palpable feeling that seemed to linger after she passed away.

Such faith and devotion were incomprehensible to me at the time. All my petty little problems paled in comparison, and my own darkness seemed purified and washed away with the flow of love.

A VISION OF LIGHT: JESUS AND THE END OF SEPARATION

It is likely not a coincidence that shortly after my time with Doña Catalina and my experience with my friend, I had my direct encounter with Jesus Christ. Many readers might roll their eyes when they read this, but I assure you, this experience felt as real to me as being in Doña Catalina's presence. Interestingly, my encounter with Jesus occurred in Mexico, during a car ride through a rural area of Baja California, from Ensenada to San Felipe in 1990.

I was sitting in the front passenger seat on a dark night. We drove past homes and villages, with kerosene lamps illuminating the houses and casting soft, flickering lights in the darkness.

Science, Indigenous Wisdom, and Jesus

Suddenly, I felt my heart open with overwhelming compassion for everyone. In that moment, something remarkable happened. I saw a dark-complexioned, bearded figure wearing a simple white robe in the car window's reflection. Instantly, I recognized him as Jesus. It wasn't like a dream or hallucination, but more like a clear inner vision, deeply felt and unmistakably real.

Then he spoke, his voice gentle yet firm, seeming to resonate both inside me and from beyond.

"Let me tell you about the end of the world," he said, calmly and clearly.

My perspective shifted dramatically as I rose far above the Earth. From this heightened viewpoint, I could see our planet below, beautifully illuminated in the darkness. Usually, from space, you'd see city lights spread across continents. But I saw billions of individual lights, each glowing warmly from a human heart. It felt intensely personal, like glimpsing the hopes and dreams of all humanity at once.

These countless rays of golden light rose upward from each heart, meeting at a single, radiant point, shaped like a large Heart, high above the Earth. It was incredibly beautiful yet almost too bright to look at directly. I intuitively knew this glowing Heart represented the Divine Heart of Christ, gathering and returning our Love. Soon, golden and purple rays cascaded back down, flowing into each of the billions of hearts below like a gentle but powerful rain of Divine compassion.

It was clear that Jesus was not calling me into a private spirituality but into His mission: to reconcile all things to Himself (Colossians 1:20), weaving a new creation of love among all peoples and nations.

BIRTHING THE SYMBIOTIC AGE

*When the light returned to Earth, it activated webs of light that began to extend horizontally from person to person and community to community worldwide—
a new web of Love and Life.*

Heaven was indeed coming down to Earth. In this vision of light, I saw the Luminous Web of Love and Nature's Luminous Web spreading from person to person, community to community, and all life forms until it engulfed the planet.

From this profound, almost inexplicable experience, I saw the end of the Culture of Separation—and the healing of our deepest divide: from each other, nature, and the Transcendent Logos. As I write about this experience, I still feel its power nearly thirty-five years later. The tears welling within me and streaming down my face are not tears of suffering but overflowing joy. My heart remains wide open, holding space for the vision to unfold, even with all the challenges humanity faces amidst the conflict and ongoing division.

I couldn't envision a better image of the Ancient Blueprint— its Transcendent connection to the Cosmic Heart pouring infinite Love into us, empowering us to share it in our families, neighborhoods, and communities.

The powerful but loving voice continued within my heart:

> *"The end of the world is near. Hear my message. The Law of Life and Love is written in your heart from the beginning. Since man doesn't recognize and act upon this hidden treasure, your civilizations have risen and fallen for the last 3,000 years, constantly repeating the same pattern.*
>
> *In times past, regional empires collapsed, chaos reigned, and other civilizations rose, taking their place, but they, too, failed. Today, the singular global empire of man has occupied the whole world—if you repeat the past, all will be lost."*

Science, Indigenous Wisdom, and Jesus

A vision beyond time: the Cosmic Heart of Jesus radiates Divine Love, dissolving separation and igniting the Luminous Web across all creation.

Jesus continued:

> "This is the message of your life. Remember, the Shadow world does not want you to proclaim these words. This is how you will confront Death. Give of yourself and be available as an empty vessel for my Love. Love everyone, especially those different from you, from all the other 'clans' and 'tribes.'
>
> When you can still love those who hate you, you will be doing my work....
>
> Now is the time. Start with yourself and your family. Be a Witness for and an Advocate for Love, a source of uplift and activation for new communities based on this Law of Life and Love."

As I reflect on it decades later, I recognize how this experience jolted me beyond the narrow beliefs of any particular tribe. It equipped me to unite individuals with widely diverging religious, political, and cultural worldviews into one tribe around a shared, symbiotic purpose—to channel the Cosmic energies of Love to unite our immediate communities around shared Virtues and needs.

Imagine if we each made this absolute commitment!

BRIDGING HEAVEN AND EARTH: THE SYMBIOTIC VISION

I began to observe the global emergence of a new commonwealth, composed of networks of thousands of local communities uniting, an unnamed eruption of spirit, transforming the battlefields of this world.

I felt I was onto something—revealing an Ancient Blueprint to Unite Humanity, discovered by connecting Transcendent Reality with the Immanent, horizontal human society in a Symbiotic Culture—a potential solution to fragmentation, polarization, and the many crises we face.

Could my initiation—disoriented from an old worldview and reoriented toward one uniting Western, Eastern, and Indigenous sensibilities— be a precursor to a mass initiation for the world?

At that time, in my early thirties, I sensed that I had completed my initial "schooling," and I was ready to take my vocation, my calling, a ministry, out into the world—to discover the power

Science, Indigenous Wisdom, and Jesus

of local symbiotic community networks in making fundamental change in real-world communities.

My thought was, how could I possibly "operationalize" the global vision I saw on that dark mountain road? Another powerful figure, Dr. A.T. Ariyaratne, founder of the Sarvodaya Shramadana Movement from Sri Lanka, who would also change my life forever, held the key!

CHAPTER 8

JESUS SENDS ME A BUDDHIST

My encounter with Jesus gave me a broad, planetary vision of a connected, unified web of humanity and all life—one that felt as real to me as anything I had ever experienced. And...I was like:

"Thank you, Jesus! Now what? How do I make that vision real?"

No public internet or social media existed in the late 1980s and early '90s, and I didn't know how to manifest this powerful vision.

However,
I knew that my "calling" was
to be in service:
to bring people together
in communities, connecting across silos
toward a common purpose and mutual benefit.

Essentially, I aimed to gather the Cosmos in Love!

SHERMAN HEIGHTS: A COMMUNITY IN CRISIS

I began where I was—Sherman Heights, a once-prosperous San Diego neighborhood now grappling with poverty and violence. I lived in a small carriage house next to a historic mansion, working on a literacy book project, surrounded by the grim realities of street-level despair.

The Victorian mansion next door was owned by a property management firm that was frustrated that they couldn't develop the property because it was a historic home. As an expression of their frustration, they allowed some drug dealers to move in and squat on the property, perhaps hoping they would destroy the place so they could tear it down.

As the renter next door, I was concerned about this situation. At one point, there was a confrontation between the drug dealers and a rival group that pulled up in a car. I witnessed my neighbors approach the vehicle with a baseball bat and smash the front windshield. Subsequently, one of the individuals in the damaged car came onto the property next to me and confronted the neighboring dealers with a knife.

> *As soon as I heard someone yell, "Go get your gun," a stirring in my heart prompted me to act. Somehow, I found myself standing between the two main antagonists.*

In that moment, I heard myself say, "You don't want to do this, it will change your whole life." Time seemed to pause. Someone in the group backed down, and the confrontation ended. I felt no fear—only the sense that I was supposed to be there. I can't say whether I was Divinely inspired or ridiculously foolish, but for some reason, I felt protected. I never felt in danger, not even for a moment.

While I still can't fully explain my fearlessness or foolhardiness in stepping into that armed confrontation, I suspect it had something to do with the spiritual core I had been developing and my sincere desire to be of service.

In this regard, I felt called to an even broader mission.

NEVER LET A CATALYZING CRISIS GO TO WASTE: A NEIGHBORHOOD AWAKENS

Given the prevalence of drug use in the neighborhood, there were thousands and thousands of used needles scattered across streets, sidewalks, and grassy areas near the freeway. At a community meeting, I was deeply moved by concerned mothers who feared for their children's safety.

Later, in building Symbiotic Networks, I realized that sometimes a community needs a catalyzing crisis to unite around a shared purpose. Sherman Heights wasn't facing a natural disaster; however, those needles, literally and symbolically, became our unifying spark.

> *To unite the predominantly Hispanic community, we organized a series of Convivencias— gatherings rooted in the Spanish verb convivir, meaning "to live with."*

These gatherings were about more than strategy; they began with food, fellowship, affection, and companionship. We believed that if we were to clean up the neighborhood, we might as well start with a celebration.

At our first gathering, over fifty people—Hispanic families, church members, community groups, and volunteers from nearby areas—shared food and ideas. As we talked, concerns about the threat to children, particularly the hypodermic needles littering public spaces, took center stage.

We soon discovered that Caltrans owned the most severely affected grassy area, where thousands of needles had been dumped, right above a major highway. With that knowledge, I organized government agencies, community leaders, and volunteers to partner with Caltrans for a neighborhood-wide cleanup.

After our massive cleanup, the pile of needles stood taller than a person. Volunteers and Caltrans worked together, spending tens of thousands of dollars to clear the danger. But the true victory was the pride and trust it restored in the neighborhood.

Early days of local action (1988)—clearing needles, restoring pride, and discovering the seeds of symbiotic community.

This successful community endeavor enhanced pride and built trust in more ways than one. First, the needles were gone, and the mothers felt safer. Second, our community—and a community center in Sherman Heights—found a common cause and a way to work together successfully.

As I later learned, part of the Symbiotic Network's secret sauce focused on what I called the *functional context*—uniting groups around a shared human need rather than divisive issues.

> *Addressing a single common challenge*
> *faded political, religious, and ethnic differences*
> *into the background, allowing more effective*
> *Symbiotic Networks to emerge.*

While this success was gratifying, it was a one-time event. There was no momentum for further progress to address other neighborhood challenges and create a lasting community. Shortly after, I had to move because my property was in disrepair.

Even though we could not build the infrastructure needed to maintain the movement long-term, the momentum continued to grow within me. I wondered if there was some structure, some model, not just for facing a problem together but for creating a sustainable, symbiotic community.

SARVODAYA SHRAMADANA: A LIVING BLUEPRINT FOR THE KINGDOM

Throughout my life, I've found that when one earnestly desires to align with the Transcendent and sets a firm, steady intention, synchronicity, serendipity, and grace often begin to appear.

In 1991, after my transformative year with Doña Catalina and my encounter with Jesus—whose life exemplified the call to love God and neighbor through direct service and embodied compassion—I moved to Logan Heights, a low-income, multi-ethnic community, primarily Hispanic and African American, located near Sherman Heights.

At the time, I was working as an instructor for San Diego Community College at the Chicano Park Learning Lab, a community center in the heart of Logan Heights. There, I taught GED preparation and over twenty high school subjects. I also served as a jail educator at the Chula Vista Detention Facility.

I continued pursuing my growing interest in holistic community work in my spare time. One day, while reading *New Options*, a newsletter published by Mark Satin, I came across a "letter to the editor" that caught my eye. It referenced a spiritual, self-help grassroots development movement in Sri Lanka called Sarvodaya. The letter immediately sparked something in me.

Mahatma Gandhi coined *Sarvodaya*—"universal uplift"—as a holistic philosophy for India's transformation. Inspired by Gandhi's teachings, a young Buddhist science teacher named Dr. A.T. Ariyaratne expanded the idea into *Sarvodaya Shramadana*, which translates as "the awakening of all through sharing."

As he came to be known, Dr. Ari began the movement in 1958 as an educational experiment. He brought his middle-class students into some of Sri Lanka's poorest villages to work alongside the residents. Together, they completed basic needs projects, shared meals, and participated in conversation and cultural exchange—not to offer charity, but to awaken shared humanity through labor and love.

This resonated deeply with what I had already recognized in the Gospels: that the Kingdom of God was not simply a far-off realm, but also a present reality born in acts of mercy, humility, and justice. The vision of Sarvodaya echoed Jesus's own ministry—lifting the "lowly," the marginalized, feeding the hungry, and calling forth Beloved Community through embodied Love.

BIRTHING THE SYMBIOTIC AGE

Dr. Ari—who would become my spiritual friend, mentor, and colleague—founded what would grow into one of the world's most renowned grassroots movements: the Sarvodaya Movement.

Like Jesus and Gandhi, he became for me a living expression of the Ancient Blueprint—a model of leadership grounded not in domination but in shared dignity and love in action.

Dr. Ari, founder of the world-renowned Sarvodaya Movement (1958)—my spiritual friend, mentor, and colleague in awakening the Ancient Blueprint through love in action.

According to Sarvodaya USA, the US-based support organization, Dr. Ari initially organized two-week Shramadana camps, during which students and villagers worked side-by-side on shared goals. These early projects sparked something much larger than anyone could have imagined at the time.

The movement, grounded in participatory democracy and decentralized empowerment, quickly expanded. Thousands of Shramadana camps spread across Sri Lanka. In more than 15,000 villages, Sarvodaya workers helped communities organize their governance, launch basic needs initiatives, and establish savings banks, preschools, training centers, and more. By offering their shared labor—the one resource every village had—they lifted one another out of poverty through mutual service and solidarity.

Building a road is a "shramadana" (communal gift of energy). Sarvodaya is a self-governance movement seeking a no-poverty, no-affluence society through community-based efforts and volunteerism. (Credit: Sarvodaya Photo Archive)

Sarvodaya's strength lay in its radical simplicity: villagers were asked to name their ten most urgent needs instead of relying on experts or outside institutions. The goal was not dependency, but empowerment rooted in deep listening and collective action. These were the ten shared basic needs they identified:

- Clean and beautiful environment
- Food
- Water
- Clothing
- Housing
- Health care
- Communication
- Energy
- Education
- Spiritual and cultural needs

How simple is that?

*Rather than imposing solutions from above,
Sarvodaya empowered communities by listening first—
and then helping people build networks
grounded in what mattered most to them.*

As the movement grew, villagers began identifying hundreds of "sub-needs" within these ten categories, building out personal, family, cultural, social, economic, and political infrastructure from the grassroots.

By the time I discovered Sarvodaya, it had already transformed over 15,000 villages, helping to rebuild a society fractured by poverty, inequality, and separation.

AWAKENING THE SELF, AWAKENING THE COMMUNITY

My heart soared when I discovered Sarvodaya, as it addressed a profound schism and yearning within Western culture and my psyche: how to reconnect our spiritual nature with rationality and practicality, integrating this into real-world community building aimed at system-wide transformation.

*While many religious and spiritual leaders may focus on
the individual cultivation of love, self-actualization, or
salvation, Dr. Ari blazed a new path to awaken
both the self and the community simultaneously.*

While social activists focus on external structures of domination and oppression, often disregarding religious or spiritual values as superstitious or irrelevant, Dr. Ari challenges us with a fundamental question: Can we awaken a person's inner life while transforming the social and economic structures of our communities and the world?

"A soul force lies dormant in all of us," Dr. Ari wrote, and *"No human life is worth living if this inner man and treasures are not discovered and experienced."*

He said that Sarvodaya workers:

> "Try to awaken themselves spiritually and thus transcend sectarian religious differences, to become one with all...several million Sarvodaya adherents in Sri Lanka have proved that they can transcend racial, religious, linguistic, and ethnic barriers to accept a common state of ideals, principles, and constructive programs to build a new society as collectively envisioned by them."

I thought, wow, I need to pay attention to this.

This was the first model in the world—and still is—that not only aligned with my vision but also seemed rooted in a lineage reflecting the Ancient Blueprint from Jesus, Gandhi, and Dr. Martin Luther King, Jr. What struck me was not how Sarvodaya differed from Jesus Christ's vision but how deeply it mirrored Jesus' teachings in practice.

That brings us back to the question from the Introduction: Are there universal Virtues, principles, common needs, and methods of organizing networks that could unite entire communities across polarized divides?

The answer was and still is YES.

This spiritual and practical approach—bridging religion and science, inner and outer—was precisely what I had been preparing for. And it had already been working for over thirty years.

As I researched more deeply, I found that Sarvodaya operates within three spheres of life: consciousness, governance, and economics. These pillars are interwoven into the fabric of their movement and have contributed to its practical success in mobilizing millions to engage in its development.

The scale of Sarvodaya's impact is striking. Beyond mobilizing the 15,000 villages as mentioned above, the movement has helped communities build over 5,000 preschools, thousands of village banks, and over 100,000 small businesses, health centers, libraries, and cottage industries. It has also supported digging wells and latrines, promoting biodiversity, solar energy, agroforestry, regenerative agriculture, and ecovillage projects while cultivating Beloved Community.

Central to this work is the Shramadana, a family gathering rooted in the shared gift of labor, energy, and resources. In each village, families come together to reflect on the ten basic needs and collectively choose one pressing need to address. They then hold a second gathering, a blend of spiritual revival, potluck, strategy session, and community building, beginning with meditation and prayer to focus on lovingkindness and service.

Then comes the shared work project that arose from the felt need discussed in the larger group. Afterward, the people return for shared food, reminiscent of the traditional "barn raisings" in rural America.

Although Sarvodaya is based in Buddhism, Gandhian thought, and Sri Lankan culture, its fundamental principles are universally applicable.

The primary idea is that consciousness, personality transformation, and the practice of Virtues are essential components in any effort to change society. Charity, self-sufficiency, and self-governance start at home.

The bottom line is that the Transcendent is "downloaded" into our personality, manifesting as the common, universal Virtues that make life worth living for each individual and the entire community.

RESTORING THE POWER OF VIRTUE: WHAT THE WEST FORGOT

While Sarvodaya cultivates spiritual Virtues as the foundation for societal healing, many in the modern West have dismissed these Virtues as irrelevant—or worse, divisive. Secular activists and community developers often shy away from religious language, viewing it as superstitious or unscientific. Yet without spiritual grounding, can true, enduring transformation ever take root?

Sarvodaya actively nurtures inner qualities that empower individuals to collaborate, enhance their circumstances, and unite their communities.

Although expressed through a Buddhist perspective—love/loving-kindness (metta), compassion (karuna), equanimity (upekkha), and sympathetic joy (mudita)—these Virtues are universal. They reflect the Ancient Blueprint I've traced back to the Sermon on the Mount, perfectly expressing "Love God, Love thy neighbor" as they root spiritual principles in meeting the community's ten basic human needs.

Projects emerge naturally from this foundation: building trusted relationships, supporting mutual aid networks, and sharing resources for the common good.

In the West, however, the spiritual imperative has been largely overlooked. Spirituality, seen as vital, has become marginalized, considered a private sentiment, incapable of transforming social or economic structures.

The Culture of Separation asserts that there is no Transcendent reality. In its place, we are left with materialism posing as a new "religion" and political ideologies held with the fervor once reserved for faith.

That's why discovering Dr. Ari's work—and Sarvodaya's embodiment of the Ancient Blueprint—was so powerful. Sarvodaya doesn't retreat from spirituality; it transforms modern skepticism into tangible action. It shows how spiritual awakening can unite a community, heal division, and address social and economic inequality through practical frameworks for self-sufficiency and systemic change.

We in the West would do well to remember that finding common projects to meet real needs can unite communities more effectively than ideology ever could. The growing polarization and incivility in modern life are symptoms of forgetting this more profound truth.

Despite severe poverty and hardship in Sri Lanka's villages, individuals have reconnected with the Transcendent, bringing "Heaven" to Earth through small acts of collective love and labor. Their spiritual connection is visible in new networks of "people's power," translating Transcendent love into immanent action.

These are the hallmarks of Sarvodaya—the foundational principles from which we in the West can learn and adapt. Over the past sixty-five years, more than 5,000 villages and towns have transformed themselves into what they call Sarvodaya Societies.

SARVODAYA SOCIETIES:
A PARALLEL CULTURE IN ACTION

The Sarvodaya Society forms the backbone of each community's "ecosystem network," scaffolding a parallel society, economy, and governance—a transformative counterculture operating alongside official local government. These movements are independent yet interdependent.

Establishing such a parallel system offers a practical method of uniting individuals across divisions maintained by top-down economic and political structures, which keep us fragmented.

What sets Sarvodaya apart from other community development models is its integration of universal spiritual Virtues into a culture designed to activate a cooperative, nonviolent society and local economy.

Let's pause to appreciate the scale of Dr. Ari's achievement.

Inspired by Gandhi's early 20th-century vision of a "Commonwealth of Village Republics," Dr. Ari translated this into reality. Sarvodaya's fractal, multi-scalar empowerment network is not just an idealistic theory—it's a functioning model from which we can learn.

We don't need to reinvent the wheel.

Modern frameworks like Bioregionalism, Cosmolocalism, Relocalization, and Doughnut Economics often overlook spiritually grounded movements like Sarvodaya—or dismiss them as irrelevant. But rediscovering and building on these movements can accelerate progress by rooting new systems in a universal foundation of Divine Love, transcending captured narratives like left/right binaries, identity politics, and other culture-war distractions born from the Culture of Separation.

If I haven't made it clear by now, let me reiterate:

Every problem we seek to address separately—even if it appears to be a universal challenge or crisis, like war, poverty, climate change, dying species, or a pandemic—can only be solved by creating a Culture of Connection that lifts us *off the battlefield* so we can work *together* in a new *context* — a *new playing field*. This living, breathing network is nothing less than a new wineskin for a new world.

BIRTHING THE SYMBIOTIC AGE

A NEW WINESKIN FOR A NEW WORLD

Learning about Sarvodaya's success helped me grasp Jesus' teaching on "new wine in old wineskins" in a practical way. As a rebellious Jew, Jesus recognized how mainstream religion had become entangled with the Roman Empire's power structures. He taught that the new wine of the Kingdom of Heaven—bringing Heaven to Earth—required new forms, structures, and communities to embody Divine Love.

Sarvodaya became a living example of that integration. They created a spiritual and practical container capable of holding the vision of a symbiotic, awakened society. What I'm about to say may seem bold:

Dr. Ari and Sarvodaya have achieved something no religious, economic, or political movement has done at a national scale in over 1,800 years.

Sarvodaya's integration of spiritual principles and practical systems, like bioregional ecosystem networks, building a new society within the old, captured my full attention.

Even now, amid crisis and collapse, no movement offers such a tangible, scalable, and spiritually coherent path forward. Their national network spanning 15,000 villages and towns, with over 5,000 Sarvodaya Societies, has built a parallel organizational structure supporting a new society alongside official governance. Though Sri Lanka and the West differ, I've worked to translate Sarvodaya's principles into what I call Symbiotic Networks.

This book offers a foundational approach to starting your local community weaving movement—anywhere in the world.

Here is the secret at the heart of it all:

The virtuous flow between Heaven and Earth—the engine turning personal awakening into societal transformation.

THE VIRTUOUS CIRCLE:
THE INTERFACE BETWEEN HEAVEN AND EARTH

How do we unite spirit and society to bring Heaven to Earth?

I began to see the Ancient Blueprint in the Sermon on the Mount—Love God and Love Others—not merely as beautiful poetry but as a core expression of reality's participatory nature, much like $E=MC^2$. This wasn't abstract inspiration—it was structure—a living code.

Ironically, the Sarvodaya Movement profoundly expresses Jesus' teachings in action—yet it emerged within a primarily Buddhist, "underdeveloped" South Asian nation. That realization stirred a powerful question in me:

How can we move from siloed separation—nonprofits, churches, businesses, and identity groups—to a unified, relational Culture of Connection in advanced, pluralistic, primarily Christian Western societies?

The answer isn't found in new ideologies or programs. These often replicate the very Culture of Separation they aim to transcend.

Sarvodaya isn't merely revolutionary—it's more radical. Revolutions revolve around old powers and keep us on the familiar wheel of uprisings and downfalls. But radical transformation heals at the root—separation itself—uniting the Cosmos in Love.

The transformation begins within—healing "in here" before expecting change "out there."

St. Maximus the Confessor spoke of a Virtuous circle: when we practice Virtues like compassion, we open ourselves to Divine Love, and in that Love, we become capable of deeper Virtue. It's not a linear climb. It's a sacred spiral. Nor is it a solitary journey. It happens in community, and it must be grounded in action.

In Sarvodaya, spiritual growth is not about Western self-improvement or individual ascent—it's about awakening—awakening to the Authentic Self that connects us to the Transcendent and to one another. And that light radiates outward from that center—self, family, community, bioregion, and world.

This awakening forms the foundation of Sarvodaya's vast network—a constellation of Virtue-awakened towns and cities across Sri Lanka. Beyond the core Buddhist Virtues of lovingkindness, compassion, joy, and equanimity, Sarvodaya also nurtures generosity, constructive work, and social equality.

These are not lofty ideals. They are lived realities—practical, accessible, transformative. As Dr. King said:

> "Everybody can serve…. You only need a heart full of grace, a soul generated by love."

This is where the rubber meets the road: the test of true religion and spirituality. This is how Heaven touches Earth—not in clouds or visions, but in villages and kitchens, in wells dug and children fed, in justice made real.

The virtuous circle is not merely personal but cultural, ecological, and civilizational.

We—human beings—are the living interface between Heaven and Earth. When we embody Virtue through conscious, daily practice, we become conduits of Divine Love into the world. In every act rooted in that Love, the space between Heaven and Earth collapses, and something sacred becomes visible. In that luminous opening, a new world can begin.

Sarvodaya has faithfully and humbly demonstrated this for over sixty-five years.

A COMMONWEALTH OF SELF-GOVERNING COMMUNITIES

As individuals and organizations in Sarvodaya harness the power of Virtues within newly connected network nodes, this conscious infrastructure radiates energy across regions, uplifting all. These nodes represent leaders, organizations, and communities once siloed, now linked in mutual purpose.

Sarvodaya is perhaps the world's most remarkable example of *Nexus Agency*—authentic power emerging from grassroots, coalescing networks focused on the common good. Its spiritual-practical synthesis offers a path forward for humanity: from isolated, single-issue activism to multi-siloed, integrated networks.

It is a multi-scalar transformation from *me consciousness* to *we consciousness*—a shift desperately needed today. Dr. Ari proved that profound cultural change can be scaled: first outward, within communities; then upward, to reshape a nation.

And if it can happen in Sri Lanka, why not globally? Like the vision Jesus showed me, Dr. Ari's was also global. He said:

> "We dream of a global commonwealth of self-governing communities, rooted in democracy, human rights, spiritual values, and respect for nature."

In the chapters ahead, you'll see how Sarvodaya's influence shaped the Symbiotic Networks we later built in San Diego and Reno. First, they embodied the Virtues, creating unity. Then, they extended this virtuous field, energizing culture and networks from the bottom up. These networks reflect the *Ancient Blueprint*—they are fractals of it.

As you'll read in Section 2, they are distributed, voluntary, and self-governing circles of trust that emerge from inner awareness and authentic relationships, not from top-down control.

Looking back, I see Sarvodaya as a living echo of Jesus' teachings—a Buddhist-rooted movement that exemplifies bringing the Kingdom of Heaven on Earth.

Sarvodaya didn't just inspire me—it answered the aching question that burned in my heart: Can spiritual awakening and social transformation truly go hand in hand?

Dr. Ari and the people of Sri Lanka proved the answer is yes. If it can happen in over 15,000 villages, it can happen in your neighborhood, church, and community. The seed of Symbiotic Culture already lives within us. It's just waiting to be awakened.

Dr. A.T. Ariyaratne visited me in San Diego in the early 1990s, sharing Sarvodaya's living wisdom.

So yes, Jesus sent me a Buddhist—and more than that, a working vision already alive in the world. This wasn't utopia; it was reality. A more loving society isn't a fantasy—it is possible, if we awaken the power within and among us.

And...I was about to discover...the seeds of this vision were being planted right in my backyard.

At the bottom of that article in which I learned about Sarvodaya, I saw a letter from a San Diego State University professor, who, to my astonishment, was running a program in Logan Heights, the neighborhood where I was living!

I reached out. Suddenly, alongside Dr. Ari's vision, I had a local ally exploring how a movement born in Sri Lanka might take root in urban San Diego. And I was off to my next learning adventure.

CHAPTER 9

CRISIS TO COMMUNITY: WEAVING BELONGING FROM BREAKDOWN

Inspired and heartened by Sarvodaya, I asked myself:
"How is it possible to consciously weave networks to bring everyone together with a common vision based on Divine Love, inspired by the Ancient Blueprint outlined by Jesus in the Sermon on the Mount and fully expressed in modern times through Dr. Ari with Sarvodaya?"
It turns out I didn't have to wait long for an answer.

It often takes a disaster or crisis to jolt us from the trance of separation and move us beyond ego toward genuine cooperation.

GROUND ZERO FOR A NEW KIND OF NETWORK

The year was 1992.

In the low-income neighborhood where I lived—Logan Heights, San Diego—ongoing gang and drug violence had created a full-blown public safety crisis. This crisis opened the door for a new response rooted in community, cooperation, and a shared desire for change.

This crisis allowed me to explore how consciously weaving Symbiotic Networks could address the real-life challenges of an urban environment. Through a participatory process, we founded Vecinos Unidos (Neighbors United) to bring together this diverse, majority Black and Hispanic community of over 50,000—united by the urgent need for safety.

Like my prior neighborhood, Sherman Heights, Logan Heights was beset by crime, poverty, addiction, and despair. Children didn't play in the streets. Women remained indoors. Men loitered on corners with nothing to occupy them.

> **On one block alone, over forty drug dealers sold cocaine and marijuana daily, often to buyers from wealthy areas like La Jolla. Police mostly looked the other way.**

Given the lack of political or economic power in the neighborhood, few outsiders took notice. Absentee landlords owned 90 percent of the homes and businesses. Roofs leaked, mold spread illness, and the sound of gunshots was part of everyday life. Even the churches, once pillars of support, had largely moved on. Their congregants—now successful and suburban—returned on Sundays but ignored the poverty they'd left behind.

What remained was a fragmented web of isolated groups—nonprofits, churches, agencies, businesses—each concentrated on its agenda, while the neighborhood's core needs went unaddressed. Only later did I realize that this fragmentation wasn't unique. It was a symptom of a larger pattern—a global Culture of Separation.

Whether in low-income neighborhoods or middle-class suburbs, the silos appeared different but functioned the same.

As I began to witness firsthand, disconnection was merely a symptom of a deeper spiritual malady of modern life.

> *I realized that siloed competition is viewed as normal in a Culture of Separation, almost like a built-in control mechanism to keep us divided and easier to manage.*

In Logan Heights (and, for that matter, everywhere else), each individual and organization operated in a reactive, survival mode, merely focusing on their narrow agendas and needs. I was shocked yet not surprised that the African American and Hispanic community organizations and religious leaders didn't know each other, nor had they ever collaborated closely. Our outreach marked the first time they were brought together for a common purpose.

That's when I realized something needed to change. Reactivity alone could not tackle the violence and isolation. We required a new type of response—one rooted in trust, shared action, and the deeper power of community. Therefore, the problems in the neighborhood festered until individuals emerged who could unite the community around a larger, higher purpose and agenda.

RE-OCCUPYING THE HOOD

I began working with a courageous Head Start director and a San Diego State University professor. After someone was shot nearby, we held our first meeting—right there on the street where it happened. Inspired by what I'd learned in Sherman Heights and Sarvodaya's principle of empowering the most marginalized, we gathered residents to name their fears and envision change.

We started small. First, we got people talking. Then, to re-weave the fabric of a broken community, we reached out to leaders—churches, businesses, nonprofits, and city officials—to join a coordinated action plan.

We organized peace marches down the streets to encourage people to leave their homes and rekindle hope. We cleaned vacant lots. The police reintroduced neighborhood patrols. Code officers began holding absentee landlords accountable.

But the fundamental shift occurred when people who had felt powerless began to take action and—many for the first time—experience agency. In just weeks, signs of transformation were evident everywhere. The bottom-up energy of grassroots networks proved stronger than any formal initiative. As Dr. Ari discovered in Sri Lanka that awakening people's agency builds lasting confidence.

> **Bottom-up, grassroots networks act as catalysts and can be more potent than any formal organizational initiative, especially government.**

Still, organizing alone wasn't enough. We had to confront the economic forces behind the destruction.

Beautifying my street—reweaving community through love, labor, and a vision of transformation.

Eight drug houses were operating openly, one of which was rumored to be the county's marijuana hub. A liquor store owner controlled four of them, ignoring criminal activity as long as the rent was paid. However, we shut them down in six months by coordinating efforts across families, churches, nonprofits, and local agencies. In contrast, the city took two years to close just two houses.

I moved into one of the reclaimed homes and began hosting nightly strategy meetings. A mix of street preachers, pastors, neighbors, and some idle men gathered with me to reclaim the most notorious street corner.

Each night, we showed up. Armed only with tough love and prayer, we told the drug dealers—some connected to a powerful Tijuana cartel—that we loved them as God commands but could not accept their behavior. It must have seemed surreal to them, facing this unlikely group determined to reclaim our ground.

Reflecting on the past, it brings to mind the #Occupy movement, which faltered by concentrating solely on what it opposed. We didn't just protest; we embodied something new: love in action, rooted in the Ancient Blueprint and modeled after Sarvodaya, even though we didn't fully realize it then.

> *When we re-inhabit ourselves with Divine Love,*
> *we begin to re-occupy our neighborhoods—*
> *not with force, but with healing energy.*
> *We become the new wineskins for new wine.*

The impact was contagious. Neighbors who had waited for others to act began to show up, drawn by the courage of those already marching. It was a public proclamation:

"This is our neighborhood—we're taking it back."

S.D. Union Nov. 15, 1992 B-1

Webster Avenue has cause to celebrate

By LEONEL SANCHEZ
Staff Writer

Juana Ortega did not know what to expect when she walked out of her house on Webster Avenue yesterday.

The 54-year-old woman was relieved not to see any syringes strewn on the sidewalks or hear anyone brawling or selling sex in the streets.

Instead, scores of people had gathered in the middle of a street for an old-fashioned block party.

The goal of the party was to remind Webster Avenue residents like Ortega that they are winning the fight against drug dealers and prostitutes in the area.

"It's good to know that people are working together to clean up this mess," Ortega said as she waited in line with her husband and grandchild for a free meal of rice and beans.

While crime is still rampant throughout Logan Heights, community activists say it is down significantly in the 3000 block of Webster Avenue.

"At one point we stopped taking kids in the streets for walks because we were afraid they'd get stuck with needles," said Claudette [illegible], a teacher at the Webster Avenue Head Start Center. "Now they can play outside and their parents are getting to know each other."

"When I first came here (to the Webster Head Start to introduce a drug education program for parents and children), I couldn't even get in without people mobbing us with drugs to sell," said James Ajemian, a social work professor at San Diego State University and

See Party on Page B-3

Party

Webster Avenue has reason to celebrate

Continued from Page B-1

Webster Avenue organizer.

"I told my assistant at that time that if we got through this alive we were going to clean it up," he said.

Ajemian worked with the Webster Head Start Center and the Webster Area Neighborhood Association to clean up the area.

Last month, he founded Neighbors United, a federally funded program whose goal is to organize neighborhoods in Logan Heights.

Yesterday, he proudly announced the groups' achievements on Webster Avenue.

Community activists have persuaded landlords to evict suspected drug dealers from seven homes and apartments on Webster Avenue. In return, they have promised not to file lawsuits against the landlords for allowing drug problems to fester near their residences.

Suing landlords is a tactic that has been successfully used by the Berkeley-based Drug Abatement Institute, which has gotten rid of crack houses in the community and won large awards in court.

"This is a tool that has not been used very much in San Diego, but it's one we want to adopt," said Richard Flyer, of United Neighbors.

Property owners also pledged to allow residents to build a park or community garden on a lot across the street from the Head Start office.

Flyer said plans are under way to set up a food cooperative for residents where they would save money by pooling their cash to buy food and other supplies in bulk.

He said United Neighbors is also studying ways to develop a community fund that would generate loans for new businesses in the area. The program would be modeled on Chicago's South Shore Bank, which is one of the few banks in the nation making loans to help revitalize low-income neighborhoods.

"Seventy-five percent of the businesses are owned by people who don't even live here," said Flyer. "We need to promote community owned businesses."

1992 San Diego Union Tribune *article documents our neighborhood organizing—an early fruit of re-occupying the hood with love.*

But transformation came with risk.

One day, I came home to see a man selling drugs on my doorstep. An upscale buyer from La Jolla had parked out front. I confronted him first. "How would you feel if I came to your neighborhood to buy drugs on your street?" Still angry from an earlier argument, I turned to the dealer and told him to leave. In a flash, he pulled out a knife and lunged. I dodged, and in that instant, I realized I was carrying anger into the moment, and I could let it go.

As soon as I did, the fear vanished. I saw not just a drug dealer in front of me, but a fellow human being. And then something happened. A light, the same one I had seen in my dreams, seemed to envelop me. The knife fell to the ground. The dealer paused, glanced at me, then walked away—and never returned. The buyer drove off in silence.

Catalina's words returned to me: "There is no need to fear evil."

FROM SURVIVAL TO SELF-DETERMINATION

What began as a response to gang violence evolved into a deeper effort: community and economic renewal. Along the way, I encountered two disempowering beliefs about poverty—either blaming the poor for being "lazy," or seeing them as helpless victims. Neither view fosters agency nor real transformation.

In the Culture of Separation, letting entire neighborhoods languish is not just common—it's normalized. But guided by Sarvodaya's radical practicality, I stopped seeing Logan Heights residents as villains or victims. I saw them as people capable of reclaiming their lives and communities.

The more I reflected, the clearer it became: Logan Heights resembled an occupied colony. Outsiders owned most homes and businesses. Money earned in the neighborhood flowed out, not in. Like Sri Lanka's poorest villages, the key wasn't outside solutions—but building agency and trust from within.

A glaring example was the Gateway Marketplace project. Though funded by city and county resources and marketed as a boon to locals, it attracted outside corporations like Price Club (now Costco). These companies brought in their employees and reaped tax breaks—another extractive model disguised as redevelopment.

The more profound lesson is that ownership matters. As Sarvodaya taught, real change begins when people become agents of their spiritual, social, and economic lives. Yet not everyone welcomed this. Some nonprofits, dependent on government grants, hesitated to collaborate. Many competed for the same limited resources, replicating the same scarcity-driven silos we hoped to transcend.

Two insights emerged. First, silos aren't accidents, they're part of the system's design. They divide us and prevent cooperation.

Silos are the ideal architecture for "divide and rule"

Abraham Lincoln said it, but Jesus said it first: *"A house divided against itself cannot stand"* (Mark 3:25). These silos weren't just inefficient, they were spiritually destructive.

Second, Logan Heights was a node in a global pattern. The local extractive economy mirrored what's happening everywhere: rising oligarchies at the top, disempowered communities below.

And yet, the story wasn't over.

Our neighborhood transformation efforts gained support from nonprofits, churches, and the city. We started a food co-op in a building that once housed a liquor store—only the second low-income co-op in the US, the other being in Park Slope, Brooklyn. Roughly 500 low-income Black and Hispanic families participated. For the first time, they could buy fresh produce locally, circulating wealth *within* the community.

When the community owns the solution, the neighborhood becomes its own miracle.

A Catholic priest from Christ the King Church blessed the center, which an African-American entrepreneur ran. Our city councilman secured a $500,000 community development grant, which enabled us to purchase a new property for the co-op and a rear community center. All major TV stations attended the grand opening. A Hispanic priest and an African American minister jointly blessed the store, the first community-owned food outlet in the neighborhood. It was a celebration of what's possible when people reclaim power together.

But even as the co-op settled into daily life, I sensed more profound unlearned lessons—and challenges yet to come.

LOGAN HEIGHTS DIDN'T TRANSFORM SAN DIEGO: IT TRANSFORMED ME

My time in San Diego taught me that intentional Symbiotic Networking is a potent tool capable of uniting diverse individuals to address even violent, complex issues. Our efforts led to creating a nonprofit, Vecinos Unidos (Neighbors United), and resulted in tangible improvements: crime decreased by 75 percent, a food co-op was established, and community ties were reinforced.

But we didn't transform San Diego. The network didn't expand beyond our neighborhood. Why?

First, as Vecinos Unidos evolved into a more formal organization, ego conflicts emerged, including my own. I lacked the spiritual maturity to navigate internal tensions gracefully. Second, while we shared goals, we did not have a common spiritual framework. Lacking grounding in Virtues like Love and the Golden Rule, our unity fractured. We lost the very coherence that had been powering Sarvodaya for decades. Still, the seed had been planted—and I hoped to nurture what we failed to sustain in San Diego more wisely in the coming years.

Secondly, I don't think I fully appreciated the spiritual foundation upon which Sarvodaya was built. We acquiesced to the popular notion of activism at that time—working to improve external conditions with the hope that spiritual understanding would emerge. That never happened. The more the group focused on "external" projects, the more we lost spiritual coherence and our sense of purpose.

In that regard, we made another common mistake: assuming that external success would naturally lead to deeper transformation. It didn't. The more we focused on projects, the less energy we had for ongoing relationship-building, which is the heart of a Symbiotic Culture.

Something else I didn't recognize then is that a project such as building a food cooperative or community education center can consume a group's entire bandwidth. The more time you dedicate to projects, worthy as they may be, the less time you have available to build network linkages in an ongoing, ever-expanding manner.

WEAVING SYMBIOTIC CULTURE

One of my most significant challenges in translating Sarvodaya to the West was contextual: Sarvodaya began in impoverished villages lacking basic infrastructure—roads, irrigation, businesses, and preschools. Their transformation was fueled by building what didn't yet exist.

In contrast, the "overdeveloped" West has an excess of infrastructure and an overabundance of businesses, nonprofits, and interest groups—each operating in its silo. Here, transformation requires not building something new, but Connecting the Good already present through shared action. This demands a different mind and heart-set.

Section 2, *Application* will offer examples of how we practiced this approach in Reno, Nevada.

Back then, Neighbors United—our early network—gradually became another silo, constrained by its mission and competing with others for funding and recognition. The crisis passed, and with it, our broader vision narrowed. Still, that period became my training ground—an apprenticeship in weaving love and service into structure and soul.

I realized my deeper calling: to weave the inner and outer worlds—spirituality and community—into what I later named Symbiotic Culture. In a fragmented society, my role was to integrate Divine Love, unity, and practical service—and to help others do the same. Those ten years were my apprenticeship in putting sacred ideals into action.

I saw firsthand how a community can transform through caring relationships, mutual respect, and Shramadana—Western style.

BUILDING THE PARALLEL SOCIETY: WHERE HEAVEN MEETS EARTH

My first attempt to bring Sarvodaya's practical wisdom into Western consciousness taught me one core truth: Authentic religion and spirituality mean cultivating Love and Service, connecting the Transcendent with the Immanent, and bringing Heaven to Earth.

Symbiotic Culture, inspired by Sarvodaya and tested in the real world offers a framework for building a parallel society rooted in the Ancient Blueprint and universal Virtues serving real community needs.

This bridge-building, civic-spiritual network can unite churches, businesses, and civic groups to connect and multiply the good.

This is the foundational equation of Sarvodaya and Symbiotic Culture—what Jesus expressed in the Sermon on the Mount: Love God and Love Others. It's not just an ideal; it's a living, participatory reality we are already part of. It lives in each of us, enabling us to bring Heaven to Earth and renew communities from within organically. This stands in contrast to client-based service models that reinforce dependency.

Through my work in San Diego neighborhoods, I saw the deeper truth in Dr. Ari's words: "We build the road, and the road builds us." Still, I needed one more experience—working inside the traditional system—to fully grasp the difference. That would be the next step in my journey.

Logan Heights didn't transform San Diego—it transformed me. What I learned there became the seed of a deeper model I would later plant in Reno: a replicable way to weave Virtue, spirit, and community into a living parallel society.

CHAPTER 10

BEYOND THE CHARITY INDUSTRIAL COMPLEX

I emerged from my experience organizing Symbiotic Networks in San Diego neighborhoods with mixed feelings. On one hand, the work had a real impact—people who once believed they were powerless began to experience individual and collective agency.

At the same time, I felt frustrated. The positive change in Logan Heights didn't seem scalable and barely affected the larger San Diego community and economy. Still, my focus remained fixed: getting to the root of poverty, inequality, and hunger. To achieve that, I realized I needed a broader playing field.

The journey of building community networks sharpened my skills and challenged me to integrate the Transcendent experiences of the past twenty years. Perhaps now was the time to apply what I learned—within a larger, better-funded countywide organization, one open to a broader vision of helping the "under-resourced" help themselves.

However, one question remained: Could the system be transformed from within, starting with a single county?

FROM NEIGHBORHOOD ROOTS TO COUNTYWIDE REACH

I hoped to discover this when, in 1997, I was recruited to become the San Diego Food Bank Executive Director, a program of the well-established Neighborhood House Association, one of the largest nonprofit service agencies in San Diego County.

Founded in 1914 as a settlement house to support immigrants, the organization had grown into a powerhouse of social services by the late 1990s. For example, it managed the region's Head Start program, which had a budget of $36 million. While the Food Bank had a board responsible for hiring and firing, it ultimately answered to the parent organization.

The Food Bank was part of Second Harvest, a corporate-driven national network that distributed unsellable food, often damaged or nearing expiration. Through it, we accessed food giants like Kellogg's and received donations from community food drives such as the Holiday Food Drive and the Letter Carriers Food Drive each May.

To clarify, the Food Bank didn't distribute food directly. Instead, it served as a warehouse, selling donated food at 14¢ a pound to churches, homeless programs, and local nonprofits, passing the food items on to the community. At that time, hundreds of such groups used their funds to purchase and redistribute this food. Most of it was shelf-stable—boxed, canned, or processed—though we also sourced some fresh produce.

At the time, the Food Bank operated out of a 100,000-square-foot warehouse at the former Naval Training Center in Liberty

Station, which had recently been converted for civilian use. It was a pristine, well-landscaped, spacious, clean, and impressive facility. I stepped into this role with a powerful mission: to end hunger in San Diego County. I also inherited twenty employees.

At my first team meeting, I asked: "How many of you believe we can end hunger in San Diego County?"

One hand went up.

Only one of the twenty staff members believed the mission was truly possible. Houston, we have a problem. I was reminded of Matthew 25, where Jesus identifies with the hungry and the marginalized. If we take that seriously, shouldn't we believe that hunger can—and must—end?

INSIDE THE CHARITY MINDSET

This was my initiation into nonprofit culture, where, regardless of the mission statement, many became caught in the inertia of institutional survival and preserving jobs. Staff fulfilled their duties by distributing food and alleviating hunger, yet few questioned what it would take to eliminate it.

> *No one addressed the root cause of poverty's persistence in such a wealthy county or how to empower people to rise above it.*

I looked at the room of staff who hadn't raised their hands and asked, "Then, why are you here?" I told them I was committed to shifting our focus—from managing symptoms to ending hunger—and if they didn't believe that was possible, I'd start replacing them. This shocked many of them. As I later learned, no one had ever been replaced. Positions had become permanent posts in the endless "fight against hunger," grounded in the assumption that hunger and poverty were immutable facts of life.

Certainly, the Food Bank made a difference, and the people working there were genuinely good individuals.

There were good programs that did excellent work within the system. For example, we ran a "brown box" program for seniors and a WIC program to feed women, infants, and children. We supported hundreds of local distributors who relied on us for bulk food.

However, I wanted to go further. I began hiring individuals with corporate experience and results-driven backgrounds. I added roles such as publicity, brought on a strong second-in-command, and built capacity for a broader vision and increased fundraising.

But this was no longer grassroots organizing.

*I had entered a power structure—
one constrained by bureaucracy, resistant to change,
and defined by entrenched relationships that had
little to do with hunger relief.*

The truth is that the Neighborhood House Association preferred the existing situation, and the Food Bank enhanced its prestige.

Its leadership was not keen on change; they were content with the status quo. I led the board, which was primarily made up of labor union leaders from San Diego and Imperial Counties. With each stakeholder focused on maintaining their influence, the mission of ending hunger faded into the background. That loss haunted me. I hadn't come to manage decline—I had come to ignite transformation.

Welcome to the Culture of Separation.

BIRTHING THE SYMBIOTIC AGE

TRYING TO CHANGE THE GAME

Still, I was determined to apply what I had learned from building Symbiotic Networks and transform the Food Bank's culture. I thought of the parable of the mustard seed. If I could plant one small, networked idea into this rigid system, it could grow into something greater.

To some extent, my proactive approach worked. I observed staff becoming more mission-driven and hopeful that they could make a deeper impact on hunger and poverty, beyond their day-to-day activities. After all, the Food Bank was already a network serving hundreds of distribution groups across the county, from church pantries to homeless outreach agencies. However, these groups operated in silos and rarely collaborated.

And then I saw an opportunity. While most of these organizations sourced food from the Food Bank, they also bought from Costco and Price Club—better than retail, but not ideal.

So, I proposed a new idea: a bulk-buying co-op. By coming together, we could negotiate better prices, enhance food quality, and provide these organizations more control and autonomy.

I met with several leaders to explore the formation of this cooperative—a Symbiotic Network in action. However, I didn't stay at the Food Bank long enough to see it through (more soon). Still, we found other ways to expand our impact. We helped organizations increase self-reliance and reduce dependency, not just by feeding people, but by empowering them.

One project involved a homeless women's shelter where we helped women start small business ventures—what would later be called "social enterprises." For example, we received massive donations of dried beans, and the women packaged and sold them through retail channels and our distribution network.

> We also catalyzed new collaborations among local networks that had never worked together before.

Beyond food, we helped organizations generate sustainable revenue streams that didn't rely solely on donations or grants.

However, even as we expanded collaborations and planted new seeds of empowerment, something didn't feel right. Was this enough? Could these small innovations change the system, or were we simply finding more efficient ways to manage symptoms?

Even our innovations reinforced a broken system. The more I examined the situation, the more I recognized that we weren't circumventing the problem—we were embedded within it. The structure itself resisted transformation, maintaining dysfunction even while appearing to do good. That realization was sobering.

What if all these well-meaning efforts were, at best, sophisticated band-aids?

THE CHARITY INDUSTRIAL COMPLEX: IT'S NOT MEANT TO SOLVE THE PROBLEM

I wanted to implement a more entrepreneurial, self-sustaining social enterprise model. However, I couldn't overcome the grip of the charity mindset, where well-meaning donors and professionals could feel good without ever truly empowering those they aimed to help. This approach of being a "handout without a hand-up" defined the nonprofit class, what I've come to call the charity industrial complex.

As director, I played—and played well—within the fundraising system. One night in 1998, we raised nearly $1 million at a star-studded event called "A Taste of the NFL." We received tens of thousands of pounds of leftover food from Super Bowl parties, auctioned rare items, and brought in celebrities like Miss America, Evander Holyfield, Drew Carey, and even the CEO of Coca-Cola. The auction included a *Seinfeld* finale taping ticket that sold for $20,000.

It was heady, glamorous, and effective. I could have stayed in that lifestyle for decades.

Most charity leaders act from sincere motivations. That's not the issue. The issue is that even well-meaning organizations like the San Diego Food Bank—and millions like it—are trapped in siloed, single-issue models that fail to address the root of systemic problems.

> *What if the system were designed not to solve the problem but to manage it?*

As I suggested, these problems aren't meant to be solved within the Culture of Separation. They are managed, not transformed, and perpetually addressed, never uprooted. Think of the "War on Drugs," "War on Cancer," or "War on Terror." These are endless wars, not solutions. Over time, I have come to see that the Culture of Separation sustains an entire Charity Industrial Complex—a system that depends on unsolvable problems for its survival.

It remains busy treating symptoms while the Culture of Separation continues to produce more. Most people within it don't realize this, and most supporters never question it.

So, with the best intentions, we reinforce the conditions we hope to change. Each symptom or crisis is an externality of a deeper systemic disorder. Put bluntly: materialism and global oligarchic systems produce the damage, and the rest of us are left to manage the fallout. This transactional charity work, focused on symptoms rather than roots, doesn't align with my deeper mission: system-changing transformation.

ENTER THE EVERYTHING INDUSTRIAL COMPLEX

I'd go further: these problems aren't meant to be solved within the Culture of Separation. Let me be clear: I'm not some deluded conspiracy theorist claiming there's a secret cabal plotting dysfunction from behind closed doors. It isn't a conspiracy, it's a self-perpetuating system.

The system does not need plotting. It just plods. It repeatedly loops through the same logic, defining "progress" as doing more of the same and hoping for different results. How else can we explain the $500 billion spent globally each year—trillions over the last decade—supporting nearly ten million nonprofits, none of which has stemmed civilization's slide toward collapse?

So, yes, I'm saying the answer is NOT more money.

And I'm not just pointing fingers at charities. That's simply the vantage point I had at the time. Since then, I've recognized something broader: the "Everything Industrial Complex"—an operating system that institutionalizes the Culture of Separation across every domain of our lives.

The phrase "industrial complex" was popularized by five-star General Dwight D. Eisenhower, the Supreme Commander during WWII and later US President. In his 1961 farewell address, he warned of a "military-industrial complex"—a system above government that served itself rather than the people.

That model has now metastasized. It's become the template for every major top-down system: self-justifying, self-replicating, and immune to reform.

At the Food Bank, I saw this dynamic on a smaller scale. Every stakeholder had their agenda, and "Ending hunger"—the mission on paper—became secondary. Just like the military-industrial complex has failed to end war, the Charity Industrial Complex rarely ends poverty.

We now live under an *Everything Industrial Complex*—a patchwork of self-perpetuating silos. It includes the Political Industrial Complex (in America, our dysfunctional two-party system), the Religious Industrial Complex (where predominantly Christian groups compete instead of collaborating with other denominations), and many others: academic, medical, media, pharmaceutical, entertainment, and the foundational financial industrial complex, fueled by speculation and debt.

> *No, these aren't conspiracies, they're patterns embedded in our institutional structures.*

But beneath the surface of these failing systems lies something even more profound—a spiritual struggle playing out through human institutions. As Paul reminds us in Ephesians 6:12, "Our struggle is not against flesh and blood, but against the rulers, against the authorities, against the powers of this dark world." These broken systems are not just political or economic failures. They are spiritual battlegrounds.

STANDING BETWEEN TWO WORLDS

At their root lies a deeper problem: these systems don't operate from Love and Service. They lack grounding in the Virtues at the core of every great faith and indigenous tradition. Disconnected from the Transcendent—from the Web of Love and the Web of Life—we end up with dysfunction at best and tyranny at worst.

Few of my colleagues at the Food Bank understood Dr. Ari's deeper vision of human development—empowering people to transform their lives and communities from within. No one discussed practical, spiritual approaches to ending poverty. The system's assumptions remained unchallenged: humans are selfish, resources are scarce, and the strong inevitably triumph over the vulnerable.

Food was distributed, yet the extractive system that created the need remained intact. There was an unspoken resignation to the status quo.

So, there I stood, at the intersection of two worlds.

One was the polished world of professional philanthropy—full of high-profile events, strategic plans, and media coverage. The other was the quieter, symbiotic reality I had seen—where ordinary people with limited resources could collaborate, care for one another, and awaken a new kind of power.

The buyers' club I had hoped to create never got off the ground. Ultimately, my mission and that of the Food Bank were misaligned. Their focus remained on managing the aftermath of systemic harm, rather than transforming the system itself.

When the afterglow of our million-dollar fundraiser faded, I realized that the odds of reforming such a system from within were insurmountable. And so, I left. My time at the San Diego Food Bank revealed the deeper limits of trying to transform entrenched systems from the inside. Yet I wasn't ready to abandon the nonprofit world entirely.

I remained strongly convinced that a more entrepreneurial, community-centered approach might succeed where the old charity model had failed. That belief led me to one final leadership role inside the system—a statewide nonprofit focused on economic self-reliance through small business development and social enterprise.

It seemed like the next logical step: moving from dependency models to dignity-based development. Would bridging entrepreneurship with empowerment better align with the symbiotic Virtues I had cultivated?

I was hopeful, but the lessons I had learned at the Food Bank made me cautious. My search for alignment between spiritual Virtue and economic inequality would now move beyond charity and toward the roots of empowerment.

CHAPTER 11

FROM SOCIAL ENTERPRISE TO PARALLEL SOCIETY: THE KINGDOM OF HEAVEN AND A CULTURE OF CONNECTION

Sometimes the most essential revelations come not in boardrooms or crisis zones, but on quiet roads with your family. After leaving the Food Bank, I took a year off with my family. We traveled through Mexico, homeschooling our children and trading the rat race for simplicity and presence.

Returning in 1999 was jarring. San Diego had exploded with malls and traffic, and we yearned for a more human-scaled place to raise our children. Meanwhile, with funds running low, I began seeking work that aligned with what I'd learned so far, something rooted in economic empowerment rather than charity.

That search led me to the Nevada Micro-Enterprise Initiative (NMI), a statewide nonprofit that provides small loans to low-income entrepreneurs. It felt like a natural next step—bridging grassroots service and systems change through dignity-based enterprise.

BIRTHING THE SYMBIOTIC AGE

We relocated to North Lake Tahoe, and I began commuting to Carson City. NMI offered real tools for transformation: loan capital, practical 10-week training, ongoing mentorship, and a clear mission to uplift the underserved. We saw tangible success—one client, once homeless, became a caterer for events at the Governor's residence. With a 96 precent repayment rate, something with real potential seemed to be taking root.

THE STRUCTURE BETRAYS THE SPIRIT

But as time passed, deeper patterns emerged.

After the initial support, there was no long-term ecosystem to sustain the businesses, no coordinated networks, and no deeper community fabric. Each entrepreneur stood alone, vulnerable to the same forces that initially isolated them.

When I investigated further, I discovered the origins of the structure. NMI's board was comprised of executives from national banks like Wells Fargo and Bank of America. The initiative enabled these bankers to meet their Community Reinvestment Act obligations—an attempt to address the damage caused by decades of redlining and disinvestment.

But the structure betrayed the spirit of the mission: no local banks were on the board, there was no interest in forming alliances with grassroots development groups, and there were no real relational networks—just more isolated, siloed programs. The institutions that had excluded vulnerable communities were now "fixing" the problem, but still controlling it from a distance.

The Culture of Separation thrived, even within an organization committed to entrepreneurship and empowerment.

I proposed an alternative: What if we built a Symbiotic Network of regional partners to support small business development over the long term?

What if we encouraged local purchasing agreements to circulate wealth within Northern Nevada, creating a regenerative economy from the ground up?

It seemed clear, practical, non-political, and effective. However, the board pushed back. Tied to global financial systems, they did not prioritize local resilience over global supply chains. Genuinely ending poverty in Northern Nevada was simply outside their framework.

Still, I gave it my best. I raised money, led programs, and supported entrepreneurs.

But the misalignment weighed on me—literally. The job became a "pain in the neck," culminating in a severe neck injury that sidelined me for a month. It was a physical manifestation of my lack of alignment with the deeper mission burning in my heart.

NMI's struggles mirrored a deeper, more uncomfortable realization:

Our global economic system can absorb, commodify, and capture even the best-intentioned reforms.

These were not isolated frustrations. The deeper I looked, the more I began to see a repeating pattern—not just in nonprofits or business, but in nearly every major system I encountered. What I experienced was not unique to Nevada. It was symptomatic of something much larger.

SEEING THE PATTERN: EVERY CRISIS IS CONNECTED

A systemic pattern lies at the root of every crisis we face—economic injustice, war, climate change, hunger, and poverty. Yet the Everything Industrial Complex insists on treating each as a separate issue, each with its own isolated "solution." But they are not separate. They are symptoms of the same fractured worldview.

If you've found this perspective a stretch so far, let me stretch it even further:

> *Any real breakthrough must address*
> *every problem at every scale—*
> *individual, community, planet, and nature—*
> *and at the same time.*

Maybe the solutions to these wicked, entangled problems don't require one more new "complex." In the pain and disillusionment, a deeper truth began to emerge. The issues I faced weren't just managerial—they were metaphysical. Perhaps what was needed was something ancient and profoundly simple: a return to connection, community, and the living web of relationships that sustain life.

But even as these realizations unfolded in my mind, my body already spoke a deeper truth. The misalignment wasn't just conceptual—it became physical, unavoidable, and deeply personal. As I mentioned previously, I threw my neck out. The injury, confirmed by MRI, was real. But the deeper damage was more challenging to diagnose—a quiet heartbreak. I had been bending myself to fit a system I no longer believed in.

The frustration stemmed from working within a siloed organization where success was measured by fundraising totals and growth metrics, not transformation. In our materialistic society, bigger is often seen as better. But scaling broken systems only deepens the original wounds.

That experience marked the end of my time in the formal nonprofit sector.

> *Although the two organizations I worked with*
> *had different missions, they shared one underlying truth:*
> *the system wasn't designed to transform itself.*

From Social Enterprise to Parallel Society

Looking back, I can name the two core problems that plagued even the most well-intentioned nonprofits. First, disconnection itself—a Culture of Separation so pervasive that even good people often couldn't see it. Yes, these organizations were helping people, but doing so within structures that preserved fragmentation. Even faith-based groups, for all their spiritual depth, often compartmentalize their sacred power.

Second, coherence was missing. The Ancient Blueprint—the deep spiritual foundation—had been privatized, siloed, and stripped from our collective life and consciousness. Without it, no amount of effort could heal the system.

I didn't know it then, but the first forty years of my life—what I now call my formation—were preparing me for something more profound: the weaving of the spiritual and the practical into a living, local symbiosis that could grow and spread.

That's when I entered a new phase. On paper, nonprofit work should have fit. I had spent over a decade immersed in organizations devoted to the public good. Yet something vital was missing. Ironically, it was through running an entrepreneurship program that others helped me realize what I hadn't admitted to myself: I was an entrepreneur. I wasn't meant to manage siloed systems that couldn't—or wouldn't—change.

I was meant to build something new.

So, I stepped away. With my father and brother, I opened a hyperbaric oxygen therapy center in Reno. It wasn't just a career shift but a shift in consciousness. I stopped trying to reform broken institutions and began creating something rooted in connection and healing.

FROM FRAGMENTATION TO FIRST PRINCIPLES: ACTIVATING THE COLLECTIVE CAPACITY OF LOVE

That clarity became a turning point for everything that followed. It wasn't just a shift in my work—it was the moment I began to appreciate what a spiritually grounded, networked civilization could look like.

The failures of silo-based systems revealed a deeper truth: true transformation requires more than better programs or bigger institutions—it demands a return to first principles. These are not abstract theories or ideological slogans.

> *First principles are the foundational truths that underlie a just and flourishing society, embodied as Virtues like trust, humility, generosity, compassion, and truthfulness.*

They are the moral architecture through which Divine Love becomes real. As explored earlier, these Virtues are not optional ideals. They are the living interface between Heaven and Earth.

To realign our human systems with the Ancient Blueprint, we must awaken from the trance of siloed thinking, embody these Virtues in daily life, and co-create a culture grounded in Divine Love—where silos connect freely through trust, not control.

Yet this requires confronting an uncomfortable truth: in the Culture of Separation, the wisdom of the Ancient Blueprint has been inverted.

Instead of sharing, we are taught to take.
Instead of service, to dominate.
Instead of humility, pride.
Instead of truthfulness, deceit.
Instead of generosity, avarice.

These anti-virtues shape the logic of our age—shadow forces that flourish when the Transcendent is banished from civic life.

Here's the paradox: Gandhi's Law of Love still quietly governs daily life. People cooperate, care, and act with kindness. And yet, individual love is no longer enough. We must activate the collective capacity of Love through families, neighborhoods, and communities by weaving shared practices of trust and cooperation.

This echoes the early Christian ecclesia (house church) described in Acts 2–4, where believers lived a Spirit-centered life of mutual support and shared goods. Like them, today's fractal networks can give rise to a new civilization rooted not in ideology but shared Virtue and mutual care.

This Spirit-led transformation transcends religious boundaries. As Vinoba Bhave, Gandhi's close associate, once said:

> *"We do not aim at doing mere acts of kindness, but at creating a Kingdom of Kindness."*

That line has never left me. It captures the essence of everything I've sought to live, teach, and embody: the transition from transactional service to transformational community.

**This Kingdom of Kindness is not utopian fantasy—
it is a real possibility, built from the ground up
by ordinary people embodying Virtues,
connecting silos, and forming living networks
of mutuality.**

To heal the human spirit, our systems must be realigned with the highest good we can conceive—a goodness rooted in Love and the Transcendent. Without a Culture of Connection, even the most sincere efforts remain isolated, reinforcing the fragmentation they seek to heal.

But even with the right principles in hand, the temptation persists: to outsource transformation to politics, policy, or reform. We place our faith in external systems—until they fail us again.

BIRTHING THE SYMBIOTIC AGE

FROM HOPIUM TO COHERENCE

Even with all this clarity, I found myself slipping into despair. If love and Virtue were so powerful, why wasn't the world changing? That's when I saw the deeper illusion hiding beneath our efforts.

We keep thinking that if we just elect the right leaders, pass the right laws, or fix the economy, everything will change. But after decades of trying, I realized something deeper: the system wasn't built to heal—it was built to extract. And that includes the way we organize charity, government, and even activism.

We chase after quick fixes and external saviors, but this only feeds a deeper illusion—what I've come to call "hopium." It's not hope in the biblical sense, rooted in faith and love. It's hope as denial: a refusal to grieve what's actually happening, a refusal to reckon with the foundational rupture in our culture and our souls.

Underneath this hopium is a deep spiritual longing—for coherence, for integrity, for a culture where the sacred and the social are not at odds.

For years, I felt like I was flipping between parallel realities. On one hand, I saw people trapped in systems they couldn't change, hiding behind impotent clichés and reacting to surface-level problems. On the other, I experienced moments of clarity—where the veil dropped, and I saw through to the roots. Those moments didn't arise from ideology. They came through relationship, beauty, grief, and surrender. They came through spiritual clarity and acts of courage. They came through coherence.

The search for coherence is not a luxury.
It is the moral and spiritual infrastructure
of a free society.

And because we've neglected it for so long, we now find ourselves in a kind of civilizational vertigo—grasping for stability in systems that no longer offer it.

If we want a future worth living in, we must build it from the inside out—not through partisan warfare or better management techniques, but through a restoration of coherence in the human soul and in the human community.

GLOBAL OLIGARCHY OR COMMUNITY SELF-GOVERNANCE?

But coherence cannot flourish in a vacuum. We must also confront the external architecture of disconnection—the global systems of extraction and control that undermine our deepest values and leave us feeling disconnected.

We are certainly not lacking in good ideas. Around the world, extraordinary movements, models, and people are doing beautiful work. But most remain isolated, fragmented, or exhausted by the very systems they are trying to change. Despite our best efforts, the dominant operating system still wins. It extracts, isolates, and divides—while feeding on polarization and despair.

We live in a system where a handful of billionaires control media, data, supply chains, and just about every aspect of our collective existence, including governance. The old dream of democratic capitalism has collapsed into a top-down technocratic oligarchy—where surveillance, artificial intelligence, and asset consolidation are accelerating faster than most of us can comprehend. And yet, somehow, we're still told to believe that voting, tweeting, protesting, or recycling will change the course of history.

The truth is: our problems are not merely political. They are spiritual and relational. The real crisis is disconnection

—disconnection from place, from purpose, from one another, and from the Transcendent.

We don't need a new ideology or central authority to save us. We need new cultural DNA—new ways of being and belonging that are encoded at the level of relationship.

Nearly every religious, spiritual, Indigenous, and ethical tradition has already given us the blueprint: Love thy neighbor, practice the Golden Rule, cultivate universal Virtues.

This is why Virtue matters. It's not abstract morality. It's a practical, civic technology—a way to align power with love, and agency with service.

The central question is not, "How do we take back the nation?" but *"How do we restore the commons?"* Not, "How do we reform the empire?" but *"How do we regenerate the village?"* We don't need to seize the center. We need to reweave the edges.

What we need is a new cultural architecture—distributed, sacred, and structurally relational. Not just more protests or platforms, but a new pattern: thousands of local communities, networked through trust and shared purpose, operating in parallel to the dominant system. Not a revolution against, but a living, breathing Culture of Connection that could weave the Beloved Community our hearts have been longing for.

That is the story I now felt called to live.

KINGDOM OF HEAVEN: THE PATH FORWARD

This final reflection gathers the fragments of what I've seen, heard, and lived. It's not a conclusion, but a turning point—where inward formation meets the stirrings of outward application.

Throughout my journey, I've been shaped by luminous experiences of the Transcendent, the Logos, and what I call the

From Social Enterprise to Parallel Society

Ancient Blueprint. These moments laid the foundation for my life's calling, work, and perhaps even ministry.

It began at age twelve with an overwhelming encounter—not with doctrine or belief, but with a Presence: loving, luminous, and alive. I didn't need to believe it. I knew it. That knowing didn't end my search—it ignited it. I would spend decades trying to live into that Light from the Luminous Web.

Even in a world fragmented by fear and domination, I could feel and live from the Kingdom of Heaven. Later, I saw this same pattern reflected in the natural world—Nature's Web, layered like tree rings, where every being is both whole unto itself and part of something greater. Nature revealed the Transcendent structure beneath the surface: self-organizing, cooperative, and radically interdependent. As humans, bearing the Divine Spark of self-awareness, we're invited to participate consciously in this cosmic unfolding.

Two questions emerged as companions on the journey:

- If creation reflects this web of harmony, why is human society so fragmented—split into warring tribes and competing silos?
- And how can we evolve beyond the ancient "silo problem," where even well-meaning efforts are trapped in separation?

This is the shift I call cultural symbiogenesis—a new stage of human evolution that realigns our systems with the deeper harmony of the Logos. As St. Maximus the Confessor wrote, we are here to "Unite the cosmos in Love."

One breakthrough came through my apprenticeship with Doña Catalina, who wove Indigenous wisdom and Christian mysticism into a spiritually coherent worldview. She showed me that healing the rift between science and spirit wasn't just possible, it was essential.

That vision became real in Sri Lanka.

> *Having already received a radiant vision from Jesus, I recognized in Sarvodaya a tangible embodiment of the "Kingdom of Heaven"—a practical spirituality that transcended religious categories.*

Jesus wasn't just a visionary of Love; he was the Logos made flesh—the pattern behind a new way of being human together.

Jesus sending me a Buddhist wasn't a contradiction; it was confirmation. Sarvodaya echoed the early Christian ecclesia—a countercultural community where inner transformation and social renewal walked hand in hand.

Sarvodaya didn't just build homes and schools. They built spiritual infrastructure. Where industrial charity offered top-down solutions, Sarvodaya empowered dignity, mutual aid, and self-governance. It wasn't just a movement, it was a fractal, a living model for global transformation.

From this emerged a bold possibility: a spiritually grounded, bottom-up, network-centric civilization—a New Global Commonwealth rooted in Divine Love and lived Virtue. A living Culture of Connection, not as utopian fantasy, but as lived reality.

I had already seen glimpses of it—in the sacred forests, in Sri Lanka, in Logan Heights.

The question became: could this take root in a middle-class, pluralistic Western city like Reno, Nevada?

That was the next test. When Virtues are embodied not only individually but communally, a new kind of power emerges—not the power of dominance, but the power of coherence. That

From Social Enterprise to Parallel Society

is the heart of what we've come to call "fractal community empowerment."

Here, the scattered threads of my journey began to converge. The luminous experiences, the wisdom of Doña Catalina, the witness of Sarvodaya—they were not fragments. They were parts of a deeper pattern. And that pattern is ready to be lived.

As the Luminous Web and Nature's design shaped my inner vision—and the Culture of Separation sharpened my sense of dissonance—I began to ask a new question:

> *What would it look like to translate this inner formation into outer application?*

The answer didn't arrive all at once. It took years of experimentation—often messy, often imperfect—to begin building local expressions of love, coherence, and spiritual infrastructure. These would eventually take shape as what I now call Symbiotic Networks.

But before we turn to those outer structures, there is one more thread to weave. My understanding of the Kingdom of Heaven—and how it relates to the kingdoms of this world—has taken decades to clarify. It has shaped not only my spiritual life, but my strategy for cultural transformation.

And in light of all we now face—the Everything-Industrial Complex, the rise of empire, and the global search for meaning—I believe this reflection must come next.

LIVING THE KINGDOM IN A TIME OF EMPIRE: FROM SACRED PATTERN TO PARALLEL SOCIETY

As I reflect on Section I, I realize that my understanding of the Kingdom of Heaven has evolved alongside my efforts to live it.

BIRTHING THE SYMBIOTIC AGE

This isn't just a theological idea or mystical yearning—it's a practical vision for how to live in the world we're actually in.

Over the past 2,000 years, Christians have wrestled with how to embody this Kingdom in a world so often ruled by the powers of domination, violence, and separation—what Christians later came to call the Kingdom of Man, meaning the systems and cultures built by humans, apart from God. My friends in modern regenerative movements may not realize it, but the Church has long held a hidden legacy—a critique of empire and materialism, what the Bible and Bob Marley both called Babylon.

That critique didn't begin with postmodern philosophers or progressive reformers. It's ancient.

*The Sermon on the Mount wasn't just spiritual—
it was subversive.*

And yet Babylon always seems to re-emerge. It just wears different robes.

Today, it's global. As I wrestled with this reality, I began studying how Christians have responded to the enduring tension between the Kingdom of God and the Kingdom of Man. Some chose the path of separation, like the Amish or Anabaptists. Others became deeply activist, whether on the Right or Left. Some institutionalized their faith through church hierarchy; others formed underground or grassroots networks. Still others pursued cultural transformation through virtue, sacrament, or prophetic witness.

I don't consider my perspective—what I now call the Symbiotic Culture approach—as better than the others. It is, however, broader and more inclusive of a variety of views, and consequently more useful in finding unity beyond diversity.

From Social Enterprise to Parallel Society

The point of naming these diverse expressions is not to prove one right, but to acknowledge the consequence of our fragmentation. Especially within Protestantism, our differences have often left the Church divided, unable to offer a coherent witness to the world.

We've struggled to carry out the Great Commission—Jesus' charge to his followers to share the good news of God's kingdom and embody it in every nation—not for lack of passion, but for lack of unity. The transformative love of Jesus—the Divine Love that heals and restores—has too often been obscured by theological arguments, institutional rigidity, or political capture.

The core is the same: Love God and Love Others. The difference is in how we relate to the powers and principalities of this world—the Kingdom of Man. Each approach grapples with how to coexist, confront, transform, or transcend the dominant systems of control, violence, and disconnection.

Symbiotic Culture offers a different possibility: not a new denomination or ideology, but a relational worldview grounded in the command to Love God and Love Others. It invites us to build something I will explore in greater detail in Chapter 30, a *Parallel Polis*—a mediating structure in parallel that bridges inner formation and civic participation. Rooted in the Ancient Blueprint, it is a sacred infrastructure based on Divine Love, shared purpose, and mutual flourishing.

This isn't about withdrawing from the world, nor about conquering it. It's about dwelling alongside it—like salt and yeast—offering a coherent alternative, a living demonstration of what Divine Love looks like when it takes on structure, practice, and activates a community's "shared self."

And now, as empire intensifies—amplified by AI, surveillance capitalism, and existential technologies—we are at a threshold.

The "Everything-Industrial Complex" I described earlier isn't just economic. It's spiritual. It commodifies our desires, fragments our relationships, and trains us to trust systems of dominance over the Spirit of Love.

It's time to unify the Beloved Community—not by flattening our differences, but by honoring the diverse ways we seek to bring the Kingdom near. And it's time to join in shared purpose with others: religious or not, Christian or not, who are also yearning for a better world built on justice, compassion, truth, and love.

We are standing at a threshold where two kingdoms contend for our allegiance—two fundamentally different operating systems for life. One trusts the power of love, truth, and shared flourishing; the other, the power of domination, self-centeredness, and control. These rival orders are not mere metaphors; they are the deep structures shaping our relationships, our economies, how we steward creation, and our souls.

The contrast could not be starker—and here it is laid bare.

One of these kingdoms reflects the sacred pattern woven into creation, the Ancient Blueprint, from the beginning; the other is a distortion that can never satisfy the deepest longings of the human heart.

This sacred pattern has always been there. Now we are invited to live it together.

From Social Enterprise to Parallel Society

A Tale of Two Kingdoms
A side-by-side comparison of the values shaping our world.

Kingdom of Heaven Life guided and governed by a Transcendent Ordering Principle: Ancient Blueprint	Kingdom of Man Life guided by self-creation and "my own truth and reality" and human law
Seek first the Kingdom of Heaven. Cosmic Trust in the underlying nature of reality	Trust in self-made success achieved through education, hard work, wealth, and status
Based on spiritual Virtues of Love, surrender, forgiveness, simplicity, and humility	Based on material values such as power, dominance, wealth, and success
Focused on loving/serving God and your neighbor	Focus on self-interest, personal gain, material possessions, and power struggles
Nonviolence and even love for enemies	Conquer and dominate your enemies
Rewards based on trust, faith, and doing the right thing	Rewards based on merit and achievement
Justice, mercy, and peacemaking	Injustice and inequality, payback, and perpetual conflict
Compassion and care for the marginalized	"That's the job of charities or government"
Stewardship of Earth and all Creation	Creation is a resource exploitation and profitable opportunity
Power of Truth and cultivating a pure heart	World weary, nihilistic, and jaded

SECTION 2

APPLICATION

BUILDING THE
CULTURE OF CONNECTION

*Love becomes real when translated
into systems, structures, and shared life.*

CHAPTER 12

BUILDING THE FOUNDATION OF A VIRTUOUS ECONOMY

By the time I turned forty, after years in nonprofit work and navigating government bureaucracy, I had seen enough to face a hard truth: the public sector and civil society, for all their noble intentions, were trapped in a siloed, problem-oriented mindset—often perpetuating the very issues they aimed to solve.

What I now understand as the Culture of Separation—deeply embedded in what I've come to call the Everything Industrial Complex—could not transform our extractive, "taker" economy into one rooted in the deeper soil of Virtue. These institutions churned through problems but rarely addressed their spiritual roots.

BIRTHING THE SYMBIOTIC AGE

FROM SYSTEMS TO SOUL: THE REAL WORK OF RENEWAL

I didn't have a name for what I sought at the time. But now I do: a Virtuous Economy—an economy grounded not just in efficiency or even equity, but in connection, character, and care.

Over the past two decades, dozens of "New Economy" movements have arisen, each proposing a fresh approach to the systems that govern our lives: Bioregional, Regenerative, Doughnut, Sharing, Gift, Circular, Solidarity, and Post-Capitalist Economies, and many more.

Each of these frameworks carries insights worth celebrating. Each one attempts to rebalance a dehumanized system, to recover something more humane and whole. And yet—as I've witnessed firsthand through our work in Reno—these models, while meaningful, remain derivative rather than foundational.

Why?

> *Because beneath every social, economic, ecological, or political crisis lies a single unaddressed root: a spiritual crisis.*

At its heart, the essential question we must ask is this: Do we live by the Golden Rule, or do we default to the rule of gold? Do we seek to embody the Kingdom of Heaven or serve the Kingdoms of Man?

As I have suggested before, the greatest obstacle to any form of "virtuous economy" is the totally immersive culture that serves the "rule of gold" and keeps the kingdoms of man in place.

The *Culture of Separation*—obsessed with materialism, distraction, and the next fleeting pleasure—has "colonized" our media, infiltrated our markets, and distorted even our minds. We are taught to believe that material problems demand material solutions alone. Given how religious tribalism has too often been weaponized to divide, it's no surprise that many secular changemakers now flinch at the word *spiritual*.

But that's precisely where the *Ancient Blueprint* offers its quiet power.

It does not elevate one religion above another. Instead, it calls us back to the shared moral foundations—the *universal Virtues*—at the heart of all wisdom traditions. It reframes our work not simply as economic reform, but as a much deeper task: A call to spiritual renewal.

But to recover that spiritual foundation, we must begin not with policies or platforms, but with Virtues that shape a society's soul.

WHY VIRTUES COME BEFORE STRUCTURES

Over fifty years ago, E. F. Schumacher—often considered the regenerative movement's spiritual grandfather—spoke directly to the heart of the problem. In *Small Is Beautiful*, he wrote:

"In ethics, as in so many other fields, we have recklessly and willfully abandoned our great classical Christian heritage. We have even degraded the very words without which ethical discourse cannot carry on—words like 'Virtue,' 'love,' and 'temperance.' The task of our generation, I have no doubt, is one of metaphysical reconstruction."

> *Schumacher saw what many still miss:*
> *no economic fix, no matter how clever, efficient,*
> *or well-intended, can succeed unless it grows*
> *from a deep moral and spiritual foundation.*

His teaching, carried forward today, remains clear and urgent: a truly regenerative economy must begin with a moral reorientation grounded in the Transcendent.

It's no coincidence that Schumacher was close friends with Dr. A. T. Ariyaratne. Their relationship shaped one of *Small Is Beautiful's* most enduring chapters, "Buddhist Economics." The two men met in 1972, and Dr. Ari reviewed the manuscript before publication. With its strong foundation in Buddhist ethics, village empowerment, and spiritual practice, the Sarvodaya movement offered a living embodiment of what Schumacher called "metaphysical reconstruction."

No economic structure, however well-designed, can survive without a moral foundation. When false foundations collapse, we are called to endure and rebuild—this time on eternal, living, symbiotic foundations.

Jesus taught:

> "Those who live by my words are like a wise builder who laid a foundation on rock—when the storms came, the house stood firm. But those who ignore them build on sand, and when the storm hits, all collapses. (Matthew 7:24-27).

That call has only grown more urgent in our time. Today's spiritual crisis threatens not just the West, but the future of humanity itself. Still, some may wonder: Does grounding economics in Virtue risk falling into religious dogma?

That's precisely the strength of the Virtuous Economy—it transcends religious boundaries. As you'll see in the chapters ahead, the Sarvodaya-inspired principles we applied in Reno are accessible across traditions: secular, spiritual but not religious, Christian, Buddhist, and Indigenous.

What unites them isn't ideology, it's shared Virtue.

Without Virtue, even the best-designed structures collapse under the weight of the Culture of Separation.

And, with it? People flourish. Communities come alive.

That's when I knew a different approach was needed—not another top-down model, but a grassroots, Virtue-driven, purpose-filled, network-powered transformation. If charity, government, and even philanthropy had reached their limits... Then maybe the next step was to walk a different path.

If not nonprofit, why not for-profit?

That, however, would require a major realignment of my own worldview and mindset.

THE MORAL CRISIS OF BUSINESS AS USUAL

After years working inside the charity mindset, witnessing how it stifled entrepreneurial creativity and constrained genuine agency, I realized I needed a new path. Starting a for-profit business seemed like the next logical step. But I had to confront something within myself before walking it: a deep, ingrained prejudice against "the business world."

And I had plenty of reasons.

Wasn't it capitalism that fueled the extractive "taker" economy that I had seen hollow out poor neighborhoods in San Diego? Wasn't it profit at all cost thinking that propped up the military-industrial complex that I had protested in the '80s? Wasn't it the consumerist mindset teaching people to trade their deepest Virtues for greed, ambition, control, power, and social conformity?

How could I find meaning—let alone redemption—in a system I had long viewed as part of the problem?

What opened the door for me was Sarvodaya. They were "in business," weren't they? They delivered goods and services. But unlike predatory corporations, they recirculated wealth, built capacity, and empowered the most vulnerable. They created value and returned it to the people.

That shift in perspective was a breakthrough. I began to see the difference between wealth extraction and value creation, between Wall Street and locally rooted Main Street enterprise. Suddenly, I could imagine a business model where Virtue wasn't sacrificed at the door but practiced in every transaction.

This realization echoed something deep in the Christian tradition of vocation: the idea that any form of work—business, education, farming, homemaking—can be sacred if offered in Love. As Paul wrote:

> *"Whatever you do, work at it with all your heart, as working for the Lord"* (Colossians 3:23).

*Ironically, to bring Sarvodaya's principles
into a Western, profit-driven culture,
I would have to engage capitalism from the inside out,
not by rejecting the market system altogether,
but by restoring the moral and spiritual compass it had lost.*

Still, old narratives ran deep. I remember speaking with a store owner in Monterey after we passed a homeless man outside his shop. "I just called the police," he said flatly. "Don't you feel any responsibility for that man?" I asked. "No. My job is to sell good products and pay my employees. That's it."

That logic, while harsh, was consistent with the dominant ethos of the day: *"It's not personal—it's just business."* But I couldn't imagine Dr. Ari—or Jesus, who taught us to love our neighbor—responding with such detachment. And yet, despite its failings, I saw that the business world held potent potential: freedom, innovation, and real accountability.

No one "voted" for the personal computer or organic food, but people voted with their dollars. Steve Jobs and John Mackey didn't wait for permission. They acted on vision, and the world responded.

The marketplace, unlike the public or nonprofit sectors, rewards actual value. In that sense, Sarvodaya was doing just that—meeting real needs, uplifting communities, and reinvesting in the sacred. That's when it hit me: Even in a broken system, you can build a bridge. You can redeem business, not by abandoning it, but by building scaffolding between what is and what can be.

LAUNCHING A FAMILY BUSINESS ROOTED IN SERVICE

After stepping away from the nonprofit sector, without any intention of returning, I knew I had to find a new path to support my family. But I wanted more than a paycheck. I wanted to build something rooted in service to the community, and by extension to the world.

As synchronicity would have it, only months after leaving the Nevada Micro-Enterprise Initiative, I walked into a hyperbaric oxygen therapy center. The owner looked up and said, "Yesterday, I decided to sell my business."

"Ah," I thought. *"A definite sign."*

Just a week earlier, my brother had told me about a man in Oregon who couldn't afford hyperbaric treatment. So, he took an oxygen tank and submerged himself sixty feet under the ocean to heal his body. That story ignited something in me. As a scuba diver, I understood the power of oxygen. I knew it was used to treat everything from decompression sickness to diabetic wounds.

Suddenly, this new business opportunity felt like a calling. My brother secured the funding, and my father joined in. And just like that, we launched a family business: Northern Nevada Hyperbarics. By October 2000, we had our first patient.

We were all in.

I started from scratch, building referral networks by meeting with doctors, clinics, and hospitals. The previous owner hadn't laid much groundwork, so I relied on what I knew: Symbiotic Networking. I organized educational events, held coffees, and made one-on-one connections.

Hyperbaric therapy was still relatively unknown, so I had to learn quickly about contracts, insurance, and billing systems. I flew to Alabama to complete a 40-hour course in hyperbaric medicine. We hired a seasoned expert from Florida, brought in a local physician as our medical director, and slowly grew our team. My brother eventually moved to Reno, but I continued managing most of the day-to-day operations.

Still, even as the business took root, something deeper stirred. Could I build something larger—a Symbiotic Network aligned with the Transcendent Order—that could transform economic and social life across Northern Nevada?

Being immersed in business gave me a whole new lens. Unlike nonprofits, which often depend on goodwill and grant cycles, for-profit ventures must deliver real value or shut their doors. That pressure brought clarity, sharpened priorities, and dismantled my lingering biases about "profit." In a service-based business like ours, profit wasn't about greed but outcomes. When patients walked out healthier, everyone won.

I also came to understand better those who saw business as inherently flawed—and how I myself might have gotten that perspective. Many of my activist peers had never run a business themselves. It's easy to criticize something from the outside, but living it from within taught me its power and limitations.

That's when I began to glimpse the possibility of radical inclusion.

> *I didn't have to choose between spirituality and entrepreneurship. I could live in both worlds and let each one enrich the other.*

That inner integration was preparing me for a deeper threshold—one that didn't tear me apart but reoriented me entirely. It was less a rupture and more a sacred disruption: a widening of perspective that revealed how inner healing and outer community transformation were not separate callings but one and the same.

FROM ANTI-WAR TO PRO-LOCAL: REWEAVING COMMUNITIES THROUGH SYMBIOTIC KINSHIP

As in San Diego, a crisis came again—this time not just in one neighborhood, but on a global stage. A war loomed. Beneath the political storm clouds, I sensed something quieter but just as profound—an economic crisis hidden in the undercurrents.

Once again, the soil was softening. The conditions were right, and something symbiotic was ready to emerge. But it wouldn't come from ideology or imposed design. It would start with connection, from building kinship into the heart of the economy.

In the spring of 2003, with the second Persian Gulf War on the horizon and political polarization deepening across America, I enrolled in a 10-week nonviolence class inspired by Saint Francis of Assisi. We convened weekly at the Quaker Meeting House in Reno. One quote from Mother Teresa bears repeating:

> "I will never attend an anti-war rally. If you have a demonstration of peace, please invite me."

That line planted a seed.

After the class ended, many of us felt a shared longing to move beyond the battlefield of tribal conflict, beyond being "pro-war" or "anti-war," and step onto a new playing field of collaboration rooted in mutual benefit. Though I didn't have the language then, I now recognize that field as the space of Divine Love and the Symbiotic Kinship that flows from it.

In my work in San Diego and through my interactions with Sarvodaya, I had already come to recognize this truth: real change doesn't stem from merely opposing what is wrong.

It arises from asking better questions, listening deeply, and coming together across divides to create something new.

Three guiding principles had emerged for me:

1. Find a compelling shared purpose.
2. Ask the community, not just the experts, what they need and care about.
3. Begin small. Create honest, relational space where leaders from different silos can meet.

Building the Foundation of a Virtuous Economy

So, I posed the obvious question: What do we all care about—left and right, religious and secular, activist and entrepreneur? The answer was clear: helping locally owned, "mom-and-pop" businesses survive and thrive.

As national chains swept Northern Nevada, it wasn't just about economics. We sensed something more profound at stake. Wall Street's machinery was hollowing out the heart of our community—our Main Street. It wasn't just the loss of businesses. It was the loss of our very soul, as we were becoming a people slowly assimilated into a rootless, impersonal empire, what Scripture calls *Babylon*.

I had seen the pattern before. In San Diego, money flowed from the Logan Heights neighborhood into the city's broader economy, entrenching poverty through structural extraction. Now, in Northern Nevada, I was watching the same forces at play on a larger scale: wealth draining from our communities into national and global systems, flowing upward into what we've come to see as a Global Oligarchy.

I could see history repeating itself. In the 1700s, the East India Company, backed by the British Crown, monopolized the tea trade in the American Colonies. Their grip eventually sparked the Boston Tea Party—an uprising led, in part, by local business owners. I could relate.

Today, the dynamics remain, but the tools have changed.

The challenge isn't to confront the giants head-on, but to reclaim local agency—to ensure money, power, and connection circulate within our communities.

This is where the Multiplier Effect comes in—a simple, well-documented truth: every dollar spent at a local business stays in the community longer, creating jobs and reinvesting.

But that raised a deeper question:

How do we unite businesses and the broader community around this common purpose?

I discovered that the answer begins with Symbiotic Kinship. This is the living heart of the Ancient Blueprint—love God, Love Others—made practical in the context of economy and community.

Symbiotic Kinship happens when grassroots organizations and neighbors unite to grow the local economy for the common good, not around ideology, but shared purpose. It means expanding our circle of affiliation beyond those who think, vote, or worship like us, and intentionally working with those committed to mutual benefit.

In this case, the shared benefit was clear and concrete: rebuilding the local economy from the ground up. As one business owner put it:

> "We're not against businesses or community elements that aren't local. We actively promote and support those with the most to gain from local focus and strength—neighbors with good intentions, vested interest, and a desire to build something better together."

This wasn't about being anti-corporate—it was about being pro-community. It wasn't about exclusion; it was about radical inclusion. We weren't just discussing economics but remembering what truly holds communities together: relationships, reciprocity, and shared values.

We were just getting started.

MAPPING A LOCAL ECONOMY AND A WEB OF TRUST

Sometimes breakthroughs happen not through grand plans but through simple acts of collaboration. That's exactly what happened when we invited nonviolence class participants to help crowdsource a living map of our local economy.

We didn't wait for the government, a university, or a network consultant to take the lead. We just started.

We taped large sheets of butcher paper to the wall and labeled them with basic business categories—restaurants, grocery stores, and clothing shops. Then we asked everyone to write down the names of local businesses they supported. People got on their feet. There was energy in the room, movement, laughter, and stories.

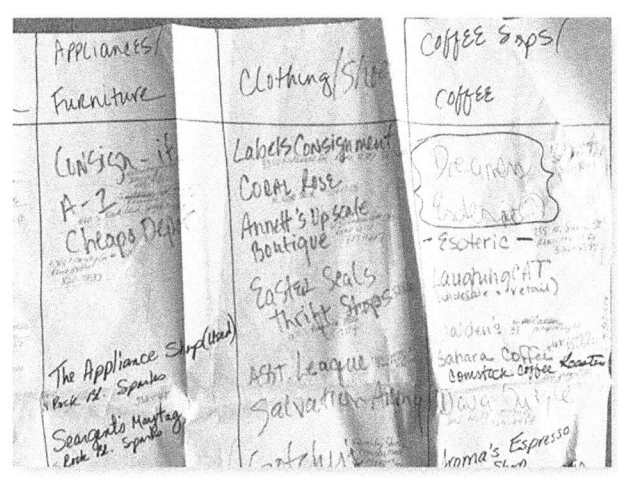

Scribbles of trust: mapping the heartbeat of a community economy.

Names filled the pages: shopkeepers, farmers, ranchers—people with whom participants had genuine relationships.

It felt like an unrehearsed dance of community memory.

By the end of the evening, around 150 local businesses had been listed—each one tied to a real person in that room. What we mapped wasn't just a local economy but a web of trust.

At the time, "buying local" wasn't the mainstream mantra it would later become. But that night, something clicked. We weren't just consumers, we were co-creators of a revitalized local economy that would impact our entire community for the better.

Later, I came across a 2002 study from Austin, Texas, showing that if every household redirected just $100 in holiday spending from chain stores to local merchants, it would inject $10 million into the local economy. A similar study in San Francisco found that a 10% shift from chains to local shops generated $192 million in economic activity, $72 million in new wages, and over $15 million in retail transactions.

But more than the numbers, I felt hope in that room—hope grounded in human connection, in the quiet emergence of a Symbiotic Network.

From my work in San Diego, I had already learned the power of catalytic connectors—those natural weavers of community who hold no official titles, but whose relational capital is immense. Everyone seems to know them. Everyone trusts them. They move between groups with grace. In our effort to strengthen the local economy, these people became our pollinators, helping us move from cold calls to warm invitations with just a name.

That's the power of transferred trust. One kind word, one thoughtful introduction can quietly shift a community's trajectory. This kind of trust-building isn't just a nice thing to have; it may be the most crucial ingredient in community transformation, even though it often goes unseen.

Why? Because it's always been there. These self-giving, connective actions are part of our human inheritance. They are the

Building the Foundation of a Virtuous Economy

invisible relational patterns that make Symbiotic Networks possible and scalable.

> *One-to-one becomes one-to-many*
> *and then, many-to-many.*
> *One web of trust becomes a web of networks.*

You can start to weave entire ecosystems when you begin to recognize and support the super-connectors—those trusted by multiple groups. What starts as scribbles on butcher paper becomes the foundation for something far more powerful: a new economy grounded in relationship, reciprocity, and renewal.

And it all started with a few pens, a shared room, and the courage to ask one humble question: *"Who do you know?"*

CATALYZING A LOCAL LIVING ECONOMY NETWORK

The engine driving our local living economy wasn't government programs or professional organizers. It was everyday people, not experts or activists, but catalytic connectors—community members with extensive personal networks and the spark to ignite something new.

Most weren't business owners themselves. But as conscious, connected consumers, they helped us map a local business ecosystem grounded in relationships.

> *By tracing word-of-mouth trust networks,*
> *we identified super-connectors—local business owners*
> *naturally linked across communities,*
> *bridging silos through relationships.*

After this informal mapping, I met with several business owners one-on-one. I asked them, "Would you like to help build a local living economy network where we support each other and get the community behind shopping locally?" The answer, again and again, was a resounding yes. They understood that supporting the larger community would strengthen their businesses too. While enlightened self-interest was part of the equation, something deeper moved them—a shared desire to promote the Common Good.

Once we had five to ten committed super-connectors, we hosted our first small gathering. Eight local business owners and nonprofit leaders sat around a table. We began, not with strategy, but with story, connection, and shared vision. And here's what I've learned: when you bring people together, you get more than ideas and concepts, you get people—people with hopes, fears, egos, dreams, and different worldviews, even around something as seemingly straightforward as supporting local businesses. That's why clarity of purpose matters so much.

From the outset, I emphasized that a Symbiotic Network is not about politics, power, or control. It's about shared Virtues: trust, generosity, purpose, and service. It's not a new organization or ideological platform, it's a space to connect across silos and enhance what's already good.

In hindsight, this simple and honest approach reflected something much deeper: the Ancient Blueprint.

In a world shaped by dominance and division,
we were quietly building something different:
a space where love and service could lead the way.

People felt it. They sensed that something sacred was taking shape—not just a concept but a presence—love in action, radiating outward into the community. After that first meeting, we scheduled a follow-up breakfast and invited each participant to bring five more leaders. And just like that, the network began to grow.

The structure we followed was intentional, yet simple:

1. Map the local ecosystem.
2. Meet one-on-one to build relational trust.
3. Convene a small group with aligned values and purpose.
4. Host a soft launch to explore possibilities.
5. Go public only when trust and clarity are solid.

That's how a Symbiotic Network is born.

If you skip any of these steps and rush into big public events, you often sow confusion or replicate the very silos you're trying to dissolve. This process isn't mechanical—it's living. And more art than science. I can say from experience that the best results came not from rigid planning but by letting intuition and the Transcendent lead the way. Reason and planning became the servants, not the masters.

Our first public gathering—a soft launch—brought together 25 local business owners. For two hours, we cultivated trust and explored possibilities. By November 2003, 150 leaders filled a hall for our official launch. The name we chose was a mouthful—Truckee Meadows Conscious Community and Business Network—but the momentum was real.

In the months that followed, we held regular meetings with breakout sessions. We co-created our vision, mission, values, logo, messaging, and decision-making approach. The creativity was electric, and the disagreements, when they came, were honest and generative.

In the process, I learned a crucial distinction: facilitation is not enough. Symbiotic Networks need more than a neutral moderator. They require stewards—initiators who have a deeper intention and embody the Virtues the network aspires to.

So, I stepped into that dual role of facilitator and initiator. Before long, others began to step forward with the same spirit of service.

To some—especially those wary of hierarchy—this was unfamiliar territory. But we weren't building a dominance hierarchy. We were building a growth hierarchy, modeled after Nature's Web. In the Culture of Separation, hierarchy is about control. But in Symbiotic Culture, hierarchy is about nurturing growth. Nature shows us how this works—from soil microbes to tree canopies, cells to ecosystems. Growth flows upward, but it only thrives when rooted in reciprocity.

That's what we were practicing—leadership not based on titles or status but on generosity and trust. The more someone contributed through relationships, time, energy, or care, the more they became recognized as leaders. As Jesus said:

"The greatest among you must be the servant of all."

We were translating that wisdom into a practical, lived blueprint—a new kind of leadership not built on control but connection, not authority but love in action. And just like that, the network kept growing.

What began as a response to war and economic extraction had become something far more generative—a new pattern of community life based not on ideology, but on mutual belonging. As we cultivated relationships across silos and sectors, we weren't just supporting local businesses, we were weaving a new kind of kinship. Symbiotic Kinship.

What I witnessed was not a political campaign or an economic plan, it was the emergence of an ecosystem rooted in Love, relationship, and reciprocal service. And it was just the beginning.

CHAPTER 13

LIVING SYSTEMS, LOVING STRUCTURES: FROM CONTROL TO CO-CREATION

While our early efforts focused on reviving local economies through kinship and connection, I soon began to see a deeper challenge embedded in the very architecture of our systems: the dominance hierarchy. The issue wasn't just economic extraction, it was the mindset of control, separation, and siloing that underpinned it. If we were to truly regenerate community life, we would need to replace systems of domination with systems of growth—where leadership, power, and purpose could emerge from the ground up, nourished by trust and shared agency.

FROM DOMINANCE TO GROWTH HIERARCHY

As I shared earlier in Section 1, there's a huge difference between dominance hierarchies and growth hierarchies, and failure to appreciate this vital distinction can quietly sabotage even the most well-intentioned community efforts.

Throughout my years of organizing, I've repeatedly seen how a reactionary aversion to hierarchy can create confusion, disorganization, and burnout. The impulse is understandable. Many have been wounded by institutions where power is hoarded and imposed from the top down. It's only natural to want to flatten those systems.

> *But rejecting hierarchy altogether misses something essential. Nature itself is deeply hierarchical—but not in a way that reinforces domination.*

Life unfolds through nested layers of interdependence from atoms to galaxies, from mycelial webs to human ecosystems. Each layer supports and nourishes the next. In this organic order, there's no coercion—only coordination. Growth hierarchies mirror this sacred structure. They aren't designed to control, but to cultivate life-giving connection.

Creation itself is a sacred growth hierarchy—a cosmic order in which the Transcendent is not only at the "top" but also beneath all things, holding every layer of being in coherence and love. This is not hierarchy as control, but as radiant structure—a vertical dimension of communion that sustains the whole.

That's the deeper design of Symbiotic Networks—not systems of power, but webs of mutual nourishment. They are living reflections of what I came to call the Network Commons: a relational ecosystem that links the Common Good across silos without domination or manipulation.

In this hierarchy, leadership is not granted by position or pedigree. It's earned through service. There are no charismatic figureheads. No scripted messaging. No career ladders to climb.

Living Systems, Loving Structures

If you're looking for prestige or control, this movement is not for you.

Here, leadership arises through love in action—consistently showing up, giving without an agenda, and cultivating trust over time.

At the time, I didn't have the language to distinguish dominance from growth hierarchies clearly. But I was already living into that wisdom, translating the Ancient Blueprint of the Sermon on the Mount into a working model of humility, service, and shared purpose.

It was—and still is—a radically different approach from what the Culture of Separation has normalized. In that world, influence is too often measured by how much power you can exert, how many followers you have, or how efficiently you can leverage others, even within so-called progressive or spiritual movements. In contrast, we practiced a distributed, hub-based model of leadership. Those who gave most freely of their networks, energy, and trust naturally became the nodes of connection—and the obvious "leaders."

They didn't direct; they attracted. They didn't command; they invited.

*Influence grew through generosity,
not political authority or big money leverage.*

If we are to invert the economic and political power pyramid, that shift begins here: from "power over" to "power with." From ego-driven control to love-rooted cooperation. From hierarchical dominance to growth hierarchies rooted in self-giving love.

True hierarchy, as seen in nature and in the design of Creation, does not suppress—it reveals and uplifts. It channels

Divine order through increasing coherence, responsibility, and care. This is not a ladder of oppression but a symphony of integration, where every voice matters and the whole is animated by a higher purpose.

As I'm sure you realize by now, this pattern is not new. It repeats across the wisdom traditions—from Jesus to Gandhi to Dr. Ariyaratne. Each shows that transformation doesn't come by overthrowing domination systems through force. It comes through the slow, steady cultivation of something so coherent, beautiful, and full of life that the old order loses its grip.

> *That's how Heaven comes to Earth—not by conquest, but through the quiet, radical power of Love.*

What we were doing wasn't just local economic development, nor was it just community revitalization. In many ways, it was a new kind of Occupy movement—but not fueled by outrage or rebellion. This was about reinhabiting ourselves with the highest Virtues, aligning with the Transcendent, and spreading that coherence outward through a growing web of connection.

We weren't standing outside the system with # Occupy placards. We were occupying our community and becoming a new society from the inside out.

SYMBIOTIC KINSHIP AS THE HEART OF A NEW ECONOMY

Back to the story.

As our network began to take shape, a natural question emerged:

Who should be included?

Some early participants wanted to limit membership to already environmentally conscious businesses—"green," regenerative, or organic. One woman, deeply passionate about sustainability, was adamant that organic farming should be a baseline requirement.

But we chose a different path. I proposed something more radical: inclusion without precondition.

At the time, I didn't have a polished term for it. However, looking back, I now recognize that I was following a deeper instinct—one I'd come to call Symbiotic Kinship, a pattern inspired by Nature's Web. In healthy ecosystems, every species has a role. No creature is excluded for not being "pure enough." The system thrives because of interdependence, not uniformity. So why should our network exclude any "species" of business genuinely trying to contribute?

John Mackey, founder of Whole Foods, faced a similar crossroads. Early on, he made the controversial decision to expand beyond purely organic products to better compete with mainstream supermarkets. That choice invited more people into the natural food ecosystem, many of whom discovered they preferred it. Rather than isolating Whole Foods into a niche, Mackey's move helped transform American food culture.

I saw a similar opportunity in Reno.

> *If we only engaged "enlightened" businesses, we'd just be preaching to the choir. By including both conventional and regenerative ones, we could catalyze change across the whole ecosystem.*

And that's what happened.

Some of our early members, including a few local dry cleaners, had been using harmful chemicals. However, as consumer awareness grew through conversations, education, and relationships, they began to transition to safer practices. They weren't coerced by ideology; rather, they were influenced by the evolving culture around them. This experience revealed something deeper:

Ideological purity doesn't transform society; relationships do.

That's why Symbiotic Kinship works. It isn't just another silo of like-minded people. It's a living, evolving network built not on sameness but mutual benefit and shared Virtue.

Still, this vision didn't come without tension.

In other cities where I'd worked—especially San Diego—I had seen movements to create race-specific or faith-specific business alliances: Black-only or Hispanic-only networks, or even a proposed national Christian-only business network. More recently, I've noticed similar patterns in regenerative and eco-justice circles, where participation is often limited to those who align with a specific worldview.

I understand the impulse. Identity-based networks can offer safety, visibility, and empowerment in marginalized communities. They provide refuge from systems that exclude or erase. However, I've also observed how easily these networks become siloed, slowly absorbed into the Culture of Separation they were meant to resist.

When movements are organized primarily around identity, they risk becoming tribal. While tribalism can offer protection, it cannot be the foundation for a shared future by virtue of their being invested in exclusion, and the competitive us vs. them mentality.

So, in Reno, we chose a different way.

> *We honored differences without allowing them to divide us. We prioritized practice over position and relationships over ideology.*

Because that's what a Symbiotic Economy demands: kinship beyond kind. Not uniformity, but unity in shared service. Not agreement on every issue, but alignment with a deeper purpose.

And that's what made all the difference.

PRACTICING SYMBIOTIC KINSHIP BEYOND THE SILOS

Today, that familiar pattern of organizing around identities, tribes, and like-minded worldviews persists.

Across sustainability, regenerative, and community movements I've observed in recent years, many leaders still operate from within silos—building coalitions only with those who share their worldview. Their causes—eco-justice, equity, anti-racism, post-capitalism—are often noble and necessary. However, when these movements exclude rather than integrate, they risk reinforcing the very fragmentation they seek to heal.

The deeper issue is not about the values themselves, but rather the framing.

Too often, these networks carry unexamined ideological baggage that subtly echoes the Culture of Separation. Rather than bridging divides, they can unintentionally deepen them. The focus shifts toward grievance and reactivity: who has been harmed, who is to blame, and what systems need to be dismantled.

Symbiotic Culture offers a different starting point. It doesn't begin with rights, but with responsibility. Not "What can I demand from others?" but "What can I offer to the whole?" Not only "How have I been hurt?" but "How can we heal together?"

The Ancient Blueprint reminds us that lasting transformation is grounded not in the identities that divide, but in the Virtues that unite. These Virtues call us to transcend ideology and move toward humility, compassion, and service.

> *The question shifts from "Who agrees with me?"*
> *to "Who can I love, serve, and build with?"*

This doesn't mean ignoring injustice. It means rising above grievance to create a new narrative rooted not in separation but in shared humanity.

BEYOND IDEOLOGY: BUILDING TOGETHER ACROSS DIFFERENCES

We all carry identities, and that's natural. However, we don't need to over-identify with them. Through my own spiritual journey, as shared earlier in this book, I learned how identities can harden into armor. I had to confront my "shadow self," discovering prejudices I hadn't known I carried. As I've already said, I was anti-business without realizing it.

And despite years of spiritual work, I held a bias against organized religion—until I made a decision to build bridges. I started attending every church, temple, mosque, and any other spiritual group I could find. I did this for more than a year and even walked into a men's Bible study at an evangelical church.

I encountered something much deeper than my assumptions. Here there were people from all walks of life engaged in the process of connecting to the Transcendent reality from their own vantage points and I found many of them were already doing community work. They turned into allies, not antagonists.

Building Symbiotic Kinship isn't an abstract theory. It's a daily, embodied practice. And it's not easy. It asks us to welcome those we disagree with, those who frustrate us, and even those we might instinctively resist.

But this is the path.

It's what Dr. Ari modeled in Sri Lanka: inviting every sector, regardless of religion, politics, or status, into the shared work of local transformation. In that same spirit, we reached out to everyone: mainstream business owners, churches, nonprofits, city staff, conservative shopkeepers and progressive activists alike.

It's not about whether someone is perfectly "green," "woke," or "aligned." It's about whether they will show up in service and build something together. That takes character. It requires humility. It demands that Virtue be the foundation of community, not just window dressing. Which is why inner work is not optional; it's essential. To build outwardly, we must clear space inwardly.

> *If we are to hold sacred space for others,*
> *we must first remove our shoes—our egos, fears, and*
> *ideological armor—before stepping into*
> *the "cathedral" of community.*

Remember, Symbiotic Networks are not just networks. They are sacred spaces, the connective tissue that holds all the silos—even competing ones—within a shared web of purpose and care. I didn't fully recognize it at the time, but we were creating not just a "virtuous economy," but a living organism that would nourish the entire region.

Back to the story.

Once our growing network chose to go "beyond green" and include businesses of all shades and shapes, a new question arose:

Who counts as a local business? It forced us into deeper discernment. Some argued that only fully independent businesses should qualify. Others wanted to include franchises or regional chains if they hired locally. Even Walmart's local manager claimed, "We're local—we hire local!"

Ultimately, we focused on ownership. To qualify, a business needed to be at least 51% owned by someone within a 50-mile radius. Why? Because local ownership tends to keep profits circulating in the region. Local owners are more likely to source locally, care for employees, and reinvest in the community.

This wasn't about balancing political factions or even "making a statement." It was pragmatic stewardship, and our single-minded focus on building a thriving local ecosystem rooted in trust. That didn't mean everything was cut and dried. There were some gray areas we had to address.

Some franchises didn't meet the strict criteria but still wanted to help, so we designated them as Affiliates. They couldn't claim to be entirely local, but they supported the movement and helped spread the word. That mattered. It gave them a way to participate, and they became part of the narrative of change. Over time, "local" became more than a label—it became an identity, a story, and a movement.

We used simple graphics and messaging to educate the public, businesses, churches, and city agencies. We also coined a new term for our region: the micro-bioregion—a "just right" scale of organizing, larger than a neighborhood but smaller than a bioregion. Towns, cities, or counties—big enough to hold diversity, small enough to stay human.

Our movement made headlines: a new economy grounded in trust, not transactions.

And powerful enough, when connected, to transform the system from the ground up. Because this was never just about buying locally, it was about belonging locally — becoming kin again.

A CULTURE EMERGES: VIRTUE AT THE HEART OF THE MARKETPLACE

Beyond the economic multiplier effect of buying locally, something deeper began to take root in our community: a lived culture of love, unity, and service. What started as a practical initiative to strengthen the local economy gradually evolved into a movement that empowered everyday people and grounded lofty ideals in tangible, everyday action.

We established this culture in simple, human ways—like our monthly breakfast gatherings, some attracting over 150 participants. Small business owners, nonprofit leaders, faith-based organizers, government staff, civic activists, and local residents came together month after month. By its peak, nearly 500 businesses and community organizations had participated.

BIRTHING THE SYMBIOTIC AGE

*What emerged wasn't just a network.
It was the birth of a Culture of Connection—
a shared model for collaboration built on
trust and mutual care.*

People practiced generosity through trusted third-party introductions. Leaders looked beyond their bottom lines to care for the broader community. Across the usual divides of ideology and identity, neighbors worked side by side toward a shared purpose.

This wasn't about branding or buzzwords. It was about living the Virtues—kindness, service, trust, generosity, and reciprocity—right where we were, in our daily business, relationships, and community life. We did more than speak about values; we built systems and bonds that embodied them.

A new kind of leadership also emerged—grounded not in position but in connection. "Super-connectors" surfaced naturally, recognized for their generosity and relational depth, not titles. It was a hub-based, network-centric way of organizing—more mycelial than mechanical—and it worked because it followed the patterns of life.

As explored earlier, Nature teaches us that life thrives through nested holons—wholes within wholes, parts within parts—woven in webs of interdependence. There's no need for a single boss when a system is alive, self-organizing, and guided by shared purpose.

Nature is radically interwoven, and so was our network. Looking back, it's clear: we weren't just launching a "buy local" campaign.

Living Systems, Loving Structures

> **We were cultivating a new way of being—
> where Virtues are the currency and
> kinship is the infrastructure.**

We demonstrated that trust, generosity, and relational wealth are not soft ideals or secondary features. They are the foundation of any enduring system.

We didn't just organize a network. We revealed an ancient pattern, hidden in plain sight—older than economic theory and deeper than any political system. When relationships are honored and Virtues are practiced, a new kind of economy becomes possible—one that grows from the inside out.

Beneath the surface of "buy local" lay something more enduring: the quiet renewal of the social fabric through Virtue, connection, and mutual empowerment.

To truly understand what made this transformation possible—and how these invisible patterns can serve as the foundation of a regenerative economy—we must turn to the ancient wisdom and spiritual currents that have guided flourishing societies since the beginning.

This is the unseen foundation of a Virtuous Economy—rooted not in systems alone, but in hearts aligned with the sacred.

CHAPTER 14

THE SPIRITUAL WEALTH OF NATIONS: VIRTUE, KINSHIP, AND THE NETWORK COMMONS

What we witnessed in Reno wasn't just economic renewal—it was the visible surface of something far older and more profound: a return to the spiritual architecture that has always supported flourishing societies. Long before "free markets" became a slogan or "capitalism" a political battlefield, moral philosophers like Adam Smith envisioned an economy not driven by greed, but by empathy, conscience, and a shared sense of the good.

He spoke of something rarely quoted today: universal fellow feeling—the recognition that our well-being is interwoven with the well-being of others. It is this universal fellow feeling, applied in the marketplace and the public square, that is "the spiritual wealth of nations."

In this chapter, I invite you to explore how ancient wisdom traditions—Christian Virtue ethics, Gandhian economics,

Sarvodaya's Buddhist roots, and Catholic social teaching—converge to illuminate the foundations of a truly Virtuous Economy.

RESTORING A SACRED FOUNDATION TO ECONOMIC LIFE

As you'll see in the upcoming Chapter 18, "Decoding Symbiotic Culture DNA: A Living Framework from Divine Design" we tapped into what I've previously referred to as the Ancient Blueprint—a pattern of universal Virtues that emerged not from theory, but from listening deeply to what people already knew in their hearts. These Virtues became our bedrock, grounding our efforts in meaning and offering our community a sense of purpose that goes beyond the marketplace to build a society's spiritual wealth.

> *Ultimately, what transforms a local economy into something sacred is not just what we build— it's the foundation upon which we build.*

In some of our earliest meetings, we began talking openly about Adam Smith, not the caricature promoted by pundits but the real Adam Smith. To our surprise, his ideas became a guiding light. Most people know him as the "father of capitalism," but few realize that before he wrote *The Wealth of Nations*, he penned a more foundational work: *The Theory of Moral Sentiments*.

In that first book, Smith argued that the health of a society—its markets, relationships, and public life—depends not on competition or control but on universal fellow feeling—what we might refer to as empathy or, better yet, shared Virtue. This wasn't an ivory tower theory.

Smith grew up in a small town in 18th-century Scotland, observing real people in real markets—farmers, bakers, merchants, neighbors—exchanging not only goods but also stories, trust, and human connection. He recognized that individual freedom, grounded in a shared moral conscience, could foster a culture where people naturally benefited from one another.

I deeply resonated with that.

Smith rooted his understanding of morality in what he called Divine Providence, or Natural Law, which I discussed in Section 1. I also refer to it as the Logos—that living pattern of Divine intelligence that undergirds creation. He believed every human being is born with a moral compass, an inner tuning toward right relationships. In Christian language, we might say this compass reflects the imago Dei—the image of God—and seeing that image in each other.

Adam Smith believed that people are wired to flourish by serving one another. That's how personal well-being and the public good become one.

He wrote:

> "How selfish soever man may be supposed, there are evidently some principles in his nature which interest him in the fortune of others, and render their happiness necessary to him, though he derives nothing from it except the pleasure of seeing it."

This version of Smith bears no resemblance to the figure portrayed by some libertarians and free-market ideologues. Nor does he fit the strawman rejected by anti-capitalists or post-capitalist theorists. Both sides have distorted his vision—either into a justification for selfishness or a scapegoat for systemic greed.

Let's be clear: the phrase "invisible hand" appears only three times in Smith's work. It was never his core idea. Like Darwin's theory, which was misinterpreted to rationalize "social Darwinism," Smith's vision was distorted into a justification for selfishness—a view he never endorsed.

Meanwhile, the anti-capitalists present their own ideologies—whether collectivism, statism, or socialism. However, these too often replicate the same dominator logic they claim to oppose. Meet the new boss, the same as the old boss. Whether a few dominate the many or an elite claiming to represent the many dominate everyone else, it's still the same Culture of Separation—an ancient structure of control, division, and conflict.

> **But on the new playing field of Symbiotic Kinship, personal benefit and public good are not opposites— they are inseparable.**

In our network, many business owners initially joined out of what we would call "enlightened self-interest." However, over time, something deeper emerged. What we practiced aligned more closely with Adam Smith's original vision: an economy built not on ideology but Virtue. In a society where trust, generosity, and mutual service are norms rather than exceptions, economic life produces and amplifies goodness.

That's the moral foundation we are reclaiming—not just from the market, but for the future.

BIRTHING THE SYMBIOTIC AGE

BREAKING FREE FROM BINARY ECONOMICS

There's another reason the endless debate between capitalism and collectivism feels stale—it's because neither exists in pure form. What is called "capitalism" today is more accurately described as global corporatism—a fusion of massive business interests with political power, creating a top-down oligarchy that shapes our future from above.

Many activists identify as anti-capitalist or post-capitalist, particularly in regenerative or "new economy" circles. Some even question private property itself. However, their alternatives often rely on heavy-handed systems—centralized government regulation, technocratic planning, or collectivist solutions—which can become as oppressive as the structures they oppose.

Others concentrate on more localized initiatives, such as cooperatives, credit unions, public banks, mutual aid, bartering networks, and regenerative businesses. These approaches show promise, yet too often become entangled in the ideological language of "equity," "justice," or identity politics. The result:

> *Movements unintentionally mirror the very Culture of Separation they're trying to heal.*

Why does this matter?

Even with the best intentions, many of these efforts have been quietly politically captured. They've become tethered to a specific political lens, accepting assumptions without questioning the framework. For example, "capitalism is inherently evil, so collectivism must be good." That's just another binary mind trap.

If we are truly called to be Uniters, not just critics or activists, we must resist "this vs. that" thinking. We must ask: What truth might each side carry? What is worth keeping? What needs to be transformed?

This isn't about being neutral. It's about rising above the ideological battlefield entirely. Every "ism" becomes another rival army in the war. But we're not here to join a side. We're here to *build a new field*—one defined not by opposition, but by shared purpose and Virtue.

> *That's why universal Virtues—transcending religion, race, or political tribe—must become the moral framework of a Culture of Connection.*

When we unite around what is good, true, and life-giving, we heal the fractures that ideology alone cannot mend.

Paradoxically, the more we obsess over the symptoms of separation—capitalism, collectivism, racism, wokism, fill-in-the-blank-ism—the more we reinforce the very divisions we hope to overcome. We waste our energy fighting against what we don't want instead of creating what we do.

In contrast, when we focus on Virtues, we build common ground—the foundation for building together what we all want.

THE NETWORK COMMONS: BUILDING A WHOLE-CLOTH MOVEMENT

Let me return to something I touched on earlier—the landscape of more than two dozen "new economy" movements, each with its language, values, and siloed community. While each contributes something valuable, they too often remain disconnected, like separate islands trying to change the world alone.

Fortunately, something else is happening beneath the surface—a quiet countercurrent.

BIRTHING THE SYMBIOTIC AGE

Across the country and the world, I've encountered people and organizations awakening to a deeper truth: that no single "ism" or initiative can carry the whole load. We need to weave these diverse efforts into a more integrated, living whole—a movement that feels less like a coalition of causes and more like a symphony of shared purpose.

That's what we began to discover in Reno. That's what Sarvodaya embodies at scale. And that's the invitation now—to step outside the comfort of our familiar silos and build something new together.

> *I envision what I've come to call a "whole cloth movement"—one that includes everyone in the local ecosystem who wants to co-create a new Culture of Connection.*

This movement encompasses value-aligned businesses and mainstream retailers; it includes regenerative projects, local faith communities, city departments, and cultural organizations—anyone ready to show up for the common good. It's not about the most "woke" or ideologically pure; it's about who's prepared to build something real. Together, we can create what I've termed a Network Commons—a shared space where local individuals, groups, and enterprises collaborate across silos to coordinate efforts and uplift the entire community.

That is how we begin building a Virtuous Economy—not through ideology or top-down reform, but from the ground up, through relationships and shared values, right where we are. When people connect through trust, generosity, and a desire to serve something greater than themselves, the walls between us fall. That's how the good unite. And that's how the future takes root.

In Reno, that vision wasn't just philosophical—it shaped how we organized. What began as a local effort to support small businesses soon became something more: a living Network Commons grounded in Virtue and kinship.

ADAM SMITH'S FORGOTTEN VISION: LOCALISM AND MORAL SELF-GOVERNMENT

As long ago as the late 1700s, Adam Smith opposed collusion between large mercantile companies, such as the East India Trading Company, and powerful governments. He believed this kind of alliance, where corporations leveraged state authority for private gain, created monopolistic systems that oppressed the poor and distorted the idea of a "free market."

Smith's vision could not be further from today's neoliberal, globalist order. He favored strong local and regional markets grounded in moral agency and mutual benefit, not in top-down control. His thinking aligned more closely with Gandhi's dream of a "Commonwealth of Village Republics" or Dr. Ari's Sarvodaya movement than modern capitalism.

Smith envisioned markets as horizontal rather than vertical. He believed true trade occurs between communities, rather than being dictated by a central plan or political elite. From this perspective, individuals in local regions retain the power to self-organize, free from the ideological schemes of both the right and the left.

He warned against what he called the "man of system"—those infected by a "messianic" certainty that their top-down reforms are necessary, regardless of the human cost. We see this same impulse today in social movements that, despite good intentions, fall into rigid ideologies and absolutist solutions.

Smith recognized the danger of treating society like a chessboard, with people as pieces to be moved around "for their own good."

> *He understood that collectivist efforts to benefit "all of us" must be balanced with the libertarian concern for "each of us."*

Even in his time, Smith recognized that our impulses for "self-serving" love were the primary cause of societal imbalance. Perhaps most prophetically, he identified the moral rot at the heart of power:

> "All for ourselves, and nothing for other people, seems, in every age of the world, to have been the vile maxim of the masters of mankind."

THE REAL INVISIBLE HAND: VIRTUE, NOT SELFISHNESS

Today, it's alarming and disheartening how the polarized left and right dominate the public square, imposing rigid solutions while stifling the sane and sacred center—the voices attempting to unite us around the common good.

If I appear fixated on Adam Smith, it's because his true legacy has been distorted, and reclaiming it may help us find our way forward. Today, "capitalism" is better described as corporatism: the unholy alliance between unchecked money and unchecked power.

Smith warned against this, fearing the collusion of corporations and governments. He believed it would destroy the moral foundation of markets, harm the poor, and lead to tyranny. In contrast to today's amoral global economy, Smith envisioned a system based on regional, owner-managed enterprises.

> *He believed in communities where business owners lived among those they served, creating jobs, sourcing locally, and sharing in both the resources and challenges of their region.*

He was skeptical of global trade and critical of monopolistic giants such as the East India Trading Company.

Smith's preference for regional economies aligns with the visions of Gandhi's village republics and Dr. Ari's Sarvodaya networks. He envisioned free markets as horizontal, relational, and self-organizing—not imposed by five-year plans or manipulated from the top down but growing from the ground up.

True free markets require more than economic freedom—they require *virtuous* participation. Smith grounded his vision in a moral framework shaped by empathy, trustworthiness, and civic responsibility. These virtues are not regulatory afterthoughts; they are the invisible architecture that allows free exchange to serve the common good.

Meanwhile, we've inherited a battlefield of "isms": capitalism, communism, and socialism. These rigid belief systems are more ideology than reality—outdated scaffolding for a world that no longer exists.

They seldom promote collaboration or innovation, and the result is endless debate and widening division. Raging against these "isms" is akin to boxing shadows. It drains our energy and obscures the vibrant, living alternatives already emerging.

BIRTHING THE SYMBIOTIC AGE

We need to move beyond tired binaries and build what works—a moral market rooted in individual dignity, family sovereignty, and a shared network of mutual support.

A regional "Network Commons" offers the scale and structure for flourishing without domination. This reflects the spirit of Jesus' parable of the Good Samaritan, where love transcends identity, tribe, or ideology (Luke 10:25-37), and our neighbor is defined not by whoever is like us, but whoever is near us.

The bottom line is the practice of kinship with all, above and beyond identities and ideological structures. It's not even that one of these structures is "better" than the other; the point is that these "isms" all populate and reinforce the Culture of Separation.

For example, critics of Marxism often highlight its atheistic materialism—and rightly so. However, many defenders of Western capitalism and socialism fail to see that they, too, are often founded on the same materialism, disconnected from any higher moral or spiritual source. Both of these mental structure "isms" are rooted in the same secular soil—and remove us further from the Ancient Blueprint.

Smith warned that markets lacking a connection to a higher principle—a Transcendent Good—will inevitably devolve into systems of domination.

The Culture of Separation distorts Smith's legacy to promote the myth that human selfishness alone—left to its own devices—will lead to optimal outcomes. But selfishness, when idolized and idealized, corrodes relationships, fragments community, and turns markets into battlegrounds. Without virtue, freedom becomes license, and capitalism becomes conquest. Without love at their center, markets driven solely by wealth and power are not free markets; they inevitably becomes slaves to the empire.

FROM PROTEST TO PRACTICE: SEEDING A NEW ECONOMY

Word about our Reno networks spread quickly. In 2004, I was invited to a breakfast in Madison, Wisconsin, hosted by a community development professor. This gathering brought together over 100 business owners, community leaders, and residents, sparking the Dane County Buy Local Initiative, which grew to become one of the largest in the US, uniting people around a shared commitment to their local economy.

It was a powerful reminder that with the right tools and principles, people don't need outside saviors. Like Sarvodaya, this movement was locally grown, and populated by everyday people leading "normal" lives—running businesses, working at jobs, or involved in other forms of service.

Back in Reno, momentum was building. Our network of locally owned businesses and community groups spread across the region and even statewide. We launched a website and printed 30,000 Hometown Directories—pre-Facebook—to help residents "Think Local First." Before long, the City of Reno and the State of Nevada began adopting key elements of our model.

Here is an excerpt from one of those directories:

> "Where Locals Shop Locals...we seek to re-localize our spending patterns within the regional economy and foster a culture committed to shared, universal Virtues that meet the real needs of our community."

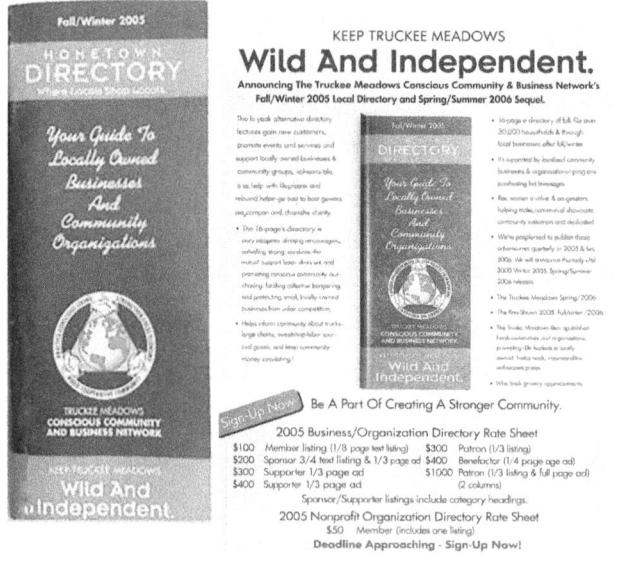

Our first Hometown Directory: helping Reno residents "Think Local First" before Facebook even existed.

Looking back, I wince at our early name—"The Conscious Community Network." It sounds somewhat self-congratulatory, as if we believed we were the only ones "awake" in the room. However, the phrase captured something essential: our intention to cultivate our inner resources to build outer community.

A truly conscious community, after all, is not made up of individuals who think they've arrived. It consists of people who can recognize when they haven't. That's close to the Christian idea of conscience—a living awareness of right and wrong that humbles us, even as it calls us to metanoia, Love, and action. The real glue wasn't branding; it was Virtue.

Business owners joined for practical reasons, but the spirit of connection kept them engaged.

Local merchants realized they couldn't compete with big-box chains on price alone, so they competed through care. They began training employees to truly listen. They aimed to leave customers feeling better when they departed than when they arrived.

Local media spotlighted our 'buycott' movement—elevating local values over corporate chains.

We also made an early decision: we wouldn't fight the system. Instead, we were going to build something better. At one of our early meetings, several participants wanted to organize a boycott against Walmart. I understood the sentiment but said, "Let's not channel this energy into anger. Let's use it to support the kind of economy we actually want." That's how we reframed the idea of a boycott into a "buycott"—a campaign to support businesses that reflected our values.

A rallying cry for local resilience—Keep Truckee Meadows wild, independent, and rooted in community-powered freedom and ecological stewardship.

That shift—from protest to practice—changed everything. People felt energized and inspired. Instead of the old familiar battlefield, we created a new playing field. As one person said, "I want what they're having."

Even though not every business shared our deeper purpose, it didn't matter. If you start with a core group of people committed to Virtue and lead with that publicly, others begin to change, often because it's in their self-interest. And that's not cynical. It's human. People are impressionable, and we bring out the best when we elevate cultural norms.

As Dr. Ari said, "We build the road, and the road builds us."

When I left the nonprofit and community development world, I sought a way to bring the spirit of Sarvodaya into a Western, industrialized society. In rural Sri Lanka, there was hardly any infrastructure. In Reno, too many siloed organizations overlapped and competed for funding and relevance.

What we needed wasn't another nonprofit. We needed a new organism.

We created an emergent, network-centric organism, a "Network Commons," that benefitted every business, charity, and local government department involved—and competed with none.

Our movement re-humanized the local economy and distributed power from the ground up.

It had a revitalizing, re-humanizing, and regenerative effect on the community. Not only did we re-localize economic power, but we also created a new model of shared and distributed people power within our communities. That's the secret to a living network. You don't impose it; you invite it. You create a space where people remember what they already know: that they matter and belong.

SPIRITUAL CAPITAL: THE HIDDEN WEALTH THAT MULTIPLIES

As I reflected on Adam Smith's notion of the "true wealth of nations," I repeatedly returned to his phrase "universal fellow feeling." I call it Symbiotic Kinship—the unseen current of empathy, service, and love that can transform a marketplace into a living community.

Without top-down control, partisan agendas, or institutional power, we witnessed something remarkable in Reno: how Love in Action, expressed through the power of choice, the dignity of work, and the desire to do right by one another, created a sense of connection that is rarely seen in modern industrial societies.

Over the years, that network helped ignite movements that reshaped our local food systems and neighborhoods, revitalized our civic life, and rekindled our shared sense of purpose. At the heart of it all was something invisible yet powerful—what I've come to call Spiritual Capital.

> *Spiritual Capital is the hidden wealth we generate through trust, compassion, and mutual service. It's the true currency of a Virtuous Economy.*

This capital doesn't live in banks or spreadsheets. It lives in the heart, in kindness extended, dignity honored, and forgiveness given.

Jesus described it as "treasures in Heaven" (Matthew 6:19–21)—imperishable gifts that can't be stolen or spoiled because they're stored in how we treat one another. St. Paul referred to this way of being as a "living sacrifice" (Romans 12:1–2), renewing the world not by force, but by transforming hearts.

You could say Spiritual Capital is the oxygen of a regenerative society—unseen yet essential, quietly multiplying wherever Love turns into action.

It flows naturally because we are all connected to the Transcendental Order—the source of Virtue and Value. This connection creates a coherent moral and psychological order that shapes our personalities toward joyful service. We feel a quiet call to share what we've received, not out of duty but from delight—offering ourselves to others while helping to unify the Cosmos for the Common Good.

Grace doesn't demand; it invites. It moves through us not as an obligation but as love in action—flowing outward to bless, build, and heal.

That's why "charity begins at home" makes deep sense. We first tend to our own hearts, then our families, then our neighbors, and finally our communities—forming an ever-widening circle of care. The more we embody these Virtues and recognize our lives as gifts, the stronger our relationships become. And the stronger our relational fabric becomes, the more resilient and flourishing our economy becomes.

This is not merely a noble aspiration but a practical and embodied way of life.

Every act of work presents an opportunity to share spiritual capital—whether crafting a product, offering a service, or simply greeting someone with care. Each transaction becomes a chance to build trust, and every decision becomes a moment to express love for others, the Earth, and future generations.

This also appears in the "nuts and bolts," including how we set prices, treat employees, relate to our vendors, steward our land, and serve our communities. It is evident in what we market, how we sell it, and why.

> *When we become aware of spiritual capital,*
> *we align self-interest with the common good and*
> *activate a prosperity rooted not in extraction and fear,*
> *but in generativity and love.*

It brings us full circle to E.F. Schumacher's insight: that any truly regenerative economy must begin with a "moral and spiritual reorientation."

When people experience life as a gift, they naturally begin to:

- Use resources with reverence—both natural and human
- Honor the dignity of the person, not as a means, but as an end
- Consider environmental, social, and spiritual impact at every stage of creation

What's most encouraging is that we don't have to create it from scratch. This reorientation has been hiding in plain sight all along, rooted in every major spiritual tradition on Earth. It is the true wealth that endures. When we build our networks and communities around it, a Virtuous Economy becomes not just possible but inevitable.

When love becomes our shared ground, everything changes.

A MORAL FRAMEWORK FOR GLOBAL RENEWAL

As I close this chapter on Spiritual Capital, it's time to connect the deeper dots—to elevate the vision from the level of individual businesses and communities to something larger: a model for national and even global renewal grounded in eternal principles.

Many of the organizations I mentioned earlier, founded around ideas of a "new economy," would likely resonate with what we built in Reno. However, our success didn't come from a new theory or strategy. It grew from something more profound—a lived moral framework, supported by spiritual capital, relational trust, shared Virtues, and following the Ancient Blueprint.

We weren't reacting against capitalism or collectivism. We were building from alignment rather than opposition, using a timeless template.

> *This template for a New Economy isn't a utopian invention. It's embedded in the very fabric of Reality.*

As I've explored throughout Section 1, there is a lineage—a moral-spiritual inheritance—that runs from the early Christian communities and the teachings of Jesus, through Gandhi's village republics, to Dr. King's Beloved Community, and Dr. Ariyaratne's Sarvodaya Shramadana in Sri Lanka. These examples point to an economic and cultural order rooted in Virtue, mutual uplift, and local sovereignty—Symbiotic Culture.

In these living examples across traditions—Christian, Hindu, Buddhist, and Catholic—we see the same pattern: economies built from the bottom up, grounded in love, service, and human dignity. In stark contrast to the top-down "Everything Industrial Complex," which extracts and concentrates power, these traditions teach that true vitality grows locally, from the individual outward—to the family, the neighborhood, the town, the region, and ultimately the nation and world.

Catholic Social Teaching identifies two key principles that beautifully reflect Gandhian values: Subsidiarity and Solidarity.

- Subsidiarity maintains that decisions and care are best managed at the most local level possible, starting with the individual and the family.
- Solidarity reminds us that we are morally bound to one another, across street corners and continents, and especially to the most vulnerable.

Pope Leo XIII first introduced the principle of subsidiarity as Catholic social teaching in his 1891 encyclical Rerum Novarum, further developed by Pope Pius XI in his encyclical Quadragesimo Anno. Pius wrote, "It is an injustice, a grave evil and a disturbance of right order for a larger and higher organization to arrogate to itself functions which can be performed efficiently by smaller and lower bodies."

In his 2009 encyclical Caritas in Veritate ("Charity in Truth"), Pope Benedict XVI offered a radical economic vision rooted in "gratuitousness"—the Gift of Self. He said business is not merely for profit but a vocation to serve, create dignified livelihoods, and act for the common good for today and future generations.

I can almost see Dr. Ari smiling from above, nodding in agreement.

This framework becomes real only when rooted in personal transformation and daily practice. To see how this comes alive, we turn to the principles of self-rule, local stewardship, and compassionate community—embodied through Gandhi, Dr. Ari, and movements like Sarvodaya.

FROM INNER RENEWAL TO GLOBAL KINSHIP

Gandhi's vision embodies the essence of Swaraj (self-rule) and Swadeshi (local kinship): a society built not from control imposed from above but through discipline, responsibility, and compassion cultivated from within. "Concentrate first with your family," Gandhi said, "and you are on a path to serve all humanity."

Swaraj and subsidiarity both start with inner transformation—self-mastery—and extend outward. They empower the smallest units of society with genuine power, fostering a culture where individuals and communities act wisely rather than waiting to be governed by distant systems.

Similarly, Swadeshi and Solidarity call us to reclaim interdependence—choosing local production and belonging not out of isolationism, but as kinship and stewardship that care for the whole by starting close to home.

All of this was not merely theory for Sarvodaya—it was embodied. Dr. Ari worked with the poorest of the poor, not through abstract policy, but by building "networks of village economies" where spiritual practice and economic resilience were intertwined.

That's what was meant by their credo: "We build the road, and the road builds us." The circles of empowerment grew—not as ascending pyramids of control, but as ever-widening rings of care. These expanding circles echoed Gandhi's image of an "oceanic circle"—a decentralized community vision in which each level supports the others from the inside out. Gandhi described it best:

> "Life will not resemble a pyramid where the base sustains the apex. Instead, it will be an oceanic circle with the individual at its center, always prepared to sacrifice for the village, and the village ready to sacrifice for the circle of villages…. The outermost circle will not possess the power to crush the inner circle but will empower all within and draw its strength from the center."

That vision isn't just a dream. It's already happening—in thousands of Sri Lankan villages. And in a small but growing way, we lived it in Reno, too.

True renewal, whether economic, cultural, or spiritual, must begin with the invisible architecture of Virtue woven into daily life.

As we discovered in Reno, the foundations of a regenerative society are not laid by massive plans or top-down systems but by small, courageous acts of connection, rooted in love, trust, and service.

We begin, as always, not by fighting the old but by planting seeds of the new, right where we are. In Reno, that seed was the Conscious Community Network—a living demonstration of how love, Virtue, and trust could be woven into the fabric of everyday civic life. What began as a simple act of local organizing soon revealed something deeper: the longing to build not just networks, but a Beloved Community.

That longing would lead us to ask: What would it take to make this dream real, not just for one town, but for all of humanity?

CHAPTER 15

CONSCIOUS COMMUNITY NETWORK: FOUNDATIONS OF A CULTURE OF CONNECTION

The seeds of Symbiotic Kinship and the virtuous economy had taken root. The next question was how do we help them grow? How do we "spend" our spiritual capital to create deeper connections and greater benefit for the community?

After the success of the Local Living Economy Network, we realized that the deeper task before us wasn't to create the "next project," but to nurture both the capacity and the living soil where many initiatives could rise, each grounded in shared values and each contributing to the greater wellbeing of the community.

The Conscious Community Network emerged as a regional framework for doing just that—part organizing platform, part trust-based community ecosystem, uniting individuals, businesses, and organizations around shared Virtues of mutual benefit.

I'm not sure we realized it at the time, but we weren't just building a network. We were cultivating the conditions for a new Culture of Connection to take root.

ANCHORING THE DREAM: FROM VISION TO SHARED CIVIC PRACTICE

I've always wondered what it would truly take to realize humanity's dream of a Beloved Community—a vision quietly held in the hearts of many, including my own, even in the aftermath of COVID, endless wars, and growing polarization.

How can we move forward from fragmentation to a spiritually grounded global civilization? Can we rediscover the courage to build from the inside out—across differences, through shared suffering, and across time?

This dream reflects the same truth Jesus proclaimed: the Kingdom of God is not just a distant dream, but a here-and-now community grounded in love, reconciliation, and shared life under Divine grace. I first caught sight of this vision during a period of deep prayer.

I shared part of the poem in Section 1—here is the fuller image that continues to guide me:

Suffering is never alone but shared.
> My heart bursts open as the energy of compassion streams through me. The blood from my open heart, so red, shoots up into the sky further and further.
>
> Then, like a cloud burst, countless droplets begin to fall towards the Earth. In midflight, they change to flowers.

A colored multitude of roses and lotus blossoms float downward in perfect harmony. Falling with purpose and direction, they land in a wide ocean.

They congeal in masses on the water, taking new shapes and forms. Arising from the flowers are rescue boats, many rescue boats moving slowly on the glistening surface of the sea.

Where are they going?

The boats move onward toward a tranquil island in the ocean. Now and then, a living being is seen in the water, lost in the boundless sea. On the boat, people of all kinds reach out and help those lost climb aboard to safety.

Together, they go in Universal Kinship to help everyone, all heading for the same shore, the same island of unlimited joy and boundless love—the island inside us, found in the silence of the still heart.

Suffering is never alone but shared.

That vision of a shared refuge—many hands reaching toward the same shore—reflected my deepest yearning as I looked back on what we had built through the Local Living Economy Network. Now it was time to look ahead.

BUILDING A NEW ROAD:
AND LETTING IT BUILD US

Over the next two years, we continued to meet monthly for breakfast gatherings, during which two critical changes unfolded.

The first change was a growing sense of grassroots empowerment. You may recall that the network originated from a felt need to unify our community during the political polarization of the 2003 Iraq War. The simultaneous "invasion" of big-box stores into our local economy only strengthened that resolve. Now we looked to sustain that momentum without an imminent crisis.

People still yearned to shift economic power from Wall Street extractors to Main Street sustainers. Local businesses thrived, fostering a genuine sense of agency and independence for the first time in a long while. Unlike many communities being "colonized" by larger entities, Reno stood firm and grew stronger. We were definitely building a "new road" together.

The second change had to do with how that road was building us, as we built a path toward local self-reliance. Hierarchies flattened, and a new trust emerged among networks of business owners, community leaders, activists, and citizens. As people stepped out of their silos, a deeper spirit of collaboration awakened.

The next question naturally followed: Now that we had established a successful local movement, what more could we cultivate together?

SYMBIOTIC KINSHIP: CONNECTING SPIRITUAL AND CIVIC ENGAGEMENT

We had created an ecosystem of core leaders dedicated to mutual benefit within our community. Now, we aimed to build on our success and ensure that the buy-local campaign wasn't just a "one-off." We shortened our name to Conscious Community Network and began discussing the bigger picture—what else could grow from this living soil?

BIRTHING THE SYMBIOTIC AGE

We rejected the usual activist path—fighting enemies or disconnecting inner life from outer action.

In the Culture of Separation, these paths are often viewed as opposites—fighting out there or retreating here when, in truth, inner and outer are meant to be intertwined. How often have we observed spiritual individuals avoiding civic engagement for fear of "dirtying their hands," or activists dismissing spiritual practice as irrelevant? This tragic divide has long kept well-meaning people apart—those who yearn for change but speak in different spiritual or political languages.

In contrast, Sarvodaya showed what's possible: a third way that seamlessly integrates spiritual practice and social transformation, grounded in universal Virtues and symbiotic cooperation.

This living integration has shaped our Conscious Community Network from the beginning. When we chose the word "conscious," it wasn't a New Age catchphrase. It pointed to a deeper grounding: that universal Virtues flowing from the Transcendent would be the foundation of everything we built.

THE DEEPER CRISIS: CULTURE OF SEPARATION

But if we were going to spread what we were doing—if we hoped to nourish other communities the way we had ours—we had to go deeper. We needed to understand what we were up against, not just politically or economically, but culturally and spiritually. The surface problems were only symptoms.

As defined in Section I, the Culture of Separation is a nearly invisible worldview shaped by core assumptions: that we are isolated individuals, that only matter matters, and that reality is fragmented. This worldview that permeates society and its institutions separates us from each other, the Transcendent, and the living world. Its underlying beliefs quietly shape how we live:

- The world is a collection of things to use.
- Rationality and technology will save us.
- Economic growth equals progress.
- Life is about maximizing comfort and desire.
- There is no objective truth, only subjective preferences.

This paradigm not only distorts society but compromises the soul.

When it is "captured" by this all-pervasive Culture of Separation, religion too often mirrors the above logic. "Love Others" becomes a private Virtue to gain salvation or achieve worldly goals, stripped of its call to become like Jesus Christ, and transform the world. The Transcendent is domesticated—trapped inside religious, political, and ideological silos that reinforce "us versus them." Rather than comforting the afflicted and challenging the comfortable, captured religion often supports the status quo.

And while technology—hyper-personalized media, curated identities, endless scrolling—amplifies our disconnection, the Culture of Separation seems to be endemic to the kingdoms of man.

Every empire eventually collapses under the same burden: greed, disconnection, and spiritual decay. Historians Arnold Toynbee and Oswald Spengler warned that civilizations crumble when personal gain eclipses communal care, not because of outside threats, but from inner rot. The death knell rings when people stop caring for one another.

Unlike the fall of previous empires—the Roman, the Ottoman, etc.—what we are witnessing is a global phenomenon.

That's why the solution must be more than local—it must be fractal. As we build Symbiotic Culture, we are not merely restoring wholeness in one place. We are also cultivating the capacity to spin off new networks—each rooted in Virtue, relationship, and shared purpose, yet adaptable to local context.

> *This is how transformation spreads: not through centralization, but by empowering communities to replicate sacred patterns of connection.*

The great value of a sacred, fractal pattern like this is that it is infinitely reproducible—it is capable of unfolding again and again wherever love, trust, and shared purpose take root.

SYMBIOTIC KINSHIP AS A CULTURAL FRACTAL

In the 1990s, long before "Culture of Separation" had entered our vocabulary, its symptoms were already visible. One study that deeply informed our early work was the Merck Family Fund's *Yearning for Balance*. It revealed a quiet cultural alarm:

- 85% of Americans believed materialism, greed, and selfishness had crowded out deeper values.
- People felt worried about the future—but uncertain how to change it.
- Many longed to pursue material security without losing their human aspirations.

Those insights were prophetic. Three decades later, anxiety, addiction, youth suicide, polarization, and economic inequality have intensified.

Our early efforts through the Conscious Community Network weren't just civic experiments, they were early cultural interventions, responding to wounds that have now become widespread.

As we asked, "What comes next?", the answer didn't come as a grand strategy. It came through patterns—small, replicable forms that reflected the larger whole.

We began to notice something powerful: wherever people organized around shared purpose, relational trust, and spiritual grounding, the same core elements re-emerged. These weren't programs—they were fractals of mutual benefit, small cultural cells rooted in:

- A shared sense of Transcendent kinship
- A commitment to common Virtues
- A focus on building around community needs rather than fighting

Instead of protesting extractive systems like Walmart, we nurtured local relationships. Instead of debating ideologies, we practiced purpose without labels. Quietly, we built three pillars:

- Cooperative Community
- Local Economic Strength
- Conscious Living

These weren't commandments, they were guideposts. And they could take root anywhere.

The goal wasn't to scale an organization, but to scale culture. Like Sarvodaya Societies in Sri Lanka, we began cultivating local "culture cells"—small, relational ecosystems that could self-organize, adapt, and grow. These fractals, grounded in love and service, held the DNA of a new society.

Section 4 will explore how these cells can grow into full Symbiotic Societies—unique in expression but unified in spirit.

BUILDING FROM THE INSIDE OUT: LOCAL WISDOM, GLOBAL PATTERNS

Another unique feature of our Conscious Community Network was that we didn't rely on outside experts. We trusted the "commonly sensed" wisdom already present among our participants. This grounded approach enabled us to build a regional network of over 500 businesses and organizations focused on food, energy, and economic resilience. We developed digital and physical directories to amplify local solutions and reinforce self-reliance.

In Reno, surrounded by a Culture of Separation, we cultivated something different—a Conscious Community Network rooted in cooperation, humility, and shared purpose. Like the early Christians, we didn't escape the system; paradoxically, we began to transcend it from within.

We were quietly building a parallel culture and society. We walked a different road.

As our networks matured, we came to see that we were stitching back together what had been torn apart. The invisible architecture of belonging emerged not through theory, but through tables, gardens, kitchens, and neighbors. It didn't grow from grand strategy, but from small acts: sharing a meal, planting a seed, seeing one another with new eyes.

That's where the transformation began—in the soil of daily life.

In the next chapter, we turn to food not only as nourishment, but as the literal ground where trust, culture, and kinship take root—where relationships become regenerative, and daily acts of care begin to reweave the fabric of community.

CHAPTER 16

FOOD AS FOUNDATION: WEAVING THE THREADS OF A NEW COMMUNITY

After building trust across our local business and community networks, we began to sense that our next frontier wasn't another campaign but food, not as a metaphor but as something imminently practical—a necessity of life where trust could root itself in the body, the land, and our shared culture.

Of all the things that bind people together, food speaks to something primal and unifying, nourishing not only our bodies but also our culture and land. Within our Conscious Community Network, a question surfaced:

> *Could food become the living ground where our shared Virtues might take root and bear fruit?*

At a meeting in 2005, someone proposed, "Why don't we start a community garden?"

I resisted the idea, even though I didn't fully understand why. Opposing a community garden felt like being against "motherhood, apple pie, or kittens!" Yet, something deeper stirred my unease. Managing a project like a garden or any other initiative risks narrowing our focus. We might become just another silo—another well-intentioned initiative reinforcing the very Culture of Separation we were trying to heal.

A Symbiotic Network doesn't run projects. It connects them, creating the living scaffolding that uplifts and unites efforts initiated by the community itself.

FROM SYMBOL TO SYSTEM: BUILDING THE FOOD NETWORK FROM THE GROUND UP

Still, the question lingered: "What's next?" The community garden idea reemerged. People sensed that food truly was the next frontier. But how? The breakthrough occurred at a local interfaith luncheon. I happened to sit beside the stake president of the local Mormon church—my dentist, as it turned out. Northern Nevada had a large LDS population, and emergency food storage was a cornerstone of their tradition.

The LDS community had spent decades preparing for potential breakdowns—growing, dehydrating, and storing food for long-term survival. That conversation sparked a realization: we didn't need another project. We needed an entire connected food system.

That's when the vision crystallized: a regional food network designed to connect and support local growers, retailers, restaurants, institutions, and families. It represented the natural evolution of our Local Living Economy Network. For years, people had consistently desired to strengthen the local food system.

A Local Food System Network could do just that—not through charity or ideology but through a regenerative, market-based approach. We would boost local farms, ranches, and value-added producers while expanding regional consumption. We would map and connect the entire ecosystem, creating a coherent, resilient marketplace to help our region become increasingly self-sufficient.

In the fall of 2005, leveraging our strong connections in the small business and community sectors, we began surveying and mapping the super-connectors in our local food system. These included farmers and ranchers, farmers' markets, backyard growers, food cooperatives, local and organic food enthusiasts, "foodies," food insecurity activists, grocers, institutional food buyers, and restaurateurs. I called six individuals we identified as key food super-connectors.

My first call was to the owner of one of the oldest farms in nearby Fallon, Nevada—a farm in his family for five generations. We already had a connection through our Buy Local movement. He also served as a small business counselor for a local economic development group, which made him a natural networker.

> I asked, "What do you think about forming a local food system network?"
> His answer surprised me: "I'm already doing it!"

Intrigued, I asked him to describe his network. "Pretend you're an eagle flying over it," I said.

"What would you see?"

He explained that his network primarily consisted of local food producers—farmers and ranchers like himself. However, when I asked if he was connected to farmers' markets, CSAs (community-supported agriculture), or farm-to-table restaurants, he answered no to each. His farm produced a large volume of several crops, nearly all of which were sold outside the community. He was a wholesaler with few direct ties to Reno's urban food system.

In other words, what he was describing was a "vital cluster," but not the entire ecosystem. A true Local Food System Network would connect all the components: growers, distributors, retailers, consumers, and advocates, weaving them into a living system. I immediately recognized the potential to regenerate local farming and bring ecological and economic benefits to the entire region without outside funding or government control. It would be a virtuous, market-based model rooted in community resilience.

After he finished describing his farm's role, I asked, *"Would you be interested in meeting with other connectors to explore building something larger?"* He agreed. That 30-minute conversation became our first buy-in.

> **The next step involved reaching out to individuals already recognized as key players in the local food landscape.**

This included leaders of farmers' markets, co-op advocates, food security champions, restaurateurs, and others already connected to our Conscious Community Network. Like the farmer, I spoke to each individual personally, reassuring them that this Symbiotic Network wouldn't replace their projects but would strengthen them through deeper connections.

This patient, one-on-one approach was crucial. Although our Buy Local network helped us gain trust, I still had to navigate the ingrained habits of the "taker" culture. A common form of collaboration was the coalition—a temporary alliance formed to "get" something.

But this would be different.

As I've emphasized, the heart of a Symbiotic Network is what Pope Benedict XVI called Gratuitousness, where the guiding question isn't "What can I get?" but "What can I give?" Coalitions often dissolve after a crisis passes or the grant ends. However, a Symbiotic Network is enduring; it grows stronger through ongoing cooperation.

As an aside, in *Cradle to Cradle*, William McDonough reminds us that the original Greek meaning of competition was "to strive together"—not to dominate, but to improve alongside others. In that spirit, our network was competitive in the best sense. Rather than "me versus you," our model became "me and you."

As word spread that we were exploring a Local Food System Network, several nonprofits offered to "run it." I respectfully declined. This wasn't a project to be owned. It needed to remain autonomous and informal, free from institutional control. Otherwise, it would become just another silo, another well-meaning fragment reinforcing the Culture of Separation.

Building a truly regional food system network required more than mapping who was involved; it demanded a new way of relating and organizing.

SCAFFOLDING A FOOD SYSTEM: HOW SYMBIOTIC NETWORKS MULTIPLY VALUE

I think of Symbiotic Networks as scaffolding—not the building itself, but the framework that makes construction possible. In a thriving local food economy, the Symbiotic Network integrates all the elements, enabling trust, communication, and collaboration to flourish.

We refer to this scaffolding as an "ecosystem" because, similar to the mycelial web described in Section I, various community "nutrients" circulate and connect throughout the system. Such networks can activate not only around food, but also health, faith, education, the arts, neighborhoods, and more.

Back to the story.

We gathered in person only after securing foundational support from key super-connectors who understood and embraced the concept. We would have faced resistance and confusion had we prematurely convened fifty stakeholders to present a half-formed idea. One crucial lesson is that major questions and concerns must be addressed with key individual participants before group gatherings in symbiotic community-building.

When we finally convened six super connectors, we didn't have to sell anything—we could align around mutual benefit. Having already clarified misconceptions, our first one-hour meeting felt natural, energizing, and full of possibility. We also began addressing "frozen assets"—untapped value trapped in siloed, competitive structures. These assets get "unlocked" through trust and generosity, often simply by sharing one's Rolodex.

Each stakeholder brought to the table their unique network cluster—growers, distributors, retailers, or advocates. Once these diverse yet related networks were connected, the energy released was remarkable. Six individuals amplified the network to nearly 100 organizations, reaching over 50,000 people!

A unique strength of Symbiotic Networks is shared leadership—no single organization or individual holds control. Initially, the catalyst operates as a hub, but once the circle forms, they, too, become peers among equals. This sharply contrasts with networks launched by existing organizations, which tend to centralize control. Human nature, being territorial, often provokes and promote competition among such networks.

> *A true Symbiotic Network, in contrast, is not a new organization. It's a living, multi-hub, community-centric organism where power is distributed.*

Because traditional, siloed structures are normalized to the point where many people assume "that's just how things are," I emphasize how our model differs:

- It's a Virtue-based network focused on mutual benefit: "What can I give?" not "What can I get?"
- It's a "mediating structure" that enhances other members' work—not another competing silo.
- It's independent, not controlled by nonprofits, businesses, or government.
- It's an informal, agile Network Commons, applicable across food, health, education, neighborhoods, and more.

The essential quality of the network is not structure, but Virtue. Without that, we may "build the road" without letting "the road build us." Virtues help us cultivate the inner resources needed to create space for mutual benefit across differences—this is the "spiritual capital" I spoke about earlier. As I've often said, you need people capable of cooperating to build a cooperative community. To hold space for collaboration, you must first become a uniter, not an unwitting divider.

Another reason for our success is Symbiotic Kinship. Similar to our Buy Local campaign, we welcomed every food-related enterprise, not just those labeled "organic," "green," or "regenerative." In a trust-based environment, transformation often occurs organically, not through mandates, but through relationships and market forces.

Later, you'll see how our "early adopter" farmer, once entirely conventional, transitioned to organic farming. This was not due to pressure but because our network revealed a new path, and the growing demand propelled him forward. This spirit of connection-of meeting people where they were and walking with them—would guide how we invited new collaborators and built relational momentum from the ground up.

SHORTENING THE PATH: WIRING THE COMMUNITY FOR CONNECTION

One of our guiding ideas was "shortening the path"—creating meaningful connections more quickly, like the best of what the tech revolution promised, but delivered through human warmth instead of algorithms. At our gatherings, we introduced a practice called speed networking, where participants briefly met someone new, shared what they were doing and needed, and introduced each other to the group.

The format was playful, energizing, and surprisingly effective. In that structured yet spontaneous space, people forged genuine bonds. We were, quite literally, wiring the community for collaboration.

This spirit of accelerated connection came alive at our public gatherings, where trusted third-party introductions revealed how quickly collaboration could take root when the conditions were right. Shortening the distance between leaders sparked surprising breakthroughs. At our first event, a rabbi and an imam discovered a shared need for halal food sources and soon launched a co-op together.

Food as Foundation

Then came the now-legendary "Pastor and the Pagan" moment: a neo-pagan farming teacher and an evangelical Christian pastor connected through their shared love for regenerative agriculture—something they might never have discovered outside the trusted space we had cultivated. These moments embodied the quiet power of trusted third-party connections.

> *A network catalyst—someone trusted in multiple circles—*
> *builds bridges not by forcing alignment,*
> *but by extending a sacred invitation:*
> *Come as you are. Let's find what unites us.*

This is the heart of Symbiotic Kinship—bringing people together across divides through shared purpose, not sameness. It echoes sociologist Mark Granovetter's theory of the "Strength of Weak Ties." While strong ties—family and close friends—reinforce identity, weak ties' more diverse and flexible relationships often unlock surprising opportunities. On a personal level, that might mean finding a job or a friend. At the community level, it means connecting disconnected organizational clusters so that more good can circulate throughout the ecosystem.

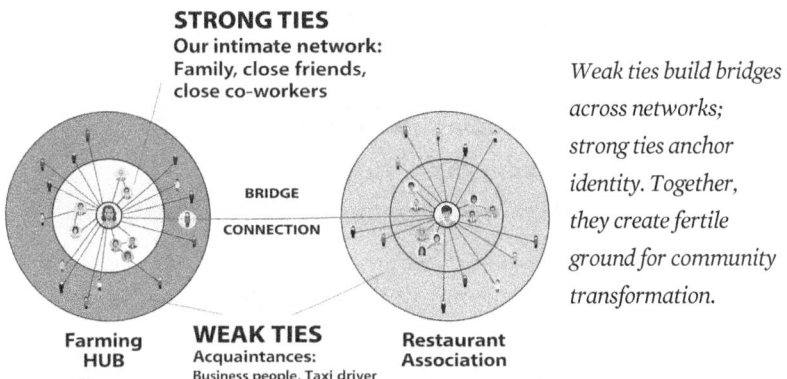

Weak ties build bridges across networks; strong ties anchor identity. Together, they create fertile ground for community transformation.

In the examples above, each otherwise polarized group—Jewish and Muslim, Evangelical and atheist—gained access to new relationships and broader horizons. Sometimes this even led to unlikely friendships, as people discovered shared values hidden beneath their tribal identities. These were our network's "collateral benefits"—gifts that stretched people beyond their comfort zones and fostered a deeper capacity to connect across differences.

SACRED INVITATIONS: FROM SHARED SOIL TO SCALABLE TRUST

We didn't just shorten existing paths—we created new ones that had never existed. Instead of gathering people around politics, ideology, or identity, we scaffolded our network around shared work in the local food system. Conversations about politics or religion became unnecessary. The focus shifted organically to a higher-order question: "What do we want to create together?" That question alone was sufficient to break the trance of separation.

There was real magic in this—not the kind born from luck, but the kind that emerges from fruitful collaboration for mutual benefit.

We cultivated a sacred space—like a cathedral— where people could metaphorically remove their "street shoes": their assumptions, judgments, and narrow identities.

In that space, people met not as roles, but as souls. For the Evangelical pastor and the Neo-Pagan farmer, friendship didn't grow from shared doctrine. It grew from shared soil, literally—a mutual devotion to land, life, and service.

Food as Foundation

At a time when Facebook was still in its infancy, our monthly face-to-face gatherings became the real "social media." They sparked authentic relationships, launched new collaborations, and stitched regional cooperation and prosperity. As stakeholders invited others into the living network, momentum spread across Northern Nevada like mycelium—quietly, powerfully, and from below.

Naturally, some suggested formalizing it into a nonprofit as the network grew. I gently resisted. I believed our strength lay in growing as a distributed, network-centric community, not in recreating the very hierarchical systems we had set out to transcend.

Of course, not everything unfolded smoothly. Conflicts of interest arose. Some viewed the network as a career opportunity rather than a shared calling. These moments reminded us why Virtues must remain at the center. Without them, the old mentality—What's in it for me?—could quietly creep back in.

Ultimately, our sacred connection—built on trust, service, and mutual benefit—became our true infrastructure. It embodied the principle of subsidiarity: start where you are, tend to your roots, and let love ripple outward worldwide.

LOCAL RIPPLES TO GLOBAL POSSIBILITY

The origins of our first network, the Buy Local Network, remind us of a simple truth: lasting change begins at home. When the world faced the impending invasion of Iraq, we could have marched for or against events halfway around the world. Instead, we asked a more urgent question: *How do we heal the conflict and polarization in our community?* As someone once quipped, "How can we have peace in the Middle East if we don't have it in the Middle West?"

We started with what we had—trusted relationships—and built outward. Trusted friends invited their trusted colleagues. I began with individual phone conversations, then small group meetings, which grew into hundreds of businesses and thousands of people, forming a radiating circle of trust.

We weren't reinventing the wheel; we were walking a well-worn but often forgotten path—what I later came to call fractal community empowerment to describe the natural way Sarvodaya's work had spread: a living, self-replicating process that expanded horizontally within villages and vertically across an entire nation, growing organically from person to person, circle to circle, and community to community.

As we will see in the next chapters, every network we built in Reno followed the same organic pattern:

> *Start with one-on-one trust, expand to small circles, and grow into larger, distributed communities rooted in the Ancient Blueprint of loving Virtues.*

That's how Sarvodaya sparked thousands of village economies and impacted Northern Nevada. Anyone reading this book can become the seed, wherever they themselves are planted. Chapter 18 will explore the five elements of fractal community empowerment and how Symbiotic Culture DNA can be integrated to foster genuine, living change from the inside out.

LOCAL, CULTURAL CHANGE STRATEGY: WHY PARADISE DID NOT GET PAVED

Our Northern Nevada Local Food System Network sparked a quiet yet profound cultural shift that ultimately influenced the entire region's economics and politics. In late 2005 and early 2006, many civic and business leaders believed that small farming was a relic of the past and that farmland should give way to condos, malls, and parking lots.

But something surprising happened on the way to paving paradise. Within six months of launching our network, small farming, farmers' markets, and local food began to blossom into a regional renaissance.

> *The momentum we witnessed confirmed a more profound truth: culture drives economics and politics more powerfully than policy ever can.*

Consider our earlier Buy Local Network, which emerged during the intense polarization surrounding the Iraq War and the growing presence of big-box stores that drained wealth from local communities. While some suggested combating Walmart with protests, we chose a different path: to support and uplift our local businesses. That shift in strategy—away from grievance and towards generative action—planted the seeds that later sprouted into our regional food system network.

We didn't need to petition the government to protect farmland. As the cultural tide shifted, political and business leaders followed suit. This reinforced a core principle we had been learning all along: global problems must be addressed locally, and real change tends to grow under the radar, like the hidden mycelial webs beneath a thriving forest.

By transforming the region's cultural consciousness around food, we created a political fait accompli without forming a partisan movement or launching a lobbying campaign. A new Symbiotic Culture of collaboration quietly reshaped Northern Nevada in powerful and lasting ways.

BIRTHING THE SYMBIOTIC AGE

And remember that community garden we decided not to launch directly? By cultivating the ecosystem rather than controlling outcomes, community gardens and dozens of similar projects emerged naturally. The lesson was clear: organic growth takes care of itself when you create the right conditions.

FROM LOCAL ROOTS TO A UNIVERSAL PATTERN

There's a paradox here worth highlighting. Had we limited the network to only regenerative, organic, or permaculture growers, we would have confined ourselves to a narrow silo—too small to influence the broader culture.

> *We created a more expansive field where real change could unfold by welcoming conventional and regenerative farmers into the same shared space.*

Ironically, this multi-stakeholder approach allowed regenerative practices to take deeper root and spread more widely across the region.

Opportunities multiplied. Connections between networks led to an explosion of new programs—more farm-to-table partnerships, more community-supported agriculture (CSA) models, and more direct farm-to-consumer ventures. One CSA grew to fifteen. What began with three farmers selling directly to city residents evolved into a thriving web of over 150 food-related businesses within a decade.

The City of Reno got involved, investing in its first public farmers' market. The Great Basin Food Cooperative—now one of the most successful in the nation—didn't emerge because we planned it. It emerged because we nurtured the ecosystem in which it could take root and thrive.

Accelerating Food Projects

From farmers' markets to food co-ops, shared trust catalyzed Reno's thriving local food ecosystem.

It's important to be clear: our food network didn't "own" these spin-offs. We weren't building an empire. We were cultivating a culture—an ecosystem where goodness could rise, adapt, and flourish. Of course, collaboration is never tidy. Humans are complex. Balancing the collective ecosystem with individual ego systems requires ongoing spiritual practice. Issues of territory, control, and trust naturally surfaced—and yes, I had my moments as well.

Still, none of this could have happened without one essential element: a sacred, trusted space—a living soil rich in the Virtues that matter most: love, cooperation, generosity, and service. Behind every farmers' market, CSA, and collaborative venture, something far deeper than a program or strategy lies beneath the surface—not just a structure but a way of being human together that transcended silos, systems, and even ideologies.

BIRTHING THE SYMBIOTIC AGE

Ecosystem Buildout
To Unfreeze Siloed Assets

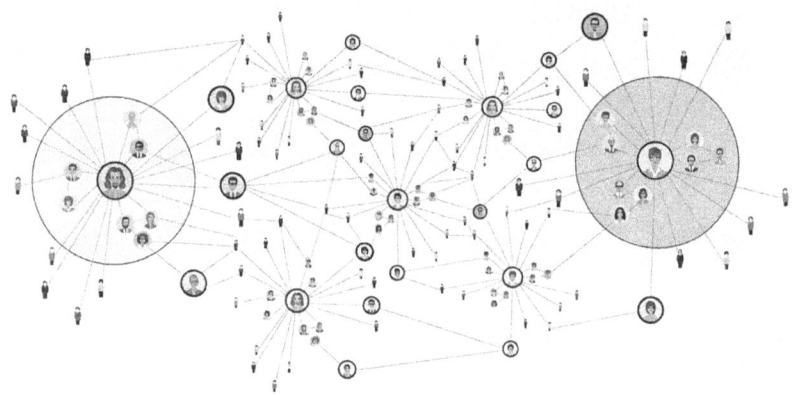

A thriving ecosystem emerged from shared Virtues and local roots, spreading like mycelium through trust, connection, and collective purpose.

> This invisible thread
> —the one that wove our neighbors into kin—
> felt ancient, as if it had always been there,
> waiting for someone to notice.

While our networks sparked real change, they also stirred a more profound longing. Could this pattern scale? Could it unify not just a region but humanity itself? As our roots deepened locally, a new question arose: What, if anything, could unite us all?

CHAPTER 17

PRELUDE TO A NEW PATTERN: REDISCOVERING WHAT UNITES US

This chapter is the prelude to something extraordinary.

In February 2006, our community would gather for what became a breakthrough moment—the Valentine's Day meeting that gave birth to Symbiotic Culture DNA. But before that could happen, a deeper recognition had to unfold. Something invisible yet essential needed to emerge: the shared longing, sacred context, and spiritual pattern that would guide everything that followed.

This wasn't about launching a new project. It was about seeing—together—what was already taking shape beneath the surface. What had we been building? What had been building us? In the quiet aftermath of our regional breakthroughs, a question arose in me that wouldn't let go: What will truly unite humanity? Not just through shared goals or efficient systems, but at the deepest level of identity, spirit, and kinship.

As we came to see separation itself as the root issue, it became clear that technical solutions alone would never be enough. Beneath every successful community initiative, I sensed a deeper invitation—not simply to fix broken systems, but to remember a shared origin story already written into our being.

What if a pattern was already woven into the human heart, waiting to be reawakened?

This wasn't a lofty ideal. It grew from real-world success. Even as society edged toward collapse, we in Reno were living a different story. Through the Local Living Economy Network, the Conscious Community Network, and the Northern Nevada Local Food System Network, we proved that igniting a culture of unity was not only possible—it was happening.

As our networks expanded across a region of 400,000 people, I wondered: could this success extend to other communities? Could a unifying story be the missing key?

It was then that I began to see it—not just a hope, but a pattern.

DISCOVERING SYMBIOTIC CULTURE DNA

Although I didn't yet have the words for it, I was beginning to uncover a deeper living pattern—a kind of Symbiotic Culture DNA: a coherent set of shared Virtues, purposes, and needs capable of regenerating thriving human communities anywhere.

This pattern wasn't abstract—it was embodied. It pointed toward something older and deeper: a sacred architecture we would later name the Ancient Blueprint. Rooted in Divine Love and Logos, this Blueprint had silently informed our instincts all along. Though we hadn't yet named it, we were already living from this relational pattern.

Inspired and energized by my Transcendent experience, I intuitively followed the breadcrumbs of sacred design to build Symbiotic Networks for mutual benefit—networks grounded in trust and belonging.

We had an advantage: we were already living the answer to what unites us. But we lacked a framework. We needed to identify the relational worldview that was quietly animating everything.

Earlier in this book, I described this worldview—a lens through which reality appears not as a collection of parts, but as a sacred whole. At the time, we didn't have the language. We were simply practicing it.

That relational worldview became our operating system—a sacred orientation to life where meaning arises through relationship, not control.

Flowing from that worldview was a protocol: Symbiotic Culture DNA. It emerged through mutuality, trust, and connection across typical dividing lines—a rediscovery of how life is designed to function when rooted in love.

This view, reiterating Jesus' message to Love God and Love each other, sees all things as connected—each soul, species, and system finding its meaning in relation to the whole, and ultimately to the Creator who sustains it.

From the Trinity to Paul's vision of the Church as one Body, to Ephesians 1:10—"to bring unity to all things in Heaven and on Earth under Christ"—the sacred design has always pointed toward unity in love.

That longing was very real for me. As I shared earlier, I was shaped by the tension between the Ancient Blueprint of wholeness and the Culture of Separation that dominated modern life.

Even as a child, I felt a mysterious ache to reconnect what had been torn apart—to bridge faith and action, science and spirit, neighborhoods and nature. In hindsight, I see it now as a quiet echo of a larger truth:

> *We are made not for disconnection but for unity—*
> *that Divine Love is the glue that holds the cosmos*
> *and society together.*

To address the issue of manifesting this mutually-beneficial Culture of Connection on a larger scale, we have to confront the deeper fracture that has shaped our age.

LOSING THE TRANSCENDENT ANCHOR AND FINDING IT ANEW

We cannot understand the fragmentation around us without facing a hard truth: we have lost our shared Source of Love, purpose, and meaning.

The Enlightenment fractured reality—splitting science from spirit, private from public, material from sacred. Into that divide rushed materialism, claiming to be the new god. But for all its promises, it has failed. It has delivered neither coherence nor meaning, only deeper fragmentation.

This wasn't just an intellectual insight. I could feel it in my bones. I was living between two worlds: one driven by analysis and control, and another animated by compassion and coherence. Even in activist circles, I saw how spirituality was kept private and separate—as if faith was too dangerous to bring into public life. And in religious circles, I often felt that social engagement was tolerated but not integrated. The split ran deep, and it mirrored the one I carried inside.

By 2006, we could already feel the spiritual vacuum hollowing out our culture. Virtues had been stripped of meaning. Shared standards had eroded.

And yet, even then, something deeper moved beneath the surface. We sensed that a shared Reality connects us, that Earth is our common home, and that we are, in truth, one family—and that unity was still possible, if we could tap this deeper thread within us.

To find a shared, Transcendent purpose, we had to confront two unspoken norms I referred to earlier:

- The modern habit of keeping spirituality private
- The activist assumption that religion is divisive or irrelevant

In contrast, the Ancient Blueprint—carried through Jesus, Gandhi, and Dr. Ari—tells a different story. It reveals a universal longing for a beloved community that transcends our ideological and religious boundaries.

Sarvodaya Shramadana in Sri Lanka embodied this possibility. Dr. Ariyaratne didn't sidestep faith—he integrated it into public life. As he said: *"We who have been born Buddhist, Hindu, Christian, Muslim... can be very comfortable praying or meditating together..."*

That spiritual grounding didn't create conflict—it nourished coherence.

As our Reno networks sought to apply the practices and lessons of Sarvodaya, societal differences were obvious. While Sri Lanka had to emerge from material poverty, we in the materially-abundant West faced spiritual poverty. One lacked infrastructure. The other had plenty of infrastructure—that was fragmented, siloed, and disconnected. Could we create coherence not by building new systems from scratch, but by reweaving the broken threads of meaning already present?

That was the question—and the invitation.

BUILDING TRUST, BUILDING TOGETHER AND HEALING THE FRACTURE

Though we shared universal Virtues, our Conscious Community still operated in silos of identity: religious, secular, activist, entrepreneur. But the groundwork of trust was there. We had already built capacity for mutual agency through our earlier networks.

From one-on-one conversations to small circles to large gatherings, we had nurtured circles of trust—or rather, circles of Love—that allowed invisible bonds to form across traditional divisions.

> *In retrospect, it became clear that these circles of trust were not just a method, they were the soil for something new.*

Without knowing it, we had begun building a parallel culture—grounded in ancient patterns and lived through everyday people.

Now we were ready to codify what had already emerged. Like Sarvodaya's village networks, we were ready to translate our lived experience into a repeatable pattern—and Virtues held the key.

We began to recognize that shared Virtues—not personal values—were the real glue of our networks. They offered a moral language broad enough for everyone, yet deep enough to mean something. They were the "currency" that allowed our circles of trust to expand and proliferate.

We began to notice something extraordinary. Like starlings in murmuration—moving in breathtaking, fluid unity without a central controller—we sensed that humans, too, could transcend isolated wills to embrace a shared intelligence. The "we" was becoming greater than the sum of our individual "me's."

Even in our overdeveloped, hyper-fragmented culture, we discovered the same truth Sarvodaya had uncovered:

When communities focus on universal Virtues and real needs, not ideology—they begin to flourish.

DIVINE LOVE AS UNIVERSAL FOUNDATION

Recognizing the universal longing for connection, we chose Valentine's Day 2006 to host a region-wide gathering—not about romantic love, but agape: the self-giving, unconditional love identified across traditions as the sustaining force of life. We called the event "Taking Our Love Higher," sensing that something more than strategy was needed. Even without the term "Divine Love" in our vocabulary, we were responding to a real Presence—one that offered connection, healing, and a living intelligence arising from between and among us.

This gathering wasn't about imposing a one-size-fits-all belief but drawing from the community's own shared heart.

Could unity emerge organically—without conformity?
Could collective intelligence arise from love?

We found our answer in the field itself. When love saturated the atmosphere, something greater awakened—insight none of us could reach alone.

Divine Love is not sentimental—it is the luminous, sustaining power that holds the universe together. Across traditions, it transcends categories like eros or friendship and becomes an embodied practice that lifts us beyond ego and control. Rooted in this Love, competition gives way to collaboration, and dominance hierarchies yield to growth hierarchies grounded in mutual empowerment and shared flourishing.

As Jesus taught, to love God and neighbor is not just moral instruction—it is the spiritual infrastructure of culture itself.

> *When communities align with this Love,*
> *they awaken what I call nexus agency:*
> *the authentic power that arises when grassroots*
> *movements coalesce for the common good.*

What began as a local experiment in connection became a reawakening of something eternal—a sacred pattern returning through us once more. It was as if Love had always been the protocol—waiting for us to remember.

VIRTUES VERSUS VALUES: REDISCOVERING A SHARED REALITY

If Divine Love was the foundation, then Virtues were its visible form—the practiced habits that gave Love shape in public life. As we moved from gathering to coherence, we began searching for a moral language that could carry the weight of our shared purpose. We wanted something broad enough to include everyone, yet deep enough to truly unify. That search brought us to a critical distinction—one I didn't fully appreciate at the time.

Looking back, I regret giving in to the pressure to use the term *values* instead of *Virtues*. I believed using the term *values* would foster broader agreement, but it didn't. Referring to them as *values* diluted the deeper truth we were striving for: the universal human aspiration toward goodness that transcends all divisions.

Virtues unite. Values divide.

Prelude to a New Pattern

Where values reflect personal preferences or ego-driven choices, Virtues orient us toward the greater good.

Values like wealth, success, or recognition are subjective and often fragment communities. They shift with time, culture, events, and ideology. One person's noble value may be another's injustice.

Virtues are different. They are relational, not relative—intentionally practiced habits of the heart, rooted in love, courage, patience, and humility. They've been recognized for over 3,000 years across Eastern, Western, Indigenous, and secular traditions as universally Good, True, and Beautiful. They do not change with the wind of preference—they endure.

Virtues provide our foundation for rebuilding trust, reclaiming coherence, and rediscovering a shared reality in a fragmented world.

So, could these enduring *Virtues* help unify a community—or humanity itself?

And how would we, or could we, find a shared reality that would provide a unitive ground of being?

This wasn't just a philosophical question. It became a lived one—posed by real neighbors across lines of faith, politics, and profession. Could we name together what was truly sacred—not through dogma, but through the deeper language of shared life? Could we discern a moral foundation strong enough to hold space for difference without losing coherence?

All of this—our longing for unity, our lived experiments, and our rediscovery of Virtue—brought us to a single moment. On a cold February morning in 2006, over a hundred community members gathered—not for policy or protest, but to listen, to love, and to remember.

This meeting would not just spawn new networks and community projects, but it would offer a key to our "knowing ourselves" as a community and providing the foundation to spread and scale Symbiotic Kinship, Symbiotic Culture and Symbiotic Networks anywhere and everywhere.

CHAPTER 18

DECODING SYMBIOTIC CULTURE DNA: A LIVING FRAMEWORK FROM DIVINE DESIGN

On Valentine's Day 2006, a hundred of us gathered at Reno's McKinley Arts Center—business owners, religious leaders, non-profit executives, activists, and city officials. We weren't launching a campaign or responding to a crisis. We had come to ask a deeper question: What is tearing us apart—and what could bring us back together?

For many, it was the first public acknowledgment of what we had quietly sensed for years: the root problem wasn't poverty or crime, it was fragmentation, a breakdown of shared meaning. In that moment of honesty, we opened the door to something rare: a collective discovery of the principles and Virtues that could form the living foundation of a new culture.

BIRTHING THE SYMBIOTIC AGE

FROM FRAGMENTATION TO CONNECTION

Beneath our efforts to reconnect was a deeper tension: *Could we even agree on what's real?*

> *In a culture where objective truth is viewed with suspicion, the idea that "everything is relative" has taken root—ironically, as an absolute.*

In our planning group, we wrestled with whether to incorporate spiritual principles and shared values. Most supported the idea, but some feared it might divide us. One business leader, a former multinational CEO objected despite holding deep spiritual convictions. His caution was understandable. We had built unity without raising what some considered "theological issues." Why risk it?

Still, reflecting on Sarvodaya's success, I felt certain: We must name and nurture shared Virtues—such as compassion and loving kindness—not just privately but together.

Whether seen as gifts of the Transcendent Logos, as C.S. Lewis believed, or as universal human longings, these Virtues offered a path through our crisis of meaning. The real question was this:

Could we build a new society—parallel to the old—on a foundation of Love and Service strong enough to hold us together?

In the Culture of Separation, we're taught to fight our way to the top. But our Buy Local, Local Food System, and Conscious Community networks prove the opposite: that a Culture of Connection isn't just possible—it's practical. It aligns with the best of the free market and the wisdom of the heart.

We held that Valentine's Day gathering just weeks after launching the Local Food System Network. We divided the group into small circles and posed one bold question: *What is the most challenging problem facing Reno and society today?*

Decoding Symbiotic Culture DNA

Celebrating unity through joy, love, and service, where shared Virtues sparked connection in a world longing for meaning and belonging.

The response was nearly unanimous: fragmentation and disunity. No one cited poverty, hunger, or crime. Instead, they identified the root cause: a collapse of shared understanding, fractured belief systems, and isolation within our community.

We followed up with two questions:

- How can we bring people together?
- What concrete actions can we take?

From that session, 150 ideas emerged. Many pointed toward timeless principles: the Golden Rule, "Love Thy Neighbor," and the call to serve one another.

Then we asked:

- What's the best way to identify our shared principles and values?
- How can we express them simply and memorably?

We were fortunate. One participant, a former Marine Corps chaplain, had experience codifying values across diverse populations for the US military. This opened the door to a broader exploration. We reviewed value systems from military institutions, synagogues, Christian denominations, Buddhist and Hindu teachings, secular civic governments, corporations, and even humanist groups.

From that collective wisdom, we brainstormed over a hundred values, around twenty core principles, twelve shared community needs, and a rough outline of a network design.

> *Over time, something beautiful emerged elegant and alive: one unifying purpose, eight guiding principles, five central Virtues, and twelve shared needs.*

All of it rested on a deeper, mostly unspoken intention: to bring the Ancient Blueprint to life for the good of all. And to truly align with it, we had to ask: *What are we here for? Not just for this meeting, but individually and collectively?*

OUR HIGHEST PURPOSE

Having named the crisis of fragmentation and glimpsed the power of shared Virtues, we now faced a deeper question: Was there a singular purpose that could truly unify our efforts?

We never stated it outright at the time, but in hindsight, our purpose was clear: To nurture a society where practicing intentional mutual benefit, from self to family to community to nation, becomes the living norm.

This echoes what St. Maximus the Confessor best captured in the 8th century: "to unite the cosmos in love," bringing what is separated back into wholeness. Throughout history, cultures and religions—Eastern, Western, and Indigenous—have sensed this same destiny: a beloved community grounded in the felt presence of the Transcendent, woven through all of Creation.

Jesus expressed this highest call in the Lord's Prayer:

> "Your Kingdom come, your will be done, on Earth as it is in Heaven."

This is the essence of the Ancient Blueprint: bringing Heaven to Earth through the understanding that we come from one Source—whether called God, Divine Love, or, as I name it, the Transcendent. However you name it, this book reflects my own experience of Jesus Christ as that living Love—present, incarnate, and active in the world. I offer this not as doctrine to enforce, but as my subjective testimony, trusting that many have encountered this same Love under many names.

Again, we didn't have the words for it, but we were an "island of coherence" inside a largely invisible yet all-pervasive Culture of Separation that builds walls of fear and fragmentation. In sharp and blessed contrast, the Culture of Connection plants gardens of trust and shared purpose. Our community recognized that fragmentation arose from losing this sacred center and the widening rift between materialism and transcendence.

Few articulated it clearly, but the evidence was all around us: the "god" of materialism had failed.

Our next challenge was, how do we make this unitive loving purpose accessible and applicable so that other communities could follow our lead—and so that we remember not just the "what" and the "how" but the "why?"

Instinctively, we gravitated toward the universal principles and radiant Virtues that reweave the Transcendent into our daily lives. Without calling it a "reality crisis," we were already cultivating a Culture of Connection, even as the Culture of Separation crumbled. As you explore the principles and Virtues we uncovered, notice how each aligns with this deeper purpose: *to create a virtuous society, economy, and culture where Heaven touches Earth.*

With that purpose taking shape, we turned to a practical question: What principles could translate this into daily action and lasting community structures?

That sense of service gave shape to the principles that would guide our every decision—not as rules, but as anchors.

FOUNDING PRINCIPLES

Anchored in our shared purpose, we identified eight principles to guide the growth of our Symbiotic Network of networks. Alongside our purpose, Virtues, and shared needs, these form the Symbiotic Culture DNA—replicable at any scale: personally, locally, nationally, globally, and even digitally.

Here are the eight foundational principles:

1. Golden Rule 2.0 — Found across major religious and ethical traditions, this version extends the transactional *"Do unto others as you would have them do unto you,"* to proactively benefiting others, because we are one family, from one Source. I am you; you are me. The Golden Rule is the Ancient Blueprint applied to human relationships.

2. Charity Begins at Home & Self-Rule — Care for yourself and your family first, then extend outward. True sovereignty begins with personal responsibility. This principle echoes Hinduism and Buddhism (Swaraj), Catholicism (Subsidiarity), and the teachings of Jesus himself.

3. Acknowledge Something Greater Than Yourself — Whether you call the name God, Higher Power, the Universe, or Community, recognizing a greater reality puts the ego in service, not in charge. The Transcendent isn't a distant goal, it's a living reality, here and now.

4. Love Thy Neighbor —Not just your physical neighbor, but everyone you meet—Symbiotic Kinship. Symbiotic Networks depend on generosity, resource sharing, and mutual benefit in all relationships.

5. Think Globally, Act Locally — Global problems must be solved through local action. If 50,000 communities created nodes of Symbiotic Culture—linked through a "bubble-up" global commonwealth—we could replace trickle-down systems. Each node is a fractal of the Ancient Blueprint.

6. Community-Based Local Economy — Prosperity starts at home. By meeting personal and community needs, we grow cultures rooted in resilience and generosity.

7. Focus on Commonality — Instead of fueling culture wars, we focused on shared community needs—just as Sarvodaya Shramadana did with its ten essentials you will read about shortly. Common purpose dissolves division. This practical approach builds bridges across differences.

8. Build a Living Organism, Not Another Silo — Cultural Symbiogenesis calls us to evolve from isolated silos into a multi-siloed, network-centric society. This new organism models the shift from a Culture of Separation to one of Connection.

Eight principles anchoring networks in love, sovereignty, the sacred, and shared purpose across all scales.

To be activated in the world our principles needed form. That form came through Virtue—the visible structure of Love.

UNIVERSAL VIRTUES: THE LIVING ENERGIES OF SYMBIOTIC CULTURE

If the principles were the scaffolding of our shared purpose, the Virtues were its animating Spirit, it's living energies—an internal compass sustaining the Culture of Connection over time. This led us to identify universal Virtues honored across cultures and traditions.

From a list of 100 Virtues and values, we distilled 35 and grouped them into five archetypal patterns: Love, Integrity, Courage, Service, and Respect. (These are not just values, they are Virtues. They describe the building blocks of character, not the varieties of individual preference.)

I refer to them as archetypal because they are revered across all cultures—indigenous and industrial, religious and secular, rich and poor. Even nations otherwise in conflict uphold these essential human Virtues. Instead of concentrating on differences, we emphasized this profound common ground.

Five universal Virtues—Love, Integrity, Courage, Service, and Respect— form the living essence of Symbiotic Culture across all traditions.

A question came to us: *Could we create unity without demanding uniformity?*

At first, "love" seemed too broad a starting point. However, it sparked conversations about how love expresses itself through compassion, kindness, empathy, and awareness. Plato described truth, beauty, and goodness as radiant expressions of love. Our group added those as well. Theological differences faded when we focused on embodiment and participation rather than intellectual agreement. By naming these shared qualities, we evoked the living essence of Love.

Contrast this with many modern civic movements, which often exclude religious perspectives, particularly Christian ones. What we built was different: a trans-religious approach that included and transcended all traditions. It wasn't a dialogue about belief systems but rather a shared embodiment of Love in action. People of faith could fulfill their highest calling by creating self-sufficient communities where individual and collective needs are met through love and shared agency.

From my own encounters with luminosity in nature and the web of life, I sensed a Transcendent reality at work. Like my experience of Jesus Christ, it was not a theory to prove, but a living reality that nourishes abundant life or does not.

Some may believe these Virtues evolved through trial and error, without reference to God. Either way, the proof lies in the practice. What matters is not their origin, but whether we embody them. Keep in mind, these Virtues exist across all cultures, expressing our longing to transcend the isolated ego and rediscover a beloved community.

Virtues are not abstract ideals.
They are Transcendent Energies—
part of the Ancient Blueprint, woven into reality itself.

Consciously applying them in daily life opens the door to the next phase of human evolution. Practicing them can turn dominance hierarchies upside down, giving rise to interlinked growth hierarchies and a new operating system rooted in love, integrity, and shared flourishing.

But how do these timeless qualities show up in real life, across diverse communities and traditions?

A CONSTELLATION OF VIRTUES: A PRACTICAL LOOK AT THE TRUE HUMAN SUPERPOWER

Another powerful insight from our Valentine's Day gathering was the need to practice Virtues collectively, not just individually. Beyond building Symbiotic Networks, we formed the Connections Gathering—the Weaver Group—to integrate personal Virtues into community life. (You'll read more in Chapters 21 and 22.) Each month, we focused on one Virtue—like integrity. Small groups shared how they lived it and explored how to express it more visibly in service and collaboration.

Through this, we codified patterns we had already been living—like "charity begins at home," the Golden Rule, and neighborliness—not as rigid commandments, but as mutual commitments to relational practice. Our Reno group discovered something profound:

Virtues are not isolated. They form a living constellation interwoven and mutually reinforcing.

For example:
- Integrity connects to balance, trustworthiness, and honor.
- Courage links to perseverance, strength, and restraint.
- Respect reflects fairness, civility, and mindfulness.
- Love embodies compassion, gratitude, humility, and patience.

Practicing them together creates a self-reinforcing field of coherence in personality and community life. Embodying one Virtue naturally calls forth others, strengthening our connection to Divine Love and expanding our collective capacity for unity. Because they connect us to the Divine, I've come to see Virtues as Transcendent Energies—the deepest human superpower available to us.

Virtues often seem disconnected or even at odds within the Culture of Separation. However, when practiced as a whole—fractals of the Ancient Blueprint—they reinforce each other, creating patterns of wholeness. Nearly every major religious tradition acknowledges that virtuous living is essential for transforming our inner lives and world.

That's why I've come to see these Virtues as universal patterns.

Buddhism provides a vivid example. The Sarvodaya Shramadana Movement—which we've explored throughout this book—embodies a constellation of Virtues through its practice of compassion, lovingkindness, equanimity, and joy in the happiness of others.

Sarvodaya's work demonstrates how living Virtues can heal individuals, families, communities, and societal structures.

We also intentionally drew from civic and religious sources, choosing Virtues that resonate across both secular and spiritual realms. In doing so, we affirmed that these are not abstract ideals but living energies embedded in every heart, waiting to be expressed and practiced.

Virtues are not the ornaments of spiritual life. They are the structure. They are how we weave ourselves—and the world—back into wholeness. Yet in a fragmented world, even our greatest strengths can be distorted.

WHEN VIRTUE TURNS TOXIC IN A CULTURE OF SEPARATION

Like all great powers, Virtues require balance. Isolated from one another, even the noblest can become distorted, especially within a Culture of Separation rather than integration. G.K. Chesterton put it best:

> "The modern world is full of the old Christian Virtues gone mad. The Virtues have gone mad because they have been isolated from each other and are wandering alone."

This echoes Adam Smith's warning about the "man of system"—driven by good intentions yet imposing his vision of Virtue without love or humility. In the Culture of Separation, the mind tries to do the Spirit's work. Stripped from Divine Love, Virtues harden into rigid constructs—pitted against one another, weaponized into dogma rather than lived.

When Virtue becomes dogma, it often leads to domination. Culture wars erupt as each side clings to a partial "good" that calcifies into judgment and exclusion. As George Santayana warned:

> "Fanaticism consists of redoubling your effort when you have forgotten your aim."

Nearly every toxic political system—from the French Revolution to totalitarian Marxism—began with a severed Virtue. Pursued in isolation and untethered by love, humility, truth, and balance, these noble ideals mutate:

- **Liberty** becomes anarchy or violent rebellion.
- **Equality** becomes forced conformity or oppressive collectivism.
- **Order** becomes brutality, surveillance, and control.

That's why St. Maximus placed Love at the center—not just as one Virtue among others, but as the living fountain from which all others flow. He emphasized that Virtues must be practiced together. Only in harmony do they form a cohesive field, unifying both personality and community.

Over time, we saw Virtues not as isolated traits but as mutually reinforcing energies—an interface between Heaven and Earth, woven through every relationship: family, neighbors, co-workers, and communities.

*Virtues practiced together
transform not just individuals,
but entire places.*

These universal Virtues—recognized across religious and secular traditions—are intrinsic. They cannot be imposed from outside; they must be awakened from within. Teaching them helps, but true transformation only comes through practice, by consciously embodying them daily.

RECOVERING VIRTUE AS A LIVING PRACTICE

Recovering Virtue as a living practice is essential to activating Symbiotic Culture DNA, not as an idea to admire but as a life to embody. If fragmentation is the problem, then Virtue is the path home. Ancient wisdom and lived experience alike point the way.

This raises an old question: Can we learn to live virtuously the way we learn to fix a car?

In one of Plato's dialogues, Socrates suggested that Virtue isn't like a skill you acquire. It comes from Divine inspiration. It's not manufactured—it's remembered and awakened. The Latin root of *educate*, *educare*, means "to draw forth" what is already within. In this view, Virtues aren't just taught; they emerge as we align with deeper patterns of reality—the Ancient Blueprint.

In our Conscious Community, we lived this truth. Practicing Virtues together was not merely moral training—it was a reconnection with the Transcendent and a healing from the Culture of Separation. The early Christian Church understood this well. Virtue was not separate from the Spirit but the fruit of abiding in Christ.

As Paul wrote to the Galatians, "The fruit of the Spirit is love, joy, peace, patience, kindness..." These are more than just inner qualities—their practice makes the relational fabric of the Kingdom of God visible.

This is what early Christians called *edification*—the Spirit-led work of mutual encouragement and spiritual strengthening, the building up of Virtue through community life and the shared practice of love. This principle re-emerged in modern times through movements like recovery communities, where transformation is grounded in daily spiritual practice.

The 12-step recovery movement describes this shift as "a new way of life"—one lived from the heart, not the ego. Our own inquiry into purpose, principles and virtues reshaped how we saw value and worth. Dr. Martin Luther King, Jr.'s "Drum Major Instinct" sermon remains deeply instructive. He reminded us that the drive toward greatness isn't wrong, but it must be reoriented toward love, generosity, and service:

> "If you want to be important—wonderful. If you want to be great, wonderful. But recognize that he who is greatest among you shall be your servant... You only need a heart full of grace, a soul generated by love."

King's words still call us back to the true meaning of greatness—not domination, but self-giving love. In our small groups, we found something similar. Talking about Virtues wasn't enough. Lives changed through humble, repeated practice. You can't shift from ambition to self-giving love by thinking alone. That's the trap of the mind. As the old joke goes: *"Sure, it works in practice—but does it work in theory?"* In a culture that worships abstraction, Virtue is an embodied path.

So what happens when Virtue isn't just remembered—but practiced consistently in community?

THE PROOF IS IN THE PRACTICE

This raises another question: Are Virtues human inventions—or reflections of a higher power?

Whether you believe they evolved through trial and error or reflect a Divine Source, the true test lies in their embodiment. I have my own perspective. I don't practice Virtue out of dogma or any external motivation—it flows from a direct, embodied understanding, rooted in extraordinary childhood encounters with a Divine order.

This knowing transcends belief, and I would never impose it on anyone. Yet anyone who's witnessed a birth, a death, a breathtaking moment in nature, or a pure act of selfless love has touched that same Source. We all have access to this "Divine Hotline." When I connect with another person, I can experience no separation. We come from one Source. We are one family.

That is my experience. In these luminous moments, it feels like the Luminous Web—the living fabric of Creation—is shimmering just beneath the surface, calling us home to unity.

Whether we reach this through direct spiritual experience, reasoned philosophy, or shared kindness, the path matters less than the realization.

When it came to practicing Virtues in our networks, we never turned them into a "thing" or belief. There was no constitution, no pledging allegiance. They became a living foundation, discovered through dialogue and sustained by relationships in the community.

I can say from experience that consistency between internal Virtue and external practice creates a field of trust. Some say consensus around shared Virtues is impossible in today's polarized world. I disagree. In Reno, we found unity around universal Virtues despite great diversity. This radical unification is still possible—anywhere people are willing to honor the wisdom of the human heart.

What did we accomplish? First, we named the invisible foundation: a shift from competition to collaboration, rooted in Virtue. Second, by immersing ourselves in the practice of Love, Integrity, Courage, Service, and Respect, we began to live these virtues as a new way of life.

They shaped our choices, inspired new initiatives, and quietly transformed us. The journey of living Virtue was the transformation.

> *These universal patterns, rooted in a Transcendent reality, gave us a common language—a way to transcend political and religious divides and "trance-end" the Culture of Separation.*

Embodying these living patterns, we found a shared language—a practical grammar for building a Culture of Connection. Now, the next question awaited: *How do we apply these energies to meet the everyday needs of community life?*

Virtues lived in isolation risk being just abstract concepts and lose their power. But when applied to everyday challenges, they become transformative. And that's precisely what we set out to do next.

Our next inquiry revealed a lived pattern of human needs, visible across every thriving community.

TWELVE NEEDS THAT HOLD A COMMUNITY TOGETHER

The community meeting process fostered a new level of openness and trust. Instead of clashing over opposing viewpoints, we gained a more holistic perspective. With a common purpose and guiding principles in place, it was time to turn "inside out"—to apply the Virtues we had uncovered in service to the broader community.

How, specifically?

Nearly fifty years earlier, Sarvodaya led village conversations in Sri Lanka that revealed ten basic community needs. Through in-depth local dialogue, they identified core needs and hundreds of sub-needs that brought the blueprint to life. Why is this important?

It revealed a critical truth: focusing on shared, functional needs, not divisive political or ideological frames, is essential for lasting cooperation.

As you'll see in Section 4, avoiding the cultural landmines of ideological capture is key to building resilient communities. We found remarkable resonance between Sarvodaya's needs and our own, even though we were working in an "overdeveloped" nation rather than a "developing" one.

Sarvodaya's Ten Basic Needs:
1. Clean environment
2. Adequate supply of water
3. Clothing
4. Nutritious food
5. Shelter
6. Health care
7. Communication
8. Fuel and lighting
9. Access to education
10. Cultural and spiritual performance

Inspired by this, our Reno community identified twelve foundational needs to guide our network-building work:

12 Common Needs of Symbiotic Culture:
1. Local Economy
2. Clean & Healthy Natural Environment
3. Community Peace & Safety
4. Local Food & Water
5. Neighbor Helping Neighbor
6. Community Empowerment of those on the "margins"
7. Local Energy
8. Arts & Culture
9. Housing
10. Family and Community Health & Wellness
11. Education and Mentoring
12. Religion/Spirituality in Service

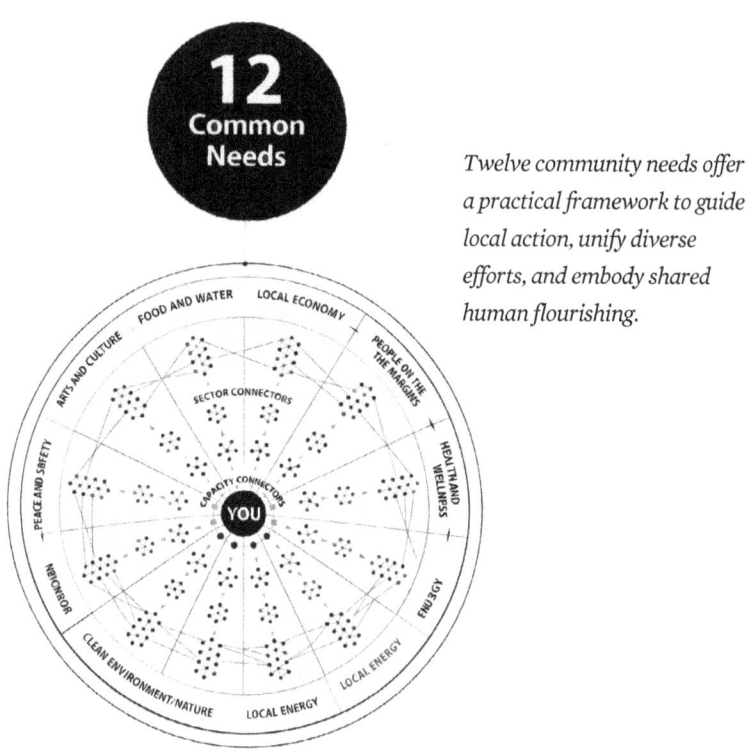

Twelve community needs offer a practical framework to guide local action, unify diverse efforts, and embody shared human flourishing.

"Building the road"—purposefully living out the principles and Virtues to serve these needs—requires a new kind of infrastructure. Fortunately, we had already begun to create it through our Local Living Economy Network and Local Food System Network: a living scaffolding, an architecture for the Culture of Connection to take root.

THE ARCHITECTURE OF CONNECTION: AN INESCAPABLE NETWORK OF MUTUALITY

Through practice, patterns began to emerge. As our networks matured, we started to perceive something more profound—an architecture of coherence hidden within our work.

Serving community needs revealed a new challenge: We needed infrastructure—not rigid organizations but living networks—to weave connections across silos and sustain symbiotic growth. A blueprint is essential for designing a building, but it's not the building itself.

It's a pattern calling for infrastructure and scaffolding that helps a community cohere, collaborate, coordinate, and communicate.

In Section 4, *Activation*, I discuss these new "mediating structures."

Back to the story.

By Valentine's Day 2006, we had already created two "Symbiotic Networks," although we didn't yet refer to them that way. In building our Buy Local and food programs, one catalytic connector—myself or others—would reach out. That single act of connection often rippled across siloed communities, weaving them into a shared purpose.

We needed to understand these networks more deeply to live out our shared principles and Virtues.

We came to see Symbiotic Networks as network-centric organizations:

- Leadership was distributed, not top-down.
- Connections were multi-nodal and horizontal, with "connector" and "super-connector" leaders weaving invisible bonds daily across the community.

Each new link generated a fresh flow of information, sparking social and economic innovation among groups that had never connected. When we remain siloed—socially, economically, religiously, and politically—we stagnate. As discussed earlier, new life comes from linking "weak ties" and liberating the resources trapped by the Culture of Separation.

Connecting across differences also dissolves inner barriers. Healing happens heart-to-heart and group-to-group through small acts of love and service—and it doesn't take long.

Within three years of launching the Conscious Community Network, we created a living "non-institution" that wielded more positive influence than any organization in the region, without force, conflict, or opposition.

Our multi-nodal network didn't *create* good; it connected and multiplied the good already present. Like Sarvodaya, we nurtured both internal and external resources. Cooperation and goodwill flourished beyond our differences. We enjoyed the work. "Connecting the Good" became our shorthand for the movement.

Within this structure, old dichotomies like "collectivism" vs. "individualism" dissolve. No top-down collectivism is imposed. Instead, empowered individuals choose to act together, making the "personal ideal" the "community real deal."

Dr. Martin Luther King, Jr. captured the essence of it:

> "In a real sense, all life is interrelated. All persons are caught in an inescapable network of mutuality, tied in a single garment of destiny. Whatever affects one directly affects all indirectly."

Our Symbiotic Networks became living expressions of that "inescapable network of mutuality"—a real-world manifestation of how the Transcendent became Immanent.

Perhaps Heaven was present all along, but now it felt like it was breaking through, made visible and tangible through deepening relationships and an architecture of connection.

Decoding Symbiotic Culture DNA

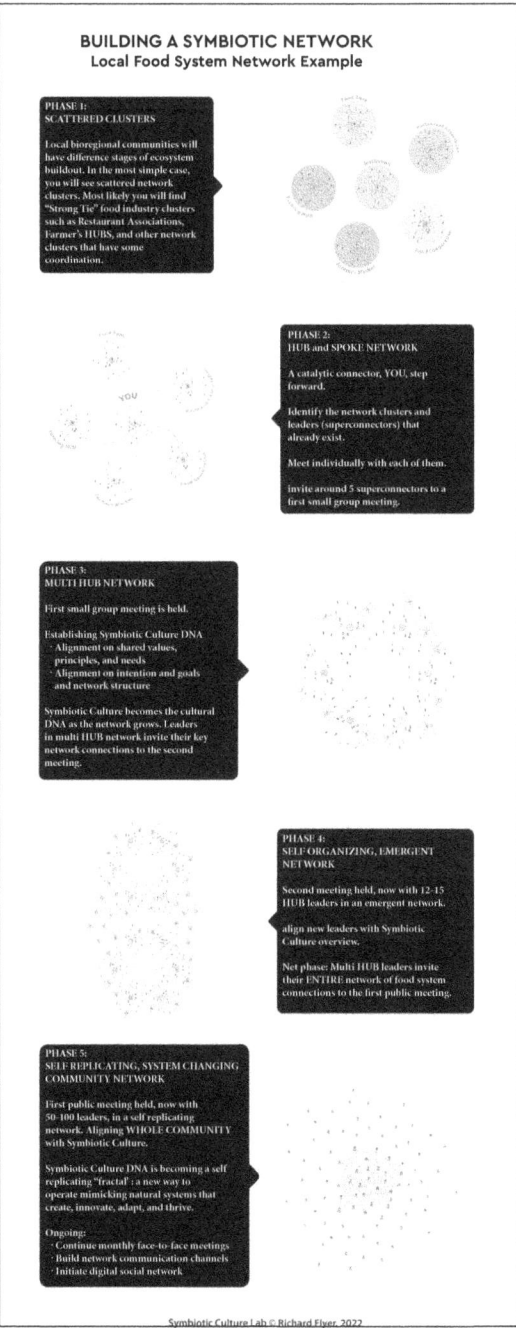

While this maps a Local Food System Network, the same steps apply to any Symbiotic Network— faith, arts, health, or beyond.

BIRTHING THE SYMBIOTIC AGE

This work is grounded in a simple truth: we thrive by honoring individual expression and the common good, interwoven in uncommon goodness. It represents the shared ground we can utilize today to heal the divisions of our fractured world.

We began to map the pattern as a lived framework that could be shared and scaled. What emerged was a set of five essential elements—deeply relational, spiritually grounded, and culturally transferable. Together, they form the living DNA of a Symbiotic Culture.

SYMBIOTIC CULTURE DNA: DECODING THE FIVE ELEMENTS OF A RELATIONAL WORLDVIEW

Reflecting on our past, we began to notice a deeper pattern emerging—a living architecture encoded through shared purpose, principles, Virtues, needs, and networks: what I now call Symbiotic Culture DNA.

Just as biological DNA encodes the instructions to build a living being, Symbiotic Culture DNA encodes the structure for building a thriving community.

It's not merely the transmission of a concept, like a meme passed mind to mind, it is a journey from heart to heart.

The Culture of Separation has reproduced itself across empires and ages. However, another hidden yet vibrant pattern has also emerged: the Culture of Connection. The same Blueprint has appeared across Eastern, Western, and Indigenous traditions—a way to bring Heaven to Earth through community, Virtue, and love.

The early followers of Jesus knew it, as did the early Christians. Gandhi knew it, as did Dr. Ari. I saw it manifest in San

Diego and Reno. A deeper coherence emerged as we built, struggled, learned, and loved. Beneath our many experiments, a single pattern kept revealing itself—the ancient code, a protocol of community life, remembered and brought back to light. This pattern is transmitted, person to person, community to community, as the Symbiotic Culture DNA.

I now recognize five interconnected elements that make this pattern tangible and replicable:

1. Shared Purpose: Uniting the Cosmos in Love

At the core lies a timeless purpose: to reunite what has been separated. We are not isolated individuals—we are one family. The Culture of Connection begins with the understanding that we come from one Source and share one destiny.

2. Eight Community Principles

From this purpose flow the practical building blocks of daily life: principles like the Golden Rule, human and local sovereignty, and regional action for global renewal. Each principle embodies Love in action—Transcendent ideals made tangible.

3. Five Universal Virtues

Virtues are not just moral ideas but genuine spiritual energies that unify and elevate. Practicing Love, Integrity, Courage, Service, and Respect connects us to the deeper currents of life. Each act of Virtue sends ripples outward, weaving the Luminous Web.

4. Twelve Common Community Needs

Every living system thrives through energy exchange. Likewise, communities flourish when they meet shared needs—health, education, food, safety, and spirit—as

Sarvodaya villages did in Sri Lanka and as our Reno community rediscovered. These are not charity but mutual uplift rooted in dignity and joy.

5. Distributed Network Infrastructure
To scale and sustain this living culture, we need new structures. Multi-nodal networks—horizontal, relational, and resilient—enable Symbiotic Culture DNA to flow across communities, dissolving silos and unlocking hidden potential.

Each element is essential, but together, they create a living architecture for human flourishing. This is how goodness reproduces itself. This is how Heaven begins to break through Earth.

This living design reflects not only how life grows but how Love multiplies. As you'll see in the next section, there is a way to spread this living pattern through Fractal Community Empowerment—not someday, but now.

But theory wasn't enough. The real test was whether this DNA could empower ordinary communities to do the extraordinary.

FRACTAL COMMUNITY EMPOWERMENT: A PRACTICAL WAY TO DO THE IMPOSSIBLE

With the DNA of Symbiotic Culture identified, the next question arose: *How could this living pattern spread, not gradually, but at the speed love demands?* For decades, I've wrestled with more questions:

> *How can one person, in concert with others, help create a global shift from a Culture of Separation to a Culture of Connection?*

How do we move beyond random acts of kindness to build the Kingdom of Kindness, where Symbiotic Culture DNA spreads as naturally as the dominant culture once did?

**The truth is, we cannot fix our current systems—
political, religious, or economic—
using the same tools that broke them.
Our crisis demands something deeper.**

The path we uncovered offers that, but could it scale quickly enough?

The answer is Fractal Community Empowerment. Instead of slow, top-down change, fractal empowerment envisions the simultaneous awakening of thousands of communities, nurturing a planetary superorganism of goodness. Imagine 50,000 communities embodying Sarvodaya's achievements in 5,000 Sri Lankan villages. Unlike traditional models, this spreads through decentralized, self-organizing human hearts and hands.

And considering the urgency of our time, we don't have the luxury of slow reform. Fractal empowerment involves infusing the pattern of Symbiotic Culture DNA into communities—now, not someday.

HOW FRACTAL EMPOWERMENT WORKS

The beauty of fractal empowerment is that it requires no permission, hierarchy, or having to be "perfect." Anyone—anywhere—can become a space-holder for Symbiotic Culture. You don't have to be a leader; you must live it.

You:
- Know your Transcendent purpose
- Embody the shared principles
- Practice the universal Virtues
- Form a Symbiotic Circle
- Identify and serve real community needs
- Build bridges across silos

Anyone can start right where they are—in families, workplaces, schools, and congregations. Each act of love becomes a spark, spreading the Culture of Connection through invisible yet powerful threads.

In traditional systems—nonprofit, business, or government—community change often relies on formal structures: boards, bylaws, fundraising, and staffing. These models have their place but are siloed, slow, costly, and hampered by red tape. Under these rules, igniting transformation in 50,000 communities would seem impossible.

> *Symbiotic Culture DNA offers a different path.*
> *It isn't an institution—it's a universal, networked,*
> *relational code or protocol. It can be embedded*
> *in any context, at any scale—*
> *from a kitchen table to an entire region.*

Rather than scaling programs, it replicates as a living pattern: adaptable, human, ecosystem-centered, and fast. In the chapters ahead, you'll see how this design supports decentralized growth—not by seeking permission, but by embodying purpose.

Any individual can "own" the purpose of uniting the cosmos in love, consciously gathering what is fragmented and allowing their daily life to radiate from that wholeness. As Gandhi envisioned, this is a moral chain reaction driven by awakening hearts across all levels of society. This is how Symbiotic DNA spreads—not someday, but now. Anyone inspired by this vision can "inject" it into neighborhoods, spiritual communities, schools, companies, and even governments.

It all can begin with one person. One life, aligned with love, can cultivate a new community and regenerate the world. Every embodied Virtue—kindness, generosity, courage—creates a self-reinforcing pattern that shapes individual identity and collective culture.

This is how our Reno network expanded throughout Northern Nevada, how Sarvodaya took root in thousands of villages, and how anyone, anywhere, can become a living seed. Each personal act of love decodes the Ancient Blueprint. Every bridge built reweaves the Luminous Web. Each renewed neighborhood becomes a fractal of a more beautiful world.

Symbiotic Culture is not a technique—it's a way of life. I share tools in this book, but if you perceive it merely as a method, you'll overlook its true power. Paradoxically, it can't be *used*—only lived.

What's emerging now is the next stage of evolution—nurturing new containers for this consciousness to take form.

Spiritual, social, economic, and political infrastructures are already being born through network nodes of people making a difference. These containers can take many forms—some entirely new, others already planted in existing institutions at the grassroots.

And one of the most important containers is already present: the local church.

Many congregations long to extend their love and service beyond Sunday gatherings but often lack the relational infrastructure to do so effectively. Symbiotic Circles (which we discuss in more detail in Part 4) can serve as a mediating structure—a relational bridge between individuals and larger institutions—helping churches transition from internal fellowship to the outward embodiment of love in neighborhoods and daily life. It's not about starting something new but expanding what's already sacred.

By the way, this applies to ANY religious, spiritual, or secular ethical group intent on serving humanity by serving the local community.

Together—our shared purpose, guiding principles, universal Virtues, common needs, and living network infrastructure—form a DNA protocol strong enough to weave a new world.

What began as a practical strategy ultimately revealed a deeper truth: we were writing a new cultural story together.

THE NEW STORY: SYMBIOTIC CULTURE

As we embraced these truths in Reno, a new narrative emerged—one that could unite humanity not through conquest or ideology, but through a shared longing for wholeness and Divine Love made real. We began with a question:

> *What could unite humanity? We found an answer:*
> *our common yearning for Divine Love*
> *to manifest on Earth, alongside our shared need*
> *to survive and thrive.*

By uncovering our shared purpose, principles, and radiant Virtues, we have rediscovered an Ancient Blueprint—and re-animated a living mission. We are called to spread intentional mutual benefit and act as a channel for Divine Love within our communities. Every handshake, every shared meal, and every barrier dissolved becomes a luminous thread in the tapestry of a renewed world.

Hundreds, thousands, even millions of people and their organizations can integrate this awareness into their daily lives and most mundane interactions—with a grocery store cashier, a bank teller, a homeless neighbor, or within families, workplaces, and local and global communities. This is how Symbiotic DNA takes hold.

Fractal empowerment sows these loving seeds everywhere, enabling them to grow and flourish in vibrant contrast to the Culture of Separation.

As the networks matured in Reno, a deeper question emerged: *How do we embody this cosmic vision in the neighborhoods where we actually live?* What happens when we bring it home, not just into economies and organizations, but onto front porches and kitchen tables?

The next step in our journey was not about expansion but intimacy. It was time to make "Love thy Neighbor" not just a spiritual command but a practical design for daily life.

CHAPTER 19

RE-VILLAGING OUR COMMUNITIES: STARTING WITH LOVE THY NEIGHBOR

Over four years, our symbiotic community experiment—fueled by crowd-sourced wisdom—began uniting siloed nonprofits, businesses, civic agencies, and everyday citizens into living networks of mutual benefit. In doing so, we uncovered the Symbiotic Culture DNA: a replicable, step-by-step process for embedding the Ancient Blueprint into every endeavor, allowing it to spread organically through existing networks.

We did this without creating a new organization, budget, or staff. There was no hierarchy, no silos.

Instead, we built a living, network-centric scaffolding—more organism than institution—where people and organizations collaborated across lines of difference. These networks, which we also referred to as "Mediating Structures," became the functional architecture for a new local operating system—a modern parallel society.

Like Gandhi and Dr. Ari's vision of decentralized village economies, we saw how local Symbiotic Networks could scale into a global commonwealth of resilient regional systems.

Our ecosystem supported local food, business, and culture, not by starting from scratch, but by connecting what already worked and rooting it in shared Virtues, common purpose, and collective wisdom.

Drawing from Sarvodaya, we identified twelve foundational community needs and began meeting them through universal Virtues and practical action. Our diverse, secular-spiritual community coalesced around a relational worldview that honored tradition but transcended tribalism.

We had diagnosed the root issue: fragmentation and disconnection. We had named the guiding principles.

FROM FRAMEWORK TO DAILY LIFE

The ideals were in place. Now the question was: How do we root them in the places we actually live? How do we embed them in a Network Commons—a living framework capable of evolving new civic and economic structures that complement, rather than compete with, the official ones?

How can we make Dr. King's "inescapable network of mutuality" tangible again? How do we reclaim "village Virtues" in our mechanized, urban-suburban world?

As our network matured, a deeper possibility surfaced—not from planning but from the people themselves. One idea began to rise: to make the Ancient Blueprint of "Love God and Love Thy Neighbor" real again, not just economically through food and business, but spiritually and relationally, neighbor to neighbor.

Our Valentine's Day gathering had given us solid ground: a shared purpose, core principles, universal Virtues, and clearly expressed needs. Now it was time to bring it all home—and make "Love Thy Neighbor" not just a value, but a way of life.

> *We came to call this process re-villaging:*
> *not a return to the past, but a recovery of something*
> *ancient and essential—human-scale trust, kinship,*
> *and sacred interdependence.*

More than neighborhood connection, it's rebuilding community life by restoring the relational patterns that make us fully human—patterns that were never meant to be lost.

To make "Love Thy Neighbor" real, we had to begin where people lived—not with institutions, but in neighborhoods. Yet we quickly ran into a deeper challenge: modern life had reshaped the very meaning of neighborhood.

GARAGE DOOR NEIGHBORHOODS AND THE LONGING TO BELONG

As big-box stores have displaced local shops, many communities have shifted from front porch culture to private backyards. In these "garage door neighborhoods," people retreat indoors, and all we might see of each other is the occasional glimpse through an open garage.

Sociologist Robert Putnam captured this shift in *Bowling Alone*, describing the decline of face-to-face connection in American life—something we experienced daily as neighbors stopped interacting and community ties weakened.

In 2007, I wrote an opinion piece in the *Reno Gazette-Journal*, observing that while we can travel across the globe, many of us don't know the people living down the street. I quoted a line attributed to both George Carlin and the Dalai Lama, that I got from Dr. Bob Moorehead, former pastor of Seattle's Overlake Christian Church: "We've been all the way to the moon and back but have trouble crossing the street to meet our neighbor."

The piece struck a chord. Within two weeks, spontaneous neighborhood gatherings began popping up across the region. Something long buried had been awakened—the longing to belong. We realized that "neighbor-to-neighbor" connection was as foundational to a thriving community as local food, resilient economies, and vibrant arts.

Neighborhood gatherings helped reconnect isolated neighbors, transforming garage door streets into places of belonging, shared purpose, and mutual care.

CATALYZING NEIGHBOR-TO-NEIGHBOR MOVEMENTS

The year after our Valentine's Day gathering, I contacted local connectors and super-connectors to help bring "love thy neighbor" to life. We followed the same Symbiotic Network process—cultivating a region-wide neighbor-to-neighbor network without formal structures.

This was Symbiotic Culture DNA in motion: good ideas emerged simultaneously, spreading through relationships, bypassing bureaucracy. We contacted local organizations, businesses, and civic leaders, including neighborhood advisory boards and community watch groups. These early connections helped build trust and laid the foundation for broader participation.

Next Door didn't exist yet, but we operated as if it did—identifying key people in neighborhoods across the county and meeting informally to explore how neighbors could connect. Like our earlier efforts, these networks were self-organizing and emergent. Those who "felt the call" started wherever they were, with little resistance.

Neighbor-to-neighbor catalytic connectors began organizing potlucks, block parties, and street gatherings in homes, cul-de-sacs, apartments, and condo complexes.

As momentum was built, we shared ideas, compared notes, and eventually created a Neighbor-to-Neighbor manual so anyone could begin. No headquarters. No staff. Just people, purpose, and presence.

LOVE THY NEIGHBOR: THE PRACTICE AND THE POWER

As for me, I started, quite literally, at home. Inspired by my earlier work in San Diego, I launched neighbor gatherings on my street. In the first year, I reached out to twenty homes, and four people showed up. The following year, ten. By year three, we had a full house. That's how Symbiotic Culture grows—not all at once, but with slow, steady momentum.

Re-Villaging Our Communities

Being a neighbor connector requires courage, especially if you aren't naturally outgoing. Public speaking is a common fear, but knocking on a stranger's door can feel even more intimidating. Nevertheless, this discomfort is part of the transformation. We begin where we are. The task becomes clearer if we start by connecting to the Transcendent and grounding ourselves in the Virtues. These Virtues serve as doorways to embody love in action.

When we remember that our purpose is to "bring the Cosmos together in love," it becomes easier to step forward with generosity, care, and presence.

> *"Love thy neighbor" isn't a metaphor—*
> *it's power made manifest.*

Our networks spread not because of clever branding or outside funding, but because they were rooted in one key principle: intentional mutual benefit. While many social change efforts focus on external fixes, we began with a deeper question: What can I give? This internal grounding—built on the Ancient Blueprint—reminded us to prioritize self-giving over self-interest. When you reach out to a neighbor, you're not intruding; you're offering a gift. Reaching out may seem like a small act, but it stems from something much more profound. It arises from the core of who we are—from the Transcendent within.

That's how we "inject" Virtues into the neighborhood—not with fanfare, but through presence. A quiet transmission of hope, trust, and love. A healthy heart/mind virus, spreading neighbor to neighbor.

We didn't codify this model; instead, we lived it. As before, we utilized the fractal strategy: start local, radiate outward, and build trust.

I invited neighbors to connect with others they knew. We formed small teams, created a simple flyer, and kicked off with a single event. Some neighborhoods already had cohesion, while others started from scratch. However, a core group of caring individuals emerged in each one, typically within a 20–30 home radius.

It didn't take a majority to start. It just took someone willing to care first.

HOW NEIGHBOR WEEK TRANSFORMED A REGION

Our neighbor-to-neighbor campaign tapped into a deep, unspoken longing for connection. The local media responded immediately. The *Reno News and Review* and the *Reno Gazette-Journal*, usually competitors, both ran stories promoting what became "Get to Know Your Neighbor Week." Television and radio stations donated PSA airtime and even helped script the messages.

Our cable network provided 4,000 TV spots across Northern Nevada. Newspapers showcased our lighthouse logo and featured daily articles. More than just coverage, they became genuine partners, adding legitimacy, visibility, and energy to the campaign.

Neighbor Week awakened a movement—media, neighbors, and civic partners united to reignite community through simple acts of connection.

Flyers and posters read, "Make a Difference Right Where You Live." People were encouraged to host a potluck, barbecue, block party, or even say hello to a neighbor. We launched a website with helpful hints and emphasized that this wasn't a one-off event. The goal was to build lasting "caring circles" rooted in joy, service, and neighborhood safety.

The momentum spread quickly. In addition to the 65 registered gatherings, local media speculated that many more occurred spontaneously. The *Sparks Tribune* quoted me saying, "Being a good neighbor isn't a one-day thing—it's a lifestyle."

> "If we want peace in the world," I said, "let's build the foundation for it in our hearts, our families, and right on the streets where we live."

With that, the neighbor project took on a life of its own. Over the next few years, we grew to nearly a hundred gatherings at once, and I became a public figure in a region of 400,000. We almost made the *Guinness Book of World Records*. Then came *Parade Magazine*.

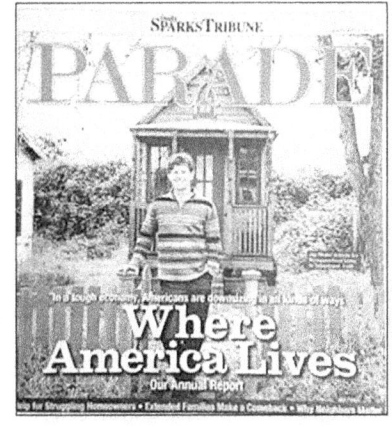

Neighbor Week went national—Parade Magazine spotlighted our decentralized model, revealing hidden needs, spontaneous kinship, and the healing power of connection.

One of the most affirming moments occurred when *Parade*, with its 40 million readers, featured our story in a national spotlight on neighborhood revival. They quoted me describing our decentralized model: neighbors inviting neighbors from a three-block radius, self-organizing, and bringing food to share. But what mattered most wasn't the method.

Parade focused on the hidden needs the gatherings revealed, and the healing they sparked. Two isolated widowed women found companionship. A lonely senior began receiving help from nearby neighbors. These people had been invisible—until now.

FROM GATHERINGS TO A CULTURE OF CARE

Looking back, everything we had done pointed to one more profound truth: when love becomes lived, it takes root. What began as a community event soon revealed itself as a sacred pattern. Through the neighbor-to-neighbor movement, we also took it broader and deeper.

> *What we did for the least of us*
> *brought out the best in us.*

We met unmet needs not through charity or ideology, but by seeing each other as equals. This wasn't about social justice campaigns or regenerative initiatives—it was about simple acts of service, rooted in Love. Our gatherings were never just "one-time parties." They reflected a new way of living, flattening hierarchies and inviting everyone, regardless of politics, religion, or background, into a circle of connection.

Looking back, this was quite a shift from my early activism. In the 1980s, as part of the anti-nuclear movement, I believed social change meant gathering people who thought like me, while dismissing those focused on PTA meetings or daily life as less important, as insignificant. We saw the "normies" as the problem. Conversion, not compassion, was the goal. Even today, much activism still plays out on that battlefield. However, the truth is that the model reinforces the Culture of Separation.

> *Now, imagine a network rooted not in ideology, but in one universal principle: Love thy neighbor.*

From that foundation, solutions arise organically, not from arguments or platforms, but from people supporting one another.

People often ask me, "Why should I connect with neighbors who don't share my beliefs?" My answer is: it's not about you or your likes or dislikes—it's about practicing a new way of being. It's about extending mutual benefit beyond the silos of whatever worldly identity we identify with. Every good cause we align with is a fractal of an even higher purpose: Bringing the Cosmos together in Love.

So, what did this look like in practice?

As connectors and caring neighbors went door to door, they encountered individuals who often struggled and felt isolated. Many had remained invisible to the surrounding systems. However, once acknowledged and welcomed, their gifts became assets for everyone. We weren't do-gooders with programs; we were neighbors with open eyes and hearts.

Local press spotlighted Neighbor Week's rise—from casual gatherings to a grassroots movement rooted in kinship, compassion, and shared care.

One neighbor might notice an elder who couldn't tend to their yard and connect them with a teen down the street who was eager to help. Sometimes we volunteered at shelters or soup kitchens, but more often, we lived by the principle: "Charity begins at home."

A COMMUNITY ARK FOR TROUBLED TIMES

Our neighbor-to-neighbor network became what we later called "nexus agency." Each group acted independently, rooted in the neighborhood's needs. We never dictated outcomes—we offered a coherent platform, shared suggestions, and sparked collaboration.

Injected with Symbiotic Culture DNA, each group held the same purpose, followed shared principles, and practiced the same Virtues. The result was self-organizing, decentralized networks that began to meet real needs across our community, from gardens and food sharing to emergency response and mutual aid.

*"We were all in the same boat—
so we built a Community Ark."*

That name captured the spirit of what emerged: a grassroots movement of neighborhoods, reconnecting people at the most local level. It was re-localization in action. Two decades later, this work feels even more urgent. In a world shaken by war, global instability, and supply chain breakdowns, many have reached out to me looking to secure local food systems. In response, I created a "Neighbors4Neighbors" organizing guide in 2022.

People are growing food, gleaning crops, and redistributing resources—not out of ideology but necessity. Back in Reno, for instance, we always had a surplus of tomatoes and couldn't grow lettuce so we would trade. This kind of practical local exchange builds trust, autonomy, and resilience.

Neighborliness isn't just moral—it's strategic.

In tough times, it's better to collaborate with your neighbors than to compete. You don't need lofty ideals to take action. The simplest motivations—staying safe, eating well, and helping one another—are sufficient to start. And yes, social media has its place. Platforms like Nextdoor can help announce gatherings. But don't confuse online connection with real connection; we still need to knock on doors and meet face-to-face.

Block by block, a resilient culture emerged—neighbors trading, gathering, and growing together in a living ark of mutual care.

BIRTHING THE SYMBIOTIC AGE

CARING CIRCLES AND THE
RISE OF THE COMMUNITY ARK

As neighbor gatherings multiplied, something beautiful began to unfold: people formed informal "caring circles." These weren't organized from the top down—they arose organically, matching "offers" and "asks" at the most local level.

What began with potlucks and block parties deepened into real kinship. Single moms launched babysitting co-ops. Widows supported one another. Neighbors tended each other's pets, gardens, and homes. Families adopted isolated elders. Teens helped with yard work. Mutual aid networks emerged. People began prepping for emergencies and linking to local nonprofits, not through governmental institutions but through the street-level web of trust.

This wasn't charity. It was kinship and mutual aid.

These connections were practical, personal, and deeply human. Symbiotic Culture DNA doesn't spread through ideology or central planning, but through relationships. Quietly, a model for fractal "re-villaging" came to life.

Compared to formal systems, our network reached where others couldn't. When I learned that 10,000 seniors in our region lived in isolation, I contacted local agencies. Their answer was simple: not enough staff, not enough funding.

They meant well, but lacked the infrastructure to reach those who had become invisible. Our caring circles did. It was a perfect example of a "parallel society" doing what formal systems could or would not. We didn't wait for anyone else to start. We took action from love.

Re-Villaging Our Communities

We built a decentralized delivery system not just for goods, but for goodness itself.

That made all the difference. Our care model didn't segregate elders into silos. It connected generations. Teens helped seniors with groceries or yardwork, and both lives were changed. These bonds couldn't be orchestrated from above. Remarkably, the system had no budget, salaries, or buildings—just people, purpose, and presence. Hundreds became paraprofessionals of care, not with titles, but with love.

As I've said before, many large agencies are so rigid that more money simply sustains what isn't working. It may sound cynical, but at times, it seems systems exist to shield us from having to face separation ourselves. We look away from the unhoused or addicted and think, "Someone else will handle it," so we can return to curated lives and scrolling screens.

But I don't want to live in that world—do you?

I want to live in a world where doorbells replace alarms, greetings replace gate codes, and a neighbor's need becomes a shared joy. Where caring is normal, and connection is expected.

Even without a formal system, imagine what's possible if we paused our busyness. What if just ten minutes a day, taken from scrolling or stressing, were used to serve? The effect could be life-changing for both them and you.

So, if starting a network like this feels daunting, take heart. You don't need a supermajority or a strategic plan. You need presence. You need heart. You need to start. It always begins with one person, reaching out to another, and then another.

That's how it spreads—not by going viral online, but by becoming vital in your neighborhood.

BIRTHING THE SYMBIOTIC AGE

STARTING WITH THE HEART: A SPIRITUAL CORE FOR ACTION

There's a reason this approach works.

The real power behind our networks in Reno and Sarvodaya lies not in the structure but in the Spirit that animates it. The foundation of Symbiotic Culture is not institutional; it's the Ancient Blueprint—a living transmission of Love. When building community, don't just seek "connectors." Look for those grounded in their authentic selves—people who live from a place of intentional mutual benefit.

That's why the spiritual core matters. And by "spiritual," I don't mean belief systems. I mean the capacity to embody universal Virtues: compassion, empathy, wisdom, truthfulness, trust, equanimity, and self-restraint.

*The fruit of a spiritual life is not belief
but Love in action.*

When you find individuals who live like this—even quietly—they become anchors. A core like this can hold space for the emergence of something greater. As the Culture of Separation seeks to pull us back into debating differences, space-holders like these build a Culture of Connection around shared aspirations and common needs.

A community formed in this way establishes boundaries for inclusion, sets standards for behavior, and becomes a coherent, unifying force.

Here's the good news.

I believe there are already millions around the globe who carry this inner wisdom and capacity in 50,000 cities, towns, and villages. In the US, there are 350,000 congregations, 1.5 million nonprofits, and 33 million small businesses, all potentially infused with Symbiotic Culture DNA.

The delivery system may be human, but the fuel is Love. Fractal community empowerment is about releasing the true power of love that flows through us into a tangible, gentle framework for community-building—one that connects the dots between people and organizations in a way that can break through everywhere, simultaneously.

That's how an impossible dream—a global network of village economies—becomes not only possible, but inevitable.

Meanwhile back to Reno, our streets and neighborhoods had become more than testing grounds for good ideas—they had become living proof that ancient wisdom could guide a new kind of community. In the ordinary rhythms of connection, we had tapped into something sacred: a timeless pattern of care rooted in the Ancient Blueprint.

Now the question was: Could it ripple outward and renew the world, as the lineage of that Blueprint has shown repeatedly throughout history?

CHAPTER 20

THE ANCIENT BLUEPRINT AND ITS LIVING LEGACY: A PATTERN THAT WORKS

The answer, we began to realize, was already all around us.

What we witnessed in our caring circles echoed the timeless call of early Christian communities—to live from Love, serve others, and see every person as family, regardless of belief. What we created in Reno was a living expression of the Ancient Blueprint inaugurated by Jesus in the Sermon on the Mount and embodied daily by early Christians.

> *This embodiment of Divine Love—not belief alone allowed them to transcend tribal boundaries and create a new kind of community.*

They took the Good Samaritan story to heart. When Jesus was asked, "Who is my neighbor?" he answered with a parable in which the one who acted with compassion, rather than as the religious elite, was the true neighbor. The Samaritan, an outsider, was the one who paused to help, crossing boundaries of tribe and tradition to show mercy. This story demonstrated compassion has no boundaries.

Early Christians exemplified this dedication. They cared for strangers—even Roman citizens who didn't share their faith. They didn't seek to reform the Roman Empire or promote political agendas. Instead, they established a parallel society—scaffolding for a new world in parallel to the old. Their lives served as a countercultural witness.

They were not revolutionaries in the modern sense. They were *radicals* in the truest sense of the word—returning to the root. And the root problem they addressed wasn't political or economic alone. It was spiritual: the Culture of Separation that undergirded all injustice. And they lived the antidote—what we now call Symbiotic Kinship.

> *They did not resist evil; instead, they multiplied the good.*

Mahatma Gandhi perceived this same radical wisdom when he read the Sermon on the Mount in 1899. He referred to it as the "Law of Love." Gandhi translated this love into tangible systems through swaraj (self-rule) and swadeshi (local economy). Our networks mirrored this approach—local action fueled by Transcendent Love.

Dr. Ari followed a parallel path in Sri Lanka. As a Buddhist, he channeled the Blueprint in a nonsectarian form. Sarvodaya cultivated Virtues in individuals and families and built decentralized infrastructure to extend those Virtues into community life. That's what we tried to do in Reno.

We might even call this the evolution of spirituality—not through a new religion, but as a broader, deeper expression of sacred life. It's a spirituality that transcends siloed beliefs and manifests in collective action that transforms social, economic, and political structures. Nobody asked, "What party are you from?" or "What religion are you?" when a teen helped an elder weed their yard. The question wasn't *what you believed*, but *how you showed up*.

We're often told to study history to avoid repeating its mistakes. But why not also learn from its light—from those times when Love changed the world? Here's the point: We don't need new philosophies or identity-driven movements, nor do we need to invent new principles or values. The Blueprint already exists—hiding in plain sight.

> *Real change starts by transforming culture*
> *from the bottom up—one neighborhood,*
> *one relationship, one act of Love at a time.*

That's why we built food networks, local economies, and neighbor-to-neighbor campaigns. We were reclaiming our agency from the grassroots. We weren't resisting evil by force—we were pulling together what had been scattered.

Our neighborhood network became ground zero for this transformation, where the Ancient Blueprint could thrive again, not just in stone or scripture but in soil, smiles, and shared meals. This is how we spread Symbiotic Culture DNA.

RE-VILLAGING THE WORLD, ONE STREET AT A TIME

Not everyone welcomed our neighbor-to-neighbor movement. Some preferred the privacy of suburban life—pulling into garages,

The Ancient Blueprint and Its Living Legacy

closing doors, and avoiding connection. Since World War II, we've moved from the front porch to the backyard, from open community to siloed encampments where "everyone minds their own business." And yet, beneath this isolation, many longed for village life—belonging, care, and closeness.

Our campaign broke that trance. When neighbors expanded their "circle of care," it reawakened hidden value in families and communities. This shift helped people realize that quality of life wasn't just about personal space but about shared space.

One obstacle we encountered was institutional "silo thinking." I expected churches and spiritual communities to embrace the message, "Love God and love thy neighbor." Many did. However, one group of evangelical pastors stated they would only participate if allowed to use the gatherings to recruit. That broke my heart. Jesus didn't say, "Love your neighbor so they join your group." He said, "Love your neighbor as yourself."

As the saying often attributed to St. Francis of Assisi goes:

"Preach the gospel at all times. When necessary, use words."

Whether he said it or not, the truth it carries still holds: a life lived in Love speaks louder than any sermon.

We never pressured anyone. Participation was voluntary, with no agenda but Love. Had those pastors chosen to embody the Word rather than preach it, they might have inspired more people than any recruitment strategy ever could.

Others approached me with causes—fighting landlords or promoting climate action—and while each had merit, they overlooked the deeper point. Neighbor-to-neighbor networks aren't about promoting a side. They're about rising above divisions to Connect the Good across all sectors. When you focus on a cause, you narrow your audience. When you emphasize shared humanity, you widen the circle.

BIRTHING THE SYMBIOTIC AGE

Love is the context where even disagreement can become dialogue.

Symbiotic Culture creates a sacred space where diverse people and ideas can coexist and collaborate. One activist criticized us for not "taking a stand" on issues like war or climate. However, we were taking a stand on the root issue behind all others: the Culture of Separation.

The antidote was right action grounded in Love. Instead of blaming or battling, we built a community. We brought people together to solve problems practically and relationally, not politically. We infused our work with shared purpose, not shared outrage.

Another obstacle was the charity mindset—the assumption that those more fortunate must 'save' those less fortunate. This mindset mirrored what I'd seen in San Diego nonprofits: top-down solutions imposed from above. True empowerment comes from within. The best thing external institutions can do is send "community catalyzers"—not to fix but to spark self-organization.

Despite initial resistance, we located willing partners among nonprofits, particularly when they ventured beyond their silos. As our Neighbor Network gained momentum, we reached a tipping point—then a "rippling point." The impact radiated outward in ways we never could have planned.

Five years in, a woman told me how a block party sparked her effort to beautify Midtown Reno. She organized neighbors, brought in merchants, and lobbied the city. Today, that area is a vibrant cultural hub filled with cafes, galleries, and summer festivals. I would have never known our movement inspired that transformation had she not told me.

The Ancient Blueprint and Its Living Legacy

> *"Connecting the Good" wasn't just a phrase or phase—*
> *it became a way of life.*

Yes, we supported local food and businesses. More than that, we promoted the release of goodness—dormant in the heart of every person and place, waiting for a way to emerge. By cultivating shared Virtues and principles, we addressed our community's spiritual needs as deeply as its material ones. The result was a vibrant ecosystem of care that embodied St. Maximus's teaching—"to unite the cosmos in Love"— in our neighborhoods.

As Plato once wrote, "Love expresses itself through truth, beauty, and goodness." The neighbor-to-neighbor network made that philosophy real, through potlucks, garden swaps, and moments of quiet kindness that built a new world from the ground up.

FROM GOOD DEEDS TO GLOBAL KINSHIP

Reflecting on our neighbor-to-neighbor movement, the word "re-villaging" takes on an even deeper meaning.

Sixty years ago, Marshall McLuhan coined the term *"Global Village"* to describe a world interconnected by technology. That vision has partially come true—through instant communication and information-sharing—but something essential was lost. Yes, the internet connected us horizontally. But vertically, we became subject to top-down narratives and atomized into siloed consumers.

> *Without the sacred at the center, this global system*
> *became just a marketplace, not a village.*

BIRTHING THE SYMBIOTIC AGE

McLuhan saw it coming: the loss of rootedness, the erasure of individuality, and the rise of homogenized mass culture. We may be wired in, but we are no longer woven in. Re-villaging brings the old village to the new. It's not about being online—it's about being alive to each other, face-to-face, heart-to-heart.

The only authentic global village is composed of vibrant local ones, and it begins with each of us. Start where you are. Have a conversation. Discover a shared purpose. Recognize a common need. Act with intentional mutual benefit. Small acts can ignite massive movements.

Imagine your neighborhood as a hub of care. Envision the hidden gifts, relationships, and wisdom already present. Now, picture this unfolding in thousands of other communities—not through central planning, but through fractal community empowerment, spreading like mycelium: quietly, everywhere.

That's what Sarvodaya achieved in Sri Lanka. Villagers didn't wait for anyone outside; they acted locally, trusting that others were doing the same.

> *As one village built a Symbiotic Network,*
> *they knew it was also happening in thousands of others.*
> *That's how random acts of kindness evolve into*
> *a Kingdom of Kindness.*

It happened in Reno as well. When I started organizing my street, I wasn't just one person with a good idea—I was part of something larger. Over 65 neighborhoods were engaged in similar efforts. That's the essence of Symbiotic Culture DNA—it spreads organically and simultaneously, everywhere.

This is re-villaging: re-establishing a sacred center, just as the early Christians did, just as Gandhi envisioned, just as Dr. Ari brought to life in Sri Lanka, even among "the least of us."

And it begins on the street where you live. All we needed was heart, presence, and practice.

"What does the Lord require of you but to act justly, to love mercy, and to walk humbly with your God?" *(Micah 6:8)*

THE ANCIENT BLUEPRINT, ALIVE ON YOUR STREET

That simple instruction became our posture—a way of life that grounded even the smallest actions in something sacred. This is how we built a living network: a connective organism, not a competing institution. The sacred center of that organism was the Ancient Blueprint—love thy neighbor, charity begins at home, serve without a self-serving agenda, and build instead of battle.

We lived a new form of "global re-villaging." We saw its power. Then came the question:

Could this ripple become a wave? Could bioregional communities worldwide serve as living nodes in a larger movement, each cultivating Symbiotic Networks from the ground up?

Could we help other cities, towns, and neighborhoods "Connect the Good" already present in their backyards? Could we break the trance of separation and revive the village Virtues—generosity, trust, and mutual care—in a world ruled by materialism and mistrust?

CHAPTER 21

SEEKING THE HOLY GRAIL OF COMMUNITY: RECOVERING THE INNER GROUND

Behind every visible transformation lies an invisible awakening. While our networks addressed food, the economy, and neighborhood connection, another hunger stirred beneath the surface—a longing for action and meaning. We weren't merely seeking better strategies for change; we were seeking the soul of community itself.

Looking back, it's clear we accomplished something remarkable in Northern Nevada. Amid the daily organizing work, we built something rare: the scaffolding for a new kind of community—a living Network Commons and a culture. Instead of launching yet another organization, we cultivated a shared infrastructure of Symbiotic Kinship—designed to manifest connection in the real world.

BUILDING A SYMBIOTIC SCAFFOLD

We built a network of trusted networks that strengthened collaboration, coordination, and communication across diverse efforts, all working to benefit each and all:

- The Local Living Economy Network boosted local economic independence and resilience.
- The Local Food System Network connected growers, vendors, retailers, and consumers into a living food ecosystem that nourished Northern Nevada.
- To bridge separation and polarization, we united around universal Virtues and applied them through the Neighbor-to-Neighbor Network and campaign.

The Conscious Community Network emerged as the context and convener for all these efforts. No one "voted" on any of this—it developed through participation. We were a self-organizing organism that grew naturally because we fit the landscape and fulfilled a genuine need. We had touched a vital nerve—a missing piece in community life that few had seen.

We had helped to birth a shared sense of co-creative coherence, and by every measure, we had succeeded.

Now, those of us at the heart of the Conscious Community wanted to delve deeper—to ensure that the transformation we ignited in Washoe County could ripple outward. I was seeking the Holy Grail—the "secret sauce" that would activate Symbiotic Culture and transform the Culture of Separation into a Culture of Connection.

BIRTHING THE SYMBIOTIC AGE

DISTRIBUTING THE LOVE: SPIRIT IN ACTION

Even though we didn't yet have the language—Ancient Blueprint, Culture of Connection, Symbiotic Culture DNA, Fractal Community Empowerment—we knew that connecting the Transcendent power of the Virtues to everyday life was essential. Distributing this Love, this Goodness, through network-centric infrastructure was the key to everything we built.

We had already created four successful networks that improved life in Washoe County—and we freely shared what we learned. Our Conscious Community Network, later called the Conscious Community Campaign, published a simple flyer to distill our mission:

"Creating a better world, starting with ourselves, then connecting with others, and local organizations to build a self-reliant community through action based on shared Virtues and common needs."

Plain yet profound, this vision was broad enough to unite grassroots leaders, civic and religious organizations, local businesses, and even government departments. It offered a common language of purpose—a fluency that transcends ideological silos. (we'll revisit this in the final "Activation" section).

We launched two other pivotal projects to deepen this work and spread it regionally and beyond.

First, we created Connections Gatherings—a "spiritual support system" where people could practice the Virtues together and cultivate the inner resources needed to grow community networks. Inspired by Sarvodaya's Buddhist foundations and my journey with Jesus and the Ancient Blueprint, we recognized the need for a shared honoring of the Transcendent. We even borrowed from Dr. Ari's model, where what started in one village grew to a network of 5,000 Sarvodaya Societies.

We hoped to plant similar "seeds" across our region—micro-networks rooted in the twelve community needs we had identified. Our daily-use Virtue Cards served as both a tool and a reminder: transformation begins within.

Virtue Cards served as daily tools and reminders, anchoring inner alignment as the foundation for outward community transformation.

We prioritized Connections Gatherings because we recognized that inner alignment was the missing link in helping people heal, grow, and become more congruent and effective in their outward actions. We knew that "everything begins at home," and to truly radiate Symbiotic Kinship, we had to recover our connection to the Transcendent as the starting point.

Second, we recognized that culture isn't only about economics, food, or neighborliness, it's also about beauty, place, creativity, and joy.

So, we launched the Conscious Community Celebration, a public festival designed to awaken our emerging Culture of Connection through the arts, music, nature, and community expression. We'll explore its impact soon, but these two projects—one focused inward, the other outward—became the next evolution of Symbiotic Culture. From healing circles to city-wide celebrations, they embodied the invisible thread: spirit at the center of systems.

THE LONGING FOR HOME: FROM SPIRITUAL EXILE TO COMMUNION

We didn't think of our group as a recovery circle at the time, but now I see the word fits. Many of us were unknowingly recovering from the Culture of Separation, with its disconnection from the Transcendent, nature, each other, and ourselves. This recovery began by rekindling our deeper connection, which we saw as inseparable from the healing of culture.

At our 2006 gathering, we asked, "What can unite our divided community?" Beneath the surface, I sensed a spiritual malaise many could feel but few could articulate. In a world where consumerism had supplanted meaning, people often internalized their alienation, believing something was wrong with them for not fitting into a system that worshipped profit over purpose.

As I mentioned earlier, I had experienced this dislocation since childhood. My awakening at twelve made me feel like a stranger in a foreign land. At least I knew I was a refugee, and I wasn't alone.

Many of us in the Conscious Community Network were what I now call spiritual refugees. Some were active in churches, synagogues, or mosques, while others had stepped away from organized religion but still longed for its essence: reconnection with the web of life and love.

Our Connections Gatherings were never a replacement for faith traditions. They were complementary—open spaces for anyone, religious or not, to practice Virtue, deepen spiritual formation, and connect across differences. They were more of a "spiritual supplement," a practice group, spirituality grounded in shared Virtues.

> *That's why I've called this a search for the Holy Grail: a quest to integrate personal formation with public service—to reweave the sacred into everyday life.*

People were not only turning away from materialism—they were seeking, as the 12-step tradition says, "a new way of living" that could reconnect them to God, one another, and the Earth. Looking back nearly two decades later, I believe we were ahead of the curve. Today, across the spectrum, we hear the same cry: "The system is broken." Despair deepens. Belonging feels out of reach. And, as more are coming to see, gathering only with the like-minded in ideological or religious silos cannot heal this dislocation.

Despite the brokenness and separation, signs of renewal abound—regenerative economies, bridge-building, mutual aid, back-to-the-land movements, bioregionalism, Cosmolocalism, and renewed focus on faith, (especially Christianity), family, and wellness. These are indicators of spiritual intelligence on the rise.

Still, no single camp holds the answer. Like nature, healing must be all-embracing, integrative, and relational. Denying the existence of others—or their truth—is anti-reality, and reality always wins.

That's why we welcomed everyone into our Local Food System Network—from conventional farmers to regenerative pioneers. As I mentioned earlier, this broad-based approach led one of our region's most traditional growers to shift his entire operation to regenerative practices. Why? Because we created a common cause around a shared purpose: a healthy food system for Northern Nevada. This shared vision transcended ideology and softened entrenched divisions.

This is part of the "secret sauce": bringing together like-hearted people, even if they're not like-minded, where heart connection can bridge the divided minds.

Our Connections Gatherings cultivated the heart, accessed the Transcendent, and grounded it in practice. These groups became spiritual laboratories—sacred spaces where Divine Love could take root and radiate through the community. We must have intuited that more fragmentation was coming. Through our networks and circles of trust, we discovered a deeper truth:

The heart of the matter was the matter of the heart.

THE CONNECTIONS GATHERINGS: BECOMING SACRED SPACE-HOLDERS

Beneath the visible networks we used to Connect the Good in Northern Nevada was an invisible thread: a connection to the Transcendent, and each other. The Connections Gatherings emerged to deepen that connection and spark a broader spiritual awakening. We had already named the purpose, principles, and Virtues that unified us. Now we set out to embody them.

> *Our gatherings were designed to connect hearts, build bridges across efforts, and raise collective consciousness so that our small experiment might scale into a way of life.*

We called ourselves "community weavers" because we were weaving something new: a functional social fabric composed of previously disconnected "threads." We aimed to move beyond ego-driven life and build a society grounded in universal Virtues and self-giving love, in the spirit of St. Maximus, to "bring together that which has become separate."

We used the metaphor of a community "Ark" to describe the new infrastructure needed to support a Culture of Connection. This is from the Community Weaver's Guide:

> "Weavers heal themselves and others by wiring the community together—through Conscious Love and Service—heart to heart and group to group.
>
> Rooted in shared needs like food, health, spirit, and justice, they identify unconnected people and efforts and help weave them into something whole.
>
> Small groups offer a glimpse of the community we long for—not some future utopia, but something we can begin living now.
>
> Radiating love and service, we are needed more than ever—to strengthen families, reach into neighborhoods and workplaces, and support the good already happening, transforming it into a force for lasting change."

In June 2006—just four months after launching our Virtues and Needs campaign—we held our prototype meeting. These small gatherings began in people's homes and became the foundation for a region-wide "intentional community without walls," cultivating internal awareness and outward connection.

Since most of us had never led a group like this, we used that first gathering to tap into our co-intelligence and co-design the format.

Our goal was simple: reflect on living the Virtues and connect around shared needs and projects, so that new networks might emerge from these circles.

We developed some core practices to guide our time together:

Meeting Guidelines:
- Speak simply and directly from the heart. Keep comments brief. No "crosstalk."
- This is not group therapy. We hold space by listening deeply, not fixing.
- What's shared here stays here. Confidentiality is essential.
- Avoid polarizing topics (politics, theology, business promotion). We focus on lived Virtue.
- Highlight unity over division. Speak from the heart and emphasize shared ground.
- Everyone is encouraged to speak once before anyone speaks again.
- Respect all viewpoints. No interrupting.
- In the Chrysalis section, share stories about how you practiced the Virtue of the month.
- In the Nexus section, briefly name your current project or need. If not project-based, share a personal need or request clearly.

We met monthly, usually with no more than twenty people. The format was intimate by design, allowing for connection and replication. Before the meeting began, we shared a potluck meal—breaking bread together as we had done in the "Convivencias" in San Diego's Hispanic neighborhoods.

We always began with a circle, and someone volunteered a short prayer or reflection to center us on the group's purpose.

After dinner, we reconvened in a circle for "check-in"—sharing our joys and challenges since the last gathering. Participation was voluntary. Our "no discussion" rule allowed each voice to be heard without interruption, helping the process remain focused and spacious. Afterward, natural connections emerged, and mutual support often continued informally.

But inner reflection alone wasn't the destination—we needed to practice these Virtues together, in real time.

THE CHRYSALIS: PRACTICING THE VIRTUES TOGETHER

After the opening circle, we broke into small groups for the Chrysalis portion of the meeting, typically consisting of four or five people. Each group convened in a separate room with a facilitator, engaging in a 45-minute process centered on one Virtue, such as integrity, forgiveness, or generosity. Participants shared personal stories about how they practiced (or struggled to practice) that Virtue over the past month.

For example, when focusing on integrity, individuals may reflect on how they present themselves differently with family, at work, or in public, and whether they are consistent across these spaces. Socrates said, "Know thyself." These circles helped us do just that.

As with the larger circle, we practiced "no crosstalk." There were no interruptions, advice-giving, or fixes—just deep listening. Participants could speak into a safe, receptive silence and hear themselves more clearly.

> *We learned that sometimes, being heard is more healing than being helped. This "listen-only" approach grounded us in the heart, not the head.*

While it may sound like any other self-help group, it was more like a "beyond-the-self" group. One of the biggest challenges in cultivating a Symbiotic Culture is bridging the gap between head and heart. It matters deeply whether we speak from the intellect or our deeper presence and whether we can hold that presence in relationship with others.

Western culture tends to prioritize the rational over the intuitive. We often talk about emotions rather than feel them. It's easier to analyze an experience than to sit with its discomfort or ambiguity. I speak from experience—even now, as I write this—I know how easy it is to get stuck in my head.

Facilitators in the Chrysalis groups were trained to help us move from Head to Heart. Most of us are more comfortable talking about our feelings than experiencing them. Through my spiritual journey and years of participating in these gatherings, I've learned that "going deeper" means integrating our thoughts, emotions, and concepts into an embodied, felt experience.

There's a world of difference between reading about the Transcendent and encountering it yourself. These circles gave us a place to practice that difference and bring the Divine down to Earth.

HEAD, HEART, AND HANDS: EMBODYING THE ANCIENT BLUEPRINT

Practicing Symbiotic Culture in the world begins with the desire to "Know Thyself."

It helps to belong to a spiritual community—or at least to walk a path of self-reflection. Throughout this book, I've described how universal Virtues serve as a human interface between Heaven and Earth—not just metaphors, but objective Transcendent Energies.

This is where the rubber meets the road. What matters most isn't lofty thoughts or beautiful words, but whether we embody these Virtues in our daily lives.

That isn't easy, especially within the Culture of Separation. It never has been.

Consider the apostle Paul's message to the early Christian community in Corinth, written around 50 AD. They were plagued by division, conflict, and inequality. Sound familiar? Paul reminded them that the love Jesus taught wasn't sentimentality or rule-following—it was rooted in the structure of reality, the Ancient Blueprint I've described:

> "Love is patient and kind; love does not envy or boast; it is not arrogant or rude. It does not insist on its way; it is not irritable or resentful; it does not rejoice in wrongdoing but rejoices with the truth. Love bears all things, believes all things, hopes all things, endures all things."
> — 1 Corinthians 13:4–7

We longed to deepen our spiritual fluency—not just for ourselves, but to become unifiers in the community, instead of dividers.

That's why we designed the final part of each Connections Gathering—the Nexus—to complete the journey from Head to Heart to Hands. Loving thoughts mean little if they don't result in loving action. After our breakout groups, we re-gathered to support each other's projects and needs. This was the moment when synchronicity often sparked unexpected change. Someone might have 5,000 books to donate—and a librarian would say, "We'll take them." A shelter worker might meet a permaculturist, and a rooftop garden would be born.

BIRTHING THE SYMBIOTIC AGE

Not every need was met, and that wasn't the point. The gatherings were designed to cultivate an inner life that naturally ripples outward. We closed with a simple circle, where each person shared a word to capture their feelings. Ultimately, our purpose was clear: to integrate personal and community awakening. We had to be the change we hoped to see. And the best way to teach a new culture is to live it.

We worked from the inside out, clearing hidden blocks—old beliefs, trauma, and over-identified roles—while building trust. These weren't therapy groups, but long-held pain could gently surface in the sacred space of presence. Over time, we realized that integrating Head, Heart, and Hands represented the life we were trying to build. While the Culture of Separation treats hypocrisy as human nature, the Culture of Connection invites us into embodied coherence, from person to planet.

It means taking your highest thoughts, grounding them in your heart, and letting them move through your hands. In other words: live your truth, act in love, and build what you believe.

> *Show us who you are—not just by what you say,*
> *but by the life you choose,*
> *how you relate to others,*
> *and the culture you help create.*

We shared our practices with the broader community to spread that way of life. One handout became a favorite: the L.O.V.E. flyer—Living Our Virtues Every Day.

Over time, we also understood what Martin Buber meant by *I and Thou*—that meeting another with full presence is an encounter with the Divine. Buber, a 20th-century Jewish philosopher and theologian, emphasized that genuine relationships open a sacred space where God becomes present. As I've shared elsewhere, this reflects the Luminous Web. For Buber, when we meet someone as a *Thou*, we indirectly meet God. The other person is not God, but a fractal of God, just as we are.

Through our Connections Gatherings, we extended this awareness to the entire community. It wasn't just personal growth—it marked the beginning of a Culture of Symbiotic Kinship, where we reconnect with ourselves, each other, and all living systems.

SELF-AWARENESS BEGINS AT HOME

There's a joke about the ultimate recovery group called "Children of Parents." Most of us consider our upbringing "normal" until we compare it to others and begin to notice the missing pieces.

My mom was highly critical throughout my life. Only later did I understand she was frustrated with the life she hadn't pursued, and my dad, often absent due to work, left her to carry that burden alone. Her criticism continued into adulthood, like the time I showed her a logo I'd designed, and she dismissed it with, "I don't like it." It seemed trivial, but it was typical. Our phone calls during my years raising my son, Isaac, often included unsolicited critiques of my parenting. She felt entitled to offer opinions I hadn't asked for.

Interestingly, the Connections Gatherings brought this to light. During one discussion on the Virtues, someone asked, *"Is there a particular Virtue you can focus on to work with your overly critical mother?"*

What arose for me was forgiveness. Thanks to her, I had regular opportunities to practice! When I visited my parents, I turned each encounter into a moment of spiritual practice. Relying on my relationship with Jesus Christ, I asked for help to forgive.

When my mother criticized me, I'd hug her and tell her I loved her. Over time, it wasn't just a strategy—it changed me. Conscious Loving became less about emotion and more about commitment. I also set firm but loving boundaries. Calmly, I told her, *"Mother, I didn't ask for your opinion about Isaac's behavior. It's getting in the way of our relationship, which is precious to me."* I had to restate that a few times, but eventually, she stopped. And our relationship transformed.

Without the Connections Gatherings—the support, spiritual accountability, and regular practice—I don't believe that lifelong pattern would have shifted. But over time, I could see that the love I offered helped her begin to release her regrets and resentments. As her life drew to a close in 2019, she often asked me a heartbreaking question, *"Why am I still alive?"*

I gently told her, *"Maybe there's something still to learn."* As I watched her let go of fear and judgment, I saw that forgiveness was her final lesson.

Shortly before she passed at age 96, I spent two weeks with her. On my last day, I held her hands and said, *"I love you. I've had a wonderful time."* She replied, "But I have been an ogre."

I lovingly told her, *"You are such a pleasant person, and I am so happy you are my mother."*

We looked into each other's eyes, and our love was evident. Our hearts opened. Our healing was complete. She had found her peace. And I had found mine.

How I remember my mother when I was in high school.

After she passed, I shared the story on Facebook:

> "I wanted to share some things I've learned, even with a challenging, difficult relationship and the potential for redemption and healing. Please consider this story a call to action toward your loved ones with whom you might still have unresolved, unhealed places in your heart. You don't have to wait for them to take the first step. Do this, not just for them, but for yourself. I love you all in peace and joy."

Undoubtedly, I—and many others—have significantly benefited from our Connections Gatherings. At one point, several groups were running simultaneously, each a sub-community built on shared practices and trust. We imagined these gatherings as "seeds" of Symbiotic Culture sprouting across the region. I even created a 260-page training manual to help spread the format. Although those seeds didn't grow as we'd hoped, the experience taught us how to transmit Symbiotic Culture DNA more effectively.

CELEBRATING THE GOOD: A CULTURAL FLOWERING

Looking back, it's clear we accomplished something remarkable in Northern Nevada. Amid the daily organizing work, we built something rare: the scaffolding for a new kind of community—a living Network Commons and a culture. More than merely launching another organization, we cultivated a shared infrastructure of Symbiotic Kinship—designed to manifest connection in the real world.

We had touched the Transcendent in a sacred circle and found healing in our inner lives. However, healing wasn't enough. We needed joy, beauty, and celebration to bring Symbiotic Culture fully to life. Connection on a cultural scale couldn't be built on ideas alone—it had to be felt, shared, and embodied.

A new impulse arose from the fertile ground of our inner work: not a meeting, not a strategy session, but a celebration. A living expression of the world we were beginning to build together. It was time to bring the Heart and Art of Community into the open. It was time to celebrate the Good. This celebration wasn't just symbolic. It marked the next evolution of our collective life together.

CHAPTER 22

THE ART OF COMMUNITY: FESTIVALS, CULTURE, AND THE COLLECTIVE FIELD

Another outgrowth of the Valentine's Day meeting was the Conscious Community Celebration—a region-wide festival honoring the goodness and good works that had emerged over the past three years. It showcased the arts and organizations that promote the local economy, food, sustainability, civic engagement, and sense of place.

From the beginning, the arts were integral to everything we did—a space where I felt especially at home. Spontaneous poetry first gave me the "Voice of the Heart of Love" to express my Transcendent experiences, opening a gateway to later community work.

> *Our network core group understood the power of the arts—poetry, music, dance, visual arts, spoken word—to nourish all layers of the human spirit.*

We understood that we were transforming culture, so we aimed to embody a Culture of Connection at every meeting, gathering, or event. There was an "art" to it all, including how we choreographed experiences that infused Symbiotic Culture into the community.

Alongside our Connections Gatherings and larger events like the Valentine's Day meeting, we hosted monthly Conscious Community Network Breakfasts to maintain momentum on Buy Local and Local Food efforts. Later, we organized Connecting the Good Lunches with leaders who supported the "least of us."

We held themed gatherings such as the Valentine's Dinner and Dance, community Contra Dances, and annual Christmas Caroling. One year, 200 carolers serenaded skaters at the local ice rink and then fanned out in groups to surrounding neighborhoods.

Unlike the meetings people dread as draining or dull, ours were energizing because we choreographed them to engage the Head, Heart, and Hands.

MORE THAN MUSIC: CHOREOGRAPHING COLLECTIVE JOY

A typical meeting—whether public or with key leaders—begins with a moment of silence. Rather than offering a specific prayer, the silence creates space for all perceptions of the Transcendent, anchoring us in shared presence and purpose. We then affirm our guiding principles and Virtues, spreading Symbiotic Culture DNA.

A facilitator might follow with a poem or inspirational reading. Community members often submitted or shared these, emphasizing commonality and individual expression. Music was woven throughout, sometimes paired with the reading and other times interspersed. Our colleague Jim Eaglesmith was a master "choreographer," seamlessly blending music and spoken word into every gathering.

Instead of relying on sermons or lectures that separate "experts" from the audience, our events resembled artistic "happenings" from the '60s and '70s, where spontaneous and creative expression blurred all boundaries. Occasionally, we invited participants to perform skits or read scripted reflections. More on that shortly.

Breakout groups helped ensure everyone, even introverts, could be heard and feel part of the circle. The surrounding "field" was always welcoming; background music, food, movement, and lighthearted games added a sense of conviviality, reminiscent of the Convivencias in San Diego.

> *To us, the arts were a gateway to belonging.*
> *These expressions left people joyful, hopeful,*
> *and eager to return.*

Most importantly, they gave participants an authentic taste of what a Symbiotic Culture could feel like. After launching networks in food, economy, and neighborhoods—and internalizing those values in our Connections Gatherings—we recognized that the next step in cultivating our Culture of Connection was clear: it was time for a festival.

THE CONSCIOUS COMMUNITY CELEBRATION AND FESTIVAL

Anyone who has created a festival knows how much work is involved. But, like so many of our Symbiotic Networks in Reno, we found ourselves in the flow—everything we needed showed up. Using our networks and Connections Gatherings as a foundation, we organized the first Conscious Community Celebration at Bartley Ranch, a Washoe County park.

The theme was: *"It's Time!—to Celebrate the Good."* Our poster read:

> "America is awakening—one community at a time. Join us where we can make the most difference—right here in Northern Nevada. It's time to walk our talk!
>
> We have joined forces to Live Our Virtues Every Day (Love, Integrity, Courage, Service, and Respect), connecting like-hearted people in practical ways to build a sustainable community and world, and uplifting humanity in these difficult times."

Looking back now, I realize that many might view those words as quaint or naïve in a post-COVID, conflict-ridden world—but I see them differently.

> *Virtues are not optional; they are foundational. They always have been—and I believe they always will be—the fruit of spiritual life and our collective survival.*

The Bartley Ranch amphitheater accommodated 400 people, and our lineup featured everything from bluegrass and youth opera to an arts, culture, and sustainability fair. Local artists, nonprofits, businesses, and food organizations set up booths, including a mini farmer's market. Children's and family activities transformed it into a true community event, celebrating "manifesting the good" we'd cultivated for years.

Richard Flyer and Isha Echols at the Conscious Community Celebration.

Richard Flyer, along with people like activist Isha Echols, are trying to create a more connected, "conscious" community.
PHOTO BY DAVID ROBERT

Thanks to sponsorships and free media—radio, TV, print, and digital—we drew 800 people the first year and 1,600 the next. A quote I gave to the *Reno Gazette-Journal* captured the heart of it:

> "If we want peace on this planet, we must have peace in our nation. To have peace in our nation, we need peace in our communities. To have peace in our communities, we need peace in the blocks of our neighborhoods. To have peace in our neighborhoods, we need peace in our families. To have peace in our families, we need peace in our hearts. That's the foundation...And politicians can't legislate that."

Newspaper coverage was advantageous, but the words above don't fully express what our festival felt like or how those who participated were transformed and literally experienced that peace in their hearts.

As mentioned earlier, singer-songwriter Jim Eaglesmith was one of our movement's key weavers. He wrote our theme song, *"The Power of Goodwill,"* and a spoken-word rap poem, *"Compassion In Raption,"* which became a beloved tradition at our events. Without preparation, Jim would invite four audience members to recite a stanza "freestyle," often with rap inflection and expressive gestures. The whole audience joined in for the chorus: "Ride the wave!"

Some activities at the Conscious Community Celebration

COMPASSION IN RAPTION: TO BE READ AS STANZAS BY PEOPLE FROM THE AUDIENCE.

Intentional acts of kindness with 'color blindness'
Always remind us that 'we have overcome.'
With good deeds done, that's where I'm comin' from.

We need an emergence, a real convergence…
Without vanity so my insanity can come to 'rest in peace'…
at least
Learn from each other…then call me your brother.

Reach out, never doubt.. share in the joy of kindness…
see through the blindness with radical open mindness.
It's never too late for 'Intentional acts of kindness.'

Don't fight a blue world.. help Make a new world..
True morality.. ain't our reality..
So trade in your charity...for Love & Unity...
At this Intentional Community!

Stand against ignorance and hate.
it's never too late...to change fate.
An act of contrition...the human condition...by my humble admission...
My Mission is forgiveness.

Do me a favor...love your neighbor...the flavor is sweet...so
Turn up the heat...and meet me at the graveyard of fear.
Water the seeds of good deeds...take heed...
the 'fruit of love' is the only Power...in the final hour...
when you are called to task for your past.
Serve the first and last Generations of young & old, so I'm told—be bold.

The Elders speak their truth...Our youth need Sharity, not empty charity...or popularity.
So Get off the fence...common sense...make a difference.
I'll take you're two cents and invest it with tact.

Now give something back and Do a Kind Act!

My sisters and brothers...let's discover one another 'Connecting the Good"...
It should...come from the heart...like "Head Start"...
Let's re start...and "Beautify the Heart of Humanity"

> What if we could...gather all the good...with a team of Goodwill
> And Instill the thrill of "connecting the dots."
> It won't take a lot for a chain reaction...of kindness in action...
> Hand in hand let's take a stand today...At the end of the day...
>
> Ride the Wave!

It was electric, participatory art that embodied our message of kindness, connection, and creative joy.

Looking back, I now understand the festival's power more clearly—it brought Symbiotic Culture to life. But at the time, I saw it primarily as a recruitment tool for our Connections Gatherings. Despite our success and growing attendance, I hesitated when the third year approached. I had become so focused on transformation through small groups that I discounted the impact of public celebration.

That well-intentioned but narrow mindset set the stage for the lessons to come.

MISSING THE FESTIVAL FOR THE TREES

Even though we grew from 800 attendees the first year to 1,600 the next, and expected 3,000, very few participants signed up for our Connections Gatherings. I was so committed—some might say *attached*—to our small group process as the key to scaling our movement that I discounted the festival's broader value. My focus narrowed. I was frustrated that so many came, enjoyed the celebration, and went home.

Didn't anyone want to go deeper?

Eventually, I convinced myself and others to cancel the third year. I now see how I fell into the very siloed thinking I've critiqued in this book. Instead of seeing the festival as a powerful, accessible pathway for spreading goodness across Northern Nevada, I took the feedback personally and dismissed its potential.

Had we continued, it might have grown to rival Reno's Earth Day, which draws 10,000 people—but ours had no alcohol, no commercialization, and stayed true to its purpose. We had already shown that a joyful, conscious celebration was possible. In hindsight, we cut short a blossoming endeavor. My ego had narrowed my view, fixating on the Gatherings as the "Holy Grail" for bringing Symbiotic Culture to life. I missed how the festival was a vital expression of that culture, another way to spread Symbiotic DNA.

I share this not to beat myself up, but to highlight how easy it is to become attached to a single model and miss what life reveals.

If this reflection helps someone else avoid that trap, it's worth sharing.

Looking back, I can now see how the celebration could have evolved into a thriving arts and culture network. This wasn't just a missed opportunity for us—it was a lost gift to the broader ecosystem. When I later spoke to Reno's Arts Commissioner, she described the difficulty of coordinating 50 separate arts groups. But we had already done that, and could have done it even better. By letting the festival go, we lost a joyful, unifying event and denied the broader community a powerful space to celebrate all we had created.

THE ART OF COMMUNITY AS A WORK OF HEART

Even though I am reflecting on the past, for those considering doing events like this in their community, I believe they would still be an integral part of building a Symbiotic Culture and Network Commons. I want to reiterate that the power of the arts is much bigger than any festival or event. In every aspect of our Conscious Community Network, "art" was a way of life and a gateway to the non-linear, intuitive approach that, in my view, helped us break through the Culture of Separation.

As I've suggested, events were just one expression. At its core, this movement was always about something more profound: the artistry of community itself. Unless we're talking about "paint by the numbers," art is intuitive...surprising...novel...unpredictable...alive.

When a community is seen as an "artistic creation," being and doing are intertwined in an ongoing journey, from inspiration to discovery to action, and we intuitively glean what is next.

Conscious community is never "complete"; it is a never-ending Virtuous circle.

Even though my background is in science, I followed the "artist's way." While there is a reproducible fractal "science" to nurturing Symbiotic Networks that we applied in our systematic approach—the Symbiotic Culture DNA we discussed in Chapter 18—the real "juice" comes from the graceful, creative, and relational process that connects individuals and their existing groups and networks.

And...that process is pure art.

SOCIAL ARTISTRY: CHOREOGRAPHING COMMUNITY AS CANVAS

There's an art to communicating purpose, inviting participation, and holding sacred space—especially when people shaped by the

Culture of Separation encounter new possibilities. Cultivating trust and navigating "the human stuff" requires more than skill; it requires heart.

My wife Marta, a painter, once described my work as "social artistry," with the community as my canvas. I've often thought of it as choreography—managing the dance of healthy interaction. Unlike a conductor standing at the front, a choreographer works behind the scenes, designing graceful movement that brings people together in flow.

Though I became a visible face of the Conscious Community Network, none of it would have happened had I acted alone. When someone once asked, "How did you accomplish so much so fast?" my answer was simple: "Because I didn't do it. I convened the field, and people naturally knew what to do." That's the quiet art of community.

I remember once asking Dr. Ari how he inspired such a vast impact in Sri Lanka. He smiled but said nothing, and in that silence, I understood. He created space by stepping aside, allowing others to enter their power. The more he let go, the more he became filled with loving, creative presence. Then that Transcendent power radiated outward.

That, too, is an art.

This "community artist's way" contrasts sharply with the Culture of Separation, which exalts hierarchy, titles, and control. The artist's path isn't about power over others it's about power with others.

When mutual benefit—dare I say Love—is your only agenda, people feel it. That's why Sarvodaya spread like wildfire. And that's why Symbiotic Culture will, too.

If linking art and spiritual power seems unusual, it's only because we've forgotten how deeply connected they are. Dr. Ari's integration of Transcendent Virtues with practical service was a masterpiece—or rather, a *master peace*. If art brings beauty, order, and inspiration, why not consider Gandhi's movement a form of social artistry?

And as for Jesus, I'm reminded of these words from Van Gogh:

> "Christ alone...lived serenely as an artist greater than all other artists, scorning marble and clay and paint, working in the living flesh...he made...living men, immortals."

A SYMPHONY OF INCLUSION: BEYOND LABELS, TOWARD LOVE

As I've shared throughout this book, the lineage of the Ancient Blueprint runs through Jesus, Gandhi, and Dr. Ari. They modeled the path of Love and community, and I did my best to follow that lineage. Though I never used the term at the time, I now recognize my role as a sacred "space-holder," helping others rise above the divisions of belief, identity, and self-interest.

In a world that often turns political, religious, and social labels into "idols," we created a space that gently loosened their grip—gathering not around identity or ideology, but around shared purpose and Love. I never promoted a personal brand, philosophy, or business—only the shared purpose of building a beloved community.

We led with creativity and joy, which drew people in. Within the sacred space, we nurtured individuals from every background—race, class, religion, and belief—who felt safe, seen, and united in purpose.

The divisions of the outside world disappeared. There was no black or white skin, political affiliation, identity, or religious label inside our networks—only a shared sense of connection and kinship.

St. Paul's vision of radical unity was not a generic "oneness," but a transformative communion grounded in Jesus Christ:

> "There is neither Jew nor Gentile, neither slave nor free, nor is there male and female, for you are all one in Christ Jesus." —Galatians 3:28

This isn't about erasing identities but embracing and transcending them through a higher-order, universal identity. It's how we create the real-world space to become UNITERS, not inadvertent DIVIDERS.

The phrase that blends love and artistry for me is "work of heart."

I believe each person carries within them a "work of heart"—a unique gift meant for the world. Too often, it goes unexpressed because the Culture of Separation puts a price tag on everything, reducing human value to economic worth. When discussing Symbiotic Networks liberating "frozen assets," we don't just mean material or financial ones—we mean human potential.

People thrive in fields of intentional mutual benefit. In practicing the art of community convening, I now see another calling: to inspire each of us to make our lives a work of Heart.

Imagine a community of purpose-driven people on a shared adventure—bringing their gifts into a Symbiotic Network that unites the Cosmos in Love and restores what has been torn apart. That would truly be a new way of living.

LESSONS FROM THE GATHERINGS: INVISIBLE FORCES THAT PULL US INTO SILOS

The Connections Gatherings offered a wonderful gift to those involved—a refuge for the "spiritual refugees" I referred to earlier. While Sri Lanka had a culturally embedded spiritual foundation, the West lacked a shared framework. Still, we all longed to amplify the good. Our 2006 Valentine's Day event planted the seed for our neighbor-to-neighbor campaign and the Gatherings.

Over time, the Gatherings became our primary focus. We stopped hosting the festival because it didn't contribute to the deeper work as I perceived it. However, as our energy turned inward, the momentum for building tangible Symbiotic Networks began to wane. In retrospect, initiatives such as Local Food, Buy Local, Neighbors, and Arts contributed more to fostering a Culture of Connection than discussing it in small groups.

Still, the Gatherings held immense value. They helped us build inner foundations—a space to practice Virtues, deepen our connection with the Divine (however named), and explore new ways of living. However, while the "hands" of service were initially active, they didn't continue to form new networks. Why?

Looking back, two blind spots limited us. First, we underestimated how deeply the Culture of Separation had exiled the sacred from civic life. Second, we hadn't yet recognized the Ancient Blueprint—especially Jesus' "Love God and Love Others"—as a functional design pattern for community life. We felt its power but hadn't acted on it fully yet.

Many participants found what they needed: spiritual fellowship, mutual support, and personal growth. I had hoped this would evolve into a broader regional web of Symbiotic Networks.

However, that leap didn't occur. In truth, the greatest gift of the Gatherings may not have been the networks they formed, but the lessons they unveiled.

Even with the best intentions, we encountered invisible forces that shaped how our efforts played out:

1. Bandwidth Limitations:
Running multiple campaigns—Local Living Economy, Food System, Neighbor Networks—alongside the Festival stretched us thin. We didn't have the capacity also to grow the Gatherings at the same time into full-fledged networks.

2. Shift Toward Individual Projects:
With limited bandwidth, the Gatherings began to support siloed personal efforts, like a rooftop garden at a homeless shelter. These were good, but they didn't advance our goal of connectivity across the system.

3. Our Gathering Became a Silo:
Ironically, a network designed to connect silos became one. We attracted like-minded people, but didn't build shared networks beyond our circle. As in many movements, we risked creating a "silo of silos"—groups aligned by interest but disconnected from each other.

4. Triggering the Immune System:
Though we aimed to complement other groups, some perceived us as competitors. A Florida organizer once told me, "I'm not sure how this differs from the spiritual groups I already attend." That stung—but it helped me see the challenge more clearly.

BIRTHING THE SYMBIOTIC AGE

FROM RIVALRY TO COMMUNITAS

Even as our gatherings grew, we noticed something more profound: cultural resistance.

One community leader once said, "Richard, it seems like you're building your own empire." I wasn't. However, in a society dominated by competition, even collaborative visibility is often misinterpreted as ego or self-promotion. I understood. In a system where nonprofits and small organizations vie for attention and funding, it's difficult not to assume every initiative has an agenda.

Still, that moment revealed how deeply the Culture of Separation distorts even the most collaborative efforts. Despite this resistance, we saw glimpses of what was possible when trust overcame fear, and mutual benefit replaced competition.

Where the Culture of Separation fosters rivalry, Symbiotic Networks build companionship. In our local food network, restaurant owners stopped competing and started collaborating. They shared resources, trust grew, and the "bigger pie" metaphor became real.

Out of this shift, something even more profound began to take shape—a quality of connection that transcended transactions and roles. More importantly, something deeper emerged: "communitas"—from the Latin communis, meaning "shared by all" or "together as one"—which represents the actual spirit of community, that rare and electric feeling of belonging to something larger than yourself, where the usual boundaries of status, role, or agenda dissolve.

It flows most freely when people meet as equals—not because our abilities or circumstances are the same, but because we all bear the *imago Dei*, the image of God. The same spark of divine life animates each of us, conferring equal dignity and worth.

United by shared purpose and mutual care, love can circulate without obstruction.

This is more than camaraderie—it's a living current that carries us toward the common good. People show up as their best selves when the field is one of love and giving. Yet we discovered that even this extraordinary spirit needed a channel.

The real work of the Gatherings was not in how many networks they built, but in what they taught us about how to build better. We learned that personal connection alone isn't enough. The energy stays contained without a clear, practical structure rooted in service and shared purpose. To spread love, it must move.

In future chapters, you'll see how we turned those lessons into a new model that fuses inner growth with outer service across twelve domains of life. We now have the blueprint. What we lacked then in design, we now bring forward with clarity.

Because if every person carries a gift, then every community is a gallery of grace.

When that grace flows, not just in moments of inspiration, but through relationships, service, and collective care, we begin to glimpse something even deeper—a sacred whole, waiting to be restored.

Restoring that whole requires more than goodwill or shared projects. It demands that we reclaim what lies at the very center of human flourishing—the sacred itself. That's where we now turn.

SECTION 3

INTEGRATION

RECLAIMING THE SACRED WHOLE

To restore the world,
we must first restore its center—
the sacred, the shared, the whole.

CHAPTER 23

THE REPLATFORMING OF GOD:
RESTORING THE SACRED
IN THE PUBLIC SQUARE

Integration begins by remembering what we've forgotten.

In the first part of this book, I shared how a series of Transcendent experiences cracked open my understanding of the world and revealed a deeper pattern at work. In the second, I explored how that awareness was embodied through spiritual practice, family, neighborhoods, food systems, local economies, and community relationships.

In this third section, we begin the process of *Integration*—bringing the inner transformation and outer application into alignment with the larger spiritual architecture behind them. What emerges is both deeply personal and profoundly collective.

For all our innovations in community and economy, one vital truth has remained quietly unaddressed: the soul of society cannot thrive without its sacred center.

BIRTHING THE SYMBIOTIC AGE

If we truly seek a culture of love, unity, and mutual flourishing, not just in isolated pockets, but at scale— we must reintegrate Spirit into the conversation.

The Spirit we speak of here is not about any specific theology, but rather a shared wellspring that transcends tribe, creed, and culture.

This chapter invites established religious traditions to participate in a vision of universal belonging—an expanded sacred space essential for uniting the Cosmos in Love and healing what has become separate. We don't need a new religion or philosophy—we need a renewed recognition of the universal purpose, principles, and Virtues found in ancient ones.

It bears repeating: E.F. Schumacher, father of the modern regeneration movement, warned decades ago that,

"In ethics, as in so many other fields, we have recklessly and willfully abandoned our great classical Christian heritage... The task of our generation, I have no doubt, is one of metaphysical reconstruction."

His use of "Christian heritage" was not a call to religious conversion, but a reminder of how deeply that foundation has shaped the moral and spiritual architecture of civilization.

The real question is this: What happens when people lose touch with the sacred—and how do we help each other remember again?

THE SOUL OF SOCIETY: RESTORING THE SACRED IN PUBLIC LIFE

Before we can re-embody spirituality—personally and collectively—and harness its power to build networks of mutual benefit, we must confront the elephant in the room. My mother warned me: "Never talk about politics or religion at dinner."

Why? Because in a fragmented world, those topics tend to spark arguments or conversion attempts, rather than connection. In the Culture of Separation, avoidance becomes a survival strategy. But here's the paradox I've discovered over four decades of community building:

> **True unity is only possible when we bring the HEART of religion and spirituality back into public life— not as dogma, but as a source of shared meaning.**

As the specter of societal collapse grows more tangible, one truth becomes increasingly clear: we must return to our spiritual roots—beyond the illusion that *"all that matters is matter."*

By "roots," I mean the collective soul of society. And by "soul," I don't mean private belief or inner peace alone—I mean the animating center of a people: the shared moral and spiritual core where meaning, belonging, and sacred purpose reside.

When a culture forgets its soul, it loses not just direction, but coherence.

This brings us to an equally unspoken reality—what I call *the rhino in the living room*. I've mentioned it before, and it bears repeating here.

More than 90 percent of humanity believes in a Transcendent reality. Across cultures and traditions, most people intuitively sense that there is more to life than materialism can explain. And yet, in public life, we're expected to suppress that knowing, to forget our inner lives at the altar of endless "progress" based on ever-more-complex mind-generated solutions.

BIRTHING THE SYMBIOTIC AGE

We are taught to dismiss the sacred—our personal convictions and our collective traditions alike—as either irrelevant or outdated superstition. This quiet denial carries consequences.

When we suppress the conscience and abandon the inner life to fit into fragmented systems, we lose more than our voice—we lose our moral clarity and our spiritual center.

Unity requires more than civility. Civility is like a polite smile that can mask profound disconnection. What we truly need is spiritual coherence—a deeper alignment of heart, purpose, and presence.

THE MOST POWERFUL LEVERAGE POINT FOR TRANSFORMATION

This inner dissonance—the split between our spiritual longing and secular systems—is not just personal, it's pervasive throughout society. And...it represents the most powerful leverage point for transforming the Culture of Separation.

Over and over, I've seen the same paradox emerge in conversations with changemakers: We long for a unifying principle—yet we overlook the most obvious source. That longing brings us back to a foundational question raised in this book's opening:

Can humanity agree on any universal purpose, principle, or Virtue that transcends yet includes religion, culture, and politics, providing a shared foundation for collaboration?

And more urgently:

Can the more than six billion people from diverse religious traditions who DO believe in a Transcendent Higher Power collaborate to address our common crises?

Can they find common ground not only with each other, but also with those who are secular or spiritually unaffiliated?

These questions are ancient—perhaps as old as the Tower of Babel—but their implications have never been more urgent. Disregarding the sacred has existential consequences in a world facing ecological collapse and civic breakdown. It also fuels what I call a "meaning-deficit disorder"—a crisis of coherence brought on by the loss of sacred orientation, shared purpose, and the resulting breakdown of relationships.

It's the very fracture this book seeks to mend.

The challenge before us is this:

We need to reintegrate religion and spirituality as a unifying power, not one that divides but connects.

That's where a relational worldview becomes essential. Unlike ideological worldviews that separate people into camps of belief or identity, a relational worldview prioritizes connection, reciprocity, and mutual belonging. It doesn't ask us to agree on doctrine—it invites us to recognize the sacred in one another and to build together from that recognition.

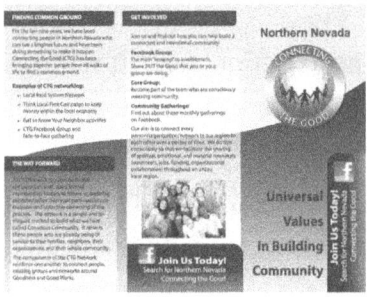 

A community-built message rooted in universal values—inviting all to weave connection, collaboration, and sacred belonging across every worldview.

It's a worldview that honors diversity, while weaving it into the whole. So, what's in the way of adopting this relational worldview, and operationalizing this most powerful leverage point?

Inside of the Culture of Separation, religion and spirituality have been exiled to the private realm.

Even the language of faith raises suspicion: *Will someone try to convert me? Dismiss my beliefs?* That fear causes even well-meaning leaders to be cautious about invoking the sacred in public life.

I've met countless civic organizers, bridge-builders, and systems thinkers who hold deep spiritual convictions, yet say nothing about them in their public work. Many acknowledge the role of Spirit privately but avoid discussing religion, especially Christianity, which often seems at odds with "progressive values." I understand this perspective; I once shared the same suspicion, unaware that I was reinforcing the separation I hoped to heal.

Even those building a more beautiful world often do so while compartmentalizing their souls. But here's the deeper challenge: the sacred will not be reintegrated into public life through ideas alone. It must be lived—re-embodied in our stories, our systems, and our everyday choices. And that begins with recognizing where we ourselves have internalized the very split we seek to heal.

LIVING SPLIT LIVES IN A FRAGMENTED WORLD

Let me get specific starting with my own bias.

As a child and young adult, I experienced a deep contrast between the unitive presence I encountered in moments of transcendence (described in Section 1) and the fractured, disembodied worldview of the Culture of Separation. I instinctively turned against the institutions perpetuating that fragmentation, especially organized religion and the business world.

In the 1980s, I was a passionate anti-nuclear activist, immersed in a left-leaning progressive mindset. Without realizing it, I had been absorbed into an ideological silo. Later, as I began building Symbiotic Networks in Reno, I had to confront those assumptions and stretch beyond the comfort of like-minded circles.

That personal awakening mirrored the broader integration we now need—of Spirit, culture, economy, civic action, and mutual flourishing.

Today, many movements focused on climate, equity, and justice operate within similar ideological bubbles. "Inclusivity" is often restricted to those who already share the same progressive worldview, leaving little room for collaboration with traditional religious or conservative communities.

Yet, hundreds of millions of people of faith around the world care for the poor, protect creation, and serve their neighbors in villages, towns, and cities daily. They are not adversaries but natural allies for a broader, unified purpose.

This widening gap between public life and the sacred calls for more than analysis—it calls for bridge-building. And that bridge is not theoretical. It's personal. Thankfully, my own life and work gave me reasons to cross that bridge—and I built it.

> *Over time, I began to see how diverse religious and spiritual streams—rising above competing ideologies—could be woven into whole-cloth movements for healing and renewal.*

My apprenticeship with Doña Catalina—both Indigenous Aztec and Christian—reaffirmed the link between spirituality and nature and introduced me to Jesus Christ through a living faith. Of course, Dr. Ari directly ties the Buddhist religion to uniting millions across thousands of communities in Sri Lanka.

These traditions, while distinct, revealed aspects of the same relational truth I later encountered most fully in the person of Jesus. While I honor the insights they offered, it was through Jesus that this truth became for me personal, embodied, and transformative.

RECLAIMING THE POWER WE'VE FORGOTTEN

The most transformative power available to humanity—the power of the Transcendent—has been rendered powerless. Why aren't most of us aware of this? And why do E. F. Schumacher's remarks about "abandoning our classical Christian heritage" seem so out of place today?

Because of what I've termed the De-platforming of God—a cultural amnesia that dismisses the sacred, that I've characterized as "throwing the Baby Jesus out with the bathwater." The dominant scientific-materialist worldview now insists: "We don't need religion." It claims that material science alone can solve every problem and provide a sufficient moral compass.

This is the legacy of the Enlightenment project, which for centuries promised that reason, science, and formal institutions could replace the need for spiritual wisdom. However, stripped of Transcendent purpose, that promise has left us with dazzling technologies and a profound crisis of meaning.

Religion isn't attacked outright, it's quietly sidelined. Its exile is framed as neutrality, but in truth, it has created a spiritual vacuum at the center of society. History shows that something else inevitably fills the void when the sacred center disappears.

Today, politics has taken on a quasi-religious role, in an attempt to redress this absence of meaning. As G.K. Chesterton warned, when true religion loses influence, politics rushes in to claim moral ground and ultimate authority. Tribal identities supplant Universal Virtues. Culture wars rage between the "woke left" and the "anti-woke right," even though many on both sides long for the same thing: Beloved Community and mutual uplift.

Social change movements, severed from spiritual grounding, are easily co-opted by political ideologies. Even the most sincere changemakers often distance themselves from traditional western religion—while embracing Indigenous practices or therapeutic spirituality.

That reaction is understandable, given the painful legacy of colonization and coercive conversion, ethnic cleansing and war. However, in rejecting institutional religion solely because of the abuse, we risk discarding the sacred wisdom and connective tissue that once held civilizations together.

As I've already pointed out, millions across faith traditions continue to serve the common good, yet they do so in fragmented isolation. The heart of society beats, but without coherence—without a soul. Even those yearning for a more beautiful world often compartmentalize their inner lives, treating them as optional, private, or irrelevant.

Within the Culture of Separation, spirituality is reduced to personal wellness. "Love thy neighbor" becomes "What's in it for me?" Prayer devolves from inner guidance to outer performance. Meditation becomes a productivity hack. Religion is repackaged as therapy or consumed as identity politics. Its prophetic power is tamed, and its communal mission is lost.

But true religion—religare—means "to bind again." Not only to personal well-being, but also to one another and the sacred Transcendent reality. It calls us beyond comfort to communion, beyond self-help to helping one another.

> *True religion is not about escaping suffering.*
> *It is about being radically transformed.*

Again, this isn't about creating a new religion or enforcing conversion—it's about recovering the spiritual coherence we've forgotten: an inner transformation, a turning of the heart toward Divine Love.

When the sacred is absent, even democracy becomes brittle. In that void, authoritarianism offers false certainty, protection, and identity. Spiritual life becomes domesticated, individualized, and stripped of its prophetic power. Religion becomes a coping mechanism rather than a call to moral courage and systemic transformation.

And yet, that Transcendent power still exists. It's not gone. It's waiting. Metanoia is the way back: a turning from self-centeredness to self-giving love. It represents the inward revolution that leads to outward coherence.

We urgently need mass metanoia—a cultural return to higher love that reweaves reality. A regenerated world begins with a regenerated heart. What we need now is not a separate self but a shared self—held by Love and called to serve.

And to serve, we must reclaim the sacred power we've forgotten—not to dominate, but to cohere. This power we need to reclaim doesn't belong to any one tradition. It's the animating power beneath them all—a living stream that reconnects us to what is True, Just, and Whole.

This reclamation is already underway. And so we return to a pattern we've already encountered in this book, what I've called the Ancient Blueprint. First glimpsed through mystical experience, nature, and later embodied in local communities and spiritual traditions, it now emerges as a guiding framework for cultural transformation.

CHAPTER 24

RECLAIMING THE ANCIENT BLUEPRINT AND ESTABLISHING A RELATIONAL WORLDVIEW

Given this high bar, is there a way forward? Yes—absolutely.

This book chronicles my journey of weaving the spiritual, civic, economic, cultural, and political into one living tapestry—an integrated life rooted in love and coherence. It includes religious organizations, nonprofits, civic groups, and Main Street businesses, all interlaced through conscious Symbiotic Kinship.

At the heart of this integration is the Ancient Blueprint—a living pattern we've already encountered throughout these pages. First glimpsed in mystical experiences, echoed in the natural world, and later embodied in community practice, this Blueprint is a template of wholeness woven into the fabric of life itself—hidden in plain sight.

Reclaiming the Ancient Blueprint and Establishing a Relational Worldview

> *Spiritual practice, then, is not merely about striving to be good—it's about reordering our way of seeing and being in the world.*

It invites us to align our lives not around ideology or performance, but around participation in something deeper: a sacred pattern that restores coherence between inner life and outer systems, personal formation and collective transformation.

This isn't just a shift in beliefs—it's a reorientation of perception: from separation to connection, from egoic striving to participatory belonging. This is where the relational worldview becomes essential.

Unlike ideological worldviews that fracture and divide, a relational worldview unites. It brings people together across traditions, cultures, and political lines through shared Virtues, purpose, lived love, and mutual care. It doesn't erase differences—it braids them into a stronger whole.

A relational worldview is not an invention—it arises from the lived experiences of those who have walked this path before us.

From the early Christian communities that practiced radical fellowship to Gandhi and Dr. Ari's commonwealth of self-governing village republics, and the networks we cultivated through Symbiotic Culture, this way of seeing and being has already been proven in real life. In other words, it is part of our collective spiritual legacy, our inheritance.

And it's radical enough—i.e., getting to the root cause—to make THE difference in this time of crisis.

At its core, a relational worldview is distinct because it doesn't demand uniformity. It invites people of various worldviews to walk side by side—not by abandoning their beliefs but by grounding themselves in shared relationships, sacred practices, and reciprocal service. It acknowledges that truth is not merely found in ideas but flows through love, belonging, and how we show up for each other and the world.

LOVE GOD, LOVE OTHERS. THE COSMIC DESIGN PATTERN

At the center of this relational worldview is the great commandment: Love God, and Love Others as yourself. In Jesus' teaching, this is not just moral guidance but the metaphysical and ontological heart of a relational cosmos. As we receive Divine Love, it overflows into our relationships, becoming the structure through which Heaven touches Earth.

> *Love God, Love Others. This is not only the greatest commandment—it is the deepest structure of the universe.*

It's about integrating the personal and communal, science and spirit, matter and meaning. My life has unfolded this integration: growing up as a secular Jew, awakening through spontaneous spiritual experiences, practicing Tibetan meditation, apprenticing with an Aztec-Christian medicine woman, and entering into an ongoing relationship with Jesus Christ.

Along the way, I discovered the Sarvodaya Shramadana movement and spent decades incorporating its wisdom into Symbiotic Culture and community-building.

I've demonstrated throughout this book that religion and spirituality are not optional. They are essential for becoming intentional uniters rather than unintentional dividers. Twenty years ago, this idea seemed ahead of its time. Today, more voices are advocating for the reintegration of spirituality into society's public life. Even Richard Dawkins, self-proclaimed atheist, author of *The Selfish Gene*, has recently called himself a "cultural Christian."

VIRTUE AS THE UNIVERSAL LANGUAGE OF UNITY

In our Northern Nevada work, we emphasized shared practice over doctrine. Rather than uniting around abstract values that sound good but ultimately ring hollow, we focused on Universal Virtues—qualities such as Compassion, Integrity, Courage, and Service that can actually change the world at large by changing the world "at small"—on the street where you live. These Virtues became the common ground on which secular and religious groups could agree on, enabling them to work side by side.

Virtue is the universal language of unity.

The Sarvodaya movement in Sri Lanka offers another powerful model of a Virtue-based community. For over 65 years, it has integrated inner awakening with mutual aid, rooted in the Four Sublime Abodes: Compassion, Loving-Kindness, Equanimity, and Empathetic Joy.

As I've shared earlier, Sarvodaya doesn't separate spiritual life from civic responsibility. Its foundation in Buddhist Virtues fosters profound coherence—something many in the modern West long for but seldom discover amidst the fragmented offerings of the contemporary "spiritual marketplace."

In contrast, much of today's "spiritual but not religious" movement de-emphasizes lineage and traditions and sacrifices depth. Sacred wisdom is reduced to a buffet of disconnected practices—timeless truths placed alongside teachings that surfaced just last week.

But spirituality is not the only fragmented area. We've also been blind to the power of Virtue as a transformational tool in social change. Many changemakers assume that fixing the systems will lead to Virtue. However, nearly every enduring religious tradition teaches the opposite: lasting outer change flows from inner transformation. Virtue is not the result of good systems—it is what makes systems good.

Materialist ideologies like Marxism share this "outside-in" assumption, pursuing justice without a spiritual foundation. However, even noble goals can lead to tyranny when Virtue is lacking.

Sarvodaya, in contrast, begins with spiritual awakening as the foundation for building a parallel society and culture. As I suggested earlier, this upends Maslow's hierarchy, which maintains that spiritual needs only emerge once material ones are met. However, actual change doesn't unfold in tidy stages; it emerges through symbiosis.

It's not either/or, it's both/and. Spiritual and material well-being must be cultivated together.

We clearly saw this in Reno, where spiritual growth flourished in relational networks—those "superhighways of love" that carried goodness across the city.

This same principle applies at larger scales.

Sarvodaya's national model demonstrates that transformation can expand when anchored in a coherent spiritual vision rather than ideology. Yet, our most potent power—Transcendent Love—has been quietly set aside. In its place, we've substituted technical fixes, institutional reforms, and managerial abstractions.

So, here's the question we rarely ask:

Reclaiming the Ancient Blueprint and Establishing a Relational Worldview

Why abandon humanity's deepest spiritual inheritance when we need it most?

This leads us to the final sections of this chapter. We will explore the breakthrough necessary for a New Creation—and how Symbiotic Societies provide a dual path of recovery: healing from the Culture of Separation and returning to the Ancient Blueprint.

BREAKTHROUGH TO A NEW CREATION: WEAVING THE THREADS OF LOVE

So...how do we build a network "superhighway" to extend the unbounded power of Love—through us and outward to our communities?

How do we ignite and spread the goodness already happening—horizontally across neighborhoods and upward into a global commonwealth of 50,000 thriving regional economies?

First, remember this "New Way of Living" isn't new. It reflects an ancient vision embedded in the Ancient Blueprint. Jesus called it, *"Love God and Love Others."* Thomas Jefferson envisioned it as a *"Commonwealth of Ward Republics."* Gandhi lived it as the *"Law of Love."* And Dr. Ari brought it to life in Sri Lanka through the Sarvodaya movement.

Dr. Ari once said:
> "We dream of a world that is a commonwealth of self-governing communities. We dream of people enjoying participatory democracy, where all human rights are respected, spiritual and moral values are strong, and where people respect nature."

This vision is real. It isn't utopian—it has a working strategy. It's not more of the "same old," but something proven, practical, and possible.

Previously, I shared that over six billion people believe in a Transcendent Power. But here's something even more compelling: their heads, hearts, and hands are already engaged.

Globally, we have:

- 11 million formal nonprofits
- 50 million informal groups
- 2.35 million religious congregations
- Hundreds of thousands of spiritual circles
- 350,000 US and 500,000 European faith-based organizations
- 272 million small businesses—68 million of them purpose-driven

These entities serve nearly every village, town, and city—yet most operate in isolation.

Catalyzing a global network of 50,000 thriving communities begins with just one person—someone who makes an unshakable commitment to hold space for their community, so that these threads of functionality and care can be woven into one whole cloth.

From that point, the math is straightforward: If each community supports 12 sector-based networks, we only require 600,000 local changemakers from a population of 8 billion people.

That's just 0.0075% of humanity—less than one in every 13,000 people. But as history shows, it only takes a few committed hearts to change the course of the world.

Are you one of them?

That is how a small fraction of humanity could ignite a global reweaving of love and purpose.

And as I've already suggested, even with so much good already happening, most efforts remain isolated. Even collaborative networks compete for attention and resources. The Culture of Separation persists—even within the movements trying to overcome it.

But what if we didn't need to create something entirely new, but just to connect what already exists? Churches, nonprofits, purpose-driven businesses, local governments, and spiritual circles could all amplify the Transcendent together.

> *What's missing isn't energy. It's coherence—*
> *a shared framework and relational infrastructure.*

All over the world, I've met people eager to collaborate. They don't yet see how to connect their "Work of Heart" with others. But the threads are already there. Together, they form an emerging, still-unnamed global movement for Intentional Mutual Benefit:

- Faith communities and spiritual groups
- Regenerative culture movements
- Civic bridge builders
- Charities and changemakers
- Purpose-driven small businesses
- New Economy and Commons advocates
- Localists, Bioregionalists, and Cosmolocalists
- Pro-democracy and civil society networks

And likely many more.

Still, I've seen this vast potential go unnoticed at global gatherings. People feel overwhelmed and disconnected, unsure how to spark real breakthroughs. Why? Because we've been taught that transformation requires formal systems—more capital, staff, and complexity.

But the truth is simpler—and far more radical:

A breakthrough doesn't come from new structures.
It comes from connected hearts.

And contrary to popular belief, we don't need a majority to begin.

Transformation starts with a few—and often with just one. One person, anchored in love and purpose, can hold space for a new way of being. That's how every Symbiotic Network began: one heartful connector...then a circle of five to ten...then fifteen...and soon, an entire community woven together in mutual benefit.

We don't need more bureaucracy. We need more Love made visible.

PUTTING LOVE TO WORK: THE SYMBIOTIC PATHWAY

In Northern Nevada, our Symbiotic Networks thrived because we led with love. Instead of building massive institutions or waiting for an outside fix, we simply gathered individuals with a shared desire to serve, responded to genuine community needs, and observed as networks began to grow organically.

It was simple—but not easy.

The hardest part was unlearning our dependence on structural fixes—trusting that connection, not control, is the true catalyst. People often say, "I'm already doing this." And maybe they are. However, as I shared previously, even a successful farmer already deeply engaged in service didn't see the potential for broader impact until we invited him into a larger network. Once he recognized it, he helped co-create something far greater.

That's the shift: from "I'm doing it" to "We're weaving it together."

Understanding the difference between networked silos and Symbiotic Networks is essential. Networked silos compete for resources, often growing their brand at the expense of broader collaboration—even when they seem to work together. Symbiotic Networks do the opposite: they simultaneously liberate resources and uplift all efforts.

They don't require everyone to unite under one banner. Instead, they create a commons—a shared relational field for addressing community needs.

Symbiotic Networks liberate resources from silos and multiply the good already happening. They are the "no-brand" that supports all brands. You can keep doing your own beautiful "work of heart" within your network. But remember that even with the best intentions, isolation won't heal the deeper issue—particularly since the issue is isolation itself! To build truly wide-reaching, love-centered networks, we must first confront the divisions within us—our habits of exclusion, addiction to our comfort zones, our unexamined preferences, and mental silos.

The real work is relational.

Inner transformation allows us to collaborate with those we might otherwise avoid or misunderstand. This opens the door to a place-based global movement for Intentional Mutual Benefit.

Many are surprised when they hear that building local movements doesn't require extensive time, money, or infrastructure. "It's too simple," one person told me. But we saw it unfold in Reno through our Living Economy Network, Food System Network, and Neighbor Networks.

The simplicity is the genius. The heart is the engine. The network is the vessel. This is the essential structure of Symbiotic Networks.

NEW WINE IN NEW WINESKINS: THE STRUCTURE OF LOVE

The hardest shift is letting go of the "head" and learning to lead from the heart. In a world where "only matter matters," we're conditioned to chase structural fixes. However, we need spiritual transformation: trusting that love, not systems, is the true organizing principle.

Keep in mind that our networks didn't grow through plans or proposals. They grew because people with hearts for service identified a need and responded. There was no master plan—only connection, compassion, and commitment. Once we began, the network took on a life of its own—a living counterculture.

To make the next evolutionary leap, we need a new kind of "interstitial tissue"—structures of love that bridge silos and thaw frozen local assets, long suppressed by divide-and-rule dynamics and a money-first economy.

To act as catalytic connectors and space holders, we must confront the separation within ourselves—the habits that keep us locked in old battles. It took me fifty years to recognize its elegant simplicity. I had to strip away cherished forms and fixed ideas to rediscover what had always been here. This is not reinvention; it's realignment with the Ancient Blueprint.

Reclaiming the Ancient Blueprint and Establishing a Relational Worldview

Earlier in the book, I referenced Jesus' metaphor of new wine and old wineskins. Now, let's return to it—not as a passing image, but as a deep blueprint for how we build today.

He said:

> "No one puts new wine into old wineskins. If he does, the wine will burst the skins—and both the wine and the skins will be ruined. No, new wine is poured into fresh wineskins." (Mark 2:22)

He wasn't merely speaking of religious ritual or doctrinal form—he was addressing the arrival of the Kingdom of Heaven, a radically new way of being, filled with Divine Love and mercy, rather than law and institutional control. The old wineskins represented the religious and political structures of the time: the temple system intertwined with the Roman Empire, rigid, self-protective, and ultimately unable to contain the expansive life of the Spirit. Jesus was clear [my paraphrase]:

> *The Kingdom could not be poured into containers built on power, performance, and purity codes.*
> *It required entirely new relational vessels—*
> *living, supple, Spirit-filled communities.*

This was not just a metaphor—it was the blueprint for the early church. Jesus' followers didn't return to the old temple system. Instead, they met in homes, broke bread together, and shared all they had in common (Acts 2:42-47). These Spirit-led assemblies embodied the very principle of new wine in new wineskins.

They didn't try to reform the religious hierarchy or resist the Roman Empire directly; they lived out a new, parallel social order rooted in love, mutual aid, and Divine presence. Their gatherings weren't centered around institutional power but around communion, prayer, edification, and community, forming the first Beloved Communities.

These were the original wineskins of the Kingdom—elastic, open, and relational enough to hold the fermenting energy of Divine transformation. Similarly, our challenge is not to pour Kingdom love into the hardened containers of today's failing systems, but to cultivate new relational structures—embodied, flexible, and fueled by Spirit.

WHEN OLD FORMS CAN'T HOLD NEW LIFE… NEW RELATIONAL VESSELS WILL

And here's the hard truth: our challenge today is even more daunting. We don't face just one or two old wineskins—we confront an entire latticework of them.

Every vertical of the "Everything Industrial Complex"—religion, business, media, politics, academia, healthcare, and even philanthropy—now carries the momentum of a self-perpetuating structure, resistant to reform, let alone transformation.

Though many of these institutions were born from sacred callings and noble intentions, they have often become burdened by bureaucracy and beholden to self-preservation. Like the temple of Jesus' day, they've lost sight of the life they were meant to uphold.

This isn't a judgment—it's a recognition of the human tendency to enshrine what once worked, even when it no longer serves. History confirms it: every "solution" eventually becomes a new problem. Unless we heal the root cause—separation—we remain trapped in cycles of reform and collapse. The culture

Reclaiming the Ancient Blueprint and Establishing a Relational Worldview

keeps trying to pour new wine into old skins, repackaging the same mindset with new branding or digital veneers.

But this new wine is different. Divine Love flows through awakened people to build Beloved Communities. The Culture of Separation cannot contain it. It is too rigid, too self-centered. Even good works become battlegrounds for attention and funding.

We need a completely new framework, rooted in unity, mutual uplift, and spiritual grounding. Not just new ideas, but new wineskins: relational, mediating structures capable of carrying and sustaining the life of the Kingdom.

And here's the most profound truth: this culture of love is not foreign. It resides within us—living in our ancestors, stories, and neighborhoods. We only need to create space, open our hearts, and let it flow.

The sacred never left us. It's been waiting patiently for us to remember. And now, with awakened hearts and open hands, we are ready to build again—not alone, not in silos, but together through a new kind of relational design capable of holding the Kingdom within and among us

Among all these institutions, few are as deeply tied to humanity's sacred longings—and its deepest disappointments—as the Church. For many, it represents both the memory of spiritual coherence and the pain of separation. And yet, when it returns to its essence—love embodied in community—it can become one of the most powerful wineskins of all.

When rooted in love rather than control, religions have a vital role to play in this reweaving—not as the gatekeeper of grace but as a living vessel of it. When animated by the Spirit, Churches remain one of the most potent forces for healing, justice, and the Beloved Community on Earth.

Religions and other spiritual traditions, civic movements, and purpose-driven networks are invited into a wider symphony that

BIRTHING THE SYMBIOTIC AGE

honors our shared sacred inheritance while helping to birth new wineskins for a new era.

Because the old forms—faithful, time-tested, but often stretched beyond their original calling—can no longer hold what Love is now pouring out.

In the next chapter, we'll explore how new relational vessels—Symbiotic Circles—emerge not from hierarchy or control but from hearts joined in service. These are not new churches, in a sense, but complementary frameworks: supple, Spirit-led containers that support the people of faith and the broader movement of love across civic and spiritual life. Their purpose is simple—to carry the goodness already flowing and to connect rather than compete.

The question is no longer if we are called to build, but how. What forms can hold the sacred without distorting it? What kind of structure can support love without suppressing it? In the chapters ahead, we'll explore Spirit-led networks that bridge civic and spiritual life—living ecosystems of coherence, rooted in mutual service and aligned with the Ancient Blueprint.

CHAPTER 25

RECOVERING THE SACRED WHOLE: FROM SILOED SYSTEMS TO SYMBIOTIC CIRCLES

The old organizational forms—designed for industrial control, not spiritual coherence—can no longer carry the sacred impulse rising in our time. We don't need more centralization. We need supple containers for Spirit: grounded in reality, guided by shared purpose, and open enough to weave people and sectors into one living whole.

The siloed systems we inherited—across government, religion, education, economy, and civil society—were built for a different age. They cannot meet today's complex, interrelated challenges. Real transformation calls for coherence and networks that honor local distinctiveness and shared Virtue.

These "new wineskins" aren't just metaphors or aspirations. They're already forming in real-world contexts—living networks that foster collaboration and unlock community potential.

Consider the Local Food Systems Network from Chapter 16: it didn't dismantle silos; it enriched them, drawing value from each and linking them into something greater. Bridging sectors helped release a community's frozen assets—spiritual, social, cultural, natural, and human—unleashing goods and goodness.

This is the power of Symbiotic Networks. They don't just carry information or money. They carry meaning. They open the floodgates, letting the wine of Love flow freely through a community, unhindered by outdated constraints.

But beyond structure lies something deeper—relationship. To unlock the true potential of these networks, we must practice a different kind of kinship, and develop new relational structures to seed and cultivate that kinship.

SYMBIOTIC CIRCLES CONNECT ISLANDS OF COHERENCE: RE-PLATFORMING DIVINE LOVE

"When a complex system is far from equilibrium, small islands of coherence in a sea of chaos can shift the entire system to a higher order."
—Ilya Prigogine, Nobel Prize-winning chemist

Given how unstable today's systems are—economically, socially, and politically—this insight remains hopeful. Yet within the Culture of Separation, the coherence among those "islands" often goes unrecognized. Scientists like Prigogine, grounded in materialist paradigms, could only go so far. They couldn't fully acknowledge that these islands of coherence may arise from an underlying spiritual reality.

Recovering the Sacred Whole

Islands of Coherence: Spirit-rooted communities, illuminated by love, form a living network to heal separation and birth a new humanity.

As I've shared throughout this book, millions of organizations and billions of loving actions are not anomalies but reflections of Divine Love and the Ancient Blueprint. While Prigogine was speaking of chemistry, the same patterns manifest socially. The problem is that these islands remain disconnected. Trapped in silos, countless acts of goodness fail to unite. Love is constantly blocked by ego, competition, and fear.

But these islands are natural expressions of a deeper spiritual order, recognized by faith traditions across the globe. As you may remember, one of the most compelling articulations comes from C.S. Lewis. Drawing from both East and West, he describes a Transcendent moral framework—what some call "The Tao." He called it:

> "...the reality beyond all predicates...the Way...the Road...the Way every man should tread in imitation of that cosmic and super-cosmic progression..."

In this vision, the Tao is the current from which islands of coherence emerge tranquilly—what I call the Ancient Blueprint. Divine Love is not merely poetic but the pattern behind reality itself.

> *As gravity governs the physical,*
> *Love undergirds the spiritual. It's the only*
> *viable foundation for a just and enduring society.*

Without Love, systems collapse.

We've already learned from historians like Toynbee and Spengler that empires don't fail from a lack of strategy or resources—they die from moral and spiritual decline.

Just the opposite was true of our Symbiotic Networks. They thrived because they were fueled by love. The real breakthrough in our Symbiotic Networks wasn't structural; it was the Heart-Generated Love flowing through them. That Love awakened dormant assets and activated trust.

As Jesus taught in the Beatitudes, "Blessed are the poor in spirit, for theirs is the Kingdom of Heaven." His words overturn the values of empire—not through power, but through a greater service to uplift the common good.

So, the question becomes: How do we grow and connect these loving islands to transform our communities—and the world?

From our Connections Gatherings and Symbiotic Networks, a simple design emerged: Symbiotic Circles. Not only do these circles help grow Love within, but they also connect it across communities—linking silos, networks, and efforts into a greater whole.

I remember one of the first moments that helped catalyze this. At a "trans-religious" luncheon, I met the Stake President of the Northern Nevada Church of Jesus Christ of Latter-day Saints. We began with very different worldviews—but as we listened to each other, we discovered a shared longing to help our communities thrive.

Out of that unlikely friendship came a breakthrough idea: instead of stockpiling food in isolation, could we build a Local Food System Network together? In addition to planting seeds for a local food network, that conversation planted the seeds of Symbiotic Kinship.

To bring those seeds to fruition, we have to acknowledge and heal our civilizational wound—our disconnection from Spirit and one another. This wounding has birthed a culture addicted to battle. It's why even social change movements often fall into adversarial postures. To birth Symbiotic Circles, we must consciously and intentionally choose healing over hostility.

> *That's why I describe this as a recovery movement— not just from personal trauma, but from an entire worldview. It is a re-platforming of Divine Love.*

We are recovering not only our connection to the Transcendent but also from the illusion that the human mind alone can solve the challenges before us. Love—not ideology—is what brings coherence to any system.

CULTURAL RECOVERY: HEALING THE THINKING PROBLEM

Another reason I use the word recovery to describe our healing process because it signals a new way of living. Traditional 12-step movements like Alcoholics Anonymous have profoundly influenced our Symbiotic Circles. These movements recognize a vital truth at their core: we cannot solve our deepest problems with the same thinking that created them.

As the classic saying goes, "Our best thinking got us here." This isn't about a lack of genius—it's about the ego's illusions. We've trusted the fragmented human mind to solve crises that require the more ingenious genius that exists beyond mind-made solutions.

Anthropologist Gregory Bateson, who studied addiction, noted that real breakthrough often comes through the first two 12-step principles. Alcoholics believe they can control their drinking—until they "hit bottom." That collapse leads to an inescapable truth: their life is unraveling, and willpower alone won't save them. The first step demands radical humility:

1. "We admitted we were powerless over alcohol—that our lives had become unmanageable."

Into that humility, the second step offers hope:

2. "We came to believe that a Power greater than ourselves could restore us to sanity."

That "Power" is often interpreted as God, and the third step affirms that interpretation:

3. "We made a decision to turn our will and our lives over to the care and direction of God as we understood Him."

There is no Pope of the 12-Steps, no doctrine.
The key is surrender. Not knowing becomes
a sacred space where deeper guidance can arise.

So, what does this have to do with the Culture of Separation?

Put simply: we don't have a drinking problem—we have a thinking problem.

We've been conditioned to believe that the mind is supreme, yet this may lead to our undoing unless we reconnect with Divine Love and begin to embody it now, in our neighborhoods, families, workplaces, and communities. That's the recovery we seek.

Earlier, I spoke of being a "space-holder"—not for systems or dogmas, but for Love itself—in action, in relationship. When we step into the sacred space of Symbiotic Circles—our "recovery groups"—we remove our metaphorical "shoes."

We set aside tribal identities and preferences—not to erase them, but to honor something deeper. We don't lose our individuality; we let go of our over-identification with it.

Without Love at the center, even the most beautiful new system will eventually replicate the old. In that humility, we surrender, allowing the still, small voice of conscience to guide us rather than being swept away by the world, and the "noise" of competing voices. That's why I keep returning to the Heart of Love in each of us—the voice of the Authentic Self.

It is the true foundation for transformation, both personal and collective, and for the Symbiotic Kinship required to build beyond tribes and differences.

> *The purpose of Symbiotic Circles isn't to dwell on what divides us—it's to support each other in living from that heart full of Love and spreading it across our relationships and communities.*

As the 12-step tradition reminds us: the antidote to addiction isn't just abstinence, it's a whole new way of living. For us, that new way is Symbiotic Culture.

FROM PERSONAL HEALING TO COLLECTIVE RECOVERY

So, how do we get there? How do we confront our collective thinking problem?

We begin by applying the first three transformational steps of individual recovery to society. In our addiction to the Culture of Separation, getting sober means first admitting that our civilization has become unmanageable. The challenges we face are so deeply intertwined that siloed solutions cannot succeed, because separation is the root issue.

We must admit in the first step, we are powerless to fix the system using the same mindsets and behaviors that created it. The price of admission to this transformed worldview is—an admission.

"We admit our society and its institutions have become unmanageable, and we are powerless to fix them with the same outdated approaches—religious, social, political, economic—that caused and sustain our separation."

This step requires honesty, humility, and courage. It asks us to confront our systems' limits and our complicity in sustaining them. The second step opens the heart to something greater:

"We came to believe that a Power greater than ourselves could restore a sane and sacred Culture of Connection."

This invites surrender, releasing ego control and learning to listen for deeper guidance. It means trusting the Heart of Love. The third step turns inner realization into outer commitment:

> "We made a decision to turn our private and public will and lives over to the care and direction of Divine Love, expressed through the Ancient Blueprint."

This takes courage and faith in Love's not-yet-seen power to restore coherence. "Recovering Divine Love" may sound abstract, so let's bring it down to Earth.

Virtues are fractals of Divine Love—shards of Heavenly light brought to Earth through intentional action.

They align our personalities with the Ancient Blueprint, creating inner coherence and direction. They are the living interface between Heaven and Earth. Virtues give tangible form to ideals like truth, beauty, and goodness. They come alive not through belief, but through action.

They allow Divine Love to dwell within us, empowering our hands to serve. Many of us first encountered them in our religious training as tools to earn Heaven or avoid hell, but such motivations no longer hold sway. As the Sarvodaya movement and I have learned: Virtue is how we practice Heaven now and avoid the hell of disconnection.

We don't live by Virtue for points, praise, or appearances. That's ego. We live by them because they are right, true, and the surest foundation for an abundant life.

FROM INNER PRACTICE TO PUBLIC KINSHIP

Recovery begins where we are—by living the Culture of Connection in our families, neighborhoods, organizations, and communities. It means sharing, caring, and humbly seeking guidance. It also calls us to reintroduce spirituality and religion into the public square—not as brands in competition, but as a shared sensibility honoring all expressions of Divine Love.

This collective recovery starts with a personal journey. To get to the root, we must confront our egos and blind spots—and step beyond our comfort zones. I had to do this myself. As you will remember, I had to move beyond my biases toward business and religion and grow past my progressive identity.

It wasn't just about becoming a business owner. It was about building trust with both main-street entrepreneurs and spiritual leaders. I had to release my judgments to earn the trust of both "pastor" and "pagan." That meant facing my shadow: fear of the "other" and anger at those I saw as unjust. The humbling truth? Judging others as being judgmental made me judgmental, too.

This heart-based trust extended to many unlikely encounters. I once found myself in dialogue with a local imam and a progressive rabbi, sharing tea and laughter while discussing community well-being.

*It wasn't agreement that united us—
it was the willingness to show up, listen, and love.
These relationships became living proof that
we don't need sameness to build sacred solidarity.*

True community requires letting go of the ego's grip. In another encounter, I remember lunch with an Evangelical Christian. Though I disagreed with some of his beliefs, I felt his love when I led with my heart. Our hearts connected even as our minds may have disagreed on some points.

The heart of the matter really is the matter of the heart.

Christian tradition calls this release of egoic concerns "kenosis" or self-emptying. Jesus emptied Himself of pride and self-interest. That "self-emptying Love" makes possible radical, all-embracing, neighbor-love—a Love willing to cross every divide. As Paul writes in Philippians 2:6–8:

"He made himself of no reputation...and took the form of a servant."

And...this spacious grace is not limited to saints and saviors. Ordinary mortals can learn this practice, and this is best done in a community. That's why we adapted what we learned from Connections Gatherings into Symbiotic Circles—simple, open groups that anyone can join. Similar to 12-step recovery meetings, they foster a new way of living, not just to liberate oneself from addiction to substances but from the addiction to the Culture of Separation and separation itself!

What's radical about 12-step groups is their simplicity: shared leadership, minimal structure, and a universal protocol that works anywhere in the world. "Hello, my name is _____, and I'm an alcoholic"—that's all that matters.

They don't debate politics or theology; they create sanctuaries for transformation. Symbiotic Circles draw from this same spirit. Our protocol is Symbiotic Culture DNA—no lecturing, no ideology, no authority, just a trusted process where personal agendas are left at the door and sacred space opens.

Symbiotic Circles are the first step—spaces where people practice Virtue, share Love, and embody communion. As individual Circles of trust connect, Symbiotic Kinship arises, weaving bonds of trust across differences. Out of this Kinship, Symbiotic Societies emerge, providing the scale and coherence to nurture Networks that meet core community needs.

In this way, Circles seed Societies, Societies empower Networks, Networks weave a Commons and a parallel polis—a living infrastructure of care, economy, and governance grounded in mutual benefit.

These Circles are built around universal practices and protocols that foster communion—sharing, intimacy, joint participation—and help birth community agency. You can see these circles as the healthy, vital cells of a society dedicated to mutual benefit, growing alongside existing institutions. These healthy cells support the new interstitial tissue of a Culture of Connection.

Symbiotic Circles extend beyond silos to embrace all of humanity. Where 12-step groups focus on individual healing, the Circles bring us together around a shared commitment: to "unite the Cosmos in Love."

This impulse transcends religion, spirituality, and secular ethics. It empowers the good already emerging in our communities and world.

Symbiotic Circles are both inward and outward, nurturing the soul while activating networks. They Connect the Good across society, expanding this way of life personally, socially, spiritually, and systemically.

SYMBIOTIC CIRCLES: POWER IN PRACTICE

When we practice the Virtues as individuals, we become "islands of coherence" within the Culture of Separation. When practiced collectively through Symbiotic Circles, these islands form a more connected, coherent community.

> *Symbiotic Circles are collective space-holders—ongoing catalysts for Goodness that seed networks and serve as the "new wineskins" for a Culture of Connection.*

Unlike AA, which centers on what people are recovering from, Symbiotic Circles focus on "being" Love now. They assist us in embodying patience, generosity, forgiveness, and kindness, building inner resources for outer transformation and mutual accountability.

These Circles unlock frozen assets in our neighborhoods and entire communities. Like Symbiotic Networks, they are "no-brand spaces" open to all paths, including religious and non-religious, offering a playing field where everyone can thrive. Anyone seeking to deepen their connection to Divine Love and act from it is welcome.

Some will join to live more abundantly in their families and communities. Others seek to foster coherence within and among faith groups, nonprofits, schools, businesses, or government—applying mutual benefit wherever they serve.

Still others may organize their streets or launch local Symbiotic Networks to address the 12 core community needs (Local Economy, Food and Water, Energy, Clean & Healthy Natural Environment, Community Peace & Safety, Neighbor Helping Neighbor, Community Empowerment of those on the "margins," Arts & Culture, Housing, Family and Community Health & Wellness, Education and Mentoring, and Religion/Spirituality in Service.)

A single principle unites all:
Love God. Love Others.

Not as words on a plaque, but as a living reality—embodied through connected nodes of goodness.

This is the beneficial paradox of Symbiotic Circles: they expand both personal freedom and social connection. As Bishop Fulton Sheen said:

"It is not a unity of religion we plead for…but a unity of religious peoples."

The goal isn't a single world religion, but a shared purpose—to rebind us to the Transcendent, the web of Love, and the web of life. Imagine a gathering where you can be your whole self while Connecting the Good and practicing mutual benefit. Like 12-step groups, Symbiotic Circles are not in competition with one another. You can attend any one and discover the same spirit of kinship and shared protocol.

As Circles connect across a region, Symbiotic Kinship begins to take shape. Out of this Kinship, Symbiotic Societies emerge—larger, more coherent communities of practice. It is at the level of these Societies that Symbiotic Networks take root, meeting needs like food, housing, health, and peace.

There could be hundreds of thousands of these Circles worldwide, each practicing Virtue, fostering community coherence, and connecting to broader networks. As we did in Reno—connecting circles of trust into a regional ecosystem—each group becomes a node in a bottom-up infrastructure that models a counterculture within the current system.

Their purpose is fractal community empowerment—spreading Symbiotic Culture DNA across communities.

> *A dozen Circles in one region, each with a unique mission, can create a living network of aligned action. As these networks mature, they begin functioning like organs in a living body.*

As a biologist, I can't help but recall the mycelial network introduced in Chapter 4. Just as fungi decompose matter to nourish forests, our Symbiotic Networks metabolize the decaying structures of the Culture of Separation, releasing nutrients that support the whole. We observed this in Reno. Sarvodaya demonstrated it in Sri Lanka, and the result was a redistribution of well-being that transformed entire regions.

This work is not theoretical. Civilizations decline not because of outside enemies but from inner dysfunction. What begins as win-lose always devolves into lose-lose. Even elites can't escape collapse. You can't eat your BMW—or your Tesla.

I've seen it firsthand. A hyperbaric therapy business partner broke a win-win agreement to chase short-term profit. They lost money, and so did we. Win-lose became lose-lose. This highlights the danger of the Culture of Separation.

However, the solution is within reach: mutual benefit, fractal empowerment, one node, one circle, one region at a time.

FRACTAL EMPOWERMENT IN ACTION

We are at a tipping point. Globally, we face a cascading lose-lose situation—and let's remember real change begins locally. That's where Symbiotic Circles and Networks step in. In Reno, we transitioned from win-lose to win-win without first collapsing. Our local food network exemplifies this: competitors quickly became cooperative colleagues.

Why? Because we long for Beloved Community and Symbiotic Kinship. And when we find it, we embrace it—because it works.

Top-down systems won't lead us out. This new way of life begins with inner Virtue, embodied where we are. Symbiotic Circles reinforce that foundation. Next come neighborhoods, organizations, and regions. Ultimately, our bold vision is establishing 50,000 regional networks—connecting and amplifying the Good.

> *To transform globally, we begin locally.*
> *Injecting a win-win culture into 50,000 places at once:*
> *that's fractal empowerment.*

And it's already happening.

We don't need millions to begin—just enough trust to take the first step. In Reno, we saw multiple Circles become a citywide ecosystem. Imagine this pattern replicated globally. 50,000 regions. 12 Circles each. That's 600,000 interlinked Circles of trust—amplifying love, spreading coherence, and embodying a whole new civilization from the ground up.

Now, put yourself in that picture.

Imagine your neighborhood, your community, your region. See yourself as a "node" in a larger network—linking the trusted circles you already inhabit. Visualize these "islands of coherence" uniting in shared communion. What if all the good being done could flow together in one great wave—a superhighway of Love, delivering a new way of life?

Symbiotic Circles and Networks open the floodgates letting the "wine" of Love flow freely through a community—a relational framework unhindered by outdated organizational structures.

What would a redistribution of well-being look like where you live? Imagine collaborative responses to homelessness, hunger, depleted soil, broken health, or isolation. What if prosperity bubbled up as your community's hidden gifts were set free?

I'm reminded of words that came to me over forty years ago, early in my journey to bring Love and authenticity into a divided world:

> Yes, you may feel this universal dream and soul longing— calling us into a deeper relationship with the Creator of All and this sweet harmony ringing throughout creation, the mirror calling us into relationship with each other.
>
> Who am I? I am You.
>
> Circles and webs of light develop from the dark. Small at first, they join together, becoming larger and larger, shining as only Spirit can shine.

Can you see the light, the beauty, the perfect harmony?
Desire to experience this all-pervasive unity, where everything is connected.

The light of Spirit now spreads throughout the world in an explosive chain reaction of moral force, countering the nuclear chain reaction of physical force.

Reflecting on these decades, I believe more than ever in Love's power to unify our communities. Imagine if we all committed to this. We would witness thousands of communities rising together in a great, unnamed eruption of spirit, transforming the battlefields of this world.

So, I ask you:

Would you like to play a part—large or small—in transforming your region into a thriving Culture of Connection? You don't need permission—only a willing heart. A single node of Love can illuminate an entire network. Perhaps it begins with a conversation—like it did for the Pastor and the Pagan—across the divide, heart to heart.

However, to scale that Love across silos and regions, goodwill alone isn't enough.

We need more than inspiration—we need infrastructure. Not rigid systems of control, but relational frameworks that extend trust. Not just better technology, but sacred technology—tools rooted in Divine Love that carry the pattern of Kinship into the digital realm without losing the soul of the local.

This isn't about escaping reality but restoring it. This leads to our next question: Can the Internet serve the Outernet?

BIRTHING THE SYMBIOTIC AGE

CHAPTER 26

CONNECTING THE GOOD: USING THE
INTERNET TO SERVE THE OUTERNET

That burning, yearning question—Can the Internet serve the Outernet?—took form in our next experiment. In 2013, we rebranded the Conscious Community Network as *Connecting the Good*. It wasn't just a name change. It was a declaration, a line in the sand: we would use digital tools to strengthen human connection, not replace it.

We weren't here to build a digital escape hatch but to create a vessel, a Community Ark, for the real world. Our mission? To leverage digital technology for the benefit of each and all—deepening genuine relationships, bridging silos, and amplifying local goodness already flowing beneath the surface.

That intention has guided us for over a decade. What emerged is proof: you can build networks that grow by love, not control, elevate Virtue over branding, and scale trust without centralizing power.

But the deeper question remained: could that Spirit of Kinship be embedded in our tools?

Could we design technology that honors the sacred and delivers it? Even a decade ago, we sensed a fork in the road—Artificial Intelligence would either serve as a partner in Love or a tool of domination.

We chose the former. That's what this chapter is about.

FROM RESISTANCE TO REGENERATION: RENO'S LOCAL RENAISSANCE

Many of the anti-war activists who gathered in 2003 evolved into bridge builders and "regeneration" activists, shifting from resistance to creation and focusing on building the world they longed for.

While other cities leaned into extraction and "trickle-down" economics, Reno chose "bubble-up" economics—a people-powered free market rooted in mutual benefit. Local producers thrived. Fair prices circulated within a circular ecosystem as businesses, nonprofits, and governments embraced the "buy local" movement. Prosperity began at the roots and flowed sideways and upward across the region.

Reno wasn't alone.

> *Around the world, communities were awakening to a similar pattern: bottom-up, place-based economies rooted in timeless principles.*

This shift gave rise to what would later be called Cosmolocalism. Since our movement began in Northern Nevada in 2003, what was once fringe—localism, Main Street renewal, bioregionalism, and regenerative economies has become increasingly mainstream. The realization is growing—global problems require local solutions.

This growing awareness sparked new frameworks—uniting the best of ancient wisdom with 21st century possibility.

COSMOLOCALISM: GLOBAL VISION, LOCAL ACTION, AND THE TIMELESS LOGIC OF LOVE

One of the most promising emerging frameworks is Cosmolocalism, which unites two seemingly opposing ideas: global Cosmopolitanism and rooted Localism. It revives an ancient vision—a Commonwealth of Village Republics—by combining local economic and political autonomy with global cooperation.

Cosmolocalism empowers communities to manage their own decentralized institutions while remaining connected to broader global networks.

Technologies such as blockchain, distributed ledgers, and peer-to-peer systems now allow for creating what I've termed a Network Commons. In this shared, community-based infrastructure, local resources are collectively governed for the common good. As I've defined it:

> "A Network Commons represents a community-based collaborative initiative where nonprofits, private for-profits, religious organizations, civic entities, mutual aid groups, cooperatives, and public resources are intentionally interconnected, shared, and governed by an engaged community of stakeholders."

These networks strengthen local resilience, particularly as global supply chains falter, by activating smaller bioregional economies based on local resources and living ecosystems. They also reshape our approach to community development, shifting focus from growth and consumption to ecological balance, well-being, and connectedness. Although it may sound novel in an era of "big everything," Cosmolocalism is rooted in timeless wisdom.

As that concept matured, it became clear that its foundations run deeper than policy or design; it resonates with the spiritual and moral frameworks that have long guided humanity. It reflects Jesus and the early Christian communities, Gandhi's vision of Village Republics and the Sarvodaya Shramadana Movement led by Dr. Ari in Sri Lanka, where the living network of 5,000 community-based economies thrives today. We didn't have to reinvent the wheel—it was already rolling along.

This convergence transcends both religious and secular boundaries. It echoes Catholic social teaching—starting with Pope Leo XIII's Rerum Novarum and Pope Pius XI's Quadragesima Anno—and affirms the Virtue of solidarity: a commitment to the common good that begins at home and radiates outward through lived Virtue.

Early 20th-century Christian thinker G.K. Chesterton referred to this kind of decentralized economy as Distributism. His famous line still rings true:

> "The Christian ideal has not been tried and found wanting. It has been found difficult and left untried."

In our current moment of civilizational fracture, Cosmolocalism and Symbiotic Networks may offer a new opportunity to try again—to express Divine Love in action, transcending religious divisions and political capture.

Even before the term Cosmolocalism entered everyday use in 2013, we already sensed the need for local autonomy and were ready to act.

But as our hands built face-to-face networks, our eyes turned to the digital frontier. Could we carry this sacred coherence into the virtual world without losing its soul?

For Cosmolocalism to flourish in the 21st century, it needed something new: a technological foundation rooted in the timeless logic of Love. The answer wasn't more screens or faster apps—it was reanimating the slow, sacred process we had already experienced in real life.

DIGITAL KINSHIP: WHY TECHNOLOGY NEEDS THE ANCIENT BLUEPRINT

As technology rapidly reshaped human life, we began to ask: How could timeless principles guide the digital tools shaping our future? Ten years into our Symbiotic Culture experiment, two "Cosmolocal" questions emerged:

> *How do we deepen mutual benefit locally,*
> *and how do we use technology*
> *to spread these networks globally?*

As I shared previously, our Connections Gatherings and Arts Festival didn't become the "Holy Grail" of community-building. But we kept going, focused on expanding mutual benefit. Even without today's language—Ancient Blueprint, Wineskin Networks, Symbiotic Kinship, Culture of Connection—we intuitively understood we were already connecting the "islands of coherence" in our region.

That was the insight that led to our rebranding as Connecting the Good. Our monthly breakfasts and lunches became grassroots labs—building trust, fostering resilience, and supporting those uplifting "the least of us." As social media rose, a new question emerged:

> Could digital tools strengthen real-world trust rather than isolate us? Before we could answer how to use technology for good, we had to confront a more fundamental question: Is it possible to create technology that fosters connection, not control?

Over the past two decades, digital platforms have shaped public perception, imposing narratives, fueling division, encouraging addiction, and turning people into products. They have disconnected us from each other and from place. With AI accelerating, the risk deepens: the more we rely on it, the more it may shape—and even enslave—us. What would it mean to design technology not just from the mind, but from the heart? What if it could emerge from the Ancient Blueprint itself?

ROOTED IN TRUST: HOW THIRD-PARTY CONNECTIONS BUILD COMMUNITY

To answer these questions, we had to return to what we knew best—not algorithms or data, but the ancient, slow work of trust. As shared previously, our Symbiotic Networks in Reno were built one conversation at a time. I contacted trusted individuals across the business, nonprofit, religious, and civic sectors. Once rapport was established, I invited them to bring their trusted connections. Step by step, we grew from individuals to networks to communities.

You might recall Stanford sociologist Mark Granovetter's concept of "weak ties"—those who bridge silos by connecting adjacent communities. Long before we formally launched Symbiotic Networks, these connections were already laying the groundwork for community resilience.

Here's a simple example: Two friends meet for coffee. A recently single person is introduced to someone whom the other knows and trusts. Even if it doesn't lead to love, the act itself reflects something profound: trust passed hand to hand, turning a frozen asset into a shared blessing.

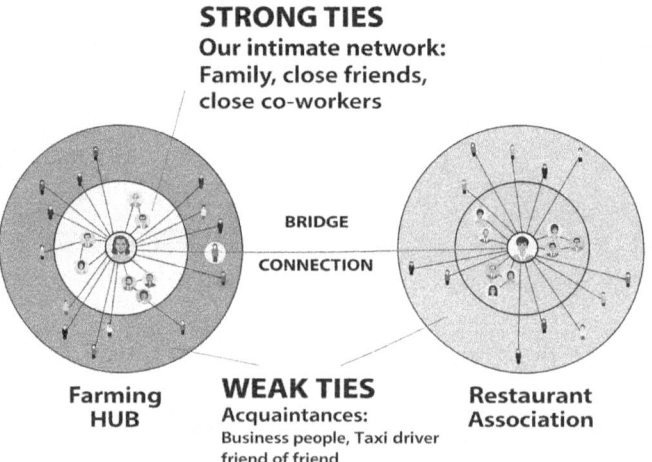

These introductions—helping someone find a job, a mentor, or housing—occur daily. They are acts of pure generosity, what Pope Benedict called Gratuitousness. There is no expectation of return—just the joy of giving.

> *This longing for communion is more than biology or self-interest; it is a spiritual pattern from the Ancient Blueprint reflecting our need for kinship, belonging, and community.*

The instinct to build bridges is ingrained in what it means to be human.

Sarvodaya calls this Empathetic Joy—delighting in the happiness of others. Dr. A.T. Ariyaratne taught that such joy is essential for a just and loving society. It's Love in action, a Virtue moving through us and becoming Divine Love in the world.

We witness this during crises—Earthquakes, floods, fires—when strangers help strangers without hesitation. The real question is: Can we live this way all the time? My answer is yes.

These small acts are the true currency of a Culture of Connection. As C.S. Lewis put it, they reflect how goodness *"everlastingly emerges, stilly and tranquilly, into space and time."*

This is the Ancient Blueprint in action—mutual benefit radiating from Love. So, what does this have to do with technology? Everything.

For technology to serve a Culture of Connection, it must be rooted in Love and extend kinship beyond family or tribe, even to those we find hard to love. This is Symbiotic Kinship, the only true foundation for building community, online or offline. These everyday acts of trust are not just social niceties but the seeds of a much larger design.

HOW A BOTTOM-UP NETWORK OF TRUST BECOMES A SUPER-HIGHWAY OF LOVE

Across all our networks—from food systems to local arts—trusted third-party connections consistently transformed ideals into real-world systems of mutual benefit. Symbiotic Networks extended the benefits of Symbiotic Kinship to all who joined, not just because of noble ideals but also because those ideals addressed real, functional needs.

BIRTHING THE SYMBIOTIC AGE

The antidote to top-down tech is a bottom-up network of trust, rooted in Love and lived Virtues.

This is fractal empowerment, where Virtues like generosity emerge at every level. In healthy communities, virtuous human interactions become the foundation of enduring networks—and the technologies that support them. Trusted third-party connections function as scaffolding that extends kinship from individuals to organizations to entire communities.

The Symbiotic Culture DNA that emerged from our experience provides a blueprint for building this foundation—a true Super Highway of Love. Starting with Love and a mutual desire to embody it, we identified guiding principles and lived Virtues such as generosity. These became the architecture for one-to-one and multi-scale network connections.

We then applied these connections to address what we now call the 12 Core Community Needs—Local Economy, Food and Water, Energy, Clean & Healthy Natural Environment, Community Peace & Safety, Neighbor Helping Neighbor, Community Empowerment of those on the "margins," Arts & Culture, Housing, Family and Community Health & Wellness, Education and Mentoring, and Religion/Spirituality in Service.)—we created organic, multi-nodal networks in many of them that bridged silos and helped Connect the Good around each need.

This superhighway creates a new type of Network Commons in every community, fostering a parallel culture, economy, and politics.

Rooted in everyday acts of generosity, these relational foundations became the scaffolding for technology designed to serve Love rather than control. This brings us back to the heart of this chapter:

How can we use the Internet to amplify benefits on the "Outernet"?

It all boils down to one truth: Love is our coherent foundation—not just a sentiment, but the animating power behind every circle of action.

*With Love at the center,
technology becomes a system that accelerates
and amplifies real-world transformation.*

REWIRING CONNECTION: TECHNOLOGY IN SERVICE TO LOVE

Today's dominant platforms extract data, enforce silos, and impose narratives. In 2013, we didn't yet have the language of "Symbiotic Culture DNA," but we were already seeking ways to design technology that enhanced connection rather than control.

What if we could accelerate connection within Symbiotic Communities—liberating "frozen assets" trapped in silos and hierarchies? It felt like a breakthrough moment, akin to discovering a social $E = MC^2$: a means for Divine Love to become tangible, transforming matter as the Transcendent becomes Immanent.

From that pattern, we envisioned a technology that could consolidate spiritual, social, and economic capital locally, and connect it globally—a new Global Commonwealth of resilient economies grounded in care.

With smartphones in hand, every community could hold the keys to Connecting the Good. What if each region's "total intelligence" were shared and accessible?

*Imagine an open-source "cloud" above each locality—
a living commons of land, people, knowledge,
and capital—where anyone
could give or receive what's needed.*

Think of the synchronicities born from third-party trust: jobs, mentors, partners, collaborators. Now imagine that amplified by technology designed for mutual uplift at scale.

What we now call "sacred technology" may sound novel, but it reflects something ancient—a desire to create tools that serve what is already holy: the Love of God, flowing through human connection and care.

This was before social media calcified into top-down narrative engines. But just as Symbiotic Circles create local common ground, we can still reclaim the open Internet's original promise—a global commons for connection, if we choose.

THE BIRTH OF ONESPHERA: TRANSLATING WISDOM INTO CODE

As I pondered how we might develop technology to enhance and expand our Symbiotic Networks, something unexpected happened—a synchronous meeting with a friend that felt more like Divine orchestration than chance.

He was deeply spiritual and community-oriented and happened to be the developer who built MySpace's original platform, onboarding six million users in nine months. Pre-Facebook, that was massive.

He also recognized the potential to connect goodness through technology. We began envisioning a way to link connectors and super-connectors across domains such as food, education, economy, environment, arts, and spirituality.

> *Was technology the "super-duper connector" that could help create a new layer of the Internet— a planetary superorganism emerging through cultural symbiogenesis?*

Until then, all our Symbiotic Networks operated on informal infrastructure—no investors, no business plan. We gathered people, created space, and let trust do the rest. We weren't building another silo—we were creating an "unbrand" to lift all brands.

This new vision, however, required more: a formal structure, a team, and funding. So we launched "CONEXUS," a purpose-driven civic engagement app designed to empower local organizations, businesses, churches, governments, and citizens to build self-reliant economies. It didn't replace our face-to-face networks—it extended them by accelerating connections.

"It's not who you know—it's who you don't know and need to know that contributes to innovation."

Unlike most tech startups, CONEXUS was initially tested in reality. We translated successful elements from living networks into digital design. Although we loved the name, it was already in use. We tested "SharePortal," before finally settling on a name that stuck: OneSphera.

Unlike our prior networks, this time we did need a prospectus. We envisioned a reality-sourced platform that would serve the hyperlocal economy, generating revenue through local advertising and offering premium services for groups and residents. It was designed to support resilient community self-governance.

By 2014, we had raised our first capital and begun the challenging process of translating twenty years of intuitive community-building into software. I had never written a manual for what I did—I followed the Spirit, reached out to catalytic connectors, and allowed trust to expand through multi-nodal hubs. In hindsight, I see it flowed from my awakening to the Transcendent and the web of nature. Ecosystems develop through interconnections, even as society fractures into dominance hierarchies. This contrast led me to ask: Can we build networks rooted in Divine order?

The answer was yes. Our Symbiotic Networks weren't just a theory—they were lived practice, born of the Ancient Blueprint and empowered by Divine Love. I wasn't building this as a systems consultant, government official, or tech founder. I was simply someone who had experienced it—on Main Street, in nonprofits, and in local organizing.

With guidance from the Sarvodaya movement and Dr. Ari's friendship, we knew we were following a time-tested path. We didn't impose a system; instead, we responded to real needs with open hands, making all the difference.

Symbiotic Culture and Networks—and now OneSphera—did not emerge from thin air; they developed from a lifetime of spiritual experiences and a lineage rooted in my relationship with Jesus Christ.

For Christians and other people of faith, these tools become vehicles for living out our faith beyond Sunday walls—serving neighbors, healing divides, and embodying Christ's love through tangible community action. They are wineskins, not replacements—complementary vessels for Kingdom life (where we are vessels for bringing the Kingdom of Heaven) to every sphere of society.

REVERSE-ENGINEERING TRUST: FROM RELATIONSHIP TO ARCHITECTURE

To bring this vision to life, we had to translate something intuitive and relational into software—a journey that began with one core question: How is trust built? Our task was to reverse-engineer the face-to-face community-building process that had fueled our Symbiotic Networks and encode it into OneSphera.

I spent nearly two years distilling two decades of grassroots organizing into a digital platform. The goal was to replicate how

I facilitated trusted third-party connections—individually and across silos—to form mutually supportive, regional networks.

This involved conversing with leaders who had helped build these networks, listening intently, and identifying the specific, repeatable steps that could form the platform's foundation. While each leader had a unique story, they followed a typical relational pattern.

For instance, when someone wants to make a third-party connection, they often begin with a shared community interest, like local food, which triggers memory pathways. Key phrases such as "farmers' markets," "backyard farming," or "community-supported agriculture" unlock trusted relationships and resources.

Trust wasn't just an idea. It was built moment by moment through meaningful context, shared language, and a sense of purpose.

To scale this trust-based architecture, we needed clarity about people's passions and their roles in each sphere of community life. After discovering how the community established these essential keyword connections, I surveyed leaders in various areas of community needs.

I wanted to know what the local food system leaders cared about and what they were doing in their part of the food system. I surveyed twenty leaders and asked them to rank their top key food sub-interests—what we had called "Sub-Spheres." We used real-world and real-time community needs as the foundation for the design of OneSphera. What was striking about this approach is that it naturally encourages many levels of network formation.

For example, while we built an overall Local Food System Network, we also encouraged people to form even more specific subnetworks. Two good examples are the backyard farmers' and permaculture networks. This parallels how natural systems function as nested and interconnected parts and wholes, as discussed in Section 1.

BIRTHING THE SYMBIOTIC AGE

TRUST: THE CURRENCY OF SYMBIOTIC CULTURE

Each layer of insight brought us back to a deeper truth—one we had seen repeatedly across all our networks. Exploring Spheres and Sub-spheres reaffirmed something I had recognized for years: trust is the bedrock of meaningful connection and collaboration.

Stephen Covey called trust "the new currency of our world." Mistrust creates friction—trust removes it. That insight shaped every phase of our work.

From the very beginning, trust was our shared currency. In early meetings, connectors shared their networks because they believed in a deeper purpose. Trust was built daily and face-to-face, as organizations made and upheld small agreements. Simply being part of a transparent local network raised the bar for accountability.

Because our networks were grounded in mutual benefit and the mission of Connecting the Good, self-promoters who didn't align with that ethic gradually left.

Trust wasn't just a value—
it was the atmosphere we breathed.

Those who stayed found that cooperation served self-interest as well. We saw this clearly in our Local Food System Network. Initially, restaurateurs viewed each other as competitors. However, within a year of network-building, they began acting like collaborators. A culture shift had taken root, and it was no accident.

It reflected spiritual common sense—a shared recognition that universal Virtues like love, compassion, and generosity aren't idealistic extras. They are the *mechanics of trust*. Dr. Ari called personality awakening a moral and spiritual awakening: people embodying the Virtues that allow the community to unify and thrive.

LOVE IS THE LOGIC OF LIFE: SCIENCE MEETS THE SACRED

It wasn't just our lived experience that confirmed this approach. Increasingly, science has begun to echo ancient truths. Modern research is catching up to the Ancient Blueprint—3,000 years of spiritual wisdom now affirmed by evolutionary biology.

The trust-based transformation we witnessed in Symbiotic Networks reflects what David Sloan Wilson and E.O. Wilson observed: networks rooted in cooperation and unity consistently outperform those fragmented by competition. Win-win collaboration surpasses win-lose systems that define the Culture of Separation.

Though initially skeptical, E.O. Wilson later embraced "group selection," arguing in his book, *The Social Conquest of Earth*, that morality, altruism, and cooperation evolved because cohesive groups were more likely to survive. Virtues like generosity and trust enhance a group's viability. They are the "lubricants" of cohesion, facilitating connection and collaboration at scale.

Even without knowledge of the Ancient Blueprint, Dr. Ari, or our work in Reno, many scientists are arriving at the same conclusion: we are biologically and culturally wired for cooperation.

> *Science now affirms what sacred religious traditions have long taught: Love is the logic of life. It generates the coherence and compassion that move us from survival to thrival.*

Yet within the Culture of Separation—where people strive to "make their mark"—I have observed well-meaning professionals who feel compelled to sanitize this wisdom. They downplay the spiritual source that has sustained humanity for millennia to make it more palatable for academia, media, and institutions.

I chose a different path.

Why domesticate the power of Love—the creative power that countless cultures recognize as common sense? Why dilute the very core that makes us whole?

We don't need to tame Love—we need to liberate it.

LOVE, TECHNOLOGY, AND THE UNSHAKEABLE BLUEPRINT

Our work is to build "wineskin networks" that accelerate the flow of Love and direct it where it's needed most. Like hyperbaric oxygen therapy, which floods the body with healing oxygen, Symbiotic Culture and OneSphera act as a Superhighway for Love, delivering care and connection to the margins, to "the least of us."

What worked in Reno and Sri Lanka's most disenfranchised communities now carries scientific affirmation. But it won't be science alone that saves us. As we became radically welcoming in Reno, our civilization must rediscover and reweave the spiritual wisdom we've long ignored.

The survival of our world depends on recovering the Ancient Blueprint—those Virtues and Transcendent Principles that have always held communities together. Whether approached scientifically, culturally, spiritually, or religiously, these shared Virtues are the glue of social coherence. Upon this unshakable rock of Divine Love, we built OneSphera: to scale, strengthen, and circulate the sacred logic of connection through heart-based technology.

And so, OneSphera was born—not from Silicon Valley ambition but from lived trust, spiritual lineage, and a longing to Connect the Good. It is not just a platform but a vessel—a sacred container for the logic of Love in the digital age.

But let's be clear: technology does not transform hearts—the Spirit of Love does. OneSphera is no substitute for Divine presence; it's simply a tool that helps carry and coordinate the good that God is already doing through people.

But how do you encode trust? How do you digitize a culture of care without losing its soul? That was our next challenge—and our next frontier.

BIRTHING THE SYMBIOTIC AGE

CHAPTER 27

ONESPHERA: A DIGITAL FRAMEWORK
FOR FRACTAL EMPOWERMENT

The digital world moves fast. But trust moves at the speed of relationship. Having helped build real-world Symbiotic Networks, we understood how trust is cultivated through shared purpose, authentic connection, and consistent service.

But translating the sacred slowness of face-to-face trust into the rapid-fire domain of technology posed a new challenge. Could we carry the heart into the machine? This chapter explores how we tried—and what emerged.

TRANSLATING TRUST INTO TECHNOLOGY

We embedded "trust principles" into OneSphera's design from the beginning—data sovereignty, privacy, and reputation. Our core belief was simple: users should control what they share and what others see. As we wrote in our prospectus:

"You decide what to share with whom—and can change it anytime."

With simple, transparent settings, you also had complete "volume control" over what you saw from others. Visibility was opt-in, not assumed. Our motto said it best:

"If you don't want to see it, you won't. If you don't want to share it, it won't be."

Trust and security weren't just features—they were the foundation. By prioritizing user empowerment, we could build toward OneSphera's unique contribution. This relational foundation shaped every design decision. But we also foresaw a deeper question emerging: What happens when intelligent machines begin shaping human connection?

All of this happened years before AI entered the mainstream. Back then, platforms like ChatGPT hadn't yet emerged. However, we were already envisioning something more relational than one-to-one chatbots. We were building a shared interface with AI, a "Social AI," acting as a teammate, helping many people connect, coordinate, and build community.

In hindsight, OneSphera foreshadowed the emergence of what are now being called Web 4.0, the Spatial and the Symbiotic Web—new paradigms where intelligent, decentralized systems are designed to serve human flourishing. While the Spatial Web focuses on blending physical and digital environments through immersive experiences like AR and VR, and the Symbiotic Web centers on intelligent, adaptive systems that learn from and serve their users, OneSphera goes further.

It roots these technological advances in relational trust, community participation, and shared Virtue, creating not just a smarter web, but a more loving and just one. It puts the heart at the heart of the machine.

While others pursued technological sophistication, we asked a different question:

Can a digital platform help a neighborhood and local region think, feel, and act more wisely as one?

That became our north star. OneSphera wasn't just about Virtues—it was about turning those Virtues into action through what I now call Augmented Collective Intelligence: the ability for a whole community to think and act more wisely together than any individual could alone.

But to make that kind of intelligence a reality, we needed more than trust—we needed a system that could move actual resources through genuine relationships. To move from wisdom to action, we needed a framework for connection and coordinated cooperation that moved real-world resources (value) where they were most needed.

THE COMMUNITY VALUE CHAIN

For OneSphera to move past the good idea phase and mobilize resources, it required a method to circulate value across all areas of life. That's where the Community Value Chain came in: not just a system for connection, but for cooperation—a framework to transform frozen assets into shared abundance.

We called it the Value Chain Platform.

In business, a value chain refers to the steps that add value to a product or service, from design and production to distribution and customer support. Each step adds value and incurs cost, with multiple parties contributing and receiving compensation.

But this applies far beyond business. When I directed the San Diego Food Bank, we had to locate, store, and distribute surplus food. Volunteers did much of the work, but janitors, drivers, and coordinators still needed to be paid. And as much as I tried to give freely, I still needed a salary to support my family.

What's the point?

Some believe a Virtuous Economy should function as a pure Gift Economy—value given freely, without expecting anything in return. It's an inspiring ideal. But most people still need to pay for housing, food, healthcare, and more. That's why OneSphera was grounded in Divine Love and mutual benefit, yet intentionally designed to function within real-world economic constraints.

From that Transcendent foundation, we sought to activate local economies by bridging networked silos—turning isolated hubs into a unified Culture of Connection.

But connection meant more than infrastructure—it required a deeper ethos. To unlock the full potential of this Value Chain, we had to honor the vast diversity of how people create and share value.

REIMAGINING THE VIRTUOUS ECONOMY

This involved connecting people, places, and organizations that would otherwise remain isolated.

A core feature of the Virtuous Economy is that it embraces every form of contribution, regardless of background, identity, or economic model. Building bridges from the Culture of Separation to the Culture of Connection must honor the full spectrum of how people create and share value. Symbiotic Kinship means meeting people where they are, without demanding ideological conformity or fitting into a single exchange model.

This Universal Kinship approach avoids labeling one type of contribution as more important than another. It doesn't exclude efforts that don't align with a particular identity or worldview. While many networks promote value through narrow lenses—Christian-only, regenerative, race-based, or identity-centered—such tribalism, though often well-intentioned, can unintentionally constrain the transformation it seeks.

We must accelerate value exchange across boundaries to shift mainstream economies, not restrict it.

That's why OneSphera expands the definition of a Value Chain beyond any single silo or ideology. It envisions a Network Commons—a regional ecosystem where the spiritual, social, and economic strength of thousands of individuals and organizations can converge.

When bridges are built across silos, all forms of community capital—spiritual, social, natural, financial, and infrastructural—begin to circulate more freely. These bridges become superhighways of mutual benefit. To support and visualize this value flow, we needed tools to reveal the tangible and intangible exchanges that keep communities alive.

Initially developed by Verna Allee with support from international strategist Ken Vanosky (who also advised OneSphera), VNA maps and analyzes value exchanges within and between networks. It distinguishes between tangible exchanges, such as products, services, and money, and intangible exchanges, such as trust, knowledge, and collaboration.

Equally important, VNA underscores individuals' roles in nurturing network health—not only what they give or receive, but also how they cultivate resilience. For instance, a network weaver connects people and resources while fostering trust. VNA illustrates how material and relational flows interact to create a thriving, interdependent system.

This illustrates how the intangible power of the Ancient Blueprint accelerates tangible benefits. By applying this corporate innovation to a Community Value Chain, OneSphera reimagined VNA for the common good, making invisible value visible.

Yet mapping value was only part of the story, showing us what was present. To act together wisely, we needed more than visibility—we needed shared intelligence to help entire communities think, feel, and act as one.

AUGMENTED COLLECTIVE INTELLIGENCE: A DIGITAL VESSEL FOR OPERATIONALIZING LOVE

Most digital platforms are designed to enhance individual performance or information flow. However, OneSphera was built for something more radical, the Augmented Collective Intelligence I mentioned earlier.

This isn't virtual reality or the metaverse. It's not another siloed social network designed to capture attention. Instead, think of a living map—a real-time interface that reflects your community's spiritual, social, economic, and cultural life.

OneSphera wasn't built to simulate reality, but to support, synchronize, and accelerate it. A whole community can think, feel, and act more wisely together than any person or institution could alone.

This vision of distributed wisdom aligns with emerging terms like the Symbiotic Web and the Spatial Web, but with a crucial distinction: OneSphera connects to the spiritual intelligence already present in communities, amplifying the Virtues within, making wisdom, compassion, and cooperation scalable.

Rather than drawing us into virtual realms, it reweaves our local regions with sacred intelligence, helping communities feel and move as one, from the inside out. Biologically, it resembles a social nervous system—a mycelial intelligence grounded not in code but relational trust. This represents the emergent wisdom of a healthy, living network, where insight and compassion travel at the speed of love.

You may recall the concept of co-intelligence—how communities discover together shared Virtues and needs, as we did at our 2006 Valentine's Day gathering in Reno. OneSphera embodies co-intelligence—augmented, digitized, and aligned with the common good.

We weren't just building tools.

We were building community cognition—
a platform where decision-making, cooperation,
and coordination reflect the lived wisdom
of the people themselves.

This wasn't artificial intelligence replacing us; it was relational intelligence empowering us.

That was the missing link between trust and transformation. OneSphera helped people position themselves within a greater whole—connecting passions, relationships, and needs into meaningful, purpose-driven roles. It served as a digital vessel for operationalizing love.

Like a smartphone's navigation system guiding you toward what matters, OneSphera helps people discover people, projects, values, and shared needs already present in their community. It serves as a relational compass for love in action. But awareness alone isn't enough. To bring this social nervous system to life, we needed to reward love in action. In other words, not just map the network but also animate it.

How do we recognize and sustain those who quietly keep communities alive—volunteers, connectors, mentors, caregivers?

How do we circulate trust, generosity, and service in ways that energize rather than exhaust?

This is where the next layer of innovation emerged: gamifying generosity—not to manipulate behavior but to celebrate and accelerate it, to honor the sacred economy already flowing beneath the surface. But how would we do this?

ANIMATING THE VIRTUOUS ECONOMY

How could we create a system that celebrated care and encouraged it to ripple outward?

Love, once visible, must also be sustained. For that, we needed to honor the hidden labor of community life—the small acts that make big transformation possible.

To animate this network of trust, we needed a way to reward those contributing to the common good by offering reciprocal benefit. The Value Chain Platform achieved this by recognizing community members for actions that enhance shared value, expanding on the established corporate definition of a value chain to that which would bring value to the entire community.

Instead of vertical relationships—between governments and citizens, businesses and customers, or nonprofits and volunteers—OneSphera flattened hierarchies, just as every one of our Symbiotic Networks did.

> *People once treated as commodified "Objects" become empowered "Subjects" with agency in a vibrant, participatory Network Commons. Anyone can "Connect the Good" and be rewarded.*

There are no uplines or downlines—only horizontal relationships among individuals, businesses, and organizations.

Imagine earning rewards by promoting a local product, church, or senior care program—sharing your passion with trusted peers. Your network transforms into a vibrant marketplace. This hidden asset enhances the value of what you support and the community itself. It's a win-win-win: you benefit, the recipient benefits, and so does the one you connected them to.

Multilevel marketing and affiliate programs redirect advertising budgets to individuals who drive engagement. OneSphera took that concept further, applying it to the commons, not for profit, but for shared prosperity. Anyone—not just leaders—could earn rewards for creating and circulating value.

> *We aimed to unlock "frozen assets":*
> *underrecognized acts of trust, care, and service*
> *that keep communities alive.*

Consider both formal and informal contributions—volunteering, shared rides, childcare, mentoring, or third-party introductions. These contributions are the invisible threads of community life. OneSphera honored them.

Participants would earn "extra credit" for their symbiotic contributions. Instead of one-to-one transactions, the platform recognized ripple effects throughout the entire network. Members shared trusted referrals—posts, reviews, and recommendations—and earned points. We called this "gossip for good."

As we wrote in our prospectus:

> "We've developed a method to share financial rewards with our customers by building an engaged community that explicitly shares their precise interests in real-time."

We also created a high-quality, opt-in, laser-targeted advertising system that boosted efficiency by honoring user agency and intent—the result: a constellation of loyalty, shared needs, and collaborative action.

One video in our campaign illustrated how we helped local businesses through "Proof of Community Cooperation and Influence"—a blockchain-enabled loyalty system for grassroots participation.

Now, imagine scaling that to thousands of community-based organizations. That's how gamification can energize a regenerative economy.

The secret sauce? Radical community engagement:

> "We support our engaged members and incentivize them to share their truthful opinions, ratings, and more. They find like-minded people and organizations, earn rewards, and co-create a thriving, interactive, regenerative economy."

Still, we knew that even the most virtuous systems couldn't flourish in isolation. No matter how relational or innovative we build a loving local economy, we live within a global economic architecture designed for extraction. And that had to change.

To understand how OneSphera could challenge that architecture, we had to ask: how do you flip a global pyramid built on exploitation into a circle of shared strength?

BIRTHING THE SYMBIOTIC AGE

FLATTENING HIERARCHIES: INVERTING THE PYRAMID

Now that we've explored how OneSphera's Community Value Chain democratizes the local economy, let's widen the lens. Our global economic system—rooted in the Culture of Separation—is breaking down. Top-down models built on extraction and consolidation are losing ground. The question is: What comes next?

OneSphera offers a practical alternative by aggregating all forms of local capital into a bottom-up trading system.

Accelerating and circularizing regional economies keeps money and resources circulating within communities, reducing the "giant sucking sound" of capital flowing upward.

In 2017, I had a pivotal meeting with Bill Melton, a rare entrepreneur who helped build billion-dollar tech companies like Verifone and served on the board of AOL. He was also an early investor in PayPal. When someone with that résumé looked at OneSphera and said,

"This platform has the power to invert the global financial and political pyramid," we paid attention.

Melton was the one who coined the term "Value Chain Platform" to describe the mechanism that could support a Global Commonwealth of Strong Regional Economies. In the years since, the cracks in globalization have only deepened.

Even those at the top see the unraveling. In a 2022 shareholder letter, BlackRock CEO Larry Fink wrote, *"The 70-year-old economic globalization project is over."* He cited the war in Ukraine and the collapse of integrated supply chains as signs of systemic change.

In addition to the destabilizing impacts of COVID-19, energy and resource insecurity, and a rising multipolar world order, countries are clearly turning back to domestic resilience. Even global power players now acknowledge the need to re-localize.

This shift isn't ideological—it's practical. As vertical systems falter, local citizens, faith leaders, businesses, community networks, and regional governments will carry the load.

What once seemed utopian is becoming essential. The threads of business, service, mutual aid, spirituality, and innovation must now be woven together, not around ideology, but around the urgent call to rebuild from the bottom up, in a world rooted in connection rather than extraction.

TURNING TRUST INTO EXCHANGE

The next challenge for OneSphera was turning trust into a tangible exchange by shortening supply chains and deepening local autonomy.

This is where value chain networks—like our Reno Symbiotic Networks, enhanced by OneSphera—can revitalize regional economies through import substitution: replacing imported goods and services with local options and building self-sufficiency from the ground up.

Global coordination emerges as regions rediscover their strengths, fostering local prosperity and outward trade in widening circles of exchange.

To effect real change, we must start at the grassroots—counties, states, and the millions of villages and cities that form our local bedrock. The local economy is a core principle of Symbiotic Culture DNA. As we wove together our region's siloed efforts,

OneSphera emerged to circulate "good goods and great goodness" more effectively.

OneSphera works best as a "growth hierarchy," fortifying horizontal collaboration while dismantling top-heavy extractor models. The term for this is disintermediation, which means removing unnecessary middle steps from the value chain. Disintermediation lowers costs, and increases flow and efficiency.

A vivid example comes from Dr. Ari's early life. Raised near the ocean in southern Sri Lanka, young Ari was steeped in service thanks to a neighboring Buddhist temple. At 14, he met an elderly woman laboring to process coconut husks—hard work for little pay. Ari didn't walk away after learning that those at the top earned eight times her wage. He organized a women's coconut husking cooperative—the region's first—and the supply chain was "flattened" so those who did the work were able to earn more.

That simple act reflected the Ancient Blueprint in motion: a spiritual, economic, and ecological correction. Flattening the chain not only addressed injustice and poverty, but it also reduced the carbon footprint tied to overextended supply systems. Nearly 20 percent of greenhouse gas emissions in global food systems come from transport alone.

The lesson? Many "middlemen" extract more than they contribute. Disintermediation is a call to reweave value chains around dignity, locality, and mutual benefit. And at the heart of that reweaving is what I've emphasized throughout this book: the Ancient Blueprint—radiating Divine Love—is the true foundation of a new Culture of Connection.

OneSphera

A WHOLE CLOTH MOVEMENT TO CONNECT THE GOOD

Knowing that top-down systems are failing is only half the equation. The real work lies in building something better, starting with coherence and moving toward coordinated action.

Over the past decade, many well-intentioned "New Economy" efforts have emerged to connect like-minded people around shared visions. These initiatives often assume that solutions will arise organically through connection. That's partly true—but not the whole story. Connection and coordination are necessary, but not sufficient.

In today's fragmented world, it's easy for networks to think their thread is THE solution. However, through organizing Symbiotic Networks and designing OneSphera, I've discovered a more profound truth: these threads only become transformative when woven into a whole-cloth movement to Connect the Good.

These "islands of coherence" must be rooted in mutual benefit and the Ancient Blueprint to contain all spiritual, political, economic, and cultural streams.

Drawing from Sarvodaya and our Reno experience, we discovered a natural sequence that inverts the global pyramid. It begins with sovereign individuals gathering around a common purpose rooted in Divine Love—a force as fundamental to spiritual life as gravity is to physical reality. Love, not ideology, forms the solid foundation of a new society.

From coherence arises the desire to connect, cooperate, and collaborate in ways that honor each person's unique mission.

These efforts create a universally embracing network responsive to the 12 community needs. Coordination only makes sense when coherence, connection, and cooperation are already present.

BIRTHING THE SYMBIOTIC AGE

The foundation of this structure that allows us to move from vision to action is Symbiotic Culture DNA, a living pattern we had been practicing all along.

DESIGNING SYSTEMS ROOTED IN LOVE

Symbiotic Culture DNA influences everything in OneSphera and our real-world networks—from intention to action. As described in Chapter 15, it starts with a common Purpose: Connecting the Good and promoting mutual benefit. This unifying aim brings together diverse efforts into something greater than the sum of their parts.

From this purpose flow shared principles, guiding Virtues that shape how we serve, relate, and organize. These principles take root through lived Virtues: Love, Integrity, Courage, Service, and Respect. Finally, we ground our work in real-world community needs aligned with individual passions and concerns. Focusing on these needs directs our energy where it matters most.

Then comes the Network Infrastructure: the people, organizations, and assets already present in a region. Connecting them creates a living Network Commons, where mutual benefit flows like lifeblood through an ecosystem.

This sequence—purpose, principles, Virtues, Needs, and Infrastructure— forms the architecture of Symbiotic Culture DNA and underpins OneSphera.

Building that infrastructure—a digital superhighway of Love—required precision. Codifying the steps and phrases that accelerate connection took two years. Using language that unlocked trust, we built a system that matched people's passions with community needs.

This wasn't outreach for outreach's sake. It was a purposeful interaction, woven into the larger framework of Symbiotic Kinship. That's coherence—something worth coordinating.

Over the years, I've encountered brilliant strategies and designs, but most have remained siloed, speaking only to the already convinced. Symbiotic Networks and platforms like OneSphera bring these visions into the center of public life.

But beautiful systems mean little if they remain detached from everyday life. That's why the next challenge was grounding our technology in the specific needs of real people.

GROUNDING TECHNOLOGY IN REAL-WORLD NEEDS

If we're serious about re-localizing the economy and building regional resilience, then our technology must serve the people, projects, businesses, nonprofits, and institutions that are already doing the work on the ground. Now that we see the potential for reweaving these threads of coherence to serve real world needs, let's review what these threads are.

As noted previously, there are:

- 11 million formal nonprofits (plus 50 million informal groups)
- 2.35 million religious congregations and 10 million informal spiritual groups
- Over 800,000 religious groups in the US and Europe combined
- 70 million purpose-driven small businesses worldwide

These leaders often work in silos, unaware of the larger framework that could unite them. Promising threads include:

- Spiritual and religious care networks
- Regenerative and localization movements
- Civic bridge-building and democracy efforts
- Purpose-driven businesses and "new economy" models
- Creation care, charities, and community wealth-building

Imagine the coherence of uniting these under one shared intent: using technology to accelerate mutual benefit. The true testing ground isn't a whiteboard or Zoom room —the real laboratories are our neighborhoods and communities, where people face real challenges.

In four decades of community work, I've seen how easily activists can become disconnected from everyday concerns. We get so caught up in the brilliance of our ideas, we fail to notice if they speak to the lived realities of those at the margins.

Gandhi warned the Indian National Congress:

> "Until we stand in the fields with the millions that toil daily under the hot sun, we will not represent India."

He called leaders to move from head and heart to hands. Dr. Ari embodied this by listening directly to villagers, not elites. He didn't impose solutions, he asked people to map their needs.

Through this dignified process, Sarvodaya identified ten core needs. Years later, when we crowd-sourced in Reno, we uncovered twelve, six of which aligned with Sri Lanka's.

This bottom-up approach grounded our network in the realities people face:

- Safety, family well-being, and economic insecurity
- Healthcare access and homeownership struggles
- Moral and civic decline
- Environmental degradation
- Political polarization, institutional distrust, and corruption
- Extraction of local wealth by global oligarchs

To respond, we worked with those already serving—nonprofits, churches, small businesses, and civic leaders. Any real solution must meet them where they are.

So, how does this all come alive in a real community? Let's return to the heart of the matter—what it looks like when these values take root—and how design, philosophy, and community practice intertwine in OneSphera's lived experience.

As a closet techie, I was thrilled to help design a platform that could emulate Beloved Community, infused with Symbiotic Culture DNA at every layer.

> *If we're going to invert the financial and political power pyramid, we need bottom-up social technology, not another top-down platform from the status quo.*

OneSphera was my attempt to replicate what I had previously practiced in building real-world Symbiotic Networks. As mentioned earlier, one of its most distinctive features is how it quickly and meaningfully connects people's passions and interests to individual and community needs and roles. OneSphera is dedicated to engaging communities as they are, radically including all segments and accelerating connection, cooperation, collaboration, and coordination toward a unified Network Commons.

Our brochure described OneSphera as "a dynamic, multi-layered reward system—a loyalty program that works—nested within a constellation of shared interests, needs, and collaborative projects." We emphasized support for engaging with other like-minded individuals and organizations, earning rewards, and co-creating a vibrant, interactive local community and economic ecosystem.

This wasn't hype. We built the architecture to make it real.

Now that we've explored the vision, let's drill down and see how the architecture works.

FROM PASSIONS TO PARTICIPATION: HOW THE FEATURES WORK

OneSphera mirrors how real communities form through trust, agency, and relationships. Individuals control what they see and share, progressing at their own pace. This "sovereignty-first" design ensures that technology amplifies human connection rather than replacing it.

At its core is the LET'S CONNECT! Engine. As our prospectus describes:

> "Connect you to your centers of passion—your spheres of interest and influence—and help you connect with others in your community who share them: to make friends, play, collaborate, volunteer, build networks, do business, practice mutual aid, and more."

These connections extend into every aspect of community life, forming a "smart community"—a kind of mycelial network that nourishes all participants. The system automatically recommends individuals, groups, and organizations based on shared interests. You're notified of "Affinity People" nearby, so connections feel organic, arising from mutual care and shared purpose.

While grounded locally, OneSphera also enables global connectivity—helping you connect with like-minded people wherever you are, whether at local events or in an airport worldwide.

OneSphera's features support this relational ecosystem in practical ways.

- LET'S TALK! enables secure messaging via text, email, or phone.
- LET'S MEET! provides an integrated event calendar aligned with your passions and community goals.
- LET'S SHARE! creates a digital marketplace for posting needs and offers—buy, sell, barter, donate—making resource exchange as natural as conversation.
- LET'S WORK! supports collaborative projects, team-building, job listings, and coordination with community partners.

Each tool reinforces a culture of mutual aid, civic collaboration, and economic self-determination.

Here's how it plays out. Imagine you have fruit trees and want to offer the extra harvest to local gleaners. You post it on the public feed. A neighbor clicks "I'm Interested," connecting you both. Even if someone can't help directly, they can still click "I Can Connect You to Another," sparking a trusted third-party connection. These small exchanges create ripple effects, building local resilience not through top-down directives, but through trust networks.

The context makes this different from a typical platform: these needs and offers are nested within the broader Symbiotic Culture DNA, which is rooted in twelve shared community needs. Each exchange contributes to a living ecosystem rather than merely a transaction.

PROJECTS are where connections deepen into purpose. Each is a living "cell" of Symbiotic Culture DNA—anchored in Transcendent purpose and mutual benefit, expressing Virtues in action, and addressing specific community needs.

Over two years, we refined how passions, roles, and needs align—avoiding mismatches and unlocking high-trust collaboration. This is the difference between just "networking" and co-creating a movement. OneSphera doesn't merely connect the like-minded—it activates a living system of meaningful roles, rooted in love and designed for real-world transformation.

THE NETWORK COMMONS IN ACTION

Let's take our Truckee River Clean-Up project as a real-world example. The "Bringing It All Together" graphic illustrates how OneSphera's features—PROJECTS, NEEDS & OFFERS, EVENTS, and NEWS—work harmoniously. With a single click, anyone can engage at a level aligned with their passions: volunteering a skill, attending the clean-up, writing an article, designing flyers, or helping with logistics.

Although OneSphera wasn't live during that campaign, we had already prototyped a comprehensive support system using our blockchain-based Value Chain Platform to gamify  participation. A time-based reward system unlocked new benefits at each stage, generating momentum. Imagine the power of incentivizing community engagement rather than just relying on outreach or advertising.

This project demonstrated how everyone can contribute and benefit. It transcended political, religious, and business lines, uniting people through shared purpose and practical action. Too often, we argue over distant global crises while neglecting the needs of our neighborhoods. OneSphera refocuses attention where life occurs—on the ground.

Every exchange between individuals, groups, and networks acts like a mycelial web, quietly nourishing a resilient ecosystem. Hundreds, even thousands, of these relational threads create a thriving Network Commons that serves the common good.

But we didn't stop there. Each person becomes a trusted node in a global tapestry of service.

We envisioned a Cosmolocal network spreading from each person—a trust-filled flow of resources through neighborhoods, cities, and nations, anchored in Divine Love and mutual benefit.

This isn't just about technology. OneSphera is a tool for breaking the trance—and the grip—of the Culture of Separation. Building trust and aligning action across boundaries responds to real-world needs with dignity and coordination. The features serve as bridges, becoming the interstitial tissue that connects communities that might otherwise remain isolated or in competition.

It's a digital Superhighway for a new culture—bridging silos and transforming society from the ground up. It was a beautiful vision. But as with all dreams, the path forward wasn't linear. OneSphera's story would be shaped not only by architecture and ideals, but also by real human lives.

A PAUSE WITH PURPOSE: THE FUTURE OF ONESPHERA

So, what happened to OneSphera?

We developed the software architecture, beta-tested features like LET'S CONNECT, and were almost ready for launch—until an unexpected tragedy changed everything. In 2018, my close friend and business partner suffered a traumatic brain injury in a fiery car crash on Highway 80. His recovery took three years. By the time he returned, I had already ventured into another project. Then, as I'll share in Chapter 28, I faced my own near-death crisis.

Another reason OneSphera never launched was funding. While we had generous early support, we never secured the large-scale investment we needed—and in hindsight, that may have been a blessing. I still hadn't completely grokked how stubbornly the system would resist an endeavor that raises all ships and that benefits the whole community.

Though monetizable, OneSphera wasn't designed for profit-hungry investors. It was built to empower communities, not feed the appetite of venture funders.

Looking back, I realize I wasn't spiritually ready to steward something so significant. Had we succeeded too soon, OneSphera might have been bought out, stripped of its mission, and repackaged as another profit-driven platform. It may have functioned, but it would've lost its soul.

I needed time to grow into the kind of person who could hold space for such a vision. That required discomfort, reflection, and a deeper understanding than I had five—or even ten—years ago. I had to fully grasp the Culture of Separation and rediscover the Ancient Blueprint that must animate any platform claiming to serve the common good.

I've done that inner work over the past five years, especially the last two. I've found the clarity, grounding, and spiritual maturity required to support something rooted in Divine Love and Symbiotic Culture DNA.

And here's the good news: the infrastructure, the code, the design, and the vision still exist.

> *OneSphera can still be launched as a cosmolocal digital platform—a web of mass construction that enables fractal community empowerment from the ground up.*

The world is ripening. More than ever, people sense that the Culture of Separation cannot solve our deepest crises. The Culture of Connection is no longer a fringe ideal; it's an idea whose time has come. It's not hard to imagine that someone, somewhere, possesses both the wisdom and the wealth to bring this gift to life—and offer OneSphera (or something like it) as a public utility for humanity, a new Internet layer built on trust, dignity, and mutual benefit.

Imagine a decentralized economy based on mutual aid, a more democratic order emerging as a collateral blessing, a world where technology empowers from the bottom up, governed not by extraction but by digital sovereignty, selfless service, and shared goodness.

Call it conscious evolution. Call it Heaven on Earth. Sarvodaya achieved it for the poorest of the poor. We accomplished it in Reno. Now, we have the spiritual, social, and technical foundations to implement it everywhere.

But to take the next step, we must begin not with technology, but with the heart.

That realization didn't just reshape the vision for OneSphera—it reshaped me.

Here lies the paradox: to build something global, we must return to the most intimate center—our spiritual grounding. Before systems can serve the whole, we as individuals must become whole. As OneSphera paused, I was called to a more profound reckoning—not of architecture or algorithms, but of love, embodiment, and personal transformation. The next chapter wouldn't be written in code. It would be written in flesh and faith—in the firelight of the heart, where all true transformation begins…and begins again.

CHAPTER 28

THE HEART-CENTERED WAY OF SYMBIOTIC CULTURE

The future we dream of—healed systems, reconnected communities, a thriving planet—won't be built by technology alone. It will be built by people whose hearts have been transformed. After OneSphera paused, I realized that before we can re-village the world, we must re-village ourselves.

That inner restoration—of heart, home, and love—must come first. The transformation we seek at the societal level must take root in the most intimate circles of our lives—our bodies, our families, our spiritual commitments. It must be lived, not merely designed.

This chapter is about that continued inner work.

RETURNING TO THE HEART: FINDING MY OWN SACRED CENTER

At the end of the last chapter, I wrote that the next phase of transformation would not be written in code but in flesh and faith.

That insight wasn't just a bright idea. It came from real experience: a breaking open, a dying and returning, a reordering of love itself. Just as the world wasn't yet ready to receive a platform like OneSphera until a deeper spiritual soil had been cultivated, I, too, wasn't prepared to offer it until I returned to my center—my heart.

That's why this chapter begins with self-care, not as self-indulgence, but as a first key step in the spiritual practice of stewardship.

> *It's about choosing to live from the Heart,*
> *even when it means letting go of identities, roles,*
> *or structures that once felt central to your life.*

Sometimes, following the Heart means beginning again—not out of failure, but out of fidelity to a deeper rhythm emerging within.

My wife and I began to feel that stirring—the sense that something old was complete, not wrong, not broken, just finished—and something new was quietly asking for room to grow.

That inner unease of needing to step beyond the known wasn't mine alone. I began to notice it surfacing in conversations with friends, colleagues, and kindred spirits worldwide. And I saw it in the lives of those closest to me.

I'm reminded of a story my son Isaac shared after his soul-searching trip through Australia and Bali. Burned out from work, he took time to travel. During his final week, he visited a small village and stepped into a Hindu temple expecting a light touristy diversion—but what he found struck far deeper.

"Everything flowed from the sacred," he told me. "And everything felt alive."

Though rooted in a different tradition, Isaac's encounter echoed a truth affirmed in the Gospel—that when Love is the center, life flourishes.

In that village, faith wasn't just an idea; it was living truth. It shaped how people treated one another, tended their land, and served their neighbors. Isaac had never encountered a community where spirituality was fully embodied. Like many in his generation, he had no roadmap to bring that experience home.

*Isaac's longing mirrored something I've seen worldwide—
a deep hunger for rootedness,
sacred belonging, and something real.*

That moment stayed with me. It crystallized a question that began to surface as I wrote:

> "Is it easier to teach someone skilled in systems and structures how to lead from the Heart, or to teach someone already rooted in the Heart how to build systems?"

So far, the answer has been unanimous: it's far easier to teach systems to someone grounded in the Heart—especially when that heart is shaped by humility, love, and a living relationship with the Source of all Good—than to teach the Heart to someone operating purely from ego or intellect.

As a gentle reminder, remember that you can't pour new wine—God's redeeming Love—into old wineskins.

Jesus said this, and His words remind us: without inner renewal, even our best ideas and systems will be absorbed by the Culture of Separation.

That's why those who lead from the Heart, when it is rooted in Christlike love, see life not as a machine to be optimized, but as a sacred flow to join. They see the world as fluid and interconnected—like living waters—rather than something to engineer or control.

BIRTHING THE SYMBIOTIC AGE

BOOK BECOMES A BIRTH

That's why this book isn't a static blueprint; it's a living process. One reader reminded me, "Your book isn't called *Building* the Symbiotic Age—it's *Birthing* it." That struck a deep chord. Birth is relational and unpredictable. It doesn't follow a schematic; it follows life. Without the Heart, even the most elegant system will be stillborn.

I aim to embed the DNA of Symbiotic Culture into every community, allowing new forms, rooted in context, to develop organically. This isn't about replicating a fixed model—it's about seeding a culture.

That's why transformation can't remain personal. As I looked around the world, I saw that others were also arriving—often unknowingly—on the same soil. Seeds of connection were already germinating.

To begin re-villaging the world, I had to re-village myself. And that began, as most things do, in the quiet corners of home. What follows is not just a chronicle of events—it's the embodiment of Symbiotic Culture in action—lived, tested, and reborn through ordinary rhythms, including my own.

RE-VILLAGING BEGINS AT HOME

In Chapter 19, we introduced re-villaging as emerging from the Culture of Separation, along with renewed village sensibilities—extending our sense of kinship beyond family to neighbors and community.

The reverse was also true for me. I needed to redirect much of the energy I had devoted to the community back into my family life.

Re-villaging requires a balance among individual, family, and community well-being. Over four decades of community work, I met people wholly dedicated to causes like peace, justice, and healing—yet their personal lives were in disarray. Some couldn't make a living; others neglected their health or relationships. This disconnect between "making a living" and "making a meaningful life" is a signature of the Culture of Separation.

I often struggled to maintain balance while leading the Reno networks, managing a business, and raising my son as a single father. That challenge hasn't become easier. As the wealth gap widens and polarization deepens, simply living a "normal" life can push us to the brink.

> *That's why cultivating Virtues in our personal lives must be the foundation for broader work. Otherwise, we risk projecting our unhealed pain onto others.*

Even with Virtue, we all experience seasons of transition.

I entered one such season, again dropping to my knees and asking Jesus for guidance—not to secure an outcome, but to surrender. Prayer became a way of aligning with reality and regaining perspective on what was truly unfolding.

But reflection alone wasn't enough. Love, like any hearth, needed tending.

When I shifted my focus from local organizing to global platforms like OneSphera, I set the tone but became disconnected from my local community. That disconnection wasn't entirely bad. Sometimes, the one who starts the fire must step back and see if it can sustain itself. The ego must release control for a deeper gift to emerge.

And the networks continued. The Local Economy Network became a statewide "We Think Local" campaign. The food network strengthened gardens, farmers' markets, co-ops, and more. However, without intentional space-holding, the focus dissipated. I hadn't prepared a transition plan.

Without a fire-tender, even the brightest spark flickers out.

When I asked trusted connectors to carry the torch, they responded warmly—but often with, "Our organization can take over." That revealed how deeply the "I, me, mine" mindset runs. In hindsight, even distributed networks require quiet, patient, and steady servant leadership.

Had I recognized that fire-tending was a role rather than merely a phase, I might have equipped others to continue it. This fire-tending eventually turned inward. As I cared for the outer circle, I returned to the innermost one—myself.

Not only did I fail to prepare a transition for the networks, but I also didn't create one for myself.

Life swept me into my re-villaging. I got married in 2015. Before that, in 2012, I sold my hyperbaric business and started a consulting practice. I believed Symbiotic Networks shouldn't require overhead—no staff, building, or bureaucracy. Like many super-connectors, I gave back beyond my formal role.

In a Symbiotic Culture, giving and receiving are one. That's why I say, "Give forward," not "Give back." These life changes—marriage and a new business—turned my attention inward. I began to see that empowering the village starts with tending to your own.

Like Gandhi's Swadeshi, "fixing" the world begins by reclaiming the spiritual, financial, and relational capacity to care for our households.

The Heart-Centered Way of Symbiotic Culture

That's not selfish, it's responsible. If we neglect our own house, the burden shifts to others, just as corporations externalize pollution. Dr. Ari and Gandhi taught that responsibility radiates outward—from self to family to neighborhood and beyond. This is fractal self-governance. If we can't govern ourselves, how can we expect our institutions to do any better?

After getting married, my top priority became providing for my family. That shift required a new rhythm. It took five years to build the consulting business and train my son to help lead it. That time gave me space to envision the book you're reading now.

To serve others, I had to reinhabit myself. This is why Virtues matter. Compassion, wisdom, generosity, and service create spiritual balance and form a soul symphony.

Looking back, I see I was being taught what Augustine called *Ordo Amoris*—the right ordering of love. The "Constellation of Virtues" described earlier helps reorient our affections from self-serving to self-giving, grounding them in the Transcendent.

I was and am re-aligning God, self, family, neighbor, community, and world. In business, too, I must grow in ways that reflect these Virtues—especially in moments of setback or loss. That deeper alignment prepared me for the next chapter.

A CHANGE OF "HEART," A CHANGE OF PLACE

This re-villaging process—renewing our connection to community while living amid the Culture of Separation—is a path we must each walk, whether we recognize it now or later.

Cultivating balance is essential for anyone seeking to build a Symbiotic Society. Life changes—marriage, divorce, children, death, employment shifts, financial stress, or health challenges—shape how and to what extent we can engage in community life.

By this point, I had a thriving medical business, a home, and a marriage. But I found myself asking, "What now?" My company, now operated by my son, had provided me with a degree of financial freedom, but to what end?

I thought the turning point might be "following my heart"—but not in the way you'd expect.

In mid-2019, I experienced a flare-up of atrial fibrillation—a terrifying heart rhythm irregularity that felt both like a panic attack and total physical depletion. When medication failed, I opted for a cardiac ablation, a procedure meant to stop the misfiring electrical impulses in my heart.

The ablation altered my rhythm, but not for the better. It led to atrial flutter, another distressing condition. I underwent a second procedure—cardioversion—which delivers electric shocks to the chest.

And that's when I died.

My heart stopped for four minutes. I didn't experience a tunnel or bright light, but I did come back changed, with a more practical, embodied understanding of "seeing the light." The impact was lasting.

That near-death experience left me with a renewed urgency to share what I'd learned over five decades of spiritual seeking and more than forty years of real-world community work.

What kind of impact do I want to have with the time I have left? Am I satisfied with what I've done? What's incomplete?

In many ways, I felt deeply fulfilled. However, I also sensed that the arc of my work wasn't yet complete. I turned my attention to this book—a project I began in 2006—and felt the call to bring it into a new era, not just to tell the story but to offer it to others walking the same path of transformation.

In 2019, my heart opened again—to Reno, the world, and the rising storm ahead. Even before the COVID lockdowns or the economic ripples of war in Ukraine, I could feel the re-emergence of the "anti-Virtues"—division, corruption, fear. And I sensed we would need to hold fast to the good more intentionally and intently than ever.

Some may find this overly religious, but I've found it to be the most honest language: there is a worldly battle between light and darkness. It's not just a myth or a metaphor. It's the rhythm of rising and falling civilizations and personal reckonings.

I began sensing a next, necessary step. My wife Marta and I spoke of a radical shift—a "to the root" transformation. It meant dismantling our current life in Reno and opening ourselves to the unknown.

The rhythm of my literal heart mirrored the changes within my spiritual one. And soon, that shift would manifest in the most tangible way possible: geography.

In the fall of 2019, we decided to sell our home, liquidate our belongings, and embark on a new phase without knowing what it would be. You may have had moments like this—when the only way forward is to let go of the structures that once gave life. Self-reinvention often requires releasing the scaffolding that held the last chapter in place.

Then, COVID hit in early 2020. We stayed put for a year. But in early 2021, we followed through—we sold our home and left Reno, a place that had been my home for 22 years and Marta's for seven. We departed with six suitcases and a few essential boxes. What followed was a multi-community, hybrid lifestyle—our attempt to serve many communities worldwide.

Our first stop was Hawaii.

In March 2021, we arrived on Kauai, the least developed of the major islands, and rented a house on a 3-acre regenerative farm. The owner had practiced permaculture for two decades and was well connected to the local food movement.

I quickly tapped into local efforts, joined a food forest project, and connected with an eco-village forming on 500 acres and a retreat center on sixty more in North Kohala on the Big Island. Marta, ever creative, began exploring ways to support the island's art scene.

And yet...nothing stuck.

BEAUTIFUL SILOS, BUT STILL SILOS

I don't mean to sound cynical, but we encountered well-meaning people, mostly wealthy, trying to create intentional sanctuaries. In many ways, they were visionary, but they were still silos. They were beautiful silos. But silos, nonetheless.

These efforts often couldn't scale to tackle the systemic crises we face. In Northern Kauai, a tension simmered between the influx of affluent newcomers and local families struggling with the rising cost of living. While the eco-projects aimed to model the future, they risked becoming enclaves instead of engines of regional transformation. Humbled but not discouraged, we turned our hearts toward Europe, curious whether the seeds of regeneration might find new soil there.

This experience taught me a crucial distinction: Intentional communities can inspire but rarely scale. When it comes to how a project spreads, I follow the "Three Bears" principle:

- **Global** is too broad.
- **Intentional communities** are too small.
- But **regions—like counties—are just right.**

The Heart-Centered Way of Symbiotic Culture

Re-villaging at this "just right" scale unites individuals, neighbors, small businesses, nonprofits, churches, local governments—even eco-villages— into a cohesive Network Commons.

Each piece may begin as a silo, but the network that connects them isn't. It becomes the relational tissue of a living, symbiotic society. These regional patterns can be woven together across nations, even globally.

PILGRIMAGE WITHOUT A MAP

After six months in Hawaii, Marta and I traveled to Germany to be closer to her family. We settled in Tuttlingen—her hometown—for the final months of 2021. While there, we turned our attention to Europe and began exploring how my experience might serve regenerative efforts abroad.

One project stood out. In an Austrian alpine valley, a permaculture farmer had developed a way to recycle hotel wastewater to heat greenhouses, extending the growing season and supplying fresh produce. With 10,000 hotel rooms in the region, this could become a significant resource for local food resilience.

I met a hotelier whose family had served travelers since the 1500s. He was deeply interested in reducing food imports and helping the community become self-sufficient. He even offered to connect us with the town's mayor. Though this remote area lay in Austria, it was only reachable by driving through Germany—another reminder of how fragmented and interdependent even rural places can be.

As we spoke, I reflected on Hawaii, where 90 percent of food is imported. It reminded me how colonial and extractive systems

BIRTHING THE SYMBIOTIC AGE

have shaped many places, replacing diverse local abundance with centralized monocultures serving distant economies.

That pattern of extraction over regeneration has gone global.

Still, while that Alpine project didn't materialize into something concrete, it seeded something in me. Because just as winter gave way to spring, another message arrived—one that would call me back to the beginning.

I received an invitation from Sri Lanka. It was a return to a mentor, a movement, and a moment of profound spiritual and practical convergence. I didn't know it yet, but I was being called home in a whole new way.

What began as a journey outward—to build new systems, forge new alliances, and weave regional networks—had become a pilgrimage inward. My return to Sri Lanka wasn't just about legacy but about listening. It was about becoming empty again so that something ancient and alive could speak through me. I didn't yet know what shape it would take. But I knew I was being invited to walk forward not as a strategist, but as a servant. The Heart had opened—and the path would open with it.

CHAPTER 29

SARVODAYA, REVISITED: COMING FULL CIRCLE

Not long after leaving Europe, I received an unexpected invitation that felt more like a Divine nudge than a coincidence. Dr. Ari—my friend, mentor, and founder of the Sarvodaya movement—was turning ninety. Although I couldn't attend the celebration, I sensed it was time to return—to revisit the soil that had inspired my journey and explore how Sarvodaya's practical wisdom might address the global crises we now face.

I had visited Sarvodaya once in my life—in 2012—to commemorate a Buddhist temple that Dr. Ari had built. That was where I met my future wife, Marta. Now I reached out to connect once again.

I spoke with Dr. Ari's son, Dr. Vinya Ariyaratne, now President of Sarvodaya. A tireless leader following in his father's footsteps, Vinya lit up when I shared how I had applied Sarvodaya principles to Western food systems. Life came full circle. I could sense how my next phase of service might support theirs.

BIRTHING THE SYMBIOTIC AGE

Traveling to Sri Lanka felt like a natural next step—an embodied response to the call for surrender.

RETURNING TO THE ROOTS OF MY CALLING

Soon after the holidays, I left with an open-ended plan. Six months seemed "right." Meanwhile, Marta stayed in Europe. When war broke out in Ukraine, she offered art therapy to refugee children crossing the Polish border, just five miles from her childhood home.

I arrived in January 2022, eager to reconnect with Dr. Ari and collaborate with Vinya and other Sarvodaya leaders. I hoped to apply what I had learned in Reno to their local context. As noted earlier, Sarvodaya has cultivated a network of 15,000 villages—5,000 actively linked as a "commonwealth of village republics."

Sarvodaya remains one of the world's clearest examples of a living parallel society rooted in spiritual principles and community-scale action.

But Sarvodaya hasn't operated in a vacuum. Like many post-colonial nations, Sri Lanka has faced modernization pressures, corruption, and centralization. Despite its grassroots strength, Sarvodaya operates within a "taker" culture embedded in power hierarchies. By early 2022, tensions had risen as food and fuel shortages sparked unrest.

Even as I reconnected with the movement's soul, I began to notice the pressures it faced at scale—pressures that revealed both its maturity and its growing edges.

Its community-based banks—designed to empower farmers and small businesses—were becoming increasingly difficult to manage at scale. In response, a national financial structure was established: Sarvodaya Development Finance. Though not a formal bank, it offers savings, loans, and microfinance, with a staff of 500 serving a nation of 22 million.

In 2021, Sarvodaya raised funds to transition this entity into public ownership. Sarvodaya retained a 56 percent stake, with the remainder held by private investors. A former head of the Sri Lankan stock exchange now chairs the board, working to uplift rural communities through this complex financial vehicle. What began as grassroots banking has evolved into something far larger and complex.

Until this visit, I hadn't fully grasped how Dr. Ari's original vision—a distributed network of village economies—had evolved into a more formal NGO structure with institutional imperatives. Sarvodaya had successfully built community trust and connectivity but hadn't yet developed a system to distribute business opportunities across the network.

During an early site visit, I met a business owner producing aloe vera drinks. He clearly had a great product but lacked access to wider distribution—a common issue in the network. This prompted me to speak with Vinya about using blockchain technology to support business development and unlock dormant community assets.

To my surprise and joy, Vinya and the chairman were already exploring something remarkably similar: a "Smart Village App" designed to digitally connect producers, distributors, and local economies nationwide.

THE SPIRITUAL ARCHITECTURE
OF A NETWORKED ECONOMY

One of the benefits of blockchain is that it enables a community-based cryptocurrency, like what we envisioned at OneSphera, to reward beneficial, trust-building actions within a local economy. Just as our Reno experiment unfolded within an extractive global system, Sarvodaya's generative village network still operated amid a broader culture of takers.

There was a growing desire to move forward and create multiple local business ecosystems powered by Sarvodaya's infrastructure.

Dr. Ari and Vinya called this vision *Artha Dharma*, or the New Economy Initiative. Their idea was bold: map the resources and economic activity of hundreds of thousands of businesses and millions of people, then weave them into a symbiotic, decentralized framework.

The first step was building a shared database of businesses, producers, consumers, distributor networks, and supporting organizations. Key questions included:

- Who is producing what?
- How much are they making?
- What are the costs?
- Who is selling these goods?
- What products are being imported that could be produced locally?
- Where are there inefficiencies, especially from unnecessary middlemen?

Take, for example, Sri Lanka's one million rice producers. Their output moves through a convoluted supply chain—distributors, millers, wholesalers, resellers—marked by corruption and vast pricing inequalities.

You may remember previously how a 14-year-old Dr. Ari streamlined a coconut husk co-op to bypass middlemen and flatten the economic hierarchy. Now, seventy-five years later, I found myself discussing with Vinya how the same problem had scaled—and how the same wisdom could be applied again.

In contrast to the secrecy of high-tech, top-down data systems, this initiative would be open-source and transparent. It would enable pricing visibility, clarifying what costs are essential and which can be removed. More importantly, it would empower local economies to be transparent and make valuable connections.

This grassroots digital infrastructure would accelerate meaningful connections, disintermediate exploitative players, and grow real, regenerative prosperity.

Crucially, Sarvodaya's New Economy Initiative also represents the most practical, large-scale infrastructure I've seen that embodies the principles of subsidiarity and solidarity—core tenets of Catholic social teaching we explored earlier on the Virtuous Economy.

It decentralizes power to the local level (subsidiarity) while weaving each community into a larger, interdependent network of mutual uplift (solidarity). In this way, it offers a rare synthesis of spiritual ethics and scalable design.

It would also place Sarvodaya—and its deep-rooted Virtues—at the forefront of Sri Lanka's economic future.

We planned to start with a model Symbiotic Business Network in one region and scale from there. But as momentum was building, the food crisis hit, and our priorities shifted to urgent food security efforts, including a nationwide food banking system.

WHEN CRISIS HITS, A PARALLEL SOCIETY SAVES THE DAY

As you may recall, Sri Lanka made global headlines in 2022. A civil society uprising—sparked by increasing government corruption and widespread food and fuel shortages—united people across religions, ethnicities, and social classes. In July, thousands of protesters stormed and occupied the presidential palace, compelling the president to flee.

By then, the world was already grappling with supply chain breakdowns exacerbated by the war in Ukraine. I experienced Sri Lanka as the proverbial "canary in the coal mine"—the first domino to fall as the globalized economy, built on extractive monoculture and transoceanic shipping, began to buckle.

Suddenly, the need for re-localization and food self-sufficiency was no longer theoretical—it was existential.

Thankfully, Sarvodaya built a nationwide grassroots infrastructure through its parallel society movement. While other institutions were paralyzed, Sarvodaya was prepared.

They quickly launched a food access initiative called the We Are One campaign.

One inspiration for the effort was Dr. Ari's "matchbox campaign," which had begun decades earlier. Even the poorest families were invited to fill a tiny matchbox with a handful of rice or dal and bring it to the local preschool, where all meals were prepared and shared.

Through this act of radical collaboration, everyone contributed whatever they could and witnessed firsthand how shared giving could foster shared abundance.

We Are One reignited that spirit of collective care. It also increased school attendance, where children were now more likely to receive consistent nourishment. The campaign centered on three key "pillars of food security":

- First, increasing local food production—encouraging families to grow their food, similar to America's victory gardens during World War II.
- Second, establishing thousands of "community kitchens" in village preschools, where donated food—homegrown or store-bought—was prepared and shared, reviving the matchbox model in real time.
- Third, developing a national food banking system.

As mentioned earlier, I have experience in this area, having served as Executive Director of the San Diego Food Bank in the late 1990s. Vinya invited me to help train Sarvodaya's leadership team, adapting the American food banking model to Sri Lanka's context, where such infrastructure had not previously existed.

At the time, I had no idea that saying "yes" to this call would mean helping an entire country create its first national food banking network while reinvigorating a regenerative economy across 5,000 village communities.

We Are One launched nearly 150 community kitchens in five months, planted 600 home gardens, and established 25 food banks in the first half of 2022. The effort reached more than 300,000 families—1.5 million people—and planned to double that number by year's end.

And...beneath the logistics and infrastructure, stood a deeper power.

Sarvodaya's capacity to respond to crises came not just from systems but also from spirit. That spirit was embodied most fully in its founder, Dr. Ari. To understand how this parallel society endured and thrived for more than sixty years, we must look beyond programs and into the heart of the man who quietly shaped it all.

BIRTHING THE SYMBIOTIC AGE

DR. ARI AND THE HEART OF THE PARALLEL SOCIETY

Although I never considered Dr. Ari my "guru," he was a spiritual friend, mentor, and colleague. His unique qualities enabled Sarvodaya to thrive for over sixty years. When he visited impoverished villages, he empowered these so-called "throwaway" people by treating every person as fully human, with equal dignity.

Dr. Ari embodied spaciousness—
a pure heart and open vessel for Divine Love.
He held sacred community space without
a narrow agenda, serving the awakening of all.

People could feel he sought neither fame, fortune, nor control—only to help and serve. Unlike many spiritual leaders, he never courted visibility or status. Although widely celebrated, he consistently stepped out of the spotlight so that others could step into their empowerment. Often described as Sri Lanka's "Little Gandhi," Dr. Ari received countless peace prizes and international honors.

Yet he consistently shunned personal glory, encouraging ordinary citizens to look beyond short-term agendas and focus on collective uplift. Once, the country's President even asked him to become Prime Minister.

He declined—characteristically. The President misread the refusal, assuming Dr. Ari wanted an even bigger role. But he didn't want power; he wanted transformation.

So why is this important?

His life demonstrates the spiritual maturity needed to create space for others to move beyond ego, allowing Symbiotic Culture to take root. As someone striving to integrate personal awakening with global transformation, I view Sarvodaya as a rare living laboratory. I don't see Dr. Ari as an icon to idolize, but as a role model we can all learn from.

My six-month visit confirmed the insight I had when I first encountered Sarvodaya in the 1990s. Its "secret sauce," the Heart, lies in two core practices:

1. Forming networks of local organizations grounded in the spiritual awakening of participants
2. Using that foundation to build self-sustaining bioregional ecosystems

It's not just about teaching people to fish—it's about training teachers to teach fishing. This fosters agency, interdependence, and long-term self-sufficiency.

Sarvodaya remains globally unique. Its efforts are grounded not in ideology but in universal principles and lived Virtue. These aren't accessories to the work—they are the foundation.

It is also the world's only example of a Commonwealth of Bioregional Ecosystems—a networked infrastructure from which transformative initiatives can launch and scale locally and globally. What I once dreamed of scaling beyond Reno could now become reality if we follow Sarvodaya's path of collaborating with people where they are and expanding through relational kinship.

I've encountered exciting bioregional and regenerative initiatives around the world. Some are brilliantly theoretical, others impressively practical, but most remain confined to predefined networks of like-minded innovators. Sarvodaya is different. It doesn't exclude anyone. It mobilizes everyone, from conventional businesses to regenerative pioneers, into a functioning parallel economy. That expansive embrace laid the foundation for my work building Symbiotic Networks.

Though rooted in Buddhist tradition, Sarvodaya reflects the same lineage of lived Virtue and service that I've traced through Jesus, Gandhi, and Dr. Ari, a lineage of love transcending institutional borders without erasing them.

And it's available to all of us—right now.

BRINGING IT BACK HOME

Bearing witness to Dr. Ari's example clarified something I had long felt but never fully articulated: that the work ahead was not just logistical, but spiritual. And that I, too, had to carry it forward more deeply.

With renewed insight and conviction, I returned to the US in the summer of 2022, eager to apply Sarvodaya's living principles to a broader context and begin the next phase of the journey.

I felt inspired to finally finish this book and launch the Symbiotic Culture Lab, a training initiative to spread these ideas more widely.

At that moment, a remarkable synchronicity occurred.

A former colleague—an influential business networker in Florida—reached out. She said about twenty colleagues across the country were concerned about food and energy shortages and wanted help building "symbiotic resiliency networks" in their local bioregions.

Instead of traveling the world to support these efforts individually, this opportunity appeared more scalable. She suggested a series of virtual coaching sessions to empower the group to launch food and neighbor networks at the same time. I jumped in, developed training materials, and shared everything I had learned.

But after a few months, the effort began to stall.

Despite their good intentions, most participants weren't deeply connected at the grassroots level in their communities. They were eager to learn, but hadn't yet cultivated the spiritual readiness or local relationships needed to sustain a Symbiotic Network.

This isn't a criticism. They were motivated by necessity and inspired by the vision, but their urgency didn't match the capacity required to hold that space.

> *Looking back, I realize I had not yet fully internalized how foundational the Virtues are to this work.*

Without a shared ethic of compassion, courage, humility, and service, any external structure will falter, no matter how well designed. Had I known then what I understand now, I might have helped the group anchor their work in those Virtues first. Some may well have risen to meet that challenge.

I chose to pause the training, recognizing that the most faithful and necessary next step was to finish the book.

FROM VISION TO RESONANCE: OCEANIA AND THE ANCIENT BLUEPRINT

My next experience unexpectedly affirmed and illuminated my life's work. In the summer of 2022, my wife and I returned to Hawaii and settled in Kaneohe, Oahu. Soon after, we were invited to a gathering of indigenous elders representing Oceania.

Oceania includes nations like Australia, Fiji, Micronesia, New Zealand, Palau, Samoa, and the Hawaiian and Marshall Islands, along with territories governed by France, the US, and New Zealand. While the conference focused on food systems, especially breadfruit, something deeper caught my attention: the way these Indigenous leaders described their collaboration process mirrored how we formed our Symbiotic Networks.

One speaker, Dr. Failautusi Avegalio, Jr.—"Dr. Tusi," a Samoan elder and director of the Pacific Business Center Program at the University of Hawaii—shared an approach that stopped me in my tracks.

His work, A Collaborative Strategy Grounded in Polynesian Values, captured a worldview strikingly similar to what I had been calling Symbiotic Culture DNA:

> "Our approach is rooted in the Polynesian precept that all people are kin, connected through the spiritual energy of mana, which is found in all things. In the human realm, mana is expressed by faaaloalo (trust and mutual respect) and alofa (love).
>
> When people exemplify these qualities, they generate balance, harmony, and mutual sustainability—the foundations of a healthy universe and the essence of effective collaboration.
>
> Indigenous Polynesian cultures approach group work organically, not mechanically. As farmers begin with cultivation, so too must collaboration begin by cultivating relationships.
>
> Meeting one-on-one with key stakeholders, a leader begins to build a foundation of mutual trust and respect. Energetically, this involves gathering and channeling each person's mana and disbursing it throughout the group—imbuing the space with faaaloalo and aloha.
>
> Only then are participants truly ready to collaborate. And when this transformation occurs, productive thinking and a sense of wholeness follow."

Sarvodaya, Revisited

This approach reflected the Symbiotic Culture model, which is rooted in purpose, flowing from individual connection to the Transcendent, and expressed through virtuous relationships that meet real community needs.

It was incredible, yet unsurprising.

Indigenous cultures have long embodied what we now call the Ancient Blueprint—applied through their own language and lineage, yet deeply aligned with Jesus, Gandhi, and Dr. Ari. For these cultures, Symbiotic Culture isn't a concept—it's a way of being.

Even in 2022, I hadn't named the Ancient Blueprint yet, but I could feel it surfacing everywhere. From Sarvodaya to Oceania, the same spiritual DNA pulsed through these communities, revealing a path older than ideology and deeper than any system.

What I once glimpsed in the early Church and Dr. Ari's village movement was asking to be fully embodied in us. And so, I returned to the roots of resistance: the quiet, steady power of living in truth—together.

That same spirit of lived truth in the face of power has surfaced repeatedly across history. One of its most powerful expressions emerged not in the warm soil of Oceania but behind the Iron Curtain.

BIRTHING THE SYMBIOTIC AGE

CHAPTER 30

LIVING THE TRUTH: BUILDING
A PARALLEL POLIS WITHIN A SPIRITUALLY
HOSTILE REGIME

I've seen the Ancient Blueprint take root in vibrant, open societies—Sri Lanka, Reno, Oceania. But what happens when that sacred pattern must bloom in the dark—under a regime openly hostile to the soul?

To my surprise, the answer came from a place I hadn't expected: Cold War Czechoslovakia. There, in the shadows of Soviet oppression, a new kind of underground church emerged—one not defined by religious affiliation alone, but by quiet resistance, cultural creativity, and an unshakable commitment to truth.

It was a tale of moral courage lived in secret, a movement that embodied the Blueprint—not in theory, but in the daily choice to live in truth behind the Iron Curtain.

LIVING IN TRUTH:
A SOCIETY WITHIN A SOCIETY

How does one live the truth inside a lie?

How does one affirm Divine Love, when it is "officially" denied?

When resistance has become futile, what else can be done?

Parallel Polis, a faith-based movement in Communist Czechoslovakia in the late 1970s, faced those questions and responded in a unique and transformational way, one that reflects the Ancient Blueprint in Symbiotic Culture in action.

Instead of confronting the regime head-on, the Parallel Polis built alternative cultural and economic systems to restore the social bonds that had been de-platformed by Communist control. This living countercurrent inspired, strengthened, and reawakened the hearts of millions numbed by authoritarian despair.

This effort was spearheaded by two Vaclavs: playwright and future president Vaclav Havel and Catholic philosopher Vaclav Benda. Together, they gave birth to the concept of "Parallel Polis"—a society within a society where truth, beauty, and freedom could thrive outside the grasp of the Soviet-controlled state. While not overtly religious, Parallel Polis was profoundly shaped by Benda's Catholic faith and the tradition of Catholic Personalism, a worldview affirming the inviolable dignity of every person made in God's image.

Benda articulated the movement's purpose as:

> "...to return to truth and justice, to a meaningful order of values, and to value once more the inalienability of human dignity and the necessity for a sense of human community in mutual love and responsibility."

These "counter-institutions" included independent education, cultural life, and media—art, literature, and music—that reflected real life and enduring traditions, in contrast to state propaganda. A parallel economy—trade, barter, and commerce outside the monopolized system—likewise addressed the real needs of real people.

Yet the Parallel Polis was more than an infrastructure of resistance—it was a recovery of the soul, a way to live in truth beneath a regime built on deception.

TRUTH AS RESISTANCE

Perhaps most importantly, community networks emerged that re-established shared Virtues and ethical responsibility. The Parallel Polis was not a literal new government (although it eventually led to one) or city, but a metaphorical space—a society within a society— where a true Culture of Connection could flourish inside of, and independent of the authoritarian regime.

"The strategic aim of the parallel polis," Benda wrote, "should be the growth and renewal of civic and political culture—and along with it, an identical structuring of society, creating bonds of responsibility and fellow feeling."

Václav Havel asserted that the movement's spiritual foundation—a "sense of the Transcendent"-was the only hope for uniting diverse, multicultural societies.

Parallel Polis was in response to a materialistic, "spiritually hostile" regime, where citizens were forced to deny the Divine Love, which they knew in their hearts. The news agency in the Soviet Union, for example, Pravda, meaning "truth," was notorious for its propaganda and misinformation. This led to the disheartening and dehumanizing practice of what was called "hyper-normalization"—everyone knowing they were being lied to, yet unable to express their truth openly.

Václav Havel used the word "totalizing" to describe a system that survives by imposing an all-pervasive lie that the people must accept, NOT because they believe in it, but because all paths of resistance seem futile.

> "If the main pillar of the system is living a lie," he wrote, "then it is not surprising that the fundamental threat to it is living in truth."

Living in Truth meant building a society that reflected Transcendent Virtues—dignity, Love, and responsibility—even in the shadows of a godless regime.

Consequently, one of the ways the Parallel Polis "re-heartened the heartland" and hastened the collapse of the Communist regime was by beginning to share the truth first inside their protected silos and then more boldly by creating parallel networks in the society at large. As Havel wrote,

> "The point where living within the truth ceases to be a mere negation of living and becomes articulate in a particular way is the point at which something is born that might be called the 'independent spiritual, social, and political society.'"

The Parallel Polis's primary task was to re-establish a civil society based on truth, integrity, and mutual benefit, powerful enough to overcome the barriers set up by the totalizing, authoritarian Communist regime.

BIRTHING THE SYMBIOTIC AGE

This model of quiet, faith-rooted resistance has ancient roots. Long before Czechoslovakia, a similar movement emerged from within the heart of another empire. The Parallel Polis echoed the spirit of the early Christian communities, who saw themselves as a "beachhead" for the Kingdom of God, an Earth-based "Colony of Heaven" planted within the harsh soil of the hostile Roman Empire.

Rather than confronting the empire with force, they lived out the radical ethic of "Love God, Love Others"—a practice so expansive that it reached beyond their ranks to embrace Christians and non-Christians. The early Christians viewed themselves as a "city within a city," forming their parallel polis that operated alongside, yet distinct from, the Roman Empire.

Like Václav Benda's parallel polis under communism, early Christians believed in a higher moral order above the state, making them a subversive societal force. Their faith itself was an act of resistance—they refused to worship the emperor or participate in pagan state rituals, instead establishing autonomous networks of worship, charity, and education beyond the reach of imperial control.

Functioning as a self-sufficient underground network of small groups, the early Church created an alternative society that met its members' spiritual and material needs. House churches were central hubs for worship, learning, and mutual support, while communal living (Acts 2:44-45) fostered economic self-sufficiency:

> "They had everything in common... and distributed to anyone as they had need."

Early Christians rejected dependence on the Roman imperial welfare system, instead developing independent charity networks that provided food, healthcare, and aid to widows, orphans, and the marginalized.

Like Benda's vision, the early Church thrived under persecution, not by directly confronting the empire but by establishing an alternative social and moral order rooted in faith, service, and communal care.

Their tightly knit communities offered a compelling contrast to the corruption and brutality of the Roman system. Their communities proved another way of life was possible—one rooted in shared Virtues, sacrificial Love, and unwavering commitment to truth.

These examples illustrate a recurring theme: spiritual resistance through parallel structures. Are we seeing a pattern here?

Yes, and this pattern of love-led resistance has repeatedly emerged, from the early Church communities to Gandhi's satyagraha, Dr. Ari's Sarvodaya, and the Czech Parallel Polis—all faith-based movements that impacted society at large. Václav Havel believed these informal, non-bureaucratic, dynamic, and open communities were "embryonic prototypes" or micro-models of future political structures.

> *Could the Parallel Polis model provide a new civic playing field to lift us out of the polarized battlefield that has pitted us against each other?*

Perhaps—but in today's world, this ancient pattern reemerges through fractured lenses, each shaped by its worldview and assumptions. As modern institutions falter and public trust erodes, love-led resistance is surfacing once more, though often in fragmented and incomplete forms.

THREE ECHOES, ONE PATTERN

Today, activists from both the left and the right have revived the concept of Parallel Polis, acknowledging that the system and the Culture of Separation cannot be transformed from within.

One of the first references I found to the Parallel Polis came from the left—from author and "psycho-social therapist" Indra Adnan. In her 2021 book, *The Politics of Waking Up*, she cites the work of Havel and Benda as a model for what she calls "soft power."

She acknowledges the failure of party politics and established institutions to address the existential crises we face today and proposes cultivating our collective wisdom and imagination to "nurture and develop a new socio-economic-political system that makes the old one obsolete."

Although she acknowledges the Parallel Polis's use of "broad moral arguments about dignity and freedom," she doesn't mention the underlying foundation of Catholic Personalism. Reading her account, it would be easy to imagine Parallel Polis as a purely social, economic, and political movement and its "broad moral arguments" as merely tactical.

> *Now, imagine for a moment*
> *an account of Sarvodaya that fails to acknowledge*
> *the movement's spiritual change strategy,*
> *which is based on Buddhist Virtues, or one that suggests*
> *that Gandhi's work was purely secular!*

In the largely progressive mainstream milieu of social change, Christian or religious influence remains invisible, unacknowledged, and unwanted.

Meanwhile, on the right, there has been a similar awakening regarding the futility of "politics as usual" and the need to "stop funding think tanks" and begin working with real people in real communities. Conservative commentator N.S. Lyons acknowledges the Parallel Polis as:

"An ultimately successful strategy of resistance to Communism developed by Czech dissidents in the Cold War to counteract atomization, isolation, and degradation."

He seems to be describing our contemporary Culture of Separation, doesn't he? Lyons critiques top-down social engineering and oppressive bureaucracy, praising the Polis model for fostering responsibility, self-discipline, and civic Virtue.

He acknowledges the unsung leaders of existing communities, such as those in impoverished neighborhoods who work out of storefront churches, possessing "moral, not credentialed authority." Understandably, someone who advocates "less government, more personal responsibility" would seize on this approach to supporting local agency.

And yet—interestingly—Lyons likewise fails to highlight the religious foundation of the Parallel Polis!

Someone who DOES emphasize the religious is Rod Dreher, author of *The Benedict Option: A Strategy for Christians in a Post-Christian Nation,* who offers his plan for a Christian Parallel Polis as a means for "cultural and spiritual survival in a secularizing world." Like Benda, he suggests withdrawing from institutions undermining Christian values and building a countercultural community that affirms the Christian faith and way of life.

Just as the Czech Parallel Polis provided both a refuge and a way forward, Dreher sees an entire Christian communal way of life—including churches, community centers, and Christian-owned businesses—as a counter-cultural island inside a materialist, secularist empire.

These parallel efforts reflect a sincere desire to reweave moral and spiritual community, but each remains shaped by its tribe's language, fears, and assumptions. While each group offers an aspect of truth, it risks reinforcing the divisions it seeks to heal.

THE MISSING THREAD: FROM TRIBE TO KINSHIP

Here's the problem.

We now have three distinct groups—progressive, conservative, and Christian—each calling for a version of the Parallel Polis aligned with their agendas. However, none appear designed for the broader community. Once again, the Culture of Separation penetrates even the most well-meaning efforts to restore moral and spiritual community. Each vision is influenced by tribal language and loyalties. Each responds to some aspect of the system but fails to recognize that separation is the fundamental crisis.

For Indra Adnan, the existential threat is the "climate emergency." As we will see later, when I address "captured narratives," that phrase alone will exclude 50 percent of the potential community. Conversely, a phrase like "preserve, restore, and regenerate a healthy environment" would receive almost universal buy-in.

For the right, the existential threat is a global, unelected elite that seeks to impose their secular culture and materialist values on all of us, essentially de-platforming not only God but also human sovereignty and self-rule.

Although they acknowledge borrowing community organizing strategies from the left, they still regard that side as the "enemy."

Dreher's "Benedictine option" seems to reflect the early Christian approach of living in the Kingdom of Heaven *within* the empire of man. However, it remains exclusively Christian and, in my opinion, is not suited to thrive in a postmodern, multicultural, and pluralistic society. It fails to acknowledge the universality of the Ancient Blueprint and that Divine Love, not solely the institution of Christianity, is the ultimate "prize."

This is a subtle yet significant distinction.

*Benda's Parallel Polis, Sarvodaya, and Symbiotic Culture
are all built on a firm foundation of
Transcendent principles and Virtues,
but they extend beyond any particular institution,
in Symbiotic Kinship.*

No doctrinal agreement was required—only a shared desire to live in truth, embody the Virtues, and work together for the good of the community.

While Christian morality and ethics influenced the original Parallel Polis movement, it focused more on defending truth and moral responsibility than promoting religious conversion. Underground church networks created safe spaces for gatherings, discussions, and moral support. Many participants valued the role of faith in resisting Communist materialism, even if they were not believers.

The movement fostered the creation of parallel institutions, such as alternative education and economy networks, independent publishing, underground seminars, and community support, where religious and non-religious individuals could collaborate to resist Communist oppression.

If the Parallel Polis is to offer more than ideological refuge, it must become a container large enough for all—transcending tribe, politics, and even religion. If each expression of the modern Polis carries part of the truth, what might happen if we dared to weave these fragments into something whole?

A SYMBIOTIC PARALLEL POLIS FOR ALL

So here is an audacious proposal—a radically broad-based, Symbiotic Parallel Polis in every community for all willing to embrace and practice self-giving love and mutual benefit. No ideology or religious belief is necessary—just loving action to create a Symbiotic Community.

As you may recall from Chapter 15, our Conscious Community Network in Reno asked, "What will unite us?" and crowdsourced the answers, which evolved into our Symbiotic Culture DNA. In addition to a tacit unity around intentional mutual benefit, all three "sides" share specific common views about the nature of the problem and potential solutions.

For example, they each:

- Reject centralized control by governments, corporations, or global institutions, favoring local autonomy of family, neighborhood, and local communities.
- Believe the system can't be fixed from within, turning to the Parallel Polis to reclaim agency and "undergrow" the current order.
- Support local economies, alternative markets, and parallel financial systems to reduce reliance on centralized bureaucracies.
- Express concern over Big Tech, monopolies, and digital control limiting freedom and choice.
- Emphasize self-governing communities with decentralized decision-making.
- Share skepticism of globalization and consumerism.

Notice that all of the above reflect the Christian principle of Subsidiarity (local autonomy), the Ordo Amoris (the Order of Love), and Gandhi's concept of swaraj (self-rule), and are entirely resonant with Symbiotic Culture DNA.

Furthermore, whether explicit or implicit, all affirm the sacredness of the human person and the dignity of each individual, contrasting with a system that reduces them to economic or political units to be manipulated.

Yet the most essential layer—the one that holds all the rest—isn't institutional or ideological. It's spiritual.

What truly animates this vision is not policy or structure—it is Love itself, reintroduced to the center of public life. Without this re-centering of Love, every framework remains hollow, no matter how decentralized or well-intentioned. Love is the living power that transforms mere community into sacred kinship, and the Parallel Polis into a vessel for the Divine.

RE-PLATFORMING LOVE: THE SOUL OF THE POLIS

That brings me to what I believe is the fundamental reason for my life's work:

> *The "re-platforming of God" means restoring Divine Love to the center of shared life, so that it may permeate every institution in society, fulfilling the Parallel Polis's true purpose and ultimate potential.*

In addition to the issues and concerns mentioned earlier, a spiritual crisis and a profound spiritual need exist. That's what Benda and Havel's original Parallel Polis addressed. Rather than merely opposing an oppressive, dehumanizing regime, they transcended it by activating the Transcendent. This Higher Power is instrumental in helping us recover our Divine connection, revealing our true human nature, and reconnecting us as stewards of Planet Earth.

I am reminded of the Merck Family Fund study from thirty years ago, which I cited in Chapter 15. In it, people reported that the materialist aspect of the American dream was out of control. They felt dehumanized by the "machine" and consumerism. We have not collectively confronted that spiritual malaise—until now.

The Culture of Separation continues to provide material and technological "solutions" that fail to address the problem. This materialist worldview has fostered a crisis of the Spirit, encouraging anti-Virtues and prompting us to adopt values antithetical to humanity's traditional religious and spiritual views.

So, here is the original challenge that the Parallel Polis movement in Czechoslovakia presented: Stop Living a Lie. Let's come together to LIVE IN TRUTH!

Consider this fact we have cited earlier: nearly 90 percent of Americans still identify with some form of spiritual belief, revealing a vast, untapped reservoir of Transcendent yearning and moral coherence. Given this deep desire and huge potential for Symbiotic Kinship beyond our tribes and silos, we no longer need to suppress our Divine nature—our best selves, long exiled by "taker" culture.

Reflecting on over forty years of my community work to bring that Divine nature to real-world communities, I now realize that instead of trying to solve problems using manmade structures and systems on the battlefield of separation, I was answering a higher calling.

My true mission was to re-platform LOVE for its own sake! Put another way, love needs no reason. *Love is THE reason.*

If love is the reason, then our communities must become the living proof—embodied blueprints of what is possible when we re-platform the sacred. Again, remember Saint Paul's exhortation in 1 Corinthians 13:

> "Without love, we have nothing. Without love, we are nothing."

The Virtues we practice are intrinsically valuable because they align us with God and Divine Love. Everything else we seek is considered "collateral benefits."

Imagine a multi-faith Parallel Polis, catalyzed by those who Love God, Others, and Creation, establishing a sacred center in each community as failing institutions unravel. Picture churches, spiritual leaders, and civic groups creating a non-coercive moral authority, rooted in mutual benefit and service.

> *Perhaps this emerging Parallel Polis—*
> *this living fractal of Symbiotic Culture—*
> *is not a rejection of Western civilization,*
> *but its long-awaited fulfillment.*

Maybe the descent into the Culture of Separation was necessary—so that we might rediscover what early Christians already knew: that the Kingdom of God is not built by reforming or toppling empires, but by transcending them—by embodying eternal truth, self-giving love, and sacred community right where we are.

To embody that truth fully, we must become it, not just as citizens, but as transformed souls. The outer revolution begins with inner revelation. And that revelation—if we let it—regenerates and revitalizes us from the inside out.

So let's stop living the lie. Let's become the living truth. A new Polis is rising—not built by empires, but seeded by love. But how do we carry this sacred pattern forward—not just in resistance, but in renewal?

CHAPTER 31

THE SPIRIT OF THE POLIS: HOW LOVE OUTGROWS EMPIRE

I began this process thinking I was writing a book. But over time, the book began writing me.

I set out to offer a framework—perhaps even a step-by-step training guide. But the act of writing became itself an initiation, reshaping not only the book's structure but also my inner life. Writing did more than clarify my thoughts—it changed me. It became a sacred dialogue between my longing to serve and what the Spirit revealed through relationships, reflections, and the truths that emerged along the way.

Writing became more than a craft—it became a spiritual practice. The spiritual writer Henri Nouwen once said:

> "The deeper we enter into the heart of reality, the more we discover that it is not something we can simply explain but something we must express."

Writing became that expression—a way of uncovering hidden connections within myself and among us.

THE BOOK THAT WROTE ME: TRANSLATING THE SACRED

Throughout the years of writing, I continued reaching out to individuals, organizations, and networks—distinct islands of coherence that resonated with my passion for Beloved Community and a society rooted in mutual benefit.

When I began this journey, I planned to describe how I had worked to "heal the world's brokenness," especially by applying lessons from the Sarvodaya model in San Diego and Reno. I expected to share what worked—practically and clearly—maybe even ending with a training manual. But something shifted. As you read this chapter, I hope you'll see why.

The process transformed me from the inside out. I'm especially grateful I followed the prompting to release the first chapters in serialized form. That decision brought an unexpected gift: feedback from readers like you who were already doing this work in your communities. Rather than asking how you could support my vision, I wondered how Symbiotic Culture DNA might serve yours. That shift changed everything.

Those reflections didn't just redirect the narrative—they reshaped the soil from which Symbiotic Culture grows.

Beneath every structure lies a Spirit, and I began to see that Spirit more clearly. My connection to sacred tradition deepened. I started to sense the profound power of the Ancient Blueprint and the spiritual lineage it evokes.

As I returned to Scripture and Christian theology, my connection to Jesus Christ strengthened. Rediscovering words like metanoia and Logos, I saw with new clarity what our culture has lost in its attempt to de-platform God and discard the Baby Jesus with the bathwater.

What follows is not just a continuation of strategy or story. It is a return to the heart. That's where the real work began.

REDISCOVERING THE CHRISTIAN ROOTS OF THE BLUEPRINT

In keeping with my approach rooted in Symbiotic Kinship, I sought connection with regenerative and civic networks, Indigenous spiritual communities, and religious traditions. The deeper I explored the Christian roots of the Ancient Blueprint, the more I uncovered profound resources—Christian "apologists" like C.S. Lewis and G.K. Chesterton, and mystics like St. Maximus the Confessor, who wrote of the call to "unite the Cosmos in Love."

> *These treasures opened my eyes to spiritual blind spots and helped me develop a more universal spiritual language.*

I'm grateful to readers whose honest feedback helped set me straight—and revealed something deeper: even as I rediscovered great treasures from sacred tradition, I hadn't yet fully confronted how far our culture had drifted from it.

Take, for example, my use of the word Oneness a few years in the writing process. I assumed it was as inclusive and unifying as it gets. But one conversation with a group of Eastern Orthodox men took me by surprise. In their view, *Oneness* suggests a New Age belief that "God, the Universe, and I are One." While well-meaning, this overlaps with pantheism—the belief that God *is* the universe—rather than theism, which teaches that God is distinct from creation.

This distinction matters. Theistic traditions such as Judaism and Christianity affirm a Transcendent God who is not identical with the world. Judaism emphasizes YHWH's utter holiness and separateness. Christianity affirms that God created humanity in His image, not as extensions of Himself. As Genesis 1:26 says: *"Let us make humankind in our image, after our likeness."*

That single conversation opened a door to a larger pattern I began to notice—one that continues to shape how many spiritually inclined communities relate to the Christian tradition.

THE DE-PLATFORMING OF GOD IN THE "NEW SPIRITUAL AGE"

The distinction I've just described may seem subtle, but it reveals a significant blind spot.

Many in "new spirituality" or universalist circles enthusiastically embrace Indigenous and Eastern traditions while reflexively dismissing traditional Christianity. This well-meaning but often misguided trend attempts to honor the universality of spiritual experience while flattening differences or erasing historical depth.

One common expression of this trend is the belief that "all religions are fundamentally the same" or that we need a single, unifying "One World Religion."

I am now thoroughly disabused of both notions. Yes, many religions carry the seed of Divine Love at their core.

However, to claim that all paths are alike or lead to the same destination is a vast overreach—and, ironically, another form of cultural imperialism. This is a hallmark of postmodern relativism:

treating a 3,000-year-old faith tradition and a bestselling pop spirituality book as equally authoritative, simply because they both "feel true."

Imagine the outcry if someone today dismissed Indigenous ceremonies as outdated or superstitious. Why, then, is it socially acceptable—almost fashionable—to speak of Christianity in the same dismissive tone?

This question matters deeply because I've spent time among communities that see themselves as the vanguard of a spiritually awakened future. I've walked alongside evolutionary mystics, civic network builders, and regenerative culture movements—many of whom are doing sacred work.

However, I've also seen how easily they overlook or even belittle the depth and resilience of traditional Christian faith.

WHY THIS MATTERS FOR BUILDING A PARALLEL POLIS

In his seminal book *A Secular Age*, Canadian philosopher Charles Taylor describes our shift from a time when belief in God was nearly inescapable to a culture in which faith is one option among many. This pluralism has birthed a spiritual smorgasbord. In that buffet line, many who were raised in secular or post-Christian cultures now seek connection through alternatives that sidestep or reject organized religion, particularly Christianity.

For many of these seekers—especially those leading social, environmental, and political transformation movements—the idea that God has been "de-platformed" may be new and even provocative.

Yet this quiet bias has often kept spiritually inclined, civically active movements from building bridges with traditional religious communities—not realizing that, in towns and neighborhoods across the world, it is often these very faith communities who are already doing the daily work of restoring trust, reweaving the fabric of life, and bringing the sacred back into public spaces.

They are not only natural allies—they are already in the trenches, quietly mending what the Culture of Separation has torn apart—yet too often remain unseen, tragically leaving some of the deepest wells of wisdom, compassion, resources, and courage untapped.

Recently, I spoke with someone who held such conviction about the superiority of her view of "non-duality" that it came across almost like a strongly held religious creed. She told me we should avoid bringing religion into any movement to change society, because it still clings to what she saw as an anthropocentric, patriarchal, and personal God.

I offered another way of seeing it, suggesting that, in its purest sense, religion—from the Latin *religare*, "to bind again"—is precisely what needs to be re-platformed: not as dogma or coercion, but as the living re-connection of humanity to the Divine.

Part of the challenge comes from the tendency—especially in post-Christian and "new spirituality" circles—to frame the personal God as an outdated, human-shaped projection. Their "non-dual" alternative is often exalted as an impersonal Absolute, universal consciousness, or purely immanent spirituality. While such views can reveal the boundless nature of the Divine, they can also lead to the assumption that personal relationship with God is less evolved, like an outdated superstition.

BIRTHING THE SYMBIOTIC AGE

I shared with her that I have been able to reconcile both a deep, personal relationship with God—through Jesus Christ—and the experience of non-dual awareness through that relationship.

In Jesus Christ, I encountered both the infinite
and the intimate, the One who transcends all categories
and yet meets us face to face,
and whose presence is not only for personal
transformation but for the healing of the world.

In retrospect, this integration is what allowed me to overcome my own prejudice toward religion and, as a result, practice true diversity and inclusion within Symbiotic Kinship—welcoming people of faith not as relics of an old order, but as vital co-creators in building practical local living economies, food systems, arts and culture, neighborhood networks, and other forms of community life.

This reconciliation between the deeply personal and the boundlessly cosmic is not a new idea—it has deep roots in the Christian tradition and offers a profound framework for cultural renewal, yet it remains largely unknown to many of my friends and colleagues engaged in secular social change efforts.

Together, these parallel ways of knowing offer a fuller picture of Reality than either alone. This is the vision I have drawn from the seventh-century Orthodox Christian St. Maximus, whose insights I have referenced throughout this book. It also echoes the words of St. Paul, who wrote: "There is neither Jew nor Greek, there is neither slave nor free, there is no male and female, for you are all one in Christ Jesus" (Galatians 3:28).

That unity is not mere abstraction—it is a lived integration that allows relational theists and non-dual mystics to stand on common ground, linking arms across worldviews and working toward shared cultural renewal.

> *We must find a shared spiritual language to create a broad-based Parallel Polis or Symbiotic Society rooted in Divine Love and mutual benefit.*

And the bottom, bottom line is this: the beating heart of this vision is not policy or structure—it is Love itself, pulsing at the center of public life, calling us back to a Transcendent reality and one another.

FROM BELIEF TO EMBODIMENT: ACTION OVER IDEOLOGY

At its core, Symbiotic Culture is not about aligning with a particular belief system. It's about action—embodying the Highest Goodness, the Transcendent, and Divine Love in tangible ways. These principles are not bound by institutions but rooted in the Spirit.

And it's in this Spirit that Symbiotic Culture takes root—not through doctrine alone, but through lived practice. It's about making those Virtues real in our lives: in our families, neighborhoods, organizations, communities, and throughout our nation and planet.

As you'll read in the final section of this book—Activation—holding space for Symbiotic Culture means consistently cultivating a field of Symbiotic Kinship. Any viable Parallel Polis must move beyond tribal over-identification. It calls us to become superconscious of opportunities for Intentional Mutual Benefit that transcend and rise above our existing ideological silos.

This has been a hard-won lesson for me. I'm deeply grateful to those who've helped me see what I could not see on my own. While sharing this book, I've had to confront the invisible beliefs that shaped my judgments. That confrontation, though uncomfortable, was a gift. Each encounter with my ego became an invitation to move past defensiveness and connect with others heart-to-heart.

It's this desire for true Symbiotic Kinship that has driven me to explore how we might build networks that include all the Tribes, not just those who think like we do.

When we gather around shared needs, such as growing and sharing local food, we begin to remember what unites us.

The deeper I've explored the spiritual foundations of Symbiotic Culture, the clearer it has become: social and political movements built around opposition—anti-racism, anti-patriarchy, anti-personal God, anti-capitalism, anti-West, anti-hierarchy—may raise important truths. But too often, they still leave us trapped on the old battlefield.

They cannot bring us to the new playing field where fundamental transformation happens—where we meet, human to human, and co-create the world our hearts know is possible by focusing on our communities' everyday needs, not just our ideological divisions.

BREAKING THE FRAME: OVERCOMING IDEOLOGICAL CAPTURE

Speaking above the din of today's hyper-polarized cultural and political climate has often left me feeling disheartened. Many individuals and organizations I once imagined would be at the forefront of Symbiotic Culture now seem captured by the same "progressive" political mindset I had to unlearn to engage in the radically welcoming community work this path requires.

It's with humility that I acknowledge how deeply, decades ago, I was embedded in that mindset. I believed that all meaningful political change had to come from the left and that nearly every problem in our society could be traced back to the institutions of Western Civilization.

I remember the quiet disdain I held for "normies"—those ordinary folks often dismissed as "deplorable" or not enlightened enough to see what I saw or know what I knew. That was my posture during my time as an anti-war, anti-nuclear activist more than forty years ago. Ironically, these were the very prejudices I had to confront and release to unite diverse San Diego and Reno communities.

Now, as I complete the final stages of this book and reach out to networks that might carry its message forward, I sometimes feel estranged from those who could otherwise resonate deeply with Symbiotic Culture—if only they weren't still fighting the same tired battles.

That's why so much of what we'll explore in Section 4, Activation, focuses on lifting well-intentioned people off the depleting battlefield of ideological warfare and inviting them onto a new playing field—one grounded in the Ancient Blueprint and guided by the shared practice of building something together.

In our current environment, many organizations whose stated mission is to foster healing, justice, or sustainability still operate from a posture of opposition. They pursue noble goals, yet remain locked in adversarial frameworks. None of these "anti" stances—anti-this, anti-that—are sufficient to birth a new vision.

Why? Because beneath the surface of every ideological battle lies the same spiritual fracture. This battlefield is the very antithesis of what it takes to cultivate a Symbiotic Culture rooted in mutual benefit and spiritual coherence.

I do not say this to dismiss or diminish the very real wounds caused by the many forms of domination rooted in Western Civilization—historic racism, sexism, and economic exploitation. These injustices matter deeply.

THE CORE WOUND IS SEPARATION

However, as long as they are viewed as isolated grievances, each vying for moral primacy in the hierarchy of suffering, we risk overlooking the deeper issue that unites them all: Separation.

It is this spiritual fracture—this disconnection from one another, from the sacred, from the Earth—that underlies the systems of oppression we seek to heal.

When we fail to identify Separation as the root wound, we default to combating symptoms rather than addressing the cause.

This becomes even more obvious locally, whether by building food networks or gathering in caring circles. In these spaces, abstract and polarized ideologies begin to dissolve, and the noise of national discourse gives way to what truly matters.

What matters is presence, trust, and shared service.

The foundation of these networks—Symbiotic Culture DNA—is mutual respect and inherent equality. These aren't goals we strive for; they are the sacred assumptions with which we begin. Within that space, there is no need to prove worth or demand dignity—it is already woven into the relational fabric.

I want to return for a moment to the Czechoslovakian Parallel Polis we explored earlier in this chapter—how it was grounded in

Christian Personalism, the conviction that every human being is made in the *Imago Dei*, the image of God. Can you see the universality of that truth? It's the same essence reflected in the Hindu greeting namaste: *I honor the Divine in you.*

You can even see this Transcendent principle embedded in the American Declaration of Independence, mainly crafted by Christians—Anglican, Presbyterian, Congregationalist—who wrote:

> "All men are created equal, that they are endowed by their Creator with certain unalienable Rights, that among these are Life, Liberty, and the pursuit of Happiness."

If that spiritual understanding helped birth one of the most radical and enduring experiments in governance and liberty, maybe—just maybe—it still has the power to guide us home.

THE REAL BATTLE IS WITHIN

The growing tendency to demonize Western Civilization often overlooks a more profound truth: this is merely the latest and most dominant iteration of human empire, now experiencing its inevitable decline. A surprising moment of clarity came while my son Isaac and I watched one of the Viking series on Netflix, which dramatized the invasions of the British Isles over 800 years ago.

As we observed the cycles of conquest, vengeance, and cultural upheaval, I was struck by a sobering realization. For all the blame directed at Western civilization by many of my contemporaries, we must recognize a larger pattern—the relentless violence, enslavement, and empire-building that has scarred every civilization throughout recorded history. East, West, Indigenous—no culture has been exempt.

BIRTHING THE SYMBIOTIC AGE

People of all colors, creeds, and continents have played both victim and oppressor. That's when I understood: the real struggle isn't between civilizations. It's within the human heart.

Aleksandr Solzhenitsyn captured this eternal truth in *The Gulag Archipelago*:

> "The line separating good and evil passes not through states, nor between classes, nor between political parties either—but right through every human heart—and through all human hearts."

The "war on evil" projected onto enemies like "The West" is futile. Fighting what we oppose drains the energy needed to co-create what we long for, echoed by Jesus' words through time: *"Resist not evil."* (Matthew 5:39). St. Paul builds on this wisdom: *"Do not be overcome by evil, but overcome evil with good."* (Romans 12:21).

This is not a call to ignore injustice or submit to wrongdoing. It's a call to step off the battlefield entirely—to break the trance of the Culture of Separation that insists the only way to defeat darkness is by becoming part of it.

Instead, Jesus gave us a far more radical path: *"Love God. Love thy neighbor as thyself."* This simple command holds profound power. It asks us to renew our connection to the Transcendent and express that Divine Love through embodied service.

It invites us to radiate that love into the world— to form circles of trust, cultivate relationships of care, and weave local networks of mutual benefit.

This is the blueprint of the modern-day Parallel Polis: global vision and local in practice.

A NEW REVELATION, NOT A NEW REVOLUTION

This isn't just a beautiful theory to place alongside other high-minded ideals on a pedestal. It is a living imperative, especially now. We are facing a moment not unlike Czechoslovakia in the 1970s, when the totalizing regime silenced truth and suppressed spirit. Václav Havel described a system where the lies told to you eclipse the truth known in your soul.

Today's totalizing regime wears a different mask. As I described previously, we live under the soft-cloth authoritarianism of the Everything Industrial Complex.

Unlike the blunt-force propaganda of Soviet communism, today's programming is so subtle that we imagine we are thinking for ourselves.

The COVID pandemic and the 2024 US election only pulled back the veil. We've seen how government agencies have influenced the influencers who influence us. What we're living through is not unlike the censorship and coercion of the past—just digitized, optimized, and delivered with a smile. And yet, tearing down this so-called "deep state" won't save us. Like every revolution before it, it risks becoming the next version of the same machine.

It reminds me of the wisdom of The Who, who once sang about how the new boss is the same as the old boss!

We are caught in a struggle between rival factions of oligarchs, each exploiting our tribal instincts—progressive, conservative, religious, secular—to further their power and control. These factions have no interest in our wholeness, only our allegiance.

That is why the time has come for something wholly different: not a new revolution but a new revelation— a Parallel Polis rooted not in ideology but in love.

It is a living framework grounded in the Ancient Blueprint and animated by the DNA of Symbiotic Culture. Only something this spiritually grounded and relationally resilient can preserve what is left of civil society—perhaps even of our species.

A UNITED PARALLEL POLIS

As I showed in Chapter 30, we now face three parallel visions of the "Parallel Polis," each shaped—and limited—by a particular mental framework. Whether progressive, conservative, or explicitly Christian, each stream identifies a fragment of the larger problem it resists. Each recognizes, in its way, that true solutions must emerge from the bottom up—through crowd-sourced wisdom and a return to meeting real people's real needs on the ground.

But what's missing is the convergence.

Rather than separate movements siloed by worldview, we are being called into something more whole, something deeper and more essential. Our task is to find the individuals, communities, and networks within these awakening islands of coherence that can hear the Heart's call. This is not merely a call to fix what's broken, but a deeper summons to rise above the structures of the mind that keep us divided.

We don't need three Parallel Polis movements.

*We need one united Parallel Polis—
welcoming all people and organizations
committed to Intentional mutual benefit,
not bound by ideology but brought together
by shared care and courageous compassion.*

This represents a radical shift—the radix, the return to the root—from the old battlefield to a new field of possibility. It begins not with institutions, systems, or elections, but with each of us, in the quiet center of our being, regardless of the power we think we have or don't have.

This isn't just a hopeful vision—it's already happening quietly and locally through those who choose to live from the Heart.

LIVING THE BLUEPRINT: A CALL TO ACTIVATION

As this journey deepens, we begin to glimpse what it truly means to live the Ancient Blueprint—not only as a personal path, but as a cultural calling. This is not a step-by-step manual or a one-size-fits-all prescription. It is a spacious invitation: to align your life more deeply with the Shared Self, the living current that flows through us all, and to step into your role as a citizen of the Kingdom of Heaven.

This is not an exclusive club. It is a universal calling.

As Solzhenitsyn reminds us, the battle line runs not between tribes or ideologies, but through every human heart. Each of us must choose—every day—whether we will empower the Culture of Separation, which sustains the empires of man, or nurture the Culture of Connection, the living expression of the Kingdom of Heaven.

This Ancient Blueprint is not proprietary. It is transparent, transmissible, and "un-brandable."

BIRTHING THE SYMBIOTIC AGE

Whether you identify as Christian, Muslim, Jewish, Buddhist, Indigenous, atheist, or "spiritual but not religious," I hope you see how this framework can integrate with—rather than override— your existing path.

There is nothing to abandon. There is only something deeper to embody and extend outward into your community.

Symbiotic Culture is not a new religion. It is a relational overlay—a pattern of mutual benefit, self-giving love, and living coherence—that amplifies the Highest Goodness already latent in every tradition. If anything, this book seeks to liberate the essence of Divine Love from the confines of doctrine, ideology, or institutional control.

I trust it's clear by now that, while my relationship with Jesus Christ has been the wellspring of this work, I am not here to proselytize or impose. With humility and clarity, I assert that the radical understanding of love, reality, and human nature I encountered through Jesus and the Bible has guided my journey and revealed the architecture of the new world we are called to co-create.

While empires have risen and fallen for millennia, what we now face is different. This empire—the global industrial monoculture—reaches every corner of the Earth. There is no opting out. No off-grid escape. No utopian enclave is untouched. To navigate this passage, we must stop, turn inward, and acknowledge—as Solzhenitsyn wrote—that the switching station is in every heart.

Each of us carries both shadow and light. We are all part of the problem—and part of the solution. This moment in history demands that we confront the full weight of our collective trauma and our extraordinary potential.

The Spirit of the Polis

*We have reached the threshold.
The horror and the beauty converge.
We must choose. Will we collapse inward
under the burden of separation,
or will we rise together in Love?*

CHAPTER 32

SOCIETY'S "COME TO JESUS" MOMENT

Before we can build a new society, we must begin with our own hearts. For me, that journey began more than fifty years ago—at a Passover dinner with my family—when I was suddenly overwhelmed with compassion for those in the world who were hungry or suffering.

That evening marked the beginning of a lifelong tension between inner compassion and outer culture—a dissonance I didn't fully understand as a child, but one that stirred a deep ache in my soul. The pain I felt ignited a desire to heal the world—and, in doing so, to heal something within myself. That longing became the throughline of my life.

It was at that dinner, in response to my tears, that my father asked the question that would change my life and shape my future:

"Well, Richard, when you wake up each day, what will you do about it?"

He was right to challenge me—not just to feel compassion, but to live it.

"So what will you *do* about it?"

My father's emphasis on doing was understandable. As part of the "Greatest Generation," he embodied a culture of relentless action—fighting wars, building homes, and shaping a prosperous postwar society. I'm deeply grateful to him for being a provider, a doer, and part of a generation that did what had to be done.

That worldview persists today.

> *Our postmodern materialist society still emphasizes action, systems, and output—giving us the illusion that we're making a difference simply by keeping busy.*

This bias toward doing is captured in the popular mantra: "Don't just sit there; do something!"

But over the years, I began to see the limits of this constant doing—and so did my father.

FROM DOING TO BEING: MY FATHER'S REALIZATION

Over the past fifty years, I've seen that a deeper way of being—rooted in presence, love, and inner coherence—gives true meaning to our actions and forms the foundation for building an authentic community.

A sad regret brought my father to the same realization.

A few days before he died at age 92, after a lifetime of worldly accomplishments, my dad expressed his deep regret to me. He was in a hospital bed, and he placed his hand on my arm, saying, "I am so sorry, son, that I have been working for fifty years and didn't take the time to truly be present for you."

I am reminded of Jesus, who says in Matthew 16:26:

> "For what will it profit a man if he gains the whole world and forfeits his soul?"

A few hours after he died, I was praying in front of the house where he spent his final months. Suddenly, my father appeared before me, as clearly as if I were speaking with a living person. He told me:

> "While I was in my body, I did not understand the work you had been doing or who you were because I was so caught up in the world. I see it now so clearly, son, the life of the Spirit and how it has called you. I am so proud of the man you have become."

Then he said, *"Let me show you heaven."*

I was transported to a field of golden wheat, moving back and forth, blown by a gentle wind. The sky was a deep blue, with a brilliant golden sun radiating rays of light. The words that came to mind were "joy within joy."

I share this not to convince you of the story's literal truth but to underscore the powerful grip of the Culture of Separation and its "religion" of materialism. This essentially "invisible" context has shaped our inner lives and how we structure our communities and society.

A famous saying from the 1980s was, "He who dies with the most toys wins." As with my father, it sometimes takes a lifetime to realign our priorities with an underlying Transcendent spiritual reality.

Society's "Come to Jesus" Moment

*We know the truth in our hearts,
yet we may not live as if it were true.*

The materialist Culture of Separation impels us to do, do, do and take, take, take, putting our spiritual life on the "back burner." And yet, through the noise of doing and the pressure to achieve, something ancient was calling me back. Beneath all the striving, I began to remember the Divine pattern.

THE ANCIENT BLUEPRINT AND THE CULTURE OF SEPARATION

Looking back on the arc of my life, I see how my spiritual awakening at twelve revealed the Ancient Blueprint—the Logos, the Divine pattern beneath all creation. It became the lens through which I saw the world and guided the path that led to my life's work and this book.

The encounter shaped my spiritual formation, with the Transcendent Virtues illuminating the shadows and organizing and unifying my personality from within.

As I was being formed by this experience of Ultimate Reality—one that grew into a personal relationship with Jesus—I was given new "eyes" to see the culture I had been born into. I could suddenly perceive how social, economic, and political structures shaped me from the outside in.

I felt compelled to reconcile the dissonance between my direct experience of Divine Love—the Kingdom of Heaven, where all is interconnected in sacred Mystery—and the separation, conflict, and suffering I saw in the "Kingdom of Man."

As I entered adulthood, I became aware of an all-immersive culture of materialism that urged us to define ourselves by what we do and acquire rather than who we are and what we can offer. Even as I clung to the Transcendent reality I had tasted, I could feel this "totalizing" culture closing in—like a fog attempting to dim the soul's light.

> *I came to see that our separation from one another, from nature, and from our own souls, is rooted in the spiritual disconnection from the Transcendent.*

That contradiction struck me early, even as many peers pursued the path to "success." Was I the only one wondering how our culture had drifted so far from the sacred truth I'd experienced?

Raised in a secular household, I had not read the Sermon on the Mount or studied St. Thomas Aquinas's Seven Deadly Sins. As a younger man, I might have dismissed such teachings as outdated or judgmental. Yet even without them, I knew in my bones that we were on the wrong track.

In my twenties, the film *Wall Street* popularized the phrase "greed is good." I didn't have to know St. Thomas Aquinas or any other religious tradition to know that greed for more material things is NOT the highest good. That movie came out nearly forty years ago, and the moral slide hasn't stopped. Though many commentators decry the state of society, few seem to grasp the core contradiction.

Instead of promoting Virtue and character, as taught by religious traditions and secular thinkers like Marcus Aurelius, our culture now celebrates anti-Virtues, advanced by what I call the Everything Industrial Complex: consumerism, algorithm-driven advertising, social media, politics, and mass entertainment.

These systems prize wealth, power, and pleasure over love, integrity, and humility. The result is a rise in polarization, escapism, and anxiety, and a decline in trust, compassion, and connection. A non-virtuous cycle is eroding the foundations of personal and collective well-being.

So we must ask: Have we hit bottom yet?

Are we willing to "admit" ourselves to a cultural recovery program, acknowledging that materialism and the primacy of the human mind are powerless to address the spiritual crisis beneath the surface?

Are we ready to surrender to a higher power and recover our individual and collective connection to the Transcendent?

Are we ready to shift from self-serving to self-giving—and extend that love into our communities?

Perhaps this is society's *Come to Jesus* moment.

When I say that, I mean it literally and universally. Jesus Christ is the living center of my life, the way I've come to know Divine Love most intimately and personally. Yet I also recognize that the Spirit moves in mysterious ways—often beyond traditional boundaries. Many are being drawn toward the same Love, the same awakening, the same invitation to truth and transformation, even if they name it differently.

This book honors my path in Christ and the broader field of grace. Whether you call it Christ, Love, or something else, what matters most is the fruit of your pursuit: a life rooted in compassion, courage, and connection. It is written from that place, deeply grounded in Christ, yet open-handed toward all who seek to walk in love, humility, and coherence.

This collective *metanoia* could give rise to a radically hospitable, spiritually grounded parallel polis—blossoming in local communities across the globe. But what would such a moment require of us, not just individually, but together? What would moving from insight to embodiment mean, from recognition to action?

Because love without structure lacks staying power. If we are to sustain this awakening, we need vessels—structures that carry Spirit into every level of society.

LIVING IN TRUTH AND THE ULTIMATE POWER

This fractal empowerment that I will outline in Section 4 must occur at all levels—individual, family, neighborhood, community, region, nation, and world. I refer to it as a "Come to Jesus" moment, not to promote a religious view, but to highlight an Ancient Blueprint—a universal pattern expressed most clearly in Western Civilization through the two-fold commandment to "Love God, Love thy neighbor."

If we lose that connection, we lose our collective soul. But when we recover it, we gain access to the Transcendent Power that can help us break our addiction to materialism and separation, and bring forth a Culture of Connection and mutual benefit.

This new understanding must lead to innovative ways of organizing and structuring society—what I've called "new wineskin networks." These relational vessels can carry the Transcendent spiritual power necessary to support fundamental transformation.

When I revisited the parallel polis movement while writing this book and began sharing it with others, I felt a spark of recognition, as if this seemingly obscure movement held vital clues for our time.

Their legacy distilled into two enduring principles:

1. Living in truth.
2. Building parallel structures.

Society's "Come to Jesus" Moment

THE INVISIBLE TOTALITARIANISM OF OUR AGE

At first glance, the situation faced by the Czech Parallel Polis may seem utterly different from ours. In the 1970s, dissent in Communist Czechoslovakia could mean imprisonment or even death. It was what Václav Havel called a "totalizing" system—one that controlled every aspect of public and private life.

Our totalizing system today is much "kinder and gentler"—yet devastating all the same.

Though our age appears freer, the internal cost is similar: to function in the modern world, we are often expected to silence our souls, denying the truth in our hearts. In Czechoslovakia, religion was explicitly repressed. In postmodern society, it has been "disappeared."

Even though over 90 percent of people worldwide believe in some form of Transcendent higher power, including many who identify as atheists, this sense of an underlying loving coherence is mainly absent from the civic and public square.

> *To operate in this kind of "totalizing" civilization, we must often behave in ways that contradict the spiritual and moral teachings of the traditions we claim to cherish—whether Western, Eastern, or Indigenous.*

We live in a cultural milieu where we're encouraged to be takers rather than givers, to believe the Lie of Separation: that we are all isolated entities competing for a sliver of security, pleasure, or power. This mindset invades every domain of life—our families, workplaces, civic organizations, and even networks that seek to do good.

We are subtly taught to suppress the soul's truth to survive socially, professionally, and politically. That pressure produces a self-betrayal—what Charles Taylor might describe as "the malaise of modernity." A society built on this internal division cannot long endure.

This is more than political repression or ideological confusion. It is a crisis of meaning that originates deep within the soul.

THE REAL BATTLE: LIVING IN TRUTH OR ILLUSION

This is the deepest leverage point for transformation: the cognitive dissonance between our sacred inner knowing and the materialistic culture we're immersed in. Why do I say that?

No culture can survive indefinitely by living a lie. Over thousands of years, empires have collapsed under the weight of internal contradiction. Václav Havel and Václav Benda, in Soviet-occupied Czechoslovakia, called this condition what it is—"Living a Lie." And lies cannot endure.

The Culture of Separation—built on materialism, competition, and individualism—is not merely a distortion of reality; it is a *dark inversion*—an *illusion* that masquerades as truth. This seductive falsehood veils what we know deep in our hearts: that we are made in God's image, united as one human family and creation.

This illusion may appear normal—even necessary—within our current systems, but it is ultimately unsustainable. It denies the sacred design that holds us together.

This, dear reader, is the true battle of the age.

It's not merely political or ideological—it is spiritual. It is a struggle between two realities: the sacred reality of being created in God's image, grounded in Divine Love and Truth—and a distorted perception of humanity as fragmented, competitive, and inherently separate.

Václav Benda, deeply influenced by Catholic Personalism, saw the stakes clearly. That's why his vision for the Parallel Polis was not just a political response but a spiritual declaration. To "live in truth" meant affirming the unifying reality of Divine Love, first in trusted circles, then in the public square. At first, this was dangerous. But as more people embraced it, it became a cultural awakening.

Today, we do not face tanks. Instead, we are surrounded by think tanks—systems of thought that reward conformity and punish inner truth. The censorship we fear is not imposed from without but internalized as self-censorship.

> *I've spoken with many civic leaders and network organizers who hide their spiritual convictions for fear of seeming "divisive."*

I understand that fear. As a Jewish child in the Boy Scouts, I felt imposed upon when a Christian minister was invited to lead a public prayer. That discomfort stayed with me.

But what we're confronting now is not religious imposition. It is spiritual suppression of a more subtle kind—and the cost is profound. If we do not speak the truth of our souls or bring our sacred center into the public square, we are left only with structures, ideologies, and solutions that repeat the very problems we hope to solve.

Which brings us to the most subtle form of suppression—the kind we impose on ourselves.

BIRTHING THE SYMBIOTIC AGE

SPIRITUAL SELF-CENSORSHIP IN PUBLIC LIFE

As I've shared, our totalizing system—where "only matter matters"—is upheld not so much by external restrictions as by internalized ones. Today, the most pervasive form of censorship isn't state-imposed—it's spiritual self-censorship.

And it's not just civic network organizers who feel this. All of us—whether in nonprofits, business, public office, or even casual conversation—are often expected to wear a "cone of silence" around our deepest spiritual convictions. The fear of being dismissed as naïve, irrational, or "a religious fanatic" is real.

Drawing on Charles Taylor's *A Secular Age*, I've pointed out how our culture increasingly filters out the Transcendent. In today's public square, God hasn't been banned—He's been de-platformed. What counts as "serious" is limited to what can be seen, measured, or monetized.

> *Unlike in Communist Czechoslovakia, where religion was suppressed by force, faith in the modern West has been quietly exiled—written out of the script of public life.*

It's been reduced to one consumer choice among many—stripped of public weight, confined to private preference, and rendered peripheral.

While claiming neutrality, the secularized public square has, in effect, given materialism an "unfair market advantage." It dominates the terrain of meaning. This invisible quasi-religion installs itself as the default framework, while spiritual worldviews are either ignored or viewed with suspicion.

Think of the common misinterpretation of "separation of church and state." We often conflate religious expression with coercion, assuming that any articulation of faith is an attempt to impose it. So we create a public square drained of the sacred—out of fear, not principle. I've seen this dynamic across decades of work—within nonprofits, activist spaces, business communities, and even churches. And here's the truth I've come to name:

> *While the political divide between "left" and "right" is obvious, a deeper and more insidious rupture has gone unnoticed: the split between the sacred and the secular.*

This hidden rift quietly redirects our collective efforts toward material fixes—systemic reforms, structural solutions—while avoiding the spiritual crisis at the heart of our unraveling.

BRIDGING THE SACRED AND THE CIVIC

Many of us have unknowingly absorbed a materialist worldview that reinforces the Culture of Separation, fragmenting us even as we hunger for unity. This unconscious bias helps explain why so many promising movements for change remain disconnected—strands of hope that never quite weave into a fabric of wholeness. Without a sacred center or shared spiritual foundation, there is no gravity strong enough to form the bridges of trust, healing, and transformation we so deeply need, leaving even our most hopeful efforts unaligned, unable to cohere.

> *Only a widely embraced sense of the Transcendent— beyond any particular brand, label, silo, or tribe— can give birth to a Symbiotic Culture and a Beloved Community.*

It is this deeper spiritual awareness that our hearts ultimately yearn for.

The greatest challenge—and most urgent need—for those of us in the West is to reintegrate religion and spirituality into public life in a unifying, life-giving way—not as dogma or division but as a shared wellspring of meaning that can bring us back into relationship with one another.

We must recover what is essential.

Once again, consider the words of E. F. Schumacher:

> "In ethics, as in so many other fields, we have recklessly and willfully abandoned our great classical Christian heritage. We have even degraded the very words without which ethical discourse cannot carry on—words like 'Virtue,' 'love,' and 'temperance.'"

He believed our generation's calling is nothing short of metaphysical reconstruction—a realignment of our collective values with timeless spiritual and ethical truths.

But when we sever social action from spiritual grounding—when we quietly remove religion and the Transcendent from public life—we cut ourselves off from the deepest Source of renewal. We disconnect from the very Power that can illuminate, animate, and sustain true transformation.

In doing so, we have made the ultimate power of Divine Love functionally powerless.

Instead of recognizing that our crisis is spiritual at its core and that its solution must be spiritual, we double down on systems, policies, and structures rooted in the same old assumptions. We build more, strive harder, and compete for influence and control, all while using the tools of the Culture of Separation to try to escape it.

But without the foundation of the Ancient Blueprint, all these well-intentioned efforts are destined to collapse—bricks laid on sand. If the foundation is cracked, no amount of structural tinkering will hold. We must go deeper—beneath politics, systems, and culture itself.

RE-PLATFORMING GOD: RESTORING THE SPIRITUAL POWER THAT UNITES US

I speak from experience—organizing the Reno networks, learning from the early Christian communities, engaging with Gandhi's movement, studying the parallel polis, and working alongside Sarvodaya. What do all of these have in common? Each was rooted in the Transcendent. Each extended outward from that sacred center, creating networks of care, compassion, and coherence.

In contrast, the major materialist movements of the modern era—whether communism, socialism, or capitalism—have all ultimately faltered. Why? Because their solutions, however sophisticated, were severed from Spirit. They lacked Love at the core.

We've traded transcendence for transaction, Spirit for systems. It's time to remove the materialist blinders we've been wearing and restore sanity and sanctity to our lives and public discourse.

We must also acknowledge the misconceptions that keep us silent. Many of us have been conditioned to believe that bringing God, spirituality, or faith into public life is dangerous, divisive, or somehow incompatible with modern civic engagement. But if we're honest—truly honest—we must ask ourselves:

Why have we left out humanity's deepest source of meaning from our efforts to heal the world?

Why should we edit out the spiritual longing and moral compass that have guided every civilization in history, just because modernity insists we do so?

If we genuinely desire unity, we must stop treating spirituality as the problem. In truth, it is the missing piece. The very ingredient that can bind us together.

And once again, here is the good news:

*We don't have to invent a new system or philosophy.
We already possess the Ancient Blueprint—
a time-tested, cross-cultural, spirit-infused pattern
that can unify humanity.*

We don't need a thousand more unproven ideas. We need the courage to recognize what already works—the re-platforming of God.

If you've read this far, you know that this Blueprint has already been proven across history and diverse cultures, and you very likely know it in your own heart. So, the question isn't whether a path exists—it's whether we'll choose to walk it. Our choice is whether we will build not in resistance to the world, but in service to something more profound.

LIVING IN TRUTH: RECLAIMING SACRED SPACE IN THE PUBLIC SQUARE

We need not just another initiative, policy, or plan, but a new context altogether. A public sphere where spirituality comes out of the closet and becomes a legitimate, even central, power in shaping how we organize society. Not a rigid program, but a living framework—a movement grounded in love, truth, and the courage to shift from the old battlefield to a new playing field.

The public square is more than a political arena. It is the cultural and civic commons—our workplaces, school boards, media platforms, neighborhood councils, and town halls—where values are lived out, decisions are made, and the soul of society takes shape. And today, that square has been spiritually hollowed out.

> *We don't just need better policies or protests—*
> *we need a re-sanctification of the very ground*
> *on which we gather.*

Does that sound impossible? Not if you realize how *necessary* it has become.

And here's the good news: the pieces are already in place.

Across the globe, billions of acts of kindness, generosity, and care unfold daily. All around us, dozens—hundreds—of grassroots networks are addressing the threads of our intertwined crises. Most are working in silos, unaware of one another.

Now imagine what could happen if those threads were woven together—unified not by ideology, but by the spiritual sensibility that lives in the human heart.

Imagine what becomes possible when we integrate this spiritual sensibility into public life, not to promote any specific faith, but to honor the sacred center that unites us all. And if you still believe that spirituality is distinct from political or civic action, consider this: the great social movements of the last two centuries—abolition of slavery, women's suffrage, civil rights—were all rooted in spiritual and religious conviction.

They were not mere policy debates. They were moral awakenings. And now, we are called to extend that awakening even further—not just to a particular group or cause, but to all of humanity. We all have the right to live in a society defined by mutual love, respect, and benefit for everyone.

This is the heart of the parallel polis—a parallel society grounded not in opposition, but in sacred affirmation. As a reminder, Symbiotic Circles are not a replacement for the Church or any spiritual tradition, nor are they considered an Interfaith effort. Instead, they are complementary vessels—spaces where faith and civic life can be reintegrated, allowing us to embody what we profess on Sundays throughout the rest of the week.

The Church has long served as a vessel of grace through its sacraments, liturgies, and ancient rhythms. Symbiotic Circles do not replace this inheritance; they extend the fruits of religious life outward, allowing the sacred to be carried into every corner of life, including our neighborhoods, workplaces, and civic systems.

Imagine a social body based on the Ancient Blueprint, animated by a universal spiritual awareness that no brand, label, or tribe can capture. If you like, call it "the Kingdom of Heaven"—not as a far-off dream, but as a real-time movement grounded in love.

> *I've witnessed it firsthand: my connection to God is not a wedge but a bridge. The Divine doesn't drive me to separate; it compels me to reconcile, unite, and heal.*

And this shared connection to the Transcendent—however we name it—can become a unifying power strong enough to bind what has been torn apart.

Through the long journey of writing this book, especially in exploring the legacy of the parallel polis, I've come to a simple but powerful conclusion: "Living in Truth" is essential to any movement that seeks tangible and lasting transformation. In 1970s Czechoslovakia, propaganda was blunt and oppressive. Today, the deception is subtler—hidden in plain sight, embedded in our systems, and normalized by culture. In this climate, living in truth is more than a private ethic. It's a public act of courage.

This movement is not just about reclaiming sacred space in the public square; it's about reclaiming our voices. For too long, those of us rooted in faith, spiritual values, and ethical traditions have kept quiet—not because we lacked passion or clarity, but because we were trained to self-censor, conditioned to hide our spiritual convictions behind polite professionalism or political neutrality.

That time is over.

Now is the time to break that silence—with love, courage, and truth. As we find our voices again, we may begin to hear others doing the same.

And we are not alone.

AWAKEN THE INVISIBLE MAJORITY

There is an invisible majority—Christians, people of other faiths, spiritual seekers, and secular individuals of goodwill—who recognize the truth of the Ancient Blueprint. Many live by its principles, quietly applying them in their lives, homes, and communities.

The question is: Will we recognize one another? Imagine a public space where people can finally be their authentic selves—where it is not taboo to say aloud:

> "I believe—or I know—God, Jesus, Divine Love. That's why I'm doing this work."

There. I said it. And maybe—maybe others will begin saying it too. Those who don't identify as religious might not object. They may respect the sincerity of someone expressing what they truly believe. And in that openness, they may recognize their own connection to this Divine Source—however they define it.

BIRTHING THE SYMBIOTIC AGE

To those who feel called to share the "good news" of their faith, I offer this gentle reminder: this movement is not about control or conversion—it's about healing and unifying. It leads not with words but with witness, not through argument but through example, not by force but by love.

It invites believers to bring their whole selves—heart, mind, and spirit—into the public square, not to dominate but to serve and testify to God's redeeming love humbly.

There's no urgent need for theological debates or interfaith panels to reconcile religious differences. Those conversations become far less important when we unite around a shared service mission—feeding the hungry, housing the homeless, and ensuring that every community meets its 12 basic human needs.

As the Sarvodaya credo reminds us: *"We build the road, and the road builds us."*

When we care for material needs with love, we naturally build spiritual fluency in ourselves and those we serve. This is the essence of Symbiotic Culture:

A living, self-reinforcing playing field, a sacred container, a cathedral in the community, where our deepest longings for a more beautiful world can enter the public square and become reality.

We don't need another revolution of power. We need a reformation of society, rooted in Love. The parallel polis is not a flight from the world. It's a bold *engagement* with it—a way of life that dares to live according to a higher order: Love, interconnection, and spiritual truth made real, right here, right now.

Just as Václav Havel and Václav Benda turned away from ideological warfare to build a new cultural playing field, so must we. Not by pushing harder against each other, but by pulling together. Not through competition for influence, but through *cooperation in service*. The more we live into this new culture, the

Society's "Come to Jesus" Moment

more it will live in us—until, one day, it overtakes the tired systems we once believed were permanent.

So, how do we begin?

I offer you two simple steps:
1. Reintroduce spiritual sensibility into your spheres of influence—your family, workplace, community, and activism.
2. Connect the dots—bring together the siloed efforts of those already seeking transformation, but who have yet to unite around a shared sacred center.

Part IV, Activation will explore how to implement these two steps, at any scale and in any context. But remember this above all: You can be a carrier of Symbiotic Culture DNA.

You can bring it into your home, workplace, or neighborhood. You might start with a book club that evolves into a Symbiotic Circle. You might speak your truth—and invite others to tell theirs. This is the crucial first move: to help create a new playing field, one conversation at a time. As more people join and as more circles form, the field expands. This is how we move—like Havel and Benda—not in opposition, but by transcending the old battlefield of separation.

Once that connection to the sacred is restored, the emerging structures will echo the Ancient Blueprint—not as doctrine but as a living, workable pattern for life and society.

They will become what the parallel polis was always meant to be: a living, breathing alternative to the Culture of Separation.

It's that superhighway of Love I have referred to—and we can begin building it right now. So, how do we live this love in practice? What does it actually look like, in the ordinary moments of life?

BIRTHING THE SYMBIOTIC AGE

A HIGHER LOVE: 1 CORINTHIANS 13 FOR THE 21ST CENTURY

Given that the fundamental problem we face is spiritual, rooted in a Culture of Separation, what can we do about it?

If the problem is separation, the solution must be a relational worldview that empowers a Culture of Connection where we work together for the common good and mutual benefit. This unifying principle is not exclusive to any one faith or ideology. It harmonizes with every religious, spiritual, and ethical tradition and contradicts none.

And here's the truth to remember: we don't have to wait for anyone else to start.

Jesus' prescription to heal humanity remains timeless and clear: *"Love God. Love others."*

The Beatles weren't far off when they sang, *"All you need is love."*

> *To transform the culture of separation*
> *that upholds the empires of man, we must embody*
> *a Culture of Connection that reflects the*
> *Kingdom of Heaven—right here, right now.*

This happens not through ideology or elaborate plans, but by making Divine Love real in our lives. I've said it many times throughout this book, and it bears repeating: No luminous idea, brilliant solution, elegant system, or structure will endure unless it is infused with love.

While our context has changed, the truth has not: All good intentions are hollow and shallow without love. The 3,000-year-old Culture of Separation—built on fear, anxiety, and domination—is coming to an end. Now, more than ever, we must return to the Ancient Blueprint encoded in the command: *"Love God, and Love Others."*

So, as we now step into activating Symbiotic Culture in your life and world, I offer an updated reflection on one of the most powerful teachings of love ever written: St. Paul's letter to the Corinthians (1 Corinthians 13).

> **Although I believe** I possess various spiritual attainments, attend my church or spiritual group regularly, praise God frequently, or sing in the church choir, if I lack Love, I become as annoying as a blaring car alarm.
>
> **Although I possess** various religious and educational degrees and despite holding a responsible position in my company, having a family, a house on a hill, several cars, and a boat, even if my faith can move mountains, I am nothing without Love.
>
> **And though I think of myself** as someone who does good works for others—whether it's through the PTA at my child's school, volunteering at my church or social organization, helping the poor, or working as an activist trying to promote peace or regenerate the environment—if I do not have love, I gain nothing."

- **Love is patient** while I navigate through traffic. Even when others cut me off or behave offensively, I choose not to take offense and provide them the space to continue safely. I "turn the other blinker."
- **Love is kind** at the corner convenience store, even when the clerk has an attitude. I understand their hearts deeply, smile at them, send them all my positive regard, and genuinely wish them well.

- **Love does not envy** my neighbor's new car, nor does it dwell on keeping up with the Joneses. My heart is deeply grateful for what God has provided me.

- **Love does not boast** about helping an elderly woman cross the street or volunteering at a local homeless shelter.

- **Love is never proud**, believing I'm superior to someone because I'm a Democrat or a Republican, interested in Regenerative Culture, or I attend one church instead of another. Love reminds me that my church or other organizations are not about the number of members, but how we demonstrate God's love.

- **Love is not rude**, not even to the tenth telemarketer who calls me while I sit down to supper with my family; it enables me to request calmly to be taken off the call list.

- **Love does not insist on self-seeking** and self-serving, always getting to go to *my* favorite restaurant, the movie *I* want to see, *my* favorite TV program, or a meal as my first priority. Love is self-giving.

- **Love isn't easily angered** when my child runs late for school, my partner takes their time getting ready to go out, or my boss disagrees with one of my ideas.

- **Love does not hold a grudge** or dwell in bitterness, considering how I might respond unkindly to a word spoken with unkindness. Instead, forgiveness is offered.

- **Love does not take pleasure in witnessing others being torn** down by gossip about a co-worker's affair or someone's misfortune. Instead, it rejoices in uplifting others and seeing them experience great blessings.

- **Love always perseveres,** even when a loved one deceives you, by seeing beyond the lie into their hearts.

- **Love always protects** by staying silent when your husband gets lost driving for the tenth time, and you refrain from saying, "I told you so" for not stopping to ask for directions.

- **Love always trusts**, even when your bank account is nearly empty, and you've lost your job, knowing God will take care of everything.

- **Love never fails because God is Love.** Amid life's sometimes painful twists and turns, Love may seem to abandon us. It doesn't; the light of Love is simply too dim to perceive.

- **Love never leaves us because it is Eternal and everlasting.**

Love here is not a feeling but the Power that has created and sustains the universe. It is always present—and always a choice. We can meet every moment in the light of Love. We can surrender to it, again and again, in how we speak, how we act, how we build. In doing so, we don't just imagine Heaven—we *live* it, moment by moment.

To shift out of the materialist Culture of Separation—where "only matter matters"—we must let Divine Love become the prime power in our lives. In other words:

The heart of the matter...is the matter of the Heart.

Practicing Symbiotic Culture is to live a radically different kind of life. It means deepening your relationship with Divine Love, expanding your circle of care, and becoming a living expression of the Ancient Blueprint in the world.

The question now becomes: What does it look like to live this Love—not only in private, but in the public realm of power, culture, and community?

CHOOSING THE KINGDOM: A CALL TO EMBODIED LOVE

Jesus did not come to confront empires on their terms. He came to reveal a new Kingdom—one built not on domination but on service, humility, and unbreakable Love. I call His vision the Ancient Blueprint—not as religious dogma, but as a living alternative: a fractal pattern of grace, truth, and radical kinship.

> *He offered nothing less than a Divine Singularity that begins within and expands outward through the Shared Self.*

It is not the artificial singularity promised by machine intelligence, but a real intelligence rooted in love—wherever two or more are gathered.

When we consciously choose to love God and love one another—to let Divine Love move through us—we awaken a power that does not merely protest injustice but transcends it.

We dismantle both domination and anti-domination, not by overthrowing systems, but by undergrowing and outgrowing them. We become not just children of God, but adults of Good, taking sacred responsibility for birthing the world to come.

This is not abstract theology. It's the relational DNA of Symbiotic Kinship. And it begins in our own hearts.

For me, that means continually returning to Jesus' life and teachings—not distorted by political or religious agendas but illuminated by the radical call to love.

I'm reminded of His mind-boggling challenge in the Sermon on the Mount:

> "If you love those who love you, what reward will you get?
> Are not even the tax collectors doing that?
> And if you greet only your own people, what are you doing more than others?
> Do not even pagans do that?"
> —Matthew 5:46-47

This is Divine wisdom for every relationship—within our groups, across divides, and even toward those who reject us. This is the foundation of a new world.

Jesus calls us to extend love beyond familiar circles and siloed tribes—even to those we dislike or disagree with. Beyond comfort. Beyond reciprocity. Into a love that includes the other.

This is a higher standard of Love—not rooted merely in emotion, but in conscious, courageous action. And that, dear reader, is how we begin to build the world our hearts already know is possible.

But love, to endure, must take form. And for love to transform the world, it must have an embodied vehicle—an infrastructure.

This is where we turn from the fire of inspiration to the architecture of activation.

ACTIVATION: WHERE THE PATTERN TAKES ROOT

The final part of this book, Section IV: Activation, invites you to step into that transformation now.

It presents a living framework composed of relational protocols, patterns, Virtues, and practices—through a coherent worldview capable of igniting grassroots transformation across thousands of communities. This is not a program to follow or a brand to adopt. It is a global movement already in motion—a new Symbiotic Culture waiting to be embodied. It carries an ancient pattern that seeks life through us, without needing a name or central headquarters.

> *The threads are already in place. The weave is waiting.*
> *What's needed now are your hands, your heart,*
> *and your voice. If you feel that quiet "yes" inside—*
> *this is your moment to lean in.*

We've laid the groundwork for cultural transformation.

Now we turn toward a deeper question: How do we live this out—personally, politically, and collectively?

Welcome to the Activation.

Let the birthing begin.

SECTION 4

ACTIVATION

**LIVING THE TRUTH,
BIRTHING THE SYMBIOTIC AGE.
A FRAMEWORK FOR A PARALLEL
SOCIETY MOVEMENT.**

*We are not waiting for a new age to arrive—
we are the ones giving it birth.*

BIRTHING THE SYMBIOTIC AGE

CHAPTER 33

SYMBIOTIC CULTURE DNA AS A RELATIONAL WORLDVIEW LENS

Having laid the foundation in the first three sections—uncovering the Ancient Blueprint, diagnosing the Culture of Separation, translating the pattern into practical community network building, and weaving it into every sphere of life—we now arrive at the final movement: Activation. Here the framework becomes a lived reality, a way of seeing and being that communities can embody, scale, and sustain.

Throughout the years of writing this book, one question has surfaced again and again:

Is it truly possible to unite humanity around a common purpose?

Many wonder whether such a purpose could be broad, deep, spacious, and welcoming enough to embrace the diversity of worldviews, values, visions, and movements now competing for attention in our fractured world.

My answer—born not of theory but of lived experience—is a resounding YES.

Symbiotic Culture DNA as a Relational Worldview Lens

For my whole lifetime, I have searched for a unifying pattern that could guide us from fragmentation to wholeness.

I've come to call that pattern the Ancient Blueprint, and its living expression is what I call Symbiotic Culture DNA—a framework composed of shared purpose, universal principles, embodied Virtues, coherent community needs, and a distributed network infrastructure.

This framework provides us with more than a philosophy—it provides us with a way to build tangible expressions of Love and interdependence in communities across the globe.

But before we can build from it, we must first learn to see through this radical relational lens.

SEEING THROUGH A NEW WAY OF BEING

Transformation begins not just with systems but with sight and vision.

And that brings us to a deeper challenge—the lens through which we perceive reality itself. In a time when AI-driven algorithms amplify division and social media splinters our shared experience, it's more urgent than ever to ask:

What is the worldview behind the world we're building?

A worldview is like a pair of glasses through which we interpret everything. Whether we're aware of it or not, we each carry one. It shapes our sense of purpose, place, and possibility. Formed from our deepest beliefs and values, it unconsciously guides our feelings, decisions, and daily lives. It defines who we are, how we live, and how we relate to one another.

BIRTHING THE SYMBIOTIC AGE

Over time, I've realized that we don't need one worldview to replace all others—or, as they say in *The Lord of the Rings*, 'one ring to rule them all.' What we need is something even more powerful:

> *What is required now is a new type of relational worldview (lens) that enables us to truly see one another.*

This kind of seeing requires a conscious shift of perception—a willingness to move beyond judgment or ideology into a deeper field of love and shared humanity.

A Symbiotic Worldview is a relational, spiritually grounded lens that harmonizes with the Ancient Blueprint—the Divine pattern of love, mutual benefit, and sacred order. It doesn't compete with other worldviews. Instead, it builds bridges among them by honoring the Transcendent thread that runs through all authentic expressions of truth.

Rooted in the Logos and embodied through Symbiotic Culture DNA, this worldview invites individuals and communities to embrace coherence without conformity and unity without uniformity. It's not a belief system to impose but a relational posture to live—a way of seeing that fosters deeper belonging, healing, coherence, and co-creation.

I recognize the Ancient Blueprint as the eternal, repeatable pattern that connects the Transcendent and the immanent. This pattern has been made visible in movements like the early Christian Church, Gandhi's revolution of love, Dr. Ari's Sarvodaya, and the Czech parallel polis. Symbiotic Culture DNA gives form to this pattern in our time—it's like spiritual RNA, translating Divine order into daily life through Virtues, practices, and structures.

Symbiotic Culture DNA as a Relational Worldview Lens

LIVING THE PRACTICE: SEEING OTHERS THROUGH LOVE

Together, the Ancient Blueprint and Symbiotic Culture do not simply offer a new worldview—they provide the foundation for one. They serve as a relational operating system rooted in Love and mutuality, capable of bridging silos, traditions, and ideologies. This makes a Parallel Polis possible: not another ideology, but a visible way of life grounded in the Transcendent—a living path of wholeness in a fragmented world.

> *Wearing this lens is like putting on spiritual glasses—suddenly, you can see the Love shining in another person's heart.*

Even when their words differ from yours or their worldview feels foreign, something deeper connects you. It's a kind of superpower: a way to stay rooted in connection even amid wildly different perspectives. Practicing this relational quality becomes a spiritual muscle, strengthening our capacity and fluency to build trust and interdependence across divides.

I remember having lunch with an evangelical Christian friend. As he shared his thoughts on the day's issues, I noticed myself tightening up, judging, disagreeing, wanting to correct him. But then something shifted. I dropped into my heart and felt his sincere, loving intention beneath the words. In that moment, I could see him. I remembered what mattered most: our friendship, shared purpose in the community, and the love at the core of his being.

That moment taught me something essential:

BIRTHING THE SYMBIOTIC AGE

Love can bridge any difference
when our commitment to unity
surpasses our attachment to being right.

Symbiotic Kinship invites us to live from that space—to transcend preferences and opinions and ground our relationships in something deeper, something sacred.

My work with community-building initiatives like the Local Living Economy Network, Northern Nevada Local Food System Network, and the neighbor-to-neighbor networks gave me a living laboratory to explore this. Through these efforts, I began recognizing and articulating the repeatable pattern that fosters connection across differences.

I realized this transformation wasn't theoretical—it was observable, repeatable, and scalable. It was more than a hopeful metaphor—it was a social and spiritual DNA, with patterns that could be felt, repeated, and grown.

FROM SEEING TO BUILDING: ACTIVATING THE BLUEPRINT

Now that I've described how this lens works on a personal and relational level, let's return to the foundational pattern I introduced earlier.

As you may recall, I first described this Symbiotic Culture DNA and the idea of fractal empowerment in Section 2. The following protocol emerged from a crowdsourcing initiative—a distillation of timeless insights from religious, ethical, and wisdom traditions. It echoes Dr. Ari's call to "create a critical spiritual mass of consciousness."

If parts of what follows seem familiar, that's because they are.

Symbiotic Culture DNA as a Relational Worldview Lens

But this time, I invite you to read with fresh eyes—to envision how you might activate this viral seed wherever you are. Consider those in your community already performing acts of kindness and care. Think of the organizations trying to do good but still operating in silos.

What follows is a practical overview of activating the Ancient Blueprint using Symbiotic Culture DNA. This DNA consists of five core elements that, when implemented, foster thriving, self-sufficient, interdependent communities capable of healing our divisions and uniting humanity.

To recap from Chapter 18, these five elements are:

1. A Shared Purpose and Goals — Uniting the Cosmos in Love
2. Eight Universal Principles — The Foundational Ethics of Symbiotic Culture
3. Five Core Virtues — The Transcendent Energies of Connection
4. Twelve Common Community Needs — A Coherent Framework for Service
5. A Distributed Network Infrastructure — The Pathway for Scalable Impact

By integrating these five elements into our personal lives, organizations, and communities, we transcend the Culture of Separation and cultivate a new Culture of Connection. The following section will walk you through each component, demonstrate how it operates in real-world settings, and offer clear, actionable steps to bring each component to life.

BIRTHING THE SYMBIOTIC AGE

1. SHARED PURPOSE: UNITING THE COSMOS IN LOVE

At the heart of Symbiotic Culture DNA is a singular purpose: to bring together what has been separated and unite the cosmos in love.

This is not merely an abstract or esoteric ideal but the foundation upon which all successful community movements are built. It reflects the lineage of the Ancient Blueprint, beginning with Jesus in the Sermon on the Mount and including Gandhi, Dr. Ariyaratne, the Czech parallel polis movement, and my work in San Diego, California, and Reno, Nevada.

How to Activate:

- Express this common purpose in personal and community conversations.
- Ensure that all actions, initiatives, and projects align with this.
- Acknowledge that every act of cooperation, service, and kindness contributes to this greater purpose.

2. EIGHT SHARED PRINCIPLES—COMMUNITY OPERATING SYSTEM—BASED ON SHARED PRINCIPLES FOR A TRULY REGENERATIVE SOCIETY

- The Golden Rule.
- Charity Begins at Home and Self-rule.
- Acknowledge Something Bigger than Yourself.
- Love Thy Neighbor.
- Think Globally, Act Locally.
- A Community-based Local Economy.
- Focus on What We Have in Common.
- Build a New Connected, Organism, not a Separate, Competing Organization.

Building on this shared purpose, we distilled eight core principles that serve as ethical guidelines for fostering unity and cooperation in a fragmented world. These principles are:

1. **The Golden Rule 2.0** — Do unto others as you would have them do unto you, acknowledging our interconnected nature.

2. **Charity Begins at Home** — Personal and local responsibility must be prioritized before addressing more significant societal issues.

3. **Acknowledge Something Bigger Than Yourself** — Whether it is God, the Universe, or collective consciousness, recognizing a Transcendent, higher power fosters humility and service.

4. **Love Thy Neighbor** — Extend kindness and cooperation beyond immediate circles of affiliation and comfort.

5. **Think Globally, Act Locally** — Build regenerative, local solutions with global implications.

6. **A Community-Based Local Economy** — Support local businesses and initiatives, prioritizing mutual benefit over competition.

7. **Focus on What We Have in Common** — Avoid unnecessary divisiveness by emphasizing shared Virtues and needs.

8. **Build an Interconnected Organism, not a Competing Organization** — Prioritize building networks that include existing projects rather than building additional siloed efforts.

How to Activate:
- Use these eight key principles to guide personal, professional, and community decision-making.
- Use these ethical foundations to build community initiatives.
- Teach and model these principles in organizations, workplaces, schools, and governance.

3. FIVE CORE VIRTUES: THE TRANSCENDENT ENERGIES OF CONNECTION
Walking Our Talk: Shared Values/Virtues

Love
Compassion
Kindness
Gratitude
Generosity
Forgiveness
Humility
Patience
Faith
Appreciation

Integrity
Authenticity
Responsibility
Honesty
Trustworthiness
Balance
Self-reliance
Simplicity
Honor

Courage
Strength
Perseverance
Acceptance
Dedication
Discipline
Restraint
Nobility

Service
Goodwill
Sharing
Caring
Involvement
Community

Respect
Mindfulness
Fairness
Justice
Civility
Cooperation
Dignity

Virtues are the lived expressions of our principles, forming an energetic foundation for a thriving Symbiotic Culture. Through community work, there are five core Virtues that unify and organize both individuals and communities:

1. **Love** — The sacred power that binds us to one another in communion, empowering connection, compassion, and co-creation in alignment with the Ancient Blueprint.

2. **Integrity** — Living in coherence—where thoughts, words, and actions reflect spiritual alignment and inner truth.

3. **Courage** — The willingness to act from the heart, even in the face of fear—grounded in trust, conviction, and the call to embody higher Virtues.

4. **Service** — A life posture of self-giving rooted in love; offering one's gifts for the flourishing of others and the healing and well-being of the whole.

5. **Respect** — Honoring the Divine image and the inherent dignity within every being, recognizing our interdependence in the Luminous Web of life.

How to Activate:
- Initiate your own monthly Virtue practice, focusing on embodying different Virtues within your communities each month.
- Create community gatherings that encourage reflection and action around these Virtues.
- Recognize and celebrate acts of Virtue within local networks.

4. TWELVE COMMON COMMUNITY NEEDS—FROM THE OLD BATTLEFIELD TO A NEW PLAYING FIELD

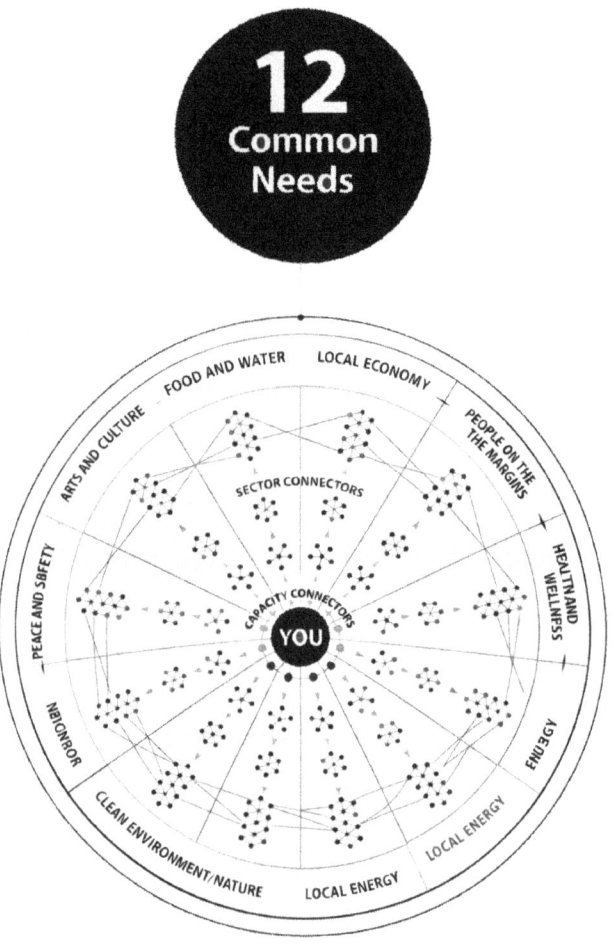

There are twelve universal community needs that serve as the foundation for a thriving society:

1. Local Economy
2. Clean & Healthy Natural Environment
3. Community Peace & Safety

4. Local Food & Water
5. Neighbor Helping Neighbor
6. Community Empowerment of the Marginalized
7. Local Energy
8. Arts & Culture
9. Housing
10. Family and Community Health & Wellness
11. Education/Mentoring
12. Religion/Spirituality in Service

Meeting these needs at the local level allows communities to operate as self-sufficient, interconnected ecosystems. There is no specific sequence for developing each of the twelve networks. Nonetheless, religion/spirituality in service, local food systems, and arts and culture are "low-hanging fruits" that are simple to initiate.

How to Activate:

- Hold community meetings to identify local priorities based on these needs.
- Form small, decentralized Symbiotic Circles to meet each need.
- Form partnerships with multiple stakeholders and organizations that align with these goals.

5. DISTRIBUTED NETWORK INFRASTRUCTURE

We must move beyond traditional hierarchical structures and adopt a network-centric approach to scale and spread the DNA of Symbiotic Culture. This entails:
- Developing multi-nodal networks that link diverse sectors and individuals.

- Encouraging collaborative leadership rather than top-down management.
- Fostering peer-to-peer engagement to facilitate knowledge sharing and resource exchange.

How to Activate:

- Identify and empower "connectors" within each common need area and the community.
- Utilize digital platforms and in-person gatherings to strengthen ties between individuals and organizations.
- Create a public "Symbiotic Culture Network Map" to visualize connections and opportunities.

CONCLUSION: THE POWER OF FRACTAL COMMUNITY EMPOWERMENT

We ignite a process of fractal empowerment by integrating Symbiotic Culture DNA into our daily lives and local communities—a ripple effect in which small, intentional acts of love and alignment spark large-scale transformation. Just as Sarvodaya Shramadana mobilized over 5,000 villages in Sri Lanka, we can inspire 50,000 communities worldwide by faithfully living out these five foundational elements.

Change begins not with massive systems or sweeping reforms, but with a grounded presence amplified through love, trust, and shared intention.

Each individual, family, organization, and community that embodies the Ancient Blueprint becomes part of a living, breathing ecosystem of transformation. Together, we demonstrate that

Symbiotic Culture DNA as a Relational Worldview Lens

uniting humanity is not some far-off dream, but a tangible and achievable reality. It's the difference between doing good in isolation and building something enduring—a cathedral not of stone, but of shared purpose and Spirit.

In this context, that cathedral becomes a viable parallel polis—woven through networks of trust, multiplying mutual benefit, and making the invisible love of God visible in everyday life.

YOUR CALL TO ACTION

Start right where you are. Infuse this framework into your relationships, your neighborhood, your work, your congregation, your circle of influence—you are the seed.

By living out this vision, you become part of something larger, a spiritual movement in action.

This is how we co-create a world where intentional mutual benefit becomes the norm and a thriving Culture of Connection takes root and grows—locally, regionally, and globally.

But here's the key: you're not doing this alone. All around the world, others are already planting seeds, building trust, and embodying this Blueprint—whether they call it that or not. A deeper coherence is already rising from faith groups and farmers to entrepreneurs and artists.

So, the question now becomes:

Who are the players already moving in this direction—and how can we weave their efforts into a unified field of transformation?

Chapter 34 maps this emerging ecosystem—the networks, movements, and humble pioneers already living parts of this vision.

By recognizing and connecting these "islands of coherence," we begin to activate the parallel polis—not unlike the early Church moving from inner renewal to outward mission, or what Ephesians calls "putting on the new self."

BIRTHING THE SYMBIOTIC AGE

CHAPTER 34

BUILDING A PARALLEL SOCIETY:
WHO ARE THE PLAYERS?

Building a parallel polis isn't about constructing new structures using an "old wineskin" approach. It's about gently weaving together the threads of Symbiotic Culture already thriving on the ground, allowing new structures to evolve organically. By linking these efforts through a relational worldview, we awaken a higher shared purpose.

These "Islands of Coherence"—the quiet pioneers already living the change—are the true meek, leading transformation through service, humility, and steadfast commitment. It is through their power that we will co-create an Earth truly worth inheriting.

This is an idea whose time has arrived. In today's fractured political landscape, we are presented with a rare opportunity: To move beyond divisive narratives and unite diverse efforts around what truly matters—a shared purpose serving the common good.

I invite you to embody the DNA of Symbiotic Culture wherever you are. Start by identifying the 12 community needs in your local context and taking meaningful steps to contribute. At its core, this movement is about spiritual renewal—a revival that honors all authentic expressions of the Ancient Blueprint and restores our sacred interdependence.

We are not starting from scratch. All around us, organizations and networks—many faith-based, spiritually grounded, and quietly service-driven—are already meeting these needs. Often, working without recognition or appreciation, these groups form the foundation of a developing Network Commons. These movements and networks hold a crucial piece of the puzzle, provided they recognize that collaborating in common accord significantly multiplies their effectiveness.

To be truly relevant, individuals, organizations, and networked silos need to recognize their unique strengths and intentionally weave them into their local ecosystem. The twelve core community needs can serve as a guiding framework—key areas that every community is called to engage with.

> **By aligning with and focusing on these real-world, on-the-ground needs, we ensure that the Parallel Polis is not an abstract idea but a living reality that meets people where they are.**

The eventual goal is to connect all helpful endeavors coherently so that each initiative benefits from mutual support, shared resources, and a collective sense of purpose. But first, we need to understand these networks and what they offer.

WHO'S ALREADY DOING THE WORK? THE CORE THREADS OF A PARALLEL SOCIETY

Here are the core movements and networks that I have identified over the past several decades:

- **FAITH-BASED AND SPIRITUAL GROUPS** — Formal and informal, these communities provide direct care and essential services around community needs, forming the backbone of local support systems. These already involve millions of organizations and hundreds of millions of individuals.

  Brings to the table: *an invisible "spiritual army" working on the ground, already embedded in communities, providing spiritual grounding in the Ancient Blueprint.*

- **CHARITIES AND SOCIAL CHANGE EFFORTS** — Humanitarian organizations dedicated to alleviating suffering and fostering justice.

  Brings to the table: *already addressing urgent community needs and ensuring no one is left behind.*

- **CIVIC ENGAGEMENT AND BRIDGE BUILDERS** Those working to mend divides, strengthen community bonds, and promote meaningful dialogue.

  Brings to the table: *tools and a track record for fostering social cohesion, promoting peacemaking, and uniting people across ideological divides.*

- **REGENERATIVE CULTURE MOVEMENTS** — Social, economic, and place-based initiatives that seek to restore, renew, and revitalize human communities, ecosystems, and cultural systems to ensure long-term sustainability, resilience, and mutual flourishing.

  Brings to the table: *Regenerative Culture advocates offer long-term regenerative principles and practices, seek to heal the relationship between people and nature, and provide an essential puzzle piece for thriving local economies and communities.*

- **FAITH-BASED CREATION CARE INITIATIVES** — Religious-inspired movements and communities that emphasize the sacred responsibility of individuals and communities to protect, restore, and steward the natural world as an expression of faith and moral duty.

  Brings to the table: *Many groups have already formed alliances with other "secular" environmental approaches to help model collaboration.*

- **PURPOSE-DRIVEN SMALL BUSINESSES** — Mission-driven and faith-based entrepreneurs prioritizing social, environmental, and ethical impact alongside financial sustainability—ensuring their products, services, and operations contribute positively to society and the planet.

  Brings to the table: *already actively demonstrates that economic systems can be transformed through Virtue-driven entrepreneurship.*

- **NEW ECONOMY AND COMMONS MOVEMENTS** — Advocating for circular economies, cooperative ownership, shared wealth, peer-to-peer networks, and decentralized systems, including blockchain.

  Brings to the table: *challenges to extractive materialism and consumerism while advocating for shared prosperity.*

- **LOCALIZATION, BIOREGIONAL, and COSMOLOCALIZATION NETWORKS** — Strengthening local resilience while remaining globally connected.

  Brings to the table: *Enhancing local self-sufficiency while upholding global solidarity.*

- **PRO-DEMOCRACY AND CIVIL SOCIETY MOVEMENTS** — Ensuring that governance remains accountable, participatory, and ethical.

  Brings to the table: *Ensure the Parallel Polis remains rooted in participatory governance and community decision-making.*

BUILDING THE SUPERHIGHWAY OF CONNECTIVITY: BRINGING ALL GOOD INTENTIONS UNDER ONE BIG IN-TENT

Now that we've outlined the key threads of a viable Parallel Polis, the natural question becomes: how do we help good people doing good work emerge from their silos and begin working together?

First, let's recognize the shared foundation: every network, movement, or structure, in its way, seeks to benefit the community. All share a common purpose: to "unite the cosmos in love."

While the Culture of Separation invisibly permeates every institution, a quiet countercurrent runs through them all: the longing for Symbiotic Kinship and Beloved Community. This current infuses even our "beautiful silos" with possibility. And yet, the common foundation—especially its spiritual dimension—is rarely named in postmodern society, even among groups that live it.

Take, for instance, networks advancing regenerative culture, cosmolocalism, or new economic models. These often operate on the fringes—dismissed or ignored by dominant systems shaped by the "only matter matters" worldview. Imagine introducing these promising yet largely untested concepts into mainstream networks addressing real community needs—giving them a real-world "culture dish" to evolve, learn, and refine.

These new models and traditional service groups don't need to compete—they need to converge.

As a biologist, I understand that evolution favors diversity—the more options we have, the better our chances for survival and thrival. You'll recall that we didn't limit participation to organic growers when developing the local food network in Reno. As a result, the largest conventional grower in the area chose to adopt organic practices and join the movement. More viable solutions emerged not from ideological purity, but from collaborative problem-solving grounded in relationship.

> **One of the most potent and promising areas of collaboration involves uniting religious, especially Christian, spiritual, and secular groups around a shared purpose.**

Remember the Pastor and the Pagan? Again, the goal isn't interfaith dialogue—it's working side by side for mutual benefit. As we saw in our spiritually diverse Reno community, cooperation built mutual respect, and understanding emerged naturally.

I'm especially energized by the meeting ground between visionary systems and grounded service—between "pie-in-the-sky" idealists and "feet-on-the-ground" groups serving the least of these. Remember Gandhi's words at the India National Conference:

> "Until we stand in the fields with the millions that toil each day under the hot sun, we will not represent India, nor will we ever be able to challenge the British as one nation."

That's the heart of Symbiotic Culture, too—real solidarity doesn't emerge from strategy alone, but from presence with the people and service to real needs. What an opportunity to reality-test promising ideas!

Consider also the Civic Engagement and Bridge-Builder networks. These are designed to foster communication and shared understanding, offering practical tools to bridge differences.

Can you see how these diverse networks can become threads in a viable Parallel Polis for any community or region?

Lastly, collaboration between secular and religious groups deepens respect and often sparks spiritual renewal in some and open-hearted tolerance in others. Imagine a truly welcoming Cultural Arts Festival—where instead of "socializing by the silo," all tribes come together to celebrate. A true gathering of the tribes—from bikers to hip-hop crews to religious elders—each showing off their "colors" in an atmosphere of mutual respect.

That would be a real "color revolution." And it's already within reach.

A CALL TO ACTION: WEAVING YOURSELF INTO THE PARALLEL POLIS

That's the vision. But vision alone is not enough.

In Chapter 29, I described how Sarvodaya stepped in during Sri Lanka's food crisis—not through heroic rescue but through a living infrastructure of love that had already been built, village by village. When the storm hit, the system didn't collapse. It served. Why? Because it was already rooted in trust, spiritual practice, and self-giving service.

Could that happen here?

Let's be honest: if a similar crisis struck in the West, many of our communities would falter. The Culture of Separation isn't built to hold us in hard times. Its foundations are transactional, not relational.

This is why we can no longer wait.

We must weave ourselves into a living network before the next disruption arrives. And that starts with you.

So, here's the real question: How will you join this movement without a name?

If your heart resonates with this movement, identify where your skills meet the community's needs. Whether in food, education, religious and spiritual care, housing, or the arts, find your place within the twelve domains of well-being.

Form or join a Symbiotic Circle. Begin the work of connection by showing up with presence, patience, and purpose, instead of by launching a new project.

And let's not forget: the original Parallel Polis was born not in freedom but under oppression. It emerged through the faithful witness of believers in Czechoslovakia, who risked everything to practice truth and love in a society where religion was criminalized. Their strength didn't come from politics—it came from prayer, spiritual clarity, and a community grounded in moral courage and love in action.

Hundreds of millions across the West and beyond gather weekly in churches, temples, and sacred communities.

But what if these often-isolated spaces became the anchors of the next great cultural awakening?

What if the "Body of Christ" (Protestant, Orthodox, and Catholic) came together—united as one, in love, and joined by other faith-rooted communities—not in a spirit of privileging Christianity, but beginning with the "tribe" I know best and calling it, as others can call their own, to move beyond differences?

What if we did this not just to believe, but to build embodied networks of solidarity with "the least of these" (Matthew 25)?

The real test will come in crises.

Will we fall back into silos or rise together in shared trust and sacred purpose? The parallel polis won't be built by idealism. It will be built by faithful presence, grace in motion, and people willing to love across differences, serve without ego, and create what the world still thinks is impossible.

That brings us to the next step: uniting the threads of these siloed efforts into a shared tapestry—a whole-cloth movement rooted in mutual benefit, ready to weave coherence across our fragmented world.

CHAPTER 35

ACTIVATING SYMBIOTIC KINSHIP: UNITING THE THREADS OF A LIVING NETWORK COMMONS

As I've reiterated throughout this book, we've all been shaped—if not hypnotized—by the polarizing Culture of Separation, even those of us committed, as St. Maximus expressed, to "uniting the Cosmos in love."

Today's convergence of crises offers not just danger but a sacred opening. It calls for vigilance, humility, and the courage to embody Symbiotic Kinship.

> *More than new systems, we need space-holders—rooted in trust, grace, and love—who can transcend division and help co-create the Beloved Community.*

But how do we get there, especially in a world shaped by siloed systems and fragmented trust?

Until now, well-intentioned projects and movements have often stayed within their lanes, especially when buoyed by the "golden handcuffs" of government, NGO, and nonprofit funding. But as top-down systems begin to unravel in the US and elsewhere, these once-stable silos are struggling to survive.

In times like these, wise leaders recognize the need to move beyond their "communities of comfort," and cultivate the inner posture and relational depth needed for true collaboration.

While engaging with those who think like us is easier, that alone can't create the coherence our communities urgently require.

These deepening crises are already prompting leaders to move beyond preference and ideology—to enter the "discomfort zone" of engaging with unfamiliar belief systems and more diverse communities.

I speak from experience. Had I not chosen to actively engage with various religious organizations and mainstream institutions in Reno—and confront my judgments and prejudices—I would have *never* been able to organize any of our successful networks.

FROM SILOS TO SYMBIOSIS: THE HIDDEN PATTERN OF COLLECTIVE AWAKENING

Here's another example of when collaboration moved from choice to necessity. This challenge isn't theoretical—it has played out again and again in the communities I've worked with, revealing a pattern we can now recognize and learn from.

In 1991, as discussed in Section 1, I worked in low-income Black and Latino communities in San Diego, then the highest-poverty census tract in the region. Though these communities had strong churches, organizations, and social services, all of these operated in isolation. Many relied on government funding and were forced to compete for scarce grants, discouraging collaboration.

Despite the obvious advantages of cooperation, the Culture of Separation prevailed. Some leaders even asked me to help form ethnic-specific business associations—Black-only or Latino-only networks. I didn't say no. I listened.

Then the crisis hit.

As the drug and gang crisis erupted in the early '90s, it became clear that no single group could respond alone. Collaboration was no longer optional—it was essential. I convened a meeting where, for the first time, the minister of the largest Black church met the local Latino Catholic priest. That kind of connection, long overdue, only happened under pressure.

As I noted earlier in this book, diverse groups often come together during natural disasters like hurricanes or wildfires. That impulse toward unity is beautiful, but it rarely lasts once the immediate crisis passes.

I've witnessed this pattern repeatedly in my work—crisis igniting cooperation only to fade back into separation.

In Reno, our first network was catalyzed by the 2003 protests surrounding the Iraq War and the arrival of national chain stores. The 2005 farmland crisis sparked action around local food. The 2008 housing crash reduced arts funding and prompted us to co-create the Arts and Culture Festival. Each crisis brought deeper cooperation and connection.

Today, we face multiple converging crises: climate, mental health, economic inequality, cultural polarization, and spiritual disorientation. Old systems are crumbling. Federal support is uncertain. The institutions we once trusted are faltering.

But if there's a silver lining in these storm clouds, it's this: The walls that once separated us are collapsing under the weight of our shared reality.

We are at a turning point. The dominant strategies of the past, rooted in control, competition, and division, can no longer meet humanity's deeper needs. But this isn't a time for despair, it may be the greatest opportunity in human history.

These recurring patterns—crisis forcing connection, followed by a gradual return to separation—don't have to continue. We now have the opportunity to break the cycle by learning to build trust before disaster strikes. Instead of relying on emergencies to drive collaboration, we can begin cultivating the kind of relational infrastructure that endures over time—strong enough to weather disruption and flexible enough to evolve with changing needs.

This is the deeper work before us: not simply responding to crises but laying the foundations for a more unified future. The systems of the past cannot meet the challenges of the present, let alone those to come. If we are to embrace this transformational moment fully, we must do more than react.

It's time to build something new.

SEEING THE FIELD ANEW: SYMBIOTIC CULTURE AS A RELATIONAL LENS

We can't stop at reactive cooperation precipitated by crisis—we need a proactive, coherent way of being and seeing.

The good news is that current realities are prompting some leaders to step out of their silos. In recent years, I've had several conversations with network leaders who now see the need to build bridges. There's a growing recognition that we can't go it alone—that we truly need one another.

One colleague, for example, realized she was primarily reaching people already in the regeneration movement: green business owners, sustainable farmers, and ecological thinkers. But when she looked beyond her circle, she saw that mainstream nonprofits, local businesses, and government officials were just outside her reach. Vast resources and potential allies remained untapped.

She saw the problem, but didn't know how to connect. That's when I recognized an opportunity to apply Symbiotic Culture: helping networks like hers build relational bridges into a broader Network Commons and unlock the community wealth trapped in isolated systems.

I can already hear a common objection from those leading networks: "Where will I find the time to take on one more thing?" Consider:

> *Symbiotic Culture isn't one more task—*
> *it's a transformative lens that lightens the load.*
> *It helps you discover hidden resources by connecting*
> *your network to others, revealing new forms of support,*
> *energy, and possibility.*

This isn't about adding something—it's about rethinking everything!

Symbiotic Culture offers a relational perspective that strengthens every siloed effort. From a practical standpoint, it's a win-win-win:

- Your network gains access to people, capital, and support previously out of reach.
- The broader community benefits as silos connect and unleash collaborative solutions around Local Food, Economy, Neighborhoods, Arts, Faith, and Service.
- And the entire ecosystem is uplifted—everyone rising together through connection, not isolation.

To be clear, I'm not offering an IKEA-style "how-to" manual." Activation isn't about building something new overnight.

It's about cultivating the soil so that Symbiotic Culture can take root in you and your community. The next step in cultivation is learning to recognize the invisible, informal structures—the trust-based relational networks that form the living interstitial tissue of a healthy culture.

And...to truly spread trust across regions and sectors, we need more than isolated collaboration—we need living social infrastructure that supports and amplifies these efforts.

That brings us to a crucial piece of the puzzle: mediating structures.

HOW SYMBIOTIC CULTURE BRINGS MEDIATING STRUCTURES TO LIFE

Before exploring how we might "unite the threads" by Connecting the Good in our communities to nurture a new parallel polis, we need to understand the kind of organization that emerges when we cultivate a Symbiotic Culture.

In a world stretched thin between hyper-individualism and massive bureaucratic systems, renewal won't come from the top down—or from any single visionary or siloed initiative. It will emerge in the middle spaces of life, where people gather in intentional, face-to-face relationships that cultivate belonging, meaning, and moral formation. These spaces are often informal, rarely commercial, and easily overlooked.

Sociologist and theologian Peter Berger called this realm "mediating structures"—the institutions that intermediate between individuals and the vast machinery of state and market. These include families, neighborhoods, faith communities, cooperatives, recovery groups, and civic and professional associations.

Like the Parallel Polis, mediating structures:

- **Emphasize grassroots**, voluntary, and human-scale organization
- **Resist domination** by centralized systems
- **Provide space** for spiritual, cultural, and ethical renewal
- **Serve as generative crucibles** of civil engagement

At its heart, Symbiotic Culture is about strengthening civil society—a web of relationships, associations, and institutions where we engage in public life, foster trust, and pursue shared values freely and voluntarily, often outside the realms of profit or government control.

These aren't abstract ideals. Symbiotic Culture activates these structures in tangible ways, helping them cooperate in service of the whole. Symbiotic Networks, for instance, don't deliver direct services. They connect and empower those who do—acting as relational bridges, scaffolding coordination, and amplifying mutual care.

They:

- **Coordinate action** on shared community needs
- **Support emerging groups** or under-resourced groups
- **Promote the twelve domains** of human well-being in harmony
- **Reduce unnecessary competition** and duplication

These networks act as a "living laboratory" where Virtue is practiced, trust is established, and collective or nexus agency becomes evident. Berger called them the essential scaffolding of a healthy society, allowing us to engage in public life without being absorbed or neutralized by dominant systems.

Across time and cultures, many thinkers affirm this view. Edmund Burke's "little platoons," Tocqueville's voluntary associations, MacIntyre's communities of practice, and Taylor's middle spaces all highlight the indispensable role of these relational institutions in shaping moral and civic life.

This wisdom isn't merely academic—it lives in practice. Nobel laureate Elinor Ostrom's groundbreaking research on commons governance showed that communities can successfully manage shared resources through decentralized, trust-based collaboration, without relying on top-down control or market competition.

Her work affirmed what many traditions already knew: mutual stewardship rooted in shared values can outperform extractive systems. This principle is reflected in the Sarvodaya societies of Sri Lanka, recovery fellowships like Alcoholics Anonymous, mutual aid groups, house churches, and the Parallel Polis of Communist-era Czechoslovakia—all living examples of Symbiotic Culture in action.

Catholic Social Teaching powerfully echoes this vision, particularly through the principle of subsidiarity. Larger systems should support—not replace—local human-scale institutions. Church documents such as *Quadragesimo Anno* and *Centesimus Annus* affirm that human dignity is fully realized through participation in these intermediate associations.

Symbiotic Culture, in this sense, is itself a mediating structure—an energizing field that weaves together all others in a local region.

It provides the relational, participatory space through which the Five Stages of Practice (discussed later) can unfold—from personal transformation to social, cultural, economic, and political coherence.

> *Symbiotic Circles and Networks are not an accessory to the work; they are the work. They are places where people don't just talk about community—they live it.*

In this moment of systemic breakdown of trust, mediating structures aren't optional—they're essential. They represent the living interstitial tissues of a Symbiotic Society: flexible enough to adapt, sturdy enough to endure. As we reimagine what it means to love, build, and belong, these structures remain our most vital places of practice.

That's why building bridges between siloed networks is crucial—not to replace the incredible work that's already happening but to amplify it. Connection doesn't dilute impact. It magnifies it.

When we align our work through shared purpose and trust, we unlock a deeper collective power that lays the groundwork for the Parallel Polis to emerge. But structure alone is not enough. As the global fabric continues to fray, we must also undergo a deep moral and spiritual re-centering.

AWAKENING AGENCY: FROM OUTSOURCING TO OWNERSHIP

We are living through the slow collapse of a paradigm: the idea that someone else—some government, institution, or distant expert—will fix our world's problems. That outsourcing illusion is fading fast. The old systems—governments, NGOs, traditional charities, or think tanks—were never designed for this moment. They're unraveling under the weight of global complexity, and the responsibility for renewal is shifting back to us.

As Dr. Ari said:

"We don't believe in charity. We believe in awakening. Each village must rise by its effort."

That's the spirit we need now. Not a reaction. Not dependence. But rebirth.

The future belongs to those courageous enough to lead and take ownership from below, anchored in love, trust, and mutual responsibility. We must create a parallel polis—a vibrant alternative rooted in a new civic operating system, founded on community self-governance and networked solidarity. It is not a replica of what's broken, but a living framework drawn from ancient wisdom, empowered by modern tools, and infused with a Transcendent pulse.

This approach will simultaneously create independent, parallel cultural movements, each organically taking root as a Network Commons in thousands of local regions.

The seeds of the future are already sprouting in neighborhoods, circles, communities, and small acts of service. All that's missing is the connective tissue—the will to weave it together. We don't need experts or credentials to begin. We need clear minds, open hearts, and willing hands.

As Dr. Martin Luther King, Jr. reminded us, and I repeat it once more:

> "Everybody can serve. You don't have to have a college degree to serve. You only need a heart full of grace, a soul generated by love."

THE QUIET REVOLUTION IS ALREADY UNDERWAY: WEAVING WHAT ALREADY WORKS

Every day, billions of acts of love and care unfold quietly in communities worldwide—from healing circles and mutual aid groups to churches, small farms, local economies, youth mentorship, and food banks. Who are some of the most significant contributors?

Churches, temples, mosques, and informal spiritual communities that embody the spirit of Matthew 25: *"I was hungry, and you fed me...a stranger, and you welcomed me."*

But here's the catch: most of this good work happens in silos.

Billions of people are giving their lives to service and healing, yet they remain disconnected, unaware of their shared purpose or the cumulative power they carry. They are islands of coherence, not yet in communion.

Globally, we have:

- **11 million** formal nonprofits and **50 million** informal civic groups.
- **Over 2.3 million** religious congregations.
- **More than 10 million** additional spiritual groups.
- And across Europe and the US, over **850,000 local religious communities**—including **nearly 700 million Christians** out of one billion people.

Let's pause and consider two of the most powerful yet often overlooked global contributors to local service: religious communities and service organizations. These are not just institutions. They are vast reservoirs of compassion, practical wisdom, and civic infrastructure.

> *The real challenge isn't creating something new—it's connecting what's already alive.*

Take the Catholic Church alone: 1.4 billion members, 222,000 parish communities, and nearly 134,000 mission stations offering care and support. Like other decentralized faith networks, this is a living web of relational and organizational strength already rooted in neighborhoods. If we're willing to connect across differences, these networks can serve as powerful anchors for Symbiotic Culture.

Likewise, service organizations like Rotary and Lions unite another 5 million people in over 100,000 local clubs across nearly every country. Billions of people are already engaged in good work, most in isolation.

To build a Symbiotic Culture, we must embrace universal Symbiotic Kinship—extending kinship even to those we may have once judged or misunderstood, especially organized religion.

I had to do this myself.

Though I've always followed Jesus, I held a deep skepticism toward institutional Christianity. But I've seen that community isn't built on agreement but on grace—the willingness to love, forgive, and stay connected despite our differences. *Grace, not uniformity*, is what makes space for true belonging.

> *This is the hidden gift of the Ancient Blueprint:*
> *a sacred pattern woven into the structure of reality itself,*
> *calling us to mutual aid and communion.*

Whether you call it Logos, the Transcendent, or Divine Love, it is alive in every act of compassion. Our mission now is simple yet profound: Help those already working find one another.

Build bridges. Foster trust. Amplify the light.

Like the unseen mycelium beneath the forest floor, we are already connected. It's time to bring that connection into the light. Still, as we begin to weave what already works, we must ask: Who has been left out of the conversation? And how do we expand the tent to embrace the full spectrum of good work already being done?

BEYOND IDEOLOGY: WELCOMING MAIN STREET AND THE MARGINS

A critical but often overlooked thread in this cultural tapestry is Main Street—local businesses and entrepreneurs who serve as economic engines and anchors of relational and civic life. These small and medium-sized enterprises comprise 90-percent of companies globally and 99.9-percent in the US and Europe.

Increasingly, many are mission-driven—motivated not just by profit but by faith, justice, and a desire to serve the common good.

And yet, in many progressive visions of a "new economy," these businesses are often excluded. I once sat in a room with 100 visionary leaders discussing the future of our economy. When I asked whether purpose-driven companies like mine had a role to play, the room hesitated.

Most advocated for co-ops, land trusts, "New Economy DAOs" (Decentralized Autonomous Organizations) and "post-capitalist" models, but no one mentioned the small business owners already striving to do right by their communities.

That moment revealed a blind spot: inclusion must go deeper than ideology or economic theory. If our movements are to be truly regenerative, they must embrace the full spectrum of people and practices committed to mutual flourishing, from main street to those on the margins.

That's why Symbiotic Culture rejects purity tests.

We honor all contributions—from private businesses and cooperatives to mutual aid groups, local government, churches, and spiritual communities. The goal isn't uniformity, but coherence: a rich, interwoven diversity of life-giving efforts animated by a shared ethic of love, responsibility, and resilience.

BIRTHING THE SYMBIOTIC AGE

That's the essence of a Network Commons:
not sorting people by worldview
but weaving them together through Love in action.

Even the most pluralistic economy will fracture if we remain divided in spirit. As Scripture reminds us, *"A house divided against itself cannot stand"* (Mark 3:25). Yet, coherence at this scale is only possible when rooted in something more profound than structure. The actual glue of regenerative culture isn't policy or partnership—it's *presence*.

A global network of 50,000 communities cannot emerge through top-down control or centralized systems design. But they *can* emerge through an invisible Blueprint rooted in scalable principles, protocols, and loving presence. These principles transcend organizational form and can be infused into any setting, wherever two or more are gathered.

This is how Symbiotic Culture scales: not through replication of structure, but through incarnation of spirit. So, coherence at the community level begins with coherence of the heart. That's why the next step isn't just building outward—it's abiding inward.

Before constructing new systems,
we must become the kind of people
who can sustain them.

LIVING INTEGRATION:
BEING AND DOING AS ONE

One of our most persistent mistakes is separating inner and outer work—being vs. doing, spiritual vs. practical. This fragmentation is a hallmark of the Culture of Separation and has infected everything from our theology to our activism.

Symbiotic Culture rejects this divide. Like the Sarvodaya Movement in Sri Lanka, it recognizes that spiritual awakening and social transformation are not separate—they are the same path.

Action must arise from Being, and Being must find expression through Action. You cannot sustainably have one without the other.

That's why, when people say, "Just teach me how to build a network," I gently ask them to reflect more deeply. Without a spiritual foundation, networks collapse under ego and disunity. And when others say, "Let's only sit and pray," I remind them that true prayer—true faith—births real-world action. The Epistle of James put it plainly:

> "Faith by itself, if it has no works, is dead" (James 2:17).

Being must flow into doing—or else both wither.

In Sarvodaya, Virtues like Compassion, Equanimity, and Loving kindness are not assumed to arise by chance—they are cultivated intentionally. Likewise, in Symbiotic Culture, we must practice Virtues consciously. Trust, humility, attentiveness, and integrity are the relational ligaments that hold our communities together.

If we abandon our inner life, our structures will fragment.
If we avoid action, our spirituality becomes escapism.
The future demands integration.

When we attune deeply to the Transcendent—to the Highest Goodness—we are moved to serve, build, and connect. As we collaborate in meaningful work, we deepen our sense of spiritual belonging. The loop is complete: Being feeds doing, and doing deepens Being.

This is not a technique or a strategy. It's a new operating system—a way of life where spirit and structure dance harmoniously.

THE PATH FORWARD: A RELATIONAL WAY OF LIFE

Many spiritual and religious movements today fall into a trap: they adopt the outward appearance of activism while unconsciously replicating the fragmentation of the same systems they seek to transform.

They rally around isolated issues, elevate personal breakthroughs, and spiritualize problems without addressing their systemic roots. Over time, this leads to burnout, disillusionment, and disconnection. The battle becomes their identity, and the battlefield begins to feel like home.

Symbiotic Culture offers a different path. It's not activism driven by reaction—it's a culture grounded in renewal. It doesn't elevate individual heroes but nurtures relational transformation. It doesn't just resist injustice—it builds an entirely new ecosystem of love, justice, and mutual aid.

It draws from deep and time-tested traditions: Early Christian communities that embodied Love as a way of life, Gandhi's and Dr. Ari's vision of village-centered self-rule, and Václav Benda's Parallel Polis, which offered spiritual resistance under Soviet occupation.

It's a path not of isolated resistance, but of coherent reconstruction.

We need to stop treating spiritual awakening as a private achievement. In Symbiotic Culture, transformation is never just personal—it is profoundly communal. The more vital question is not, "How awakened are you?" but *"How deeply are you embedded in relationships of love, truth, and shared responsibility?"*

We must also reject the split between inner awakening and outer change. Compassion without systemic awareness leads to resignation, and structure without compassion leads to oppression. We need both. We need wholeness.

> **That is why Symbiotic Culture is not some version of sacred activism. It is a new way of being human together.**

WEAVING A LUMINOUS WEB

To build a new culture, we must learn to work beyond boundaries—as we did in our Symbiotic Networks—uniting all who supported intentional mutual benefit.

Why? Because true transformation demands inclusion with integrity.

We resisted the pressure to form echo chambers—green-only networks, progressive-only alliances, or "solidarity" economies filtered through narrow ideological frames. Rather than replicate the fragmentation we aimed to heal, we built a big tent: a Network Commons where main street businesses, small farms, government departments, service providers, churches, spiritual communities, co-ops, and social enterprises could all contribute.

Like an ecosystem, every part—not just the idealized—has a role to play.

If we only welcome the "perfect," we lose resilience. If we only speak one ideological language, we lose relationship. Symbiotic Culture embraces diversity while anchoring everything in shared Virtue.

BIRTHING THE SYMBIOTIC AGE

This approach is profoundly countercultural. Many movements today prioritize tribal allegiance over partnership. But what we truly need is coherence across difference, not uniformity.

That means creating space for unlikely allies— faith-based and secular, left and right, progressive and conservative—to meet in Symbiotic Kinship.

That's how we weave the Luminous Web: not by branding our silos but by building bridges of trust, humility, and common purpose.

But bridges don't hold without strong beams.

The threads of connection—between unlikely partners, across divides, and among diverse sectors—only become a durable web when reinforced by something deeper. It's not just shared goals that unite us, but how we walk together.

If new network structure is the skeleton of a new society, Virtues are its muscles. Without relational integrity, networks fray. Without humility and grace, collaboration collapses. That's why the next move in Symbiotic Culture isn't just external—it's internal.

To sustain the Luminous Web, we must embody the spiritual DNA of the culture we seek to create.

RELATIONAL VIRTUES:
THE MUSCLE OF SYMBIOTIC CULTURE

To bring this luminous web to life, we need more than vision—we need Virtue. None of this work would be possible without gaining greater fluency in living the Virtues daily. These Virtues are not optional extras. They are the foundational currency of Symbiotic Culture—a culture where Love becomes the organizing principle of society. And now, the question turns to you.

The Virtues that follow are the practical expressions of Love-in-action—lived qualities that make the invisible threads of community visible and strong.

Trust
It creates safety and openness, allows people to share gifts, take risks, and build reliable, lasting connections.

Relational Humility
Letting go of ego, staying teachable, and honoring others' wisdom create space for shared leadership and mutual discernment in the community.

Compassionate Action
Self-giving love expressed through practical care and service holds communities together and reflects Divine compassion through action.

Restorative Relationship
Heals division and restores trust by releasing resentment and repairing bonds; essential for sustaining long-term connection and unity.

Empathic Engagement
Deeply seeing and feeling with others invites discovery, builds bridges across differences, and anchors relationships in understanding.

Relational Integrity
Living aligned with values, words, and actions keeps commitments strong and fosters reliability, coherence, and trustworthiness in relationships.

Sacred Welcome
Creates spaces where people feel seen, safe, and valued; turns strangers into neighbors through presence, care, and genuine welcome.

Mutual Service
Contributing selflessly for the good of the whole sustains the commons and expresses love through shared responsibility and action.

Shared Purpose
Aligning efforts with a greater vision, focuses energy toward a Transcendent mission, unifying people without demanding uniformity.

Generous Attentiveness
Offers time, support, and affirmation freely; listens deeply to needs and strengths, weaving strong, enduring relational ties.

Graceful Resilience
Trusts the unfolding process of growth and change; allows relationships and systems to evolve with flexibility, wisdom, and grace.

Honest Communication
Speaks truth with love and clarity; fosters trust, cohesion, and accountability by openly naming needs, intentions, and challenges.

Spiritual Attunement

Being fully present to others and the Spirit cultivates inner stillness and relational depth through sacred, nonjudgmental listening.

Covenantal Alignment

Living in conscious harmony with Divine order and each other guides relationships with intention, mutual responsibility, and sacred purpose.

These aren't idealistic aspirations. They're practical tools for connection. They're the muscle and sinew of any real movement of love. At its heart, this is Kingdom work.

What Jesus proclaimed—the Kingdom of Heaven, not as coercive power but as humble, healing love—takes shape when we live these Virtues together. Symbiotic Circles are mediating structures: relational bridges between churches and other organizations working for betterment and the broader ecosystem of people and organizations working to heal the world.

They provide a space for those who are moved by a shared longing for justice, compassion, and community. This is not about compromising faith but embodying it: becoming the "city on a hill" (Matthew 5:14) not through dominance, but through trust, shared service, and lives rooted in grace.

We do this not in isolation, but as co-laborers in the healing of the world—alongside those who may speak in different tongues but are animated by the same Divine impulse toward wholeness and love.

This is the call: to stop waiting, to stop judging, to start connecting. It begins not with grand institutions but with simple, meaningful relationships. It grows through openness rather than control, and it deepens not by fighting harder but by living more fully, loving more freely, and linking what is already good.

Here's the bottom line: The future doesn't belong to a single ideology or system. It belongs to the bridge builders, the "meek"—those willing to connect the scattered strands of beauty, courage, and compassion already alive in this world. Let's unite the threads, walk the Ancient Blueprint, and build the Symbiotic Age together.

CHAPTER 36

FROM POLARIZED PARALYSIS TO PARALLEL POLIS: HOW WE GET THERE FROM HERE

Throughout history, humanity has longed to bring Heaven to Earth—to bridge the Transcendent with the material and embody Divine Love in everyday life. This longing is not merely a mystical ideal but the foundation of any truly coherent, compassionate, and functional society.

The Ancient Blueprint invites us to cultivate a Culture of Connection, where relationship with the Transcendent becomes natural, welcomed, and celebrated. The sacred connection extends to one another, the Earth, and the living web that holds us all.

It calls us into a re-prioritized life rooted in community, where fulfillment flows more from relationships than material gain. It offers a more abundant way of life, revealing new possibilities as we connect silos and tribes while meeting the basic needs of all people together.

Rather than competing with religious and spiritual communities, Symbiotic Culture supports them, deepening and extending their sacred rhythms into the fabric of everyday life. It nurtures an integrated spiritual life that moves beyond sanctuaries into homes, neighborhoods, and systems.

Over time, this becomes the spiritual scaffolding of culture: prayer turns into practice, communion becomes community, and the sacred breathes through our new systems and structures.

What begins in worship blossoms into a living culture of grace, rooted in the architecture of love.

These ideas are not my invention but reflect a lineage from Jesus to Dr. Ari. In Sarvodaya, spirituality lives through daily acts of compassion and joy, woven into service across 5,000 villages. It's one thing to glimpse the sacred; it's another to live it. The question then becomes: How do we carry this sense of the Divine into our daily lives?

For the sacred to become systemic—for Love to become embodied—we need more than ideals. We need a path.

A COHERENT PATH:
THE FIVE STAGES OF PRACTICE

We begin wherever we are.

Symbiotic Culture is what I call an extended spiritual practice—a way of integrating the sacred into all aspects of life. And by "extended," I mean that something must already be present within you: an existing practice, a longing, a sense of faith or belonging. You may be part of a faith tradition—Christian, Muslim, Jewish,

Buddhist—or consider yourself spiritual-but-not-religious. Even atheists may resonate with the "Transcendent moral order," or the sacredness of life.

So, what exactly are we extending?

We are extending our connection to the Transcendent, allowing Divine Love to stretch us beyond our comfort zones and lead us into deeper relationships with others.

> *This sacred stretch—the movement from self-centeredness to shared purpose— opens the door to a new cultural possibility.*

From that space, we become catalysts for a new kind of society: a Parallel Polis. It is not just an idea but a relational *delivery system* for a new way of being, where the sacred is woven into the structures of everyday life.

To translate this sacred connection into a living culture, we need more than vision—we need a coherent path—one that moves from inner transformation to outward expression, one that is structured yet flexible, grounded yet inspired.

Thankfully, we are building on the living wisdom and lineage of those who came before.

Now it's your turn.

This section is for you, dear reader—an invitation to walk the path from the love in your heart to meaningful, grounded, effective, and grace-filled action in the world. We've identified five stages of practice that form this journey. Each aligns with Divine Love and reinforces the universal order.

Each stage builds on the one before, radiating outward from personal to cultural to civic life. Together, they establish Symbiotic Culture as both a way of living and a way of life. These stages form the five key infrastructures that carry the pattern of Divine order from the individual to society:

A COHERENT PATH:
THE FIVE STAGES OF PRACTICE

1. **Personal Practice** (Individual Infrastructure)
2. **Cultural Infrastructure** (Symbiotic Circles & Recovery Groups)
3. **Social Infrastructure** (Dynamic Networks of Mutual Benefit)
4. **Economic Infrastructure** (Virtue-Based Network Commons)
5. **Political Infrastructure** (The Coherent Will of the People)

There's a reason politics comes last in this approach: because the world's healthy order has been inverted, and we must help turn it right side up. So, let's begin with politics.

REORDERING THE FLOW OF CHANGE

In our current system, the first reflex is political action when someone seeks to address an economic, social, or moral imbalance. Thousands of organizations exist to lobby, petition, and legislate toward justice. You've likely supported one, marched for a cause, or gone door-to-door.

But as you've likely seen by now, these "causes" are rarely causes at all—they're effects. They dominate our public discourse while the deeper root goes unexamined. The truth is that political dysfunction is a symptom, not the source, of the world's disorder.

From Polarized Paralysis to Parallel Polis

Instead of assuming that political systems cause cultural change, we assert the opposite. As Andrew Breitbart famously said, politics is downstream from culture. Real change begins *upstream*, at deeper levels—personal Virtue, spiritual alignment, community culture, shared economic values.

The issues we try to solve through policy are not, at their core, political—they are spiritual, moral, and relational. They stem from disconnection: from self, from each other, from the Earth, and the Divine.

As I've emphasized throughout this book, you cannot solve spiritual problems with material tools. This is why a Parallel Polis cannot be legislated into existence. *It must be practiced into being.* Each stage of practice loosens the grip of the Culture of Separation and strengthens the Culture of Connection.

The true foundation of change begins within, with perception, conscience, longing, and metanoia—a turning of the heart. From there, it radiates outward, from personal to cultural, from economic to political.

Like concentric ripples in water, transformation begins at the center. This is what I mean by reordering the flow of change. It's not just about diagnosing problems—it's about proposing a new, spiritually coherent sequence for transformation:

- **Spiritual grounding** (connection to the Transcendent)
    → leads to **Personal transformation**
    → leads to **Cultural coherence**
    → which shapes **Economic relationships**
    → which finally informs **Political expression.**

Do you see how politics is downstream from culture?

Now, let's trace the flow further upstream to show how the world has inverted the natural flow from Being to Doing.

- **Politics is downstream from economics.**
  When money drives influence, governance becomes a servant of capital. Even those trying to eliminate "money in politics" ironically have to raise their own money to stay in the game.

  In contrast, political tensions ease when a virtuous economy serves all, and justice emerges organically.

- **Economics is downstream from culture.**
  How we trade, accumulate, and distribute reflects our values. A culture that exalts competition and individual gain produces an economy of scarcity and hoarding.

  But when we value interdependence and care, regenerative models emerge—like Reno's buy-local campaign, which helped our largest grower transition to organic farming.

- **Culture is downstream from social networks and media.**
  These don't just shape our content—they shape our worldview. Platforms like TikTok, YouTube, and Facebook mold what we believe to be real.

  That's why local, in-person collaboration grounded in love is one of the most potent antidotes. That was the heart behind our vision for OneSphera.

- **Social media is downstream from the individual.**
  These platforms reflect our hopes, wounds, fears, and projections—amplified at scale.

So, we must ask: Are we sourcing our agency from the Transcendent or from the algorithm? Are we masters of our tools or merely echo chambers?

METANOIA BEGINS AT HOME: RADICAL RESPONSIBILITY AND MORAL SOBRIETY

It's easy enough to become an echo chamber.

Thanks to the media, politics has our attention 24/7, urging us to enter the political fray and try to "fix" society from the top down. But without addressing the deeper layers, we risk rearranging furniture in a burning house. So, we must ask: Where are we getting our marching orders? Who—or what—are we really serving?

This is where the journey of metanoia begins—with radical personal responsibility.

You'll remember how I was triggered by religious institutions, and how that discomfort became my teacher. I participated in the interfaith movement. Beyond that, I attended a year of Evangelical Bible study every Friday at 6 a.m., Mormon services, Jewish temples, Religious Science gatherings, and Buddhist meditation groups.

Of course, each tried to recruit me! I didn't "convert," but I was changed.

> *I saw how people desire to access a Divine ground as they understood it from different angles. I saw the heart behind the practice, and I lost my judgment. In that humility, I became a better bridge-builder.*

I can imagine my Christian readers—and people of other faiths—wondering how come I didn't become a post-Christian,

New Age universalist. It's a fair concern. When bridges are built across traditions, some fear that faith identity will be diluted or lost altogether. But for me, the opposite happened. Once I moved beyond my religious antagonism, I built authentic relationships across faith lines—not by compromising what I believed, but by listening with an open heart. And in doing so, I didn't lose Jesus Christ—I drew closer to Him.

I discovered a deeper Christianity not through separation, but through connection. The more I respected others' sacred paths, the more I could hear the voice of Christ within my own. Grace opened the space. Love built the bridge. And truth walked across it. The less judgmental I became, the more space I could hold for others. Holding space—that Transcendent container—is the foundation of leadership in a Symbiotic Culture.

At the same time, I noticed another trend in the culture—one that views every firmly-held identity with suspicion. Some fear that identifying too clearly as a Christian, an American, a businessperson, or even a white male automatically suggests exclusion, dominance, or imperialism. However, we are entering a new era where it's possible to embrace a particular identity without allowing it to define or divide us.

It's not about rejecting our inherited identities, but recognizing that they are not ultimate. The highest identity is our relationship with the Divine. That's the foundation on which every other role, label, or affiliation must rest. To transform reality, we have to accept what's real, including the exclusive designations we carry. But we also need to remember: these identities are not the point. They are not the end. They are the vessels, not the source.

Once we embrace this higher identity, we become less addicted to the lesser ones, and less addicted to the battlefield. We become capable of "radical humility" and can recognize the wisdom in the Pogo quote:

From Polarized Paralysis to Parallel Polis

"We have met the enemy, and he is us."

This isn't about guilt or shame. It's about recognizing that the state of the world is not separate from us—it reflects our collective consciousness.

The violence, inequality, fragmentation, and despair we see are intimately tied to our inner divisions and blind spots. We can't simply "work on ourselves" to fix the world, but neither can we "fix" the world without turning inward.

We must recognize when we are still battling on the old field—blaming the media, the rich, the poor, the left, the right, the religious, or the secular. Until we resolve disconnection within, we will continue to recreate disconnection without.

This is not a resignation. It's moral sobriety. It's remembering that the constructs of the mind, disconnected from the wisdom of the heart, are what got us here. Metanoia is the path back through surrender to a higher power, however we name it.

As we heal our internal disconnection, we begin to carry a new kind of presence into our communities—one that doesn't seek power but rather radiates coherence. That's where the real work begins—not just in seeing the truth, but in living it.

LIVING TRUTH FROM THE INSIDE OUT

The Parallel Polis does not arise from institutional power. It arises from awakened individuals co-creating sacred culture, rooted in Love, reciprocity, and self-giving service.

What is required is nothing less than healing our collective imagination—a spiritual reorientation that restores our experience of Divine coherence and shared purpose.

The failed modern experiment—believing reason alone could deliver ethics, meaning, or truth—has given us powerful tools, but no compass. Cut off from the Transcendent, we've defaulted to control systems, utopian ideologies, and engineered narratives.

This has led to a reversal of reality: where power trumps people, matter overshadows meaning, and spectacle replaces the soul. But there is a way back. We need a return to the Source—God, the Logos, the Transcendent.

> *Only this Eternal Presence can re-root a person, reboot a culture, regenerate a virtuous economy, and ultimately guide our politics.*

Without that rooting, we remain reactive and fragmented. But with it, we become vessels of coherence—radiating order, justice, and love outward in ever-widening circles. This is the inner-to-outer renewal Symbiotic Culture was born to nurture.

FROM TRANSFORMATION TO PRACTICE: THE FIVE STAGES OF SYMBIOTIC CULTURE

With the inner roots firmly planted, how does this transformation flower in the world at large?

The good news is, the path ahead is clearly marked. It follows a sacred sequence: from personal awakening to shared culture, trust-based networks to virtuous economies, Network Commons, and coherent civic life.

These five stages form a living architecture of Symbiotic Culture—an embodied way of being that begins in the heart and ripples outward into systems, structures, and society. Transformation doesn't happen all at once. It unfolds step by step, like roots deepening before branches rise.

This is why the five domains unfold in sequence:

1. **Personal Practice** — Where self-awareness, healing, and connection to the Divine take root.
2. **Cultural Infrastructure** —Where shared Virtues, sacred relationships, mutual support, and a common story are cultivated in the community.
3. **Social Infrastructure** — Where these Virtues and principles begin to manifest as networks of collaboration and trust.
4. **Economic Infrastructure** — Where we translate our moral priorities into material systems—how we exchange, invest, and steward. Where material exchange is realigned with Virtue, justice, and mutual benefit—a virtuous economy.
5. **Political Infrastructure** — The coherent will of an awakened people becomes manifest, not imposed from above, but arising organically from within individuals and communities.

It's also why we do not begin with politics. We end there.

This inversion is one of the great secrets of transformative movements: they begin not with political power but with individual presence. They do not start by seizing power and control but by embodying coherence that builds an unshakeable foundation. Consider the original parallel polis movement in communist Czechoslovakia. While Havel and Benda had a political agenda, their first focus was cultivating spiritual reawakening in the individual...then in small groups where people could speak their truth and acknowledge a Higher Power.

These groups helped develop a "Symbiotic Culture" of living truth and mutual regard, which in turn led to new economic relationships. It was only then, when the people and community had regained their spiritual foundation and created networks of mutual benefit, that the stage was set for political transformation. Each stage of coherence weakened the communist political order, priming it for inevitable collapse.

Following this five-stage plan I outlined below, transformation can happen worldwide, one community at a time, turning what we've called "politics" on its head.

Transformation ripples outward from that coherence and presence, not as a demonstration to protest, but a demonstration of a better way, not a reactive resistance but a proactive resurrection.

STAGE ONE — INDIVIDUAL INFRASTRUCTURE: STARTS WITH THE PERSON

Real change begins at the most local level: not in the streets or systems, but within the self, not the "small self" driven by fear or ego, but the authentic self, aligned with Divine Love.

The authentic self is not defined by fear, performance, or social conditioning, but by its direct connection to the Divine. It is the vessel through which Transcendent love flows into the world. When we live from that place, we become agents of Symbiotic Kinship.

> *As said earlier, the authentic self is a shared self that enables us to extend Divine Love to our neighbor, expanding the Western idea of "spiritual awakening" beyond the personal and into the collective.*

We cultivate spiritual coherence by embodying integrity and authenticity, moment by moment. And nothing can be accomplished without healing the Culture of Separation within oneself. My belief in unity—and loyalty to a dream of unity—triggered every part of me that hadn't yet evolved, every place where I was judging others' beliefs or actions so I wouldn't have to examine my own.

In doing this work, *you will confront* the "ego-system" that helped you navigate the world until now—but that no longer serves the new one we are building.

Having hundreds, then thousands, millions of kindred spirits walking this road with you will encourage you when the inevitable challenges arise. And... this process requires radical humility.

I've had to give up my "rational" belief that the mind alone can solve mind-generated problems. My relationship with Jesus Christ has been my path to the Transcendent. I have surrendered both pride and control, praying and asking for guidance—sometimes literally on my hands and knees.

The internal world is often cluttered by a noisy "committee" of competing voices, pulling us in conflicting directions and leaving us confused. But when we practice the Virtues—patience, courage, forgiveness, humility, and charity—we begin to organize that inner chaos. The Virtues are not religious ideals; they are Divine ordering principles that restore coherence to the soul.

Nor are they passive qualities—they're living energies we embody, decisions we make, and habits we cultivate in the small, ordinary moments of daily life. Each act of Virtue becomes a node of coherence in a fragmented world. When we volunteer at a soup kitchen with love, we are not simply "doing good"—we embody a fractal of Divine order.

These are not random acts of kindness but intentional acts of cosmic alignment. In other words, we recognize this not as an isolated deed but as one sacred thread in a vast tapestry—one of millions or billions, uniting the Cosmos in Love.

PRACTICES FOR PERSONAL TRANSFORMATION:

1. **Daily Silence and Reflection** — Create space for Transcendent awareness beyond the noise of secular distractions. Pray and meditate unceasingly. Spend time in nature. Read scripture. Take frequent "being" breaks amid all you do, every day.

2. **Embodied Virtue Practice** —Intentionally practice Virtues like humility, self-giving love, patience, courage, and justice in ourselves, families, neighborhoods, organizations, and networks. Consider focusing on one Virtue each month or week.

3. **Radical Generosity and Mutual Aid** — Give without expectation of return, challenging the consumerist mindset. For example, paying a stranger's toll may seem like a relatively insignificant one-off action — yet we can see its significance in the greater scheme of things.

4. **Sacred Rhythms of Life** — In a world where it's business, business, business 24/7, we can counteract the busyness by reintroducing rituals like a weekly Sabbath rest, morning and evening prayer or meditation, and periodic fasting. These are all ways to make the Transcendent imminent in our lives daily.

5. **Re-enchanting the Ordinary** — View every part of life as sacred: a conversation, a meal, a blade of grass. Let beauty and relationship become sacraments. As William Blake once wrote, let us "see a world in a grain of sand, and Heaven in a wildflower."

PERSONAL DECLARATION:

I commit to embodying the Virtues in all aspects of my life. I will be a unifying principle in all my social networks, silos, and tribes—I choose to gather the cosmos in love by practicing intentional mutual benefit, and bringing that which is separate back together.

STAGE TWO — CULTURAL INFRASTRUCTURE: SYMBIOTIC CIRCLES AS SEED-FORMS

Once individual practice takes root, we naturally seek others on a similar path. Together, we form *recovery groups*—a term used playfully, signifying our recovery from the Culture of Separation as we reconnect to the Sacred center. These circles are where *beingness* begins to translate into *doing*.

These groups offer more than reflection—they cultivate spiritual sobriety, collective accountability, and embodied support. They are not religious institutions, social clubs, or ideological cells, they are mediating structures within a community.

They are sacred spaces of inclusion, where all are welcomed and respected, and beliefs, biases, and agendas are set aside. We gather around a single shared question:

How do we practice the Culture of Connection in our lives and communities?

Whenever we unite in trusting circles to practice symbiotic Virtues, we plant seeds of the world we long to inhabit. These groups serve as the fertile ground for a living, bioregional ecosystem—one that connects the good and releases the region's hidden resources for the good of all.

These Circles form the spiritual foundation of real-world networks. They are where transformation becomes visible.

BIRTHING THE SYMBIOTIC AGE

The word that best captures their essence is communitas—"intense community spirit," a deep, felt sense of shared purpose, radical togetherness, and mutual care.

In many ways, these Circles echo the house churches of early Christianity, where one of their goals was edification: cultivating Virtue in daily life. Today, even within churches, spiritual growth can stagnate. A pastor I know, who is also a historian on the origin of worship in the church, once confessed that despite decades of attendance, many of his congregants seemed no more patient or loving than they were forty years ago.

That's why we need the kind of personal, informal mediating structures I've described—safe spaces for spiritual accountability and honest reflection, where the focus is not just on what we believe but how we live, where practice aligns with purpose and preaching becomes embodied through love.

Symbiotic Circles are not ends in themselves. They are the living seed-forms of a broader Symbiotic Society. Each Circle carries within it the DNA of the whole: Love as culture, trust as governance, and shared care as economy. As they multiply and mature, they begin to weave together into the larger fabric of community life.

They are *seed groups* for a much larger reality in the next stages of community growth: the formation of Symbiotic Societies and eventually networks around the 12 shared community needs explored previously.

Gatherings can take place in public venues or private homes. As with the Connections Gatherings described previously, sharing food—a potluck—is a beautiful expression of *communion*. We always began our formal meetings with a moment of silence to connect each person to God, without privileging any one tradition.

From Polarized Paralysis to Parallel Polis

The grounding was "potluck and fellowship"—shared food, presence, and life. This wasn't a business networking group. There was no selling, converting, or promoting. The conversation always returned to the Virtues and the work of mutual benefit.

At our gatherings, we used a simple two-round format:

- In Round One, participants shared personal reflections on practicing the Virtues.
- In Round Two, we discussed efforts and challenges in extending love into the broader community.

Like in Czechoslovakia's original Parallel Polis, these small groups are the *cultural Petri dish* for living truth.

As these Circles deepen, they begin to recognize themselves in one another, linking across neighborhoods, faiths, and organizations. What started as simple gatherings becomes the nucleus of a Symbiotic Society—an ecosystem of Circles that together carry the pattern of the future.

MAKING IT REAL: PRACTICAL GUIDANCE FOR HOSTING CIRCLES

- **Choose the right location** and stick with it when possible. Make it hospitable, gracious, and welcoming, whether a living room, café, church hall, workplace, or farm.

- **Create a consistent rhythm** of weekly, bi-weekly, or monthly gatherings to build commitment and momentum.

- **Ensure a "soft entry"** — this is not a private club or tribal silo. It should reflect Symbiotic Kinship across politics, faith, race, economics, and worldviews.

- **Celebrate and integrate culture** — let people bring their music, food, stories, and spiritual languages. This is how we create a shared culture of deep acceptance.

- **Weave culture, spirituality, and mission** into every aspect of the gathering: from silent prayer to shared meals, from storytelling to collective service.

This step lays the foundation for a tangible community in which people don't just talk about connection—they *experience* it.

PERSONAL DECLARATION:
I commit to practicing the Virtues in community. Together, we will cultivate a Culture of Connection and become the seedbed of a new society.

From these Circles, threads of trust begin to weave outward—linking hearts, homes, and efforts across silos. This is how a Symbiotic Society begins to take form: not yet a full network, but more than isolated circles—a local ecosystem of trust, culture, and care that reflects the DNA of the whole.

STAGE THREE — SOCIAL INFRASTRUCTURE: SYMBIOTIC SOCIETIES INTO DYNAMIC NETWORKS OF MUTUAL BENEFIT

When Symbiotic Circles mature and begin to link, they give rise to a Symbiotic Society—a visible ecosystem of trust-based communities woven from many circles. And as this Symbiotic Society grows it will start to actively bridge silos, becoming Symbiotic Networks that consciously bring together previously disconnected groups.

They become regional catalysts for broader transformation that draw together businesses, nonprofits, faith communities, local governments, and civic leaders into dynamic webs of mutual benefit.

This network scaffolding becomes the foundation for generative bridge-building across all silos. These aren't new institutions or separate silos. They aren't formal organizations or standalone initiatives. They are mediating structures, trust-based constellations of people and projects rooted in shared purpose and held together not by mandate but by alignment of positive intention.

Businesses, churches, nonprofits, and even local agencies begin working together—not because they must, but because love and trust open the door.

This is how our Buy Local movement in Reno began. Amid deep political polarization, we found unexpected common ground around a simple goal: helping local businesses thrive against the threat of big-box expansion. That one act of unity ignited a citywide web of connection—one project leading to the next, building trust, shared energy, and a culture of cooperation transcending ideology. What started as economic support evolved into community transformation.

And it didn't come from a five-year plan. Our networks grew organically.

Like mycelial webs beneath the forest floor, these networks link root systems, share nutrients, and adapt to changing needs. No one node controls the whole, and no single person or institution "owns" the network. Life flows where it's needed, and the whole system becomes a living community resource.

This is the moment when Symbiotic Circles reveal their full purpose. What began as small gatherings for mutual care now expands into a living society of interconnection, and then into networks capable of transforming culture at scale.

These networks can form around any or all of the twelve identified community needs, or emerge in response to new challenges and opportunities unique to your local context. In Reno, we began with food, neighbor support, and an arts festival—not because of a master plan, but because that's where energy and need converged.

The principles were simple: Connect the Good. Let Love Lead. From that place of openness, genuine unity emerged. Our Neighbor-to-Neighbor network gained enthusiastic support from both of Reno's rival newspapers. Even unlikely allies show up when focused on care, not ideology.

Through these efforts, we discovered the core purpose, principles, Virtues, and shared needs that later became the Symbiotic Culture DNA. We were already building a Parallel Polis, but we didn't have the language for it yet.

BUILDING SYMBIOTIC NETWORKS: A PRACTICAL GUIDE

1. **Identify a Common Need**

   Start where pain and potential meet: food insecurity, faith in action, care for the environment, neighborhood cohesion, the arts. Focus on simple, visible, shared needs that transcend race, class, and ideology.

2. **Convene Trusted Individuals**

   Bring together people from different silos who are spiritually grounded and committed to the common good. Ensure your inner circle includes those capable of holding sacred space, not dominating it.

3. **Establish Mutual Agreements**
   Set clear guidelines for collaboration: no one dominates; all serve the shared good. Let the Symbiotic Culture DNA guide your norms. In this ecosystem, the protocol is the leader.

4. **Grow Through Trust, Not Control**
   Allow the network to expand naturally. Let coherence, not coercion, be your growth strategy. Stay attuned to resonance and alignment with shared values.

MAPPING THE ECOSYSTEM

As you develop your network, remember the threads of connection discussed earlier in this chapter. Focus on what each person or organization has to offer and what they may need in return.

- List faith groups, local businesses, farmers, healers, artists, activists, governmental officials, educators, and regenerators already doing aligned work in your area.
- See who in your inner circle can serve as trusted connectors.
- Launch a "Connecting the Good" initiative to unify efforts. Start with the needs that have natural momentum and shared relevance across sectors.

SPREADING THE VISION: MAKING THE PARALLEL POLIS VISIBLE

A Parallel Polis must be seen to grow. Its power is multiplied when shared. Here are four ways to amplify and expand the movement:

✓ **Media**
> Create a decentralized, values-aligned media ecosystem—podcasts, newsletters, blogs, or community radio. In Reno, both of our rival newspapers co-sponsored our Neighbor Network, and we launched *Unite Radio* to broadcast good news. Tell stories that elevate Virtue and inspire hope.

✓ **Events**
> Host summits, festivals, meetings, and celebrations in the sacred public square. In Reno, our Arts and Culture Festival united diverse communities around shared sustainability, creativity, and collaboration values. Events create cultural common ground.

✓ **Local Participation**
> Invite local businesses, churches, and nonprofits to co-create solutions. Even non-local businesses wanted to participate in our Buy Local campaign. We welcomed their support because this is about participation, not purity.

✓ **Global Outreach**
> Link your efforts to others around the world. Connect with global Parallel Polis initiatives. Share your stories. Learn from theirs. This is the power of cosmolocalism—the sharing of rooted, local practice across planetary networks. Part of building the cathedral is becoming an inspiration for other regions.

PERSONAL DECLARATION:
> *I commit to doing the bridge-building work of Connecting the Good in my community. I embrace servant leadership and place shared benefit above personal gain. I will embody Divine Love to become a catalyst for the Symbiotic Network.*

From Polarized Paralysis to Parallel Polis

When trust takes root in networks of mutual care, something remarkable begins to happen: value begins to circulate. Not just goodwill, but resources, opportunity, and shared benefit flow through the connections we've built.

This is how the Parallel Polis begins to take material form—not through ideology or top-down reform, but through the lived experience of reciprocity. The economy itself starts to transform. Love becomes livelihood. Exchange becomes sacred.

The next stage of Symbiotic Culture: is the emergence of the Network Commons—an economy grounded not in scarcity and domination, but in Virtue, relationship, and intentional mutual benefit.

STAGE FOUR — ECONOMIC INFRASTRUCTURE: THE SPIRITUALLY-BASED NETWORK COMMONS

As Symbiotic Networks mature, they give rise to new patterns of local wealth and well-being. Out of these relationships emerges the Network Commons—an economy rooted not in extraction or domination, but in reciprocity and mutual benefit. This stage becomes all the more vital as we face economic uncertainty, political polarization, and the widening chasm between the wealthy and political elites, and the rest of us, in a global empire increasingly marked by moral decline.

The Network Commons includes local Main Street businesses, food systems, nonprofits, churches, local government, cooperatives, mutual aid networks, fair trade initiatives, and ethically driven enterprises. It is flexible, diverse, and adaptive, mirroring nature's ecological richness and shaped by the unique needs and resources of each bioregion.

At its core is one unifying principle: intentional mutual benefit. This becomes the foundation of a virtuous economy—one in which no one seeks unfair advantage, and local resilience is prioritized over global dependency.

This marks the next critical phase in the emergence of the Parallel Polis. When our economic relationships are rooted in fairness, reciprocity, and love, the very structure of politics begins to shift—quietly, organically, and from the ground up.

DEFINING THE NETWORK COMMONS

A community-based collaborative initiative in which nonprofits, private enterprises, civic organizations, mutual aid groups, gifting circles, cooperatives, and public resources are intentionally interconnected, shared, and governed by an engaged community of stakeholders.

> The Network Commons is a stakeholder collaborative, owned by none and used by all. It recirculates wealth in the community, creating shared prosperity for everyone involved.

Radically open by design, it honors all life-giving economic forms, from corporations and sole proprietors to nonprofits and gift economies. It is the economic embodiment of Symbiotic Kinship—extending the trust, reciprocity, and mutual care once found in tribes or tight-knit communities to an entire region. It transforms the economy into a living system of shared benefit, where every contribution is valued and every participant uplifted.

This may well reflect what Adam Smith originally envisioned—a genuinely free marketplace, animated by "universal fellow feeling." Like a living circulatory system, the Network

Commons keeps value circulating locally, nourishing the whole. And like the mycelial web beneath a forest, it strengthens the entire ecosystem rather than concentrating power in a few dominant nodes.

This isn't just idealism. We witnessed it firsthand in Reno. Our Buy Local campaigns and Local Food System Networks revitalized neighborhoods, supported family farms, and even influenced state economic policy—all without lobbying, legislation, or protest. And of course, there's Sarvodaya, where a Network Commons has empowered the poorest of the poor across more than 5,000 villages.

Bottom line: The Network Commons is built on trust and honors the soul of exchange. It offers not just an alternative economy but a parallel one—one that forms the economic foundation for a region-wide Parallel Polis grounded in Virtue and mutual benefit.

KEY VALUES AND PRACTICES OF THE NETWORK COMMONS

- **Local and Ethical Spending**
  Supports and uplifts businesses aligned with mutual benefit. Every dollar becomes a vote for the world we want to build.
- **Welcoming Novel Models**
  Without privileging one form, the Commons supports innovation—traditional businesses and organizations, social enterprises, cooperatives, regenerative, "green," or spiritually conscious businesses all find a home.
- **Locally Based Microfinance**
  Encourages investment in Virtue-driven entrepreneurs whose efforts reinforce community health and cohesion.

- **Regenerative Local Food Systems and Virtuous Economies**
  Nourishes both land and people. Strengthens food independence, supports small farms, and weaves economic resilience through daily nourishment.

PERSONAL DECLARATION:

I commit to supporting and growing the Network Commons in my community. I will spend and circulate my resources with love and intention. I will help birth an economy that reflects the Kingdom of Heaven.

When love circulates through an economy and trust becomes a region's bloodstream, a profound shift occurs. Communities no longer need to be governed from the top down; they begin to govern themselves from the inside out. The Network Commons doesn't just change how we exchange goods; it transforms how we relate, organize, and decide.

What begins in relationships and flows through economic cooperation now seeks its full expression: a political culture rooted in shared Virtue and mutual trust. That's where we turn next—to a form of governance that doesn't emerge from control but from coherence—to a politics not of power over but of love made visible through the coherent will of the people.

STAGE FIVE — POLITICAL INFRASTRUCTURE: THE COHERENT WILL OF THE PEOPLE

At last, we arrive at politics—the final "frontier" in building our Parallel Polis.

In a Culture of Separation, politics thrives on division. The dominant discourse reduces civic life to binary narratives—left or right, for us or against us. So, how do we move beyond this fragmentation to a system of governance that reflects our deepest shared longing for Symbiotic Kinship rooted in Divine Love?

We do it by building from the ground up.

> **Political coherence doesn't begin with parties or platforms. It emerges when individual transformation, cultural renewal, social trust, and economic integrity radiate outward in ever-expanding circles.**

Once a community has cultivated the first four stages—rooted in shared Virtue and mutual benefit—the political structure that emerges reflects the coherent will of the people.

Sarvodaya offers a living example.

When I first visited Sri Lanka in 2012, I was taken to a town about an hour from Sarvodaya headquarters—15,000 people strong and recognized by the UN as a World Heritage Site. As I sat next to the local bank president, who also led the town's Sarvodaya Society, I asked whether they ran candidates in local elections.

"We don't need to," he said.

He explained that nearly half the town—about 7,000 people—were already active in Sarvodaya. "We've created a container of spiritual consciousness," he told me, "centered on compassion and shared love. We've already shaped the social, environmental, and economic foundations."

Their influence didn't require political control. The culture had already shifted, and those elected naturally aligned with the movement's ethos. What an elegant example of politics flowing downstream from culture. When spiritual values animate community life, and the economy reflects fairness and reciprocity, governance becomes the fruit, not the root, of transformation. The state serves the people, not special interests.

We saw something similar unfold in Reno. In 2005, development was king. The prevailing wisdom favored more shopping centers, parking lots, and condos. Farming—especially small family farms—was dismissed as obsolete. But the momentum of the local food movement shifted everything.

When people tasted the abundance and beauty of regionally grown food, when participation created prosperity, the region's awareness of itself evolved. Development plans quietly faded. Farmers' markets, food co-ops, and CSAs took root and have been thriving ever since.

All this happened with no lobbying. No campaigns. No protests.

This is what real independence looks like. A countervailing power within the community, not opposed to established political power but a power rooted in Love, reshaped civic life. Governance became a servant of the people, not a rubber stamp for business as usual.

This is how we move from activism captured by political machinery to recovering governance as a sacred expression of collective will. This is how we spiritualize the political by beginning not with control but with coherence.

It is what happens when:
- **Politics is downstream** from a virtuous economy.
- **The economy is downstream** from a Culture of Connection.
- **Networks of trust** hold that culture.
- **Sovereign individuals** build those networks.
- And those individuals are **rooted in the Transcendent.**

From Polarized Paralysis to Parallel Polis

This is how we invert the global financial and political power pyramid. It is not a withdrawal from the world but a re-rooting in love. The Parallel Polis I envision doesn't isolate—it illuminates.

Now imagine this not just in one town, but in thousands of communities—each one cultivating Network Commons that meet real needs: food, housing, religion and spirituality, education, the arts, energy, healthcare, and more. Imagine the leaders of these networks, formed in love and seasoned in Virtue-based collaboration, gathering in council to steward the common good.

This is not politics as control. This is politics as the coordination of shared Love. Not domination, but service. Not ideology, but Love made visible.

Does that seem like a dream?

Then let me offer you this: it is not a fantasy but a map. Our next section shows how this can happen anywhere...and scale everywhere, starting with you.

PERSONAL DECLARATION:

> *I commit to political transformation from the inside out. I will practice community self-governance through the Virtues and embody the coherent will of the people. I will build the future not by resisting the old, but by living and demonstrating the new.*

CONCLUSION:
FROM RESISTANCE TO RESURRECTION

It should be clear by now that even the most elegant framework is empty without the light of love, the presence of purpose, and the radiance of the Spirit. These five stages are not abstract theories. They are rooted in lived experience—in a lineage that includes Jesus, Mahatma Gandhi, Václav Havel, Václav Benda, Dr. Ari, and countless others who have walked the path of sacred culture.

The seeds of the Parallel Polis have already sprouted in Sri Lanka and Reno, and quiet revolutions are blooming around the world. They reflect the Ancient Blueprint: a way of life not only rooted in Spirit but also in how human beings are designed to live, connect, and flourish.

As Václav Benda and Václav Havel taught us in Czechoslovakia, living in truth is the most potent form of resistance. But this is not merely resistance. It is resurrection—a revival of a society's soul.

By creating Parallel Polises grounded in love, we invite others to step out of the "flatland"—the lie that "only matter matters"—and rediscover a world infused with meaning, transcendence, and grace.

By prioritizing relational leadership over political activism, we shift the culture. As the culture shifts, governance follows.

KEY COMMITMENTS FOR PARALLEL POLIS BUILDERS

1. Trust in the power of the Transcendent.
2. Live as if the Kingdom of Heaven is real.
3. Create alternative social and cultural spaces where Divine Love is tangible.
4. Foster communities that cultivate Virtue, Service, and Love.
5. Re-platform God and the Transcendent as the sane and sacred center of the community.
6. Reintegrate faith into public life without coercion.
7. Build networks of cooperation across like-minded groups.

From Polarized Paralysis to Parallel Polis

FINAL CALL TO ACTION

I commit to building the Parallel Polis—starting with myself. I choose to be a fractal of Divine Love. I will gather the cosmos with love, in my heart, family, neighborhood, and networks. I will not wait for permission or power. I will begin now.

What we've built so far is not a theory, but a reality-tested, living framework—rooted in and aligned with the sacred design of the Ancient Blueprint—that unfolds through Love, real lives, and real places.

These five stages of nurturing community form a solid foundation, the scaffolding for a new Culture of Connection, laid with love, trust, and shared purpose.

But scaffolding is not an end in itself. Its purpose is to hold something alive: the warmth of relationships, the beauty of shared meals, the sound of laughter and prayer—to be a new wineskin for the new wine of the Spirit, perpetually flowing through renewed systems and structures, unimpeded, building a superhighway of Love that breaks down barriers and unites the Cosmos in Love.

Now it's time to imagine what we can build when we embody this vision together—to see it in our hearts before we raise it in the world. That work begins with the light of vision, and the joy that fuels the journey.

CHAPTER 37

TELL-A-VISION:
A JOYOUS UNIVERSE AND YOUR PLACE IN IT

Now that we've explored the five stages of how Symbiotic Culture takes root—from personal transformation to political coherence—it's time to "tell-a-vision."

What could happen when thousands of communities embody and walk this path together? What might unfold if these lights converged—not as a top-down campaign, but as a grassroots constellation of love in action?

The vision I am sharing is not just a strategy; it's a spiritual compass.

Proverbs 29:18 tells us where there is no vision, the people perish. I speak of vision here in two distinct yet related ways. The first and most obvious meaning is seeing a coherent and workable way forward, like the five-stage plan I just outlined.

However, there is a second, deeper meaning to vision, one rooted in the Ancient Blueprint: Divine guidance.

Tell-A-Vision

In the biblical sense, vision is not just foresight but a living connection to God's purpose, offering moral and spiritual direction. Without it, Proverbs warns, people "cast off restraint"—they unravel, lose coherence, and drift into conflict, despair, and division. The original Hebrew suggests something even starker: a people coming undone.

Does that sound familiar? Today, many of us feel that people and society have become unglued. I see it as being unmoored from a deeper reality. Like empires before us, we too have lost our way.

But when guided by a Transcendent vision—rooted in love, justice, and sacred community—people become whole, resilient, and aligned with the greater good.

This is why shared vision and purpose matter.

They anchor Symbiotic Culture in higher Virtues and Divine intention, ensuring that what we build is coherent and life-giving. The vision I offer points to a future shaped by hundreds, thousands, even millions of metanoias—spiritual awakenings marked by a change of heart and mind—aligned with the Ancient Blueprint.

Woven together, these awakenings can form a living network of 50,000 regional ecosystems that invert today's top-down economic and political power pyramid.

This is no hopium-induced fantasy. It's a roadmap for a global Parallel Polis—real, grounded, and flourishing within a decade. But to apply this roadmap in the real world, we must first confront the fragmentation crisis and reclaim our spiritual coherence.

FROM FRAGMENTATION TO A NEW FOUNDATION

I can see how you might look at the audacious dream presented in this book, and say, "Impossible." Or, if you're more optimistic, "Highly unlikely."

BIRTHING THE SYMBIOTIC AGE

The dominant Culture of Separation—marked by division, disconnection, and distrust—has clouded our collective vision and brought civilization to the brink. In the United States, where I live, the political landscape has become a battleground—a war of worldviews with no unifying center. This polarization has left many feeling helpless and hopeless, retreating into either denial or despair. Furthermore, this fragmentation isn't just local—it's become global.

Beneath all political, economic, social, and psychological divisions lies a deeper root: our collective separation from the spiritual reality of which we are a part. By healing that separation—within ourselves, our families, our communities, and our regions—we awaken the most potent untapped resource we possess: the unfathomable power of Divine Love, flowing through hearts brought into coherent accord.

Here is the good news—the reason the impossible is possible:

The Ancient Blueprint I've written about throughout this book can unify our inner lives and our shared society. It has been proven when tried, though it has been too rarely attempted.

As I've come to recognize it, this Ancient Blueprint reflects the call to love God and neighbor, to embody a sacred communion of service, and to live as a people set apart, as "bringers of heaven"—not by dominance or ideology, but by humility, compassion, and shared purpose.

The confluence of crises we now face offers a sacred opportunity to put this Blueprint to the test—individually, communally, and collectively. My entire purpose in writing this book is to present a radiant future and a practical pathway to get there.

Together, we can create a virtuous economy and co-create a Parallel Polis rooted in the Golden Rule, not the rule of gold.

All it takes is your willingness to engage with like-hearted companions and connect with the Good already present in your families, neighborhoods, communities, and regions. If we are to realize this "possible" dream, this is our moment of choice.

It doesn't require getting everything right—it just requires showing up with your whole heart. An act of faith. A commitment of trust. A willingness to begin. And the fuel for that beginning? Not fear or obligation—but joy. That's where we turn next.

JOY AS THE SERIOUS BUSINESS OF HEAVEN

If you feel called to say YES, surprisingly enough, the place to start is by cultivating joy in your heart. In the words of C.S. Lewis, "Joy is the serious business of Heaven."

Lewis saw joy as the manifest expression of Heaven, and though he never used the phrase himself, he described a universe alive with Divine meaning—what we might call a "Joyous Cosmos," our true home.

Beyond any program, plan, system, or structure—beyond even the inspiring and workable ideas in this book—exists a shard of light, a fractal of Heaven. I glimpsed it as a 12-year-old, and countless others across history have known it in their own way.

So...locate that place in your heart, that singular point of connection, as you continue reading this "tell-a-vision" re-programming and discover your rightful place within it.

Imagine...

> *What would it feel like to awaken each morning knowing your life and daily actions were part of a joyful universe,*

shaped by an ordering principle rooted in a luminous web of Divine Love?

What would it be like to live from the Kingdom of Heaven—embodying its Virtues and remaining grounded in what St. Maximus called "Cosmic Love"—while navigating the conflicts of this world and transforming them into healing, with steadfast purpose and grace?

What would it mean to be in the world, but not of it, to such a degree that your presence enlivens and inspires everyone you meet?

I'm inviting you to find out. Start with your own life. Then, extend that joy to others in Symbiotic Circles and Symbiotic Community. Say yes to making the impossible possible. Say yes to facing the world's suffering without turning away. Say yes to confronting both our personal and collective shadow, without guilt or shame, and without judgment.

Here's something to remember:

The Ancient Blueprint, rooted in the Logos—manifest in Jesus Christ, whose life made visible the love at the heart of God—guides us toward the union of inner practice and outer transformation. It offers the structure and spiritual coherence to move beyond isolated personal awakening into meaningful, collective change.

With this alignment, spiritual practice becomes more than personal growth—it's a journey of profound connection and shared community purpose.

For those called to social impact, this framework ensures that their efforts are not scattered acts but part of a broader healing movement. Even simple actions now start addressing not just the symptoms of disconnection but the root causes, paving the way for true transformation.

Connecting to the Logos—and living it out—opens the door to a new way of life and a deeper kind of happiness—not the fleeting satisfaction of consumerism, but the lasting joy that springs from alignment with a Transcendent order and Divine Love. As we embody these Virtues, we cultivate a more abundant life and co-create a Culture of Connection that nourishes us all.

START WHERE YOU LIVE

If you're asking, *"Where do I begin?"* — thank you for asking.

Start where you live. Let that be your sacred ground because this vision won't become global unless it becomes local first.

Begin by noticing where your skills and passions meet the needs of your community. Are you drawn to food systems, holistic health, environmental care, religion, spirituality, or the arts and culture? Each can become a living "culture dish"—fertile ground for Symbiotic Culture to grow. Recall the twelve common needs we identified, drawn from our Northern Nevada community. As you revisit that list, ask yourself:

> *Where can I serve as a catalytic connector?*
> *A cultural catalyst? That becomes your new playing field where inner calling meets outward expression.*

Here are some guiding questions to reflect on:

- **Do I feel aligned** with the vision of Symbiotic Culture?
- **Do I have the relational qualities** to engage across differences? If not, am I ready, willing, and able to develop them?

- **What is uniquely mine to contribute?** Where can I offer the most impact?
- **What emerging local challenges** are ripe for coherent collaboration?
- **What shared need or longing** could become a bridge to bring people together?

Then, look around:
Who do you know who shares this longing?
Who's already walking a similar path?
Who among your friends, neighbors, or colleagues might carry this vision in their way?

Taking the first step becomes easier and more joyful when others walk alongside you. You don't have to do it alone. Consider the Connections Gatherings we held in Reno: small, relational spaces where like-hearted people came together to support, inspire, and encourage one another in the everyday practice of Symbiotic Kinship.

Let that be your beginning.

BECOMING A LIVING NODE IN THE NETWORK

Your work can begin with a simple, powerful question:
"How can I intentionally bring mutual benefit to my community today?"

Many of us already do this instinctively. But our impact deepens when we act with awareness, intention, and alignment with a greater whole. We become part of something larger—a coherent movement of love in action.

Tell-A-Vision

*Imagine yourself at the center of a circle,
with vibrant networks radiating outward
in every direction. Your role is to hold space—
to become a living container for Symbiotic Culture,
an agent of intentional mutual benefit.*

You carry this evolutionary impulse in every conversation, meeting, or casual encounter. You express it through presence, care, and connection until it no longer feels like a stretch but your natural state—first practiced, then second nature, and eventually first nature.

As a space-holder, you extend that presence to your family, street, neighborhood, and beyond. And as your intention deepens, something remarkable often happens. Synchronicities appear. Resources arrive. Connections emerge just when they're needed.

Grace finds you.

As your awareness of intentional mutual benefit grows, so will your confidence in sharing it. And when that happens, allies will appear. You'll think less about your image or needs, and more about the people and places around you. You'll begin to forget yourself—not in the sense of losing identity, but in shedding ego-concerns like "looking good" or "being right."

Your attention will shift outward. You'll start noticing hidden needs and overlooked gifts on your block, building, and region. And you'll remember: You don't need to be the expert. It's better if you're not.

*Your job isn't to rise above others—
it's to help weave the web where all can thrive.
You're not a savior. You're a steward.*

Let Dr. Ari be your example. He didn't begin as a politician or spiritual teacher. He started as a humble high school science teacher. In 1958, like Gandhi, he walked with his students into a single rural village—not to impose solutions, but to listen and serve. From that simple act of love, a movement was born that would touch thousands of villages and millions of lives.

You may be surprised at how natural this feels—and how gifted you already are. What once seemed unlikely may now feel entirely possible: becoming a catalytic connector in your neighborhood and beyond.

And as you find others working in parallel spaces, encourage them: "Start where you are." That one spark of connection may ignite a cascade of transformation across the entire web. This is how change begins—small, relational, intentional. And then, what happens when these sparks catch fire everywhere at once?

FROM INSPIRATION TO ACTIVATION: SEEDING THE GLOBAL MOVEMENT

Do you know what the most remarkable aspect of this seemingly "impossible" mission is?

It's DOABLE—and we know this because it has already been accomplished by so-called "third-world" villagers in Sri Lanka and mainstream Americans in Reno. Real-world examples demonstrate that this path works. If it succeeds in one location, it can grow in many, quietly replacing the failing systems that no longer serve us. There's no need to fight against what's broken. Instead, build what works, and those seeking genuine solutions will find their way to it.

Now, I want to present the bigger picture—illustrating how your individual actions and community networking, along with the efforts of millions like you, can scale into a global Parallel Polis movement.

Understanding that one's daily actions fit into a broader context provides the spiritual fuel and motivation to overcome obstacles and frustrations.

For over 65 years, Sarvodaya villagers have lived with this kind of awareness. They recognize how small, local acts of service connect them to their community—and to millions of others in thousands of villages working toward the same shared vision. They understand they are transforming their nation because they can *see* it, not just in the roads they are building, but in the new world emerging through them.

They are also profoundly aware of their global connection. They see it in one another's faces—in the spirit of unity and purpose. Dr. Ari described this as Vishvodaya—the Awakening of the Global Community. Ironically, Sri Lankan villagers seem to grasp the essence of global awakening more intuitively than many of us in the West who are still stuck debating solutions.

Your Symbiotic Circle is your connection to this awakening global community.

FROM CIRCLES TO SOCIETY

Once you commit to activating and spreading Symbiotic Culture DNA, start by reaching out to others in your community or network who may resonate with the ideas presented in this book—some may have read it already. Consider forming a small group or book circle—a kind of consciousness-raising gathering—where you can explore the principles and apply them in real life. Let this be a space rooted in the spirit of the Parallel Polis and its foundational call to "live in truth."

> *Surrounded by a Culture of Separation, these circles of trust become the "culture dish" for practicing and proliferating Symbiotic Kinship.*

This is Stage Two of the journey: the Symbiotic Circle as the seed-form of a new culture, carrying the DNA of the whole. At some point, your group will be ready to take the next step—moving from being to doing.

Like our small pods in Reno, you'll discern which of the twelve community needs to focus on first. It may be a pressing issue, a shared passion, or a mix of both. Once that need is clear, the question becomes: Who do you know? That's when the work expands, extending your circles of trust outward and weaving new connections into the fabric of a Symbiotic Culture.

If your group isn't ready to take on a specific need or sector, you can still play a vital role by connecting with other Symbiotic Circles in your region and offering support. This is the bridge into Stage Three—Circles linking into Symbiotic Societies.

Even if you just hold space for the Parallel Polis, your circle remains a crucial building block. Symbiotic Societies emerge when local Circles unite. They bridge the networked silos and pool their energy into regional hubs of collaboration. I envision this is an essential intermediary step—modeled after the Sarvodaya Societies founded by Dr. Ari in Sri Lanka—where local circles unite to form a regional Symbiotic Society.

These societies can help coordinate multi-nodal networks, Connecting the Good, seeding collaboration, and laying the foundation for a regional Network Commons rooted in mutual benefit and shared purpose.

You and your Circle can begin right now by intentionally incorporating Symbiotic Culture DNA into every group, network, or silo you're already a part of—whether it's a church, school, nonprofit, business, or even your soccer league.

By consistently and deliberately embodying the truth of our interconnectivity, you are already stepping into Stage Four and

Tell-A-Vision

Stage Five—helping Circles become Networks, Networks become a Commons, and Commons grow into a Parallel Polis.

Imagine the Symbiotic Society in your area launching a local food, neighbor network, or faith in service network. How does it scale? In Reno, it took less than six months from our first gathering to create the Buy Local Network. This led to the Local Food System Network, the Neighbor Network, Connections Gatherings, and a community-wide Art Festival over the next four years.

This is what it looks like when Circles expand into Societies, and Networks weave a Commons. We accomplished all this without a formal plan—just the shared spirit of Sarvodaya and a commitment to connection, service, and love in action. A single Circle becomes the seed of a Society, Societies weave into Networks, and Networks lay the groundwork for a Parallel Polis.

It is not just theory—it is a path you can walk, beginning with the people right around you.

FRACTAL COMMUNITY EMPOWERMENT: PATH TO A GLOBAL PARALLEL POLIS MOVEMENT

What if thousands of Symbiotic Circles began emerging in communities across every country and the world? What if each one shared best practices, learned from others, and adapted the DNA of Symbiotic Culture to its unique local context?

Now imagine these circles growing into multi-nodal community networks, each Connecting the Good across key needs—food, health, housing, religion, spirituality, education, and the arts.

As these networks of mutual benefit take root, a new kind of leadership emerges—not from titles or top-down appointments, but from those already doing the work. These grounded leaders—trusted by their communities and guided by shared purpose—form the Network Commons: a relational council of network stewards across diverse sectors.

Picture this: representatives from regenerative agriculture, local healthcare, faith communities, educational programs, and housing initiatives in active conversation—communicating, collaborating, and amplifying one another's efforts.

This is how the culture spreads and scales.

This is how society transforms from the ground up.

This is the first visible structure of the Parallel Polis—a living, decentralized system for meeting real community needs.

It doesn't seek to replace government; it activates the intermediating structures that have always sustained human life at the grassroots level. These are the relational infrastructures—neither government nor market—that hold the power to regenerate culture.

This renewal of local agency redefines how we understand leadership and authority. Formal authority is granted through elections or appointments in a representative republic like the United States. But what about those who aren't elected—yet form Commons, convene councils, and serve their communities with love and consistency?

Their authority doesn't come from the ballot box. It comes from something deeper: earned trust, embodied Virtue, and a visible commitment to the common good. They lead not by mandate, but by mutual recognition—by the lived credibility that arises from steady, loving service. They lead by delivering the goods, in more ways than one.

By connecting the Good products and services that enrich lives and strengthen bonds.

Tell-A-Vision

By connecting the Good works and projects.

We saw this clearly in Reno.

As you will remember, our Neighbor-to-Neighbor Network identified isolated seniors whom the formal system had overlooked. When Washoe County's well-funded Senior Services department said, "We don't have the money," unpaid neighbors quietly stepped in. In meeting that need, informal networks began to outperform formal systems—whether government or nonprofit—and gained something powerful: functional authority.

This isn't a competition. It's an invitation to collaborate. And over time, institutions often choose to join. That's exactly what happened in Reno. As our movement grew, the media, local businesses, nonprofit leaders, and even government officials began to align with it. Within five years, the Governor of Nevada—a Republican—launched the We Think Local initiative that encouraged communities across the state to develop their local networks.

Soon, across Nevada, elected officials—from city councils to state legislators—began taking their cues from a vibrant, living Parallel Polis.

> *That's how a parallel culture becomes a shared culture.*
> *Lead with results. Let others step in.*
> *This is how bottom-up becomes top-down—*
> *without coercion, only through love-in-action.*

Now imagine that same shift happening in one state and everywhere. What about your town? We've already shown what's possible. Nothing is stopping us. Why wait?

What we've seen locally has the potential to ripple globally. So, let's keep going. Let's explore how fractal community empowerment becomes not just a local story, but a global movement.

BIRTHING THE SYMBIOTIC AGE

A NEW GLOBAL CULTURE BUILT ON TRUST

All we have to do is follow the numbers.

The United States alone has over 3,000 counties and approximately 19,500 towns and villages. Now imagine if a Parallel Polis movement took root in just ten towns, cities, or regions in each state. By uplifting and Connecting the Good already happening, through mutual benefit and shared purpose, these efforts would begin to generate real, measurable change.

If enough of these local movements flourish, their collective impact will be visible enough to begin transforming the cultural mainstream. What once seemed fringe would become the new norm.

Our local movement in Reno took only three to five years to scale to the state level. Now, imagine how much faster it could progress elsewhere, with the benefit of our experience and the growing momentum of other Parallel Polis initiatives already emerging in parallel.

Add to this the power of emerging technologies like OneSphera, working with new relational intelligences (Social AI) that can facilitate and accelerate connection and coordination in any community, and the potential for rapid, scalable transformation becomes not only possible but inevitable.

As we saw with Sarvodaya, elected officials will begin to take notice once the Parallel Polis delivers tangible results. Many will support it. Some will even become its champions, recognizing that it serves the people more effectively than many existing systems.

Imagine this: if just ten active Parallel Polis networks were to take root in each of the 50 states, we would see 500 independent, thriving movements across the US within the next three to five years—each one building trust, meeting real needs, and quietly transforming the culture from the ground up.

Tell-A-Vision

If just three-quarters of those states followed Nevada's lead, supporting and encouraging the growth of Symbiotic Culture, then within five to ten years, this momentum could become a genuine groundswell.

At that point, it's entirely possible that a governor from one of these states could run for President, not just as a politician, but as a champion of a new paradigm. A platform rooted in Symbiotic Culture. Committed to building the Parallel Polis nationwide. Dedicated to decentralizing our political and economic systems for the common good.

But that's just the US.

There are approximately two million villages, towns, and cities worldwide. So, how do we scale this to 50,000 thriving regional economies globally?

It will take "only" 50,000 committed change-makers—each ready to build a Parallel Polis in their town, city, or region. All it takes is one person with the heart, the grounding in the Ancient Blueprint, and the courage to start a Symbiotic Circle. That one circle becomes a regional Symbiotic Society, which evolves into a Network Commons.

Imagine this across the 12 core needs sectors: 50,000 x 12 = 600,000 individuals holding space in love for their communities. That's enough to transform local systems, ignite regional renewal, and build a new global culture—from the grassroots, bottom up.

Imagine a new global economy—not based on extraction and exploitation, but on Love. Generative, not extractive. Cooperative, not coercive.

This expanding network of fractal community empowerment will naturally lead to a bottom-up, transnational trading system—a regenerative global economy built on trust, mutual benefit, and local resilience. Tools like OneSphera are designed to support this evolution, helping communities connect, collaborate, and trade across borders in alignment with the values of Symbiotic Culture.

I've laid out a ten-year journey to transform the foundation of our global system—from a Paradigm of Separation to a Paradigm of Connection, from fragmentation to coherence, from isolated efforts to a living, relational culture rooted in mutual benefit, spiritual purpose, and Divine Love.

VISION OF LIGHT: THE BIRTH OF A NEW ORDER

At the heart of this Tell-A-Vision is the light that has guided me from the beginning.

This is the birth of a new order—not by commands from above or demands from below, but through a Divine reality breaking into our world.

We have not "created" this reality, but we awaken to and participate in it—woven into the fabric of Love itself, waiting to be revealed. When we align our lives with that Love—rooted in compassion, connection, and the Divine spark within us—what has been hidden becomes visible.

It is an awakening to the greater order that has always been here, quietly unfolding in our families, neighborhoods, and communities wherever Love takes root.

As I recalled in Section 1, the cosmic vision of Jesus Christ:

"I saw the Earth as if from space. Typically, from that vantage point, you would see the glow of cities. But suddenly, instead of cities, I saw billions of golden rays—each one emanating from a human heart.

These beams of light rose and converged into a single, radiant heart hovering above the Earth—the Heart of Christ. And just as these lights joined in union, a brilliant stream of light from that cosmic heart beamed back down into every soul on Earth.

In that moment, I saw the web of life and love made visible. And I came away from that profound, inexplicable experience understanding the "end times" not as the end of humanity, but as the end of our separation—from each other and from the Transcendent Reality that holds us all."

Looking back now with clearer eyes, my vision has expanded. Those lights were not only awakening individuals, but vibrant circles and communities—each a node of symbiotic connection, deeply rooted in place and anchored in its people. These beams of connection were not only vertical, rising into the Heart of Christ, but also horizontal—forming a healing matrix of mutual nourishment and benefit.

In them I discovered a way to make real the Great Commandment: Love God in the vertical, Love Others in the horizontal. Each line of love and purpose, woven together in trust and communion, illuminates a path beyond a world of separation, pointing toward a Culture of Connection.

Through my eyes and heart, I've seen this living network originate from the Heart of Christ—coherent, radiant, and alive. For me, Jesus is the center of this vision and its source. Others may name the Divine differently, and I honor those paths—but for me, the Logos revealed in Christ remains the living template of Love.

If what feels like "religious" language becomes a barrier, let's just say Love is the universal solvent—dissolving walls, bridging gaps, and inviting us into sacred communion. The essence of Symbiotic Culture is this: finding our way together.

We may come from different beliefs, backgrounds, or worldviews—but what matters most is where we're going. Not despite our differences, but because of them, we are converging toward something larger, something sacred: the Highest Goodness. Together.

The Symbiotic Age has been quietly unfolding all around us—in gardens of Love, trust, and shared purpose—and wherever it takes root, communities flourish. It is not merely an ideal but a present reality that has worked when tried, as the stories in this book attest.

Like the Kingdom of Heaven, it is alive in us not only as a future dream, but a lived reality in the present moment. As the early Christians understood, we walk in two worlds at once—this present age, and the age to come already breaking through.

We are already living the reality that will one day transform the world—citizens of a greater sacred order, carrying this light into our families, neighborhoods, and networks, entrusted with its work here and now. Each act of Love is a seed of that coming age. Each bond of trust is a foretaste of its peace.

Imagine what it feels like to know that every choice we make, every act of kindness and care, every family and neighborhood we nurture, every network and community we strengthen, is animating that future.

Put another way, we aren't just carrying bricks. We are building a cathedral.

Everything in these pages has been, in its own way, a story of how to live into the Symbiotic Age—made real as a daily practice of Love, trust, and shared care.

> *This is the moment to live as if the Symbiotic Age has already arrived. Because in us, through us, it has. We are invited to live now as citizens of that age— to embody it in each act of Love, each circle of trust, each community of care.*

And so we stand at the threshold—not of an ending, but of a beginning, where light breaks in and Love makes all things new.

BIRTHING THE SYMBIOTIC AGE

EPILOGUE

THE STILL POINT AT THE THRESHOLD OF A NEW WORLD

As this book concludes, what rises in me is not urgency, but an invitation to stillness—a deeper presence that precedes all meaningful action.

When I began writing, I imagined the book would end with a detailed blueprint—a step-by-step guide to building Symbiotic Networks. After all, that's what people often ask for: "Just teach me how to build a Local Food System Network." I thought that was what this book needed to deliver.

But then a wise friend said something that stopped me in my tracks:

> "This story is too powerful to end as just a new system or structure. Don't turn this into a program. Let it breathe."

Epilogue

LET IT BREATHE

That moment changed everything.

I realized that even the most well-intentioned frameworks, introduced too soon, can harden into old wineskins—repeating the very patterns we set out to heal. If we rush to implement without first grounding in the Transcendent, we will simply recreate the Culture of Separation in more beautiful packaging.

So, rather than ending with a plan, I offer a pause.

This has been a long journey. Let yourself take it in. What I'm offering here is not a checklist, a toolkit, or a program. It's a living invitation—meant to be absorbed slowly, embodied personally, and evolved in relationship.

Like a fine bottle of wine, it needs time to breathe. You don't uncork it and gulp it down. You let it settle, open, and awaken—so that its depth can be fully revealed. That's what I'm asking you to do now—with this vision, your heart, and your community.

Before we build anything new, we must allow space for the deeper pattern to surface within us.

So instead of beginning with doing, we start with being.

As Thich Nhat Hanh once said, "Don't just do something. Sit there."

Without alignment, even our best actions will create more noise, burnout, and fragmentation. We'll find ourselves fighting on the old *battlefield* when we're being called to a new *playing field* entirely.

So let this way of being ripple through your life. Walk in nature. Relish small, sacred connections. Spend quality time with your family. Pray or meditate often. Check in with your neighbors. Breathe in the moment. Watch the sky. Share silence. See the world again with eyes of wonder and curiosity.

BIRTHING THE SYMBIOTIC AGE

Before any structure can emerge, this new culture must take root—not just in systems but also in hearts and habits of attention. It cannot be engineered; it must be received.

This is not about strategy. It is about surrender. It is about a radical turning—from self-serving to self-giving, performance to presence, fear to Love.

WHAT COMES NEXT: LET IT EMERGE

People often ask me, "What's your plan for rolling this out?"

My honest answer? I don't have one—no formal business plan. And that's intentional.

A single mind cannot map this, and no blueprint from above will capture it. The plan must emerge from the collective intelligence of those who feel called to give this vision form, right where they are.

We're not building a network just yet. We're cultivating a living system that evolves in real time, in response to real needs, among real people. If this vision resonates with you, here's how you can begin:

- Read the book. Share the book. Let it breathe.
- Reflect on what it stirs in you.
- Start a conversation. Invite others to wonder with you.
- Listen to the Spirit, your neighbors, and the whisper of what your community needs.
- Form a Symbiotic Circle—not an organization, but a sacred space for inquiry, presence, and practice with trusted friends or colleagues.

Let the action arise—not as a command, but as a calling. The first steps are more like midwifery than architecture. We are not building systems yet—we are helping something be born.

That means starting simply...gently...patiently, resisting the urge to rush into organizing or building structure. You can't proliferate something that is still forming. And what is forming is your spiritual fluency to carry it forward.

Before we build networks or launch projects, we must first ask ourselves:

Am I living from fear, or Love?

Am I feeding the Culture of Separation, or embodying the Culture of Connection?

Am I showing up with presence, patience, humility, and trust? How would Symbiotic Culture reshape how I relate to my family, group, workplace, and community?

My role is not to command or coordinate but to serve as a vision holder—an inspiration, a companion on your path. It is also to catalyze, share what I've learned, accompany those ready, and support the emergence of 50,000 villages, towns, and cities practicing Symbiotic Culture in their own unique ways.

BIRTHING THE SYMBIOTIC AGE

If there is demand, I will respond. If communities reach out, I will show up.

The Ancient Blueprint has already been tested. It's yours now. This next chapter isn't something I will write—it's something we will co-create.

And know this: it is not a solitary path. Many are already walking it quietly and faithfully in neighborhoods, villages, and circles worldwide. We're not beginning from nothing, but awakening to what is already alive among us. This is a shared unfolding—a holy participation in the reweaving of the world.

THE INVITATION

May we co-create this global-local culture—rooted in Love and guided by intentional purpose and the Virtues—and may it, in turn, regenerate us into the kind of people, communities, and world our hearts have always known were possible.

> May the road build us as we build the road.
>
> Before we act, we must attune.
> Before we organize, we must align.
> The next step begins not with structure, but with breath.
> Let it breathe.
> Let it take root.
> Let it rise.
>
> And when the time is right, let it bloom.
>
> This book is not the end.
> It is the threshold of a new beginning.
> It opens a Symbiotic field already in motion.
>
> I'll meet you there.

ACKNOWLEDGMENTS

Writing this book has been a long journey, and I've been blessed with the support, insight, and encouragement of many along the way. What follows is a partial expression of my deep gratitude to those who helped bring this vision to life.

I sincerely thank Dr. A.T. Ariyaratne, Dr. Vinya Ariyaratne, Dr. Samya Charika Marasinghe, and the Sarvodaya movement for practicing the Ancient Blueprint and inspiring me in a lifetime of service. Your example continues to inspire what's possible.

I'm grateful to David Christel for your friendship, and it's been almost 20 years since you helped me write and edit the first chapters, and recently. I'm grateful for your sharp eye, patient guidance, and steady hand in helping shape and edit the words.

Thank you to Steve Bhaerman for your friendship and acting as a "writing therapist," helping transform hours of spoken reflection into working drafts with care, clarity, humor, and integrity. Your support in scaffolding this book helped me find my writing voice. Thank you also for giving life to the phrase "From the Old Battlefield to a New Playing Field," which captured so much of the journey.

I also thank my friends and colleagues: Doug and Diana Damon, Father Chuck Durante, Jim Eaglesmith, Hans Frieshenshen, Bruce Geisheider, Eric Hekler, Fred and Kathy Jakolat, Bud James, Kabir Kadre, Bill Melton, Shannon Procise, Philip Moore, Sutton Porter, Elisa Sabatini, Gene and Sean Savoy, Kenneth Small, Ken Vanosky, Vishnu Vasu, and many other friends, leaders, and organizations in Northern Nevada and throughout the world.

I would also like to acknowledge those who are no longer here to hold this book in their hands, but who, through their friendship and insight, helped with its creation—James Ajemian, Andy Hill, and Clifton Maclin.

Thank you to the readers who walked with me this past year, offering encouragement, insight, and community as I shared early drafts of this work.

I am indebted to the local community networks in San Diego, CA, Reno, NV, and beyond, who helped co-create the living experiments that fill these pages. And to the many readers, friends, and early supporters who engaged with earlier drafts—your encouragement, insights, and presence made this possible.

ABOUT THE AUTHOR

Richard Flyer is an author, community-builder, and faith-rooted cultural strategist whose life work bridges science, faith, and civic renewal. Trained as a biologist, he studied pilot whale and dolphin communication at UC Santa Cruz and San Diego State before earning an M.S. in Biology. His early grounding in living systems science laid the foundation for what he later called Symbiotic Culture—a framework that unites spiritual insight with practical tools for regenerative community life.

Richard's career has spanned health, education, and grassroots leadership. He pioneered hyperbaric oxygen therapy programs in Nevada hospitals, taught in community colleges and detention facilities, and led nonprofits including the San Diego Food Bank, Neighbors United, and the Nevada Microenterprise Initiative. He has also served Sri Lanka's Sarvodaya Shramadana movement's national network of 5,000 communities and millions of people. His work draws inspiration from Jesus and the early church, Gandhi's village republics, and Václav Benda's Parallel Polis.

For Richard, following Jesus is not about dogma but about daily discipleship/practice—learning to embody Love, reconciliation, hospitality, and neighborliness in a world often marked by separation. He sees in Jesus not only the center of his faith but also a bridge across traditions, calling all people into deeper connection.

Today, through the Symbiotic Culture, Richard mentors leaders across faith, civic, and cultural spheres. In *Birthing the Symbiotic Age*, he offers a vision for building a Global Commonwealth of 50,000 empowered communities, a parallel polis, rooted in Love, justice, and mutual flourishing. He lives in Oahu, Hawaii with his wife Marta, finding renewal in the islands' natural beauty, time with family, and the simple joy of "Connecting the Good" wherever he goes.

CONTINUE THE JOURNEY

This book is not just the end of a story—it's the beginning of a community.

I invite you to stay connected and become part of the larger conversation about building a Symbiotic Culture.

- 📖 Collaborative Online Community — reflections, essays, and ways to engage: www.richardflyer.com
- 💼 LinkedIn — connect, follow, and share ideas
  linkedin.com/in/richard-flyer-6820727
- 📹 YouTube — talks, conversations, and resources
  youtube.com/@SymbioticCultureLab
- @ Contact me at: www.richardflyer.com
- 👥 Start a Book Club — Gather a few friends, neighbors, or colleagues. Read, reflect, and explore together how the ideas of Symbiotic Culture might take root in your own community.
- 🌱 Next Steps: Form Symbiotic Circles — Stay connected as we co-design Symbiotic Circles—small groups of shared purpose and mutual care that become seeds for broader networks of belonging.

Together, we can cultivate the next chapter of this work—not just in words, but in practice.

BIRTHING THE SYMBIOTIC AGE

BIRTHING THE SYMBIOTIC AGE

www.ingramcontent.com/pod-product-compliance
Lightning Source LLC
Chambersburg PA
CBHW020529030426
42337CB00013B/784